Rationality and the Reflective Mind

Rationality and the Reflective Mind

KEITH E. STANOVICH

OXFORD
UNIVERSITY PRESS

2011

OXFORD
UNIVERSITY PRESS

Oxford University Press, Inc., publishes works that further
Oxford University's objective of excellence
in research, scholarship, and education.

Oxford New York
Auckland   Cape Town   Dar es Salaam   Hong Kong   Karachi
Kuala Lumpur   Madrid   Melbourne   Mexico City   Nairobi
New Delhi   Shanghai   Taipei   Toronto

With offices in
Argentina   Austria   Brazil   Chile   Czech Republic   France   Greece
Guatemala   Hungary   Italy   Japan Poland Portugal   Singapore
South Korea   Switzerland   Thailand   Turkey Ukraine   Vietnam

Published by Oxford University Press, Inc.
198 Madison Avenue, New York, New York 10016
www.oup.com

Oxford is a registered trademark of Oxford University Press

Library of Congress Cataloging-in-Publication Data

Stanovich, Keith E., 1950-
Rationality and the reflective mind / Keith Stanovich.
p. cm.
ISBN 978-0-19-534114-0
1. Reasoning (Psychology) 2. Individual differences. 3. Intellect. 4. Cognition. I. Title.
BF442.S727 2010
153.4'3—dc22
2010036746

For my friend Marilyn

Preface

In this book, I explore how data on individual differences in reasoning have implications for dual-process theory and the Great Rationality Debate in cognitive science. These same data on individual differences also have profound implications for how we understand the relationship between the concepts of intelligence and rationality, and the latter chapters of the book explore this relationship. My longtime colleague, Richard West, has worked with me on all of these issues and co-authors several of the chapters. More recently, Maggie Toplak of York University, has worked with us on the intelligence/rationality relationship and on a conceptual framework for assessing rational thought and is the co-author of Chapter 10. No one could ask for two more dedicated colleagues who make every day we work together full of anticipation and fun.

My intellectual debts in writing this book are immense and are represented in the wide literature that I cite. Special note, though, goes to the work of Daniel Kahneman and Amos Tversky. Their early studies inspired my interest in rational thinking tasks that were new to psychology at the time. More recently, the work of Jonathan Evans and David Over provoked me to make my own contributions to dual-process theory. Jonathan was one of Oxford's reviewer's for this book, and went way beyond the call of duty with his review. He provided many pages of extremely apt suggestions that have been incorporated during several revisions of this book. Jonathan is a truly generous scholar. Oxford's other reviewer was anonymous, but that scholar provided many useful suggestions as well.

My editor at Oxford University Press, Catharine Carlin, is thanked for her enthusiasm for the project and for her patience in waiting for me to bring it to completion. Several conferences were seminal in allowing me to discuss these ideas at length: the Fourth International Thinking Conference in Durham, England; the Conference on Dual-Process Theories of Reasoning and Rationality in Cambridge, England, organized by Jonathan Evans and Keith Frankish; a workshop on dual-process theory at the University of Virginia organized by Tim Wilson and Jonathan Evans; the Sixth International Thinking Conference in Venice, Italy; and the NSF Workshop on Higher Cognition in Adolescents and Young Adults organized by Valerie Reyna.

My empirical research on some of the issues discussed in this volume was made possible by support received from the Social Sciences and Humanities Research Council of Canada and by the Canada Research Chairs program. Many members of the Stanovich/West/Toplak lab (a joint lab linking the University of Toronto, James Madison University, and York University) in the past decade have contributed in some way to the research of our own that is cited in this volume. Lab members, past and present, thanked for their participation are Maria Grunewald, Caroline Ho, Carol Kelley, Judi Kokis, Eleanor Liu, Robyn Macpherson, Sarah Mannino, Kimberly Marsh, Russ Meserve, Laura Page, George Potworowski, Walter Sá, and Geoff Sorge.

Contents

Rationality and the Reflective Mind

I

Dual-Process Theory and the Great Rationality Debate

The term *rationality* has a strong and a weak sense. The strong sense of the term is the one used in cognitive science and it will be the one used throughout this book. However, a weaker sense of the term has sometimes influenced—and hence confused—arguments in the so-called "Great Rationality Debate" in cognitive science. The influence of the weak sense of the term has also impeded investigation into individual differences in rational thought which, as I hope to show in this book, has important implications for arguments in the Great Rationality Debate.

Dictionary definitions of rationality tend to be of the weak sort—often seeming quite lame and unspecific ("the state or quality of being in accord with reason"). The meaning of rationality in modern cognitive science (the strong sense) is, in contrast, much more specific and prescriptive than this. The weak definitions of rationality derive from a categorical notion of rationality tracing to Aristotle (man as the rational animal). As de Sousa (2007) has noted, such a notion of rationality as "based on reason" has as its opposite not irrationality but *arationality*. Aristotle's characterization is categorical—the behavior of entities is either based on thought or it is not. Animals are either rational or arational.

In its stronger sense (the sense employed in cognitive science and in this book), rational thought is a normative notion. Its opposite is irrationality, and irrationality comes in degrees. Normative models of optimal judgment and decision making define perfect rationality in the non-categorical view employed in cognitive science. Rationality (and irrationality) come in degrees defined by the distance of the thought or behavior from the optimum defined by a normative model. de Sousa (2007) points out that the notion of rationality in Aristotle's sense cannot be normative. Other animals may be arational, but only humans can be irrational. As de Sousa (2007) puts it, "if human beings can indeed be described as rational animals, it is precisely in virtue of the fact that humans, of all the animals, are the only ones capable of irrational thoughts and actions" (p. 7).

Hurley and Nudds (2006) make a similar point when they argue that, for a strong sense of the term:

> "ironically, rationality requires the possibility that the animal might err. It can't be automatically right, no matter what it does. . ... when we say that an agent has acted rationally, we imply that it would have been a mistake in some sense to have acted in certain different ways. It can't be the case that anything the agent might do would count as rational. This is normativity in a quite weak sense." (p. 2)

The weak sense they are referring to is an Aristotelian (categorical) sense, and no cognitive scientist is using rationality in this sense when claiming that an experiment has demonstrated human irrationality.

When a cognitive scientist terms a behavior irrational he/she means that the behavior departs from the optimum prescribed by a particular normative model. The scientist is not implying that no thought or reason was behind the behavior. Some of the hostility that has been engendered by experimental claims of human irrationality no doubt derive from an influence (perhaps tacit) of the Aristotelian view—the thought that cognitive psychologists are saying that certain people are somehow less than human when they are said to behave irrationally. Nothing could be further from the case. All cognitive psychologists accept the de Sousa (2007) view that "man the rational animal" deserves Aristotle's appellation and its corollary that humans are the only animal that can potentially display irrationality.

Some of the heat in the Great Rationality Debate is no doubt caused by reactions to the term irrationality being applied to humans. As mentioned, lingering associations with the Aristotelian categorical view make charges of irrationality sound more cutting than they actually are. In the literature, we could do better to signal that it is the noncategorical, continuous sense of rationality and irrationality that is employed in cognitive science. When we find a behavioral pattern that is less than optimally rational, we could easily say that it is "less than perfectly rational," rather than that it is irrational—with no loss of meaning. Perhaps if this had been the habit in the literature, the rationality debate in cognitive science would not have become so heated. For this reason, I will use the term irrationality sparingly (except for the descriptions of the Great Rationality Debate in this chapter and in Chapter 8) and instead refer more often to continuous variation in rational thought. Such an emphasis also highlights the theme of the volume—that there are indeed individual differences in rational thought and that understanding the nature of these differences might have important theoretical implications.

It should also be noted that in the view of rationality taken in this volume, rationality is a personal entity and not a subpersonal one (Bermudez, 2001; Davies, 2000; Frankish, 2009). A memory system in the human brain is not rational or irrational—it is merely efficient or inefficient (or of high or low capacity). Thus, subprocesses of the brain do not display rational or irrational properties *per se*, although they may contribute in one way or another to personal decisions or beliefs that could be characterized as such. Rationality concerns the actions of an entity in its environment that serve its goals. Of course, one could extrapolate the notion of environment to include the interior of the brain itself and then talk of a submodule that chose strategies rationally or not. This move creates two problems. First, what are the goals of this subpersonal entity—what are its interests that its rationality is trying to serve? This is unclear in the case of a subpersonal entity. Second, such a move regresses all the way down. We would need to talk of a neuron firing being either rational or irrational ("turtles all the way down!")[1]. As Oaksford and Chater (1998) put it, "the fact that a model is optimizing something does not mean that the model is a rational model. Optimality is not the same as rationality. . ... Stomachs may be well or poorly adapted to their function (digestion), but they have no beliefs, desires or knowledge, and hence the question of their rationality does not arise" (p. 4, 5).

---

1 I am referring here to a joke that has circulated widely. A version of it is in Steven Hawking's *A Brief History of Time* (1988). One version has philosopher William James after a lecture on the solar system being approached by a determined elderly lady. "We don't live on a ball rotating around the sun," she says. "We live on a crust of earth on the back of a giant turtle." James decides to be gentle: "If your theory is correct, madam, what does this turtle stand on?" The lady says, "The first turtle stands on the back of a second, far larger turtle, of course." "But what does this second turtle stand on?" says James. The old lady crows triumphantly. "It's no use, Mr. James—it's turtles all the way down!"

The Great Rationality Debate

Cognitive scientists recognize two types of rationality: epistemic and instrumental. *Epistemic rationality* concerns how well beliefs map onto the actual structure of the world. It is sometimes called theoretical rationality or evidential rationality (*see* Audi, 1993, 2001; Foley, 1987; Harman, 1995; Manktelow, 2004; Over, 2004).

The simplest definition of *instrumental rationality* is: Behaving in the world so that you get exactly what you most want, given the resources (physical and mental) available to you. Somewhat more technically, we could characterize instrumental rationality as the optimization of the individual's goal fulfillment. Economists and cognitive scientists have refined the notion of optimization of goal fulfillment into the technical notion of expected utility. The model of rational judgment used by decision scientists is one in which a person chooses options based on which option has the largest expected utility (*see* Baron, 2008; Dawes, 1998; Hastie & Dawes, 2001; Wu, Zhang, & Gonzalez, 2004). One of the fundamental advances in the history of modern decision science was the demonstration that if people's preferences follow certain patterns (the so-called "axioms of choice"—things like transitivity and freedom from certain kinds of context effects), then they are behaving as if they are maximizing utility—they are acting to get what they most want (Edwards, 1954; Jeffrey, 1983; Luce & Raiffa, 1957; Savage, 1954; von Neumann & Morgenstern, 1944). This is what makes people's degrees of rationality measurable by the experimental methods of cognitive science. Although it is difficult to assess utility directly, it is much easier to assess whether one of the axioms of rational choice is being violated. This is why the seminal heuristics and biases research program inaugurated by Kahneman and Tversky has focused on the causes of thinking *errors*.

As will be apparent in the remainder of this book, rationality has multiple components. It is hard to measure the optimal functioning of all these components—that is, to specify whether "perfect" rationality has been attained. Researchers have found it much easier to measure whether a particular rational stricture is being *violated*—that is, whether a person is committing a thinking error, rather than whether their thinking is as good as it can be. This is much like our judgments at a sporting event, where, for example, it might be difficult to discern whether a quarterback has put the ball perfectly on the money, but it is not at all difficult to detect a bad throw.

In fact, in many domains of life this is often the case as well. It is often difficult to specify what the best type of performance might be, but performance errors are much easier to spot. Essayist Neil Postman (1988) has argued, for example, that educators and other advocates of good thinking might adopt a stance more similar to that of physicians or attorneys. He points out that doctors would find it hard to define "perfect health," but despite this, they are quite good at spotting disease. Likewise, lawyers are much better at spotting injustice and lack of citizenship than defining "perfect justice" or ideal citizenship. Postman argues that like physicians and attorneys, educators might best focus on instances of poor thinking that are much easier to identify as opposed to trying to define ideal thinking. The literature on the psychology of rationality has followed this logic in that the empirical literature has focused on identifying thinking errors, just as physicians focus on disease. Degrees of rationality can be assessed in terms of the number and severity of such cognitive biases that individuals display. Failure to display a cognitive bias becomes a measure of rational thought.

A substantial research literature—one comprising literally hundreds of empirical studies conducted over several decades—has firmly established that people's responses sometimes deviate from the performance considered normative on many reasoning tasks. For example, people assess probabilities incorrectly, they test hypotheses inefficiently, they violate the axioms of utility theory, they do not properly calibrate degrees of belief, their choices are affected by irrelevant context, they ignore the alternative hypothesis when evaluating data, and they display numerous other information processing biases (Baron, 2008, Evans, 2007a; Kahneman & Tversky, 2000). Demonstrating that descriptive accounts of human behavior diverged from normative models was a main theme of the heuristics and biases research program inaugurated by Kahneman and Tversky in the early 1970s (Kahneman & Tversky, 1972, 1973; Tversky & Kahneman, 1974). The term *heuristics* refers to *why* people often make errors in choosing actions and in estimating probabilities—because they use mental shortcuts (heuristics) to solve many problems.

Researchers working in the heuristics and biases tradition tend to be so-called Meliorists (Stanovich, 1999, 2004). They assume that human reasoning is not as good as it could be, and that thinking could be improved. The dictionary definition of meliorism is "the doctrine that the world tends to become better or may be made better by human effort." Thus, a Meliorist is one who feels that education and the provision of information could help make people more rational—could help them more efficiently further their goals and bring their beliefs more in line with the actual state of the world[2]. Stated this way, Meliorism seems to be an optimistic doctrine, and in one sense it is. But this optimistic part of the Meliorist message derives from the fact that Meliorists see a large gap between normative models of rational responding and descriptive models of what people actually do. Emphasizing the gap, of course, entails that Meliorists will be attributing a good deal of irrationality to human cognition.

Over the last two decades, an alternative interpretation of the findings from the heuristics and biases research program has been championed. Contributing to this alternative interpretation have been evolutionary psychologists, adaptationist modelers, and ecological theorists (Anderson, 1990; Cosmides & Tooby, 1996; Gigerenzer, 2007; Oaksford & Chater, 2007; Todd & Gigerenzer, 2000). They have reinterpreted the modal response in most of the classic heuristics and biases experiments as indicating an optimal information processing adaptation on the part of the subjects. These investigators have argued that the research in the heuristics and biases tradition has not demonstrated human irrationality at all. This group of theorists—who argue that an assumption of maximal

---

2 It is important to note that the Meliorist recognizes two different ways in which human decision-making performance might be improved. These might be termed cognitive change and environmental change. First, it might be possible to teach people better reasoning strategies and to have them learn rules of decision making that are helpful (see Stanovich, 2009b). These would represent instances of cognitive change. Additionally, however, research has shown that it is possible to change the environment so that natural human reasoning strategies will not lead to error (Gigerenzer, 2002; Milkman, Chugh, & Bazerman, 2009; Thaler & Sunstein, 2008). For example, choosing the right default values for a decision would be an example of an environmental change. In short, environmental alterations (as well as cognitive changes) can prevent rational thinking problems. Thus, in cases where teaching people the correct reasoning strategies might be difficult, it may well be easier to change the environment so that decision making errors are less likely to occur.

human rationality is the proper default position to take—have been termed the *Panglossians*. This position posits no difference between descriptive and normative models of performance because human performance is actually normative.

But how could a Panglossian position be maintained in light of the findings mentioned previously—particularly the many demonstrations that human performance deviates from normative models of rationality? The Panglossian theorists have several responses to this question, but two predominate. First, they argue that the normative model being applied is not appropriate because the subject's interpretation of the task is different from what the researcher assumes it is. Second, they argue that the modal response in the task makes perfect sense from an evolutionary perspective.

The contrasting positions of the Panglossians and Meliorists define the differing poles in what has been termed the Great Rationality Debate in cognitive science—the debate about how much irrationality to attribute to human cognition[3]. Tetlock and Mellers (2002) have noted that "the debate over human rationality is a high-stakes controversy that mixes primordial political and psychological prejudices in combustible combinations" (p. 97). The great debate about human rationality is a "high-stakes controversy" because it involves nothing less than the models of human nature that underlie economics, moral philosophy, and the personal theories (folk theories) we use to understand the behavior of other humans. For example, a very influential part of the Panglossian camp is represented by the mainstream of the discipline of economics that is notable for using strong rationality assumptions as fundamental tools.

The difference between the Panglossian and the Meliorist was captured colloquially in an article in *The Economist* magazine (February 14, 1998), where a subheading asked "Economists Make Sense of the World

---

3 This debate has generated a very substantial literature of often heated arguments (Cohen, 1981; Doherty, 2003; Edwards & von Winterfeldt, 1986; Evans & Over, 1996; Gigerenzer, 1996; Jungermann, 1986; Kahneman & Tversky, 1983, 1996; Koehler, 1996; Koehler & James, 2009; Krueger & Funder, 2004; Kuhberger, 2002; Lee, 2006; Samuels & Stich, 2004; Stanovich, 1999, 2004, 2010a; Stanovich & West, 2000; Stein, 1996; Stich, 1990; Vranas, 2000).

by Assuming that People Know What they Want. Advertisers Assume that They Do Not. Who Is Right?" The Meliorist thinks that the advertisers are right—people often do not know what they want and can be influenced so as to maximize the advertiser's profits rather than their own personal utility. A Panglossian view of perfect rationality in the marketplace would need to defend the view that people take only from advertising what optimizes their consumption utility. In contrast, the Meliorist does not assume that consumers will process the advertiser's information in a way that optimizes things for the consumer (as opposed to the advertiser). Thus, Meliorists are much more sympathetic to government attempts to regulate advertising because, in the Meliorist view, such regulation can act to increase the utility of the total population. This is just one example of how the Great Rationality Debate has profound political implications.

A reconciliation of the views of the Panglossians and Meliorists is possible, however, if we take two scientific steps. First, we must consider data patterns long ignored in the heuristics and biases literature—individual differences on rational thinking tasks. Second, we must understand the empirical patterns obtained through the lens of a modified and updated dual-process theory. A concern for individual differences has also led me to posit a substantial modification of dual-process theory and to emphasize a tripartite model of mind. Together, an updated dual-process theory and individual difference analyses provide a way to reconcile the warring camps in the Great Rational Debate in cognitive science.

Individual Differences in the Great Rationality Debate

Panglossians and Meliorists often argue about the appropriate normative model to apply to a particular task. Interestingly, these disputes sometimes rely on empirical outcomes, although this reliance on empirical data is rarely noticed because it is often implicit. For example, Panglossian theorists use data patterns to justify their critiques, but they rely exclusively on the modal response. Some Panglossians argue that because the descriptive is simply indexed to the normative, the latter can simply be "read off" from a competence model of the former (Cohen, 1982, terms this the Norm Extraction Method). For example, Stein (1996) noted that this seems to follow from the Panglossian view that "whatever human reasoning competence turns out to be, the principles embodied in it are the normative principles of reasoning. . . .This argument sees the reasoning experiments as revealing human reasoning competence, and, thereby, as also revealing the norms" (p. 231). Panglossians taking this stance view the response that most people make (the modal response) also as the normative response.

Stein (1996) notes that this type of Panglossian position "rejects the standard picture of rationality and takes the reasoning experiments as giving insight not just into human reasoning competence but also into the normative principles of reasoning. . . .The norms just are what we have in our reasoning competence; if the (actual) norms do not match our preconceived notion of what the norms should be, so much the worse for our reconceived notions." (pp. 233–234). Stein (1996, p. 239) terms an extreme form of this strategy—that of explaining away all normative/descriptive gaps in terms of incorrect norm application—the "reject-the-norm strategy." Notably, this strategy is used exclusively by the Panglossian camp in the rationality debate, although this connection is not a necessary one.

Specifically, the reject-the-norm strategy is exclusively used to *eliminate* gaps between descriptive models of performance and normative models. When this type of critique is employed, the normative model that is suggested as a substitute for the normative model is one that coincides perfectly with the descriptive model of the subjects' performance—thus preserving a view of human rationality as ideal. It is rarely noted that the strategy could be used in just the opposite way—to *create* gaps between the normative and descriptive. Situations where the modal response *coincides* with the standard normative model could be critiqued, and alternative normative models could be suggested that would result in a new normative/descriptive gap. But this is never done. The Panglossian camp, often highly critical of empirical psychologists ("Kahneman and Tversky . . . and not their experimental subjects, commit the fallacies" Levi, 1983, p. 502), is never critical of psychologists who design reasoning tasks in instances where the modal subject gives the response the experimenters deem correct. Ironically, in these cases, according to the Panglossians, the same psychologists seem never to err in their task designs and interpretations.

It is quite clear that Cohen's (1979, 1981, 1986) trenchant criticisms of experimental psychologists would never have been written had human performance coincided with the standard normative models that the psychologists were using. The fact that the use of the reject-the-norm strategy is entirely contingent on the existence or nonexistence of a normative/descriptive gap suggests that the strategy is *empirically*, not conceptually, triggered (norms are never rejected for purely conceptual reasons when they coincide with the modal human response). This means that in an important sense, the norms being endorsed by the Panglossian camp are conditioned (if not indexed entirely) by descriptive facts about human behavior. Gigerenzer (1991) is clear about his adherence to an empirically driven reject-the-norm strategy:

> "Since its origins in the mid-seventeenth century....When there was a striking discrepancy between the judgment of reasonable men and what probability theory dictated—as with the famous St. Petersburg paradox—then the mathematicians went back to the blackboard and changed the equations (Daston, 1980). Those good old days have gone.... If, in studies on social cognition, researchers find a discrepancy between human judgment and what probability theory seems to dictate, the blame is now put on the human mind, not the statistical model." (p. 109)

That Gigerenzer and Cohen concur here—even though they have somewhat different positions on normative justification—simply shows how widespread is the acceptance of the principle that descriptive facts about human behavior should condition our notions about the appropriateness of the normative models used to evaluate behavior.

Interestingly, the descriptive component of performance around which Panglossian theorists almost always build their competence models (which, recall, index the *normative* in their view) is the central tendency of the responses (usually the mean or modal performance tendency). But if we are going to "read off" the normative from the descriptive in this way, why is this the only aspect of group performance that is relevant? Do the pattern of responses around the mode tell us anything? What about the rich covariance patterns that would be present in any multivariate experiment? Are these totally superfluous—all norm-relevant behavioral information residing in the mode? My research group

(Stanovich & West, 1999, 2000) has argued in several papers that if something about the normative must be inferred from the descriptive, then there is more information available than has traditionally been relied upon.

How should we interpret situations where the majority of individuals respond in ways that depart from the normative model applied to the problem by reasoning experts? Thagard (1982) calls the two different interpretations the populist strategy and the elitist strategy: "The populist strategy, favored by Cohen (1981), is to emphasize the reflective equilibrium of the average person. . . .. The elitist strategy, favored by Stich and Nisbett (1980), is to emphasize the reflective equilibrium of experts." (p. 39) Thus, Thagard (1982) identifies the populist strategy with the Panglossian position and the elitist strategy with the Meliorist position.

But there are few controversial tasks in the heuristics and biases literature where all untutored laypersons disagree with the experts. There are always some who agree. Thus, the issue is not the untutored average person versus experts (as suggested by Thagard's formulation), but experts plus some laypersons versus other untutored individuals. What has largely been ignored is that although the average person in the classic heuristics and biases experiments might well display an overconfidence effect, underutilize base rates, ignore $P(D/\sim H)$, violate the axioms of utility theory, choose P and Q in the selection task, commit the conjunction fallacy, and so forth, on each of these tasks, *some people give the standard normative response.* For example, in knowledge calibration studies, although the mean performance level of the entire sample may be represented by a calibration curve that indicates overconfidence, some people do display near perfect calibration. Likewise, in probabilistic assessment, although the majority of subjects might well ignore the noncausal baserate evidence, a minority of subjects often makes use of this information in exactly the way prescribed by Bayes' theorem. A few people even respond correctly on the notoriously difficult abstract selection task (Evans, Newstead, & Byrne, 1993; Stanovich & West, 1998a, 2008b).

In short, some people give the response traditionally considered normative, and others do not. There is variability in responding on all of these tasks. So it is incorrect to say that a specific experiment shows that people, in general, display a particular irrational thought pattern or response pattern. The experiment might instead be said to show that the average person, or perhaps the modal person, displays suboptimal thinking. Other people, often a minority to be sure, do not. Might anything be learned from this variability?

One aspect of this variability that researchers have examined is whether it is correlated at all with cognitive sophistication. The question has been: Do people who display more complex cognition tend to give the response traditionally considered normative? Or, alternatively: Do people who display more complex cognition tend to give the modal response—the response that is justified by the alternative interpretations of these tasks favored by the Panglossians? We might take the direction of this association as a validation of the alternative normative models of either the Panglossian or the Meliorist. Stanovich and West (1999) termed this the *understanding/acceptance assumption*—that those who more fully understand the normative issues at stake are more likely to accept the correct normative model[4]. In short, the point is that more reflective and engaged reasoners are more likely to affirm the appropriate normative model for a particular situation.

From an individual differences standpoint, more sophisticated reasoners tend to be more reflective and engaged reasoners. Individual differences in cognitive sophistication have been indexed in three different ways in the research literature—developmentally, by intelligence, and by cognitive style. Developmentally, it is straightforward to assume that adolescents are more cognitively sophisticated than young children and that,

---

4 We derived this assumption from an argument that Slovic and Tversky (1974) made years ago, although it was couched in very different terms in their paper and thus was hard to discern. Slovic and Tversky (1974) argued that descriptive facts about argument endorsement should condition the inductive inferences of experts regarding appropriate normative principles. In response to the argument that there is "no valid way to distinguish between outright rejection of the axiom and failure to understand it" (p. 372), Slovic and Tversky observed that "the deeper the understanding of the axiom, the greater the readiness to accept it" (pp. 372–373). We named their argument and turned it into an individual difference prediction (Stanovich & West, 1999). Note that another way of framing the understanding/acceptance principle is to view it as stressing that a normative/descriptive gap that is disproportionately created by subjects with a superficial understanding of the problem provides no warrant for amending the application of standard normative models (in the manner that the Panglossians who attack the standard norm advise).

in turn, adults are more cognitively advanced than adolescents. The question then becomes whether cognitive developmental level, as indexed by age, is correlated with performance on rational thinking tasks. In contrast, for a group of subjects of the same age, the natural index of cognitive ability is intelligence test performance. The question then becomes whether cognitive developmental level, as indexed by intelligence, is correlated with performance on rational thinking tasks. Intelligence, however, is not an exhaustive measure of cognitive functioning. For one thing, intelligence tests fail to tap important metacognitive strategies and cognitive styles that are critical components of what has been termed *the reflective mind* (*see* Chapter 2 and Stanovich, 2009a, 2009b; Sternberg, 2003). These components of cognition travel under a variety of names in psychology; thinking dispositions or cognitive styles are the two most popular, and I will use the former here. These are the third measure of cognitive sophistication that has been employed in this literature.

What do the data say about these relationships—about the correlations between performance on rational thinking tasks and age, intelligence, and thinking dispositions? The data on intelligence are most extensive, and this has been the individual differences variable employed in most of the work in my own lab. Intelligence displays positive correlations with rational thinking on a variety of heuristics and biases tasks, but not all (Stanovich & West, 1998c, 2000, 2008b; West & Stanovich, 2003; West et al., 2008). On some tasks, there is no correlation. However, there is never a negative correlation—that is, it is never the case that subjects giving the non-normative response that is defended by the Panglossians are higher in intelligence than those giving the normative response[5].

---

5 The data on thinking dispositions largely parallels that on intelligence. A variety of the thinking dispositions display positive correlations with rational thinking on a variety of heuristics and biases tasks, but not all. On some tasks, there is no correlation. However, there is never a negative correlation—that is, it is never the case that subjects giving the non-normative response that is defended by the Panglossians are higher on efficacious thinking dispositions (e.g., need for cognition) than those giving the normative response (Bruine de Bruin, Parker, & Fischhoff, 2007; Klaczynski & Lavellee, 2005; Kokis et al., 2002; Ku & Ho, 2010; LeBoeuf & Shafir, 2003; Parker & Fischhoff, 2005; Ricco, 2007; Smith & Levin, 1996; Stanovich & West, 1999; Toplak & Stanovich, 2002; West et al., 2008). The data on developmental trends are not quite so consistent, however (see Stanovich, Toplak, West, 2008), in part because

The two sides of the great debate about human rationality can be reconciled if these findings are set within the context of dual-process theory.

Dual-Process Theory: The Current State of Play

The idea that the brain is composed of many different subsystems (*see* Aunger & Curtis, 2008) has recurred in conceptualizations in many different disciplines—from the society of minds view in artificial intelligence (Minsky, 1985); to Freudian analogies (Ainslie, 1982); to discussions of the concept of multiple selves in philosophy, economics, and decision science (Ainslie, 2001; Schelling, 1984). In fact, the notion of many different systems in the brain is by no means new. Plato (1945) argued: "we may call that part of the soul whereby it reflects, rational; and the other, with which it feels hunger and thirst and is distracted by sexual passion and all the other desires, we will call irrational appetite, associated with pleasure in the replenishment of certain wants" (p. 137).

What *is* new, however, is that cognitive scientists are beginning to understand the biology and cognitive structure of these systems (Evans & Frankish, 2009) and are beginning to posit some testable speculations about their evolutionary and experiential origins. I will build on the current consensus that the functioning of the brain can be characterized by two different types of cognition having somewhat different functions and different strengths and weaknesses. There is a wide variety of evidence[6] that has converged on the conclusion that some type of

---

there are many fewer developmental comparisons than there are studies of intelligence or thinking dispositions. Age is correlated with the use of causal baserates (Jacobs & Potenza, 1991; Kokis et al., 2002). However, the developmental research on framing effects is quite confusing. Some studies have failed to find a developmental trend (Levin & Hart, 2003; Levin, Hart, Weller, & Harshman, 2007) and others have actually found that sometimes framing effects increase with age (Reyna & Ellis, 1994). In contrast, belief bias does attenuate with age (Kokis et al., 2002), as does the gamblers fallacy (Klaczynski, 2000, 2001; Klaczynski & Narasimham, 1998). Performance on the four-card selection task improves with age (Overton, Byrnes, & O'Brien, 1985).

6 The evidence for a dual-process view encompasses a variety of specialty areas (Brainerd & Reyna, 2001; Evans, 1984, 2003, 2006a, 2006b, 2008, 2009; Evans &

dual-process notion is needed in a diverse set of specialty areas not limited to: cognitive psychology, social psychology, neuropsychology, naturalistic philosophy, decision theory, and clinical psychology. Evolutionary theorizing and neurophysiological work also have supported a dual-process conception. In fact, a dual-process view was implicit within the early writings in the groundbreaking heuristics and biases research program[7]. As Kahneman (2000) notes, "Tversky and I always thought of the heuristics and biases approach as a two-process theory" (p. 682).

Table 1–1 illustrates how ubiquitous dual-process models are in psychology and related fields by listing a variety of such theories that have appeared during the last couple of decades. Table 1–1 also lists some common terms for the dual processes. The details and terminology of the various dual-process theories differ, but they all share a family resemblance. My purpose here is not to adjudicate the differences among the models. Instead, I will gloss over differences and instead start with a model that emphasizes the family resemblances.

The family resemblances extend to the names for the two classes of process. The terms *heuristic* and *analytic* are two of the oldest and most popular (*see* Evans, 1984, 1989). However, to attenuate the proliferation

---

Over, 1996; Evans & Wason, 1976; Feldman Barrett, Tugade, & Engle, 2004; Ferreira, Garcia-Marques, Sherman, & Sherman, 2006; Frankish, 2004; Haidt, 2001; Hofmann, Friese, & Strack, 2009; Johnson-Laird, 1983; Lieberman, 2007, 2009; Metcalfe & Mischel, 1999; Sloman, 1996, 2002; Schneider & Chein, 2003; Smith & Decoster, 2000; Stanovich, 1999; Stanovich & West, 2000; Sun, Lane, & Mathews, 2009). The wide convergence includes a growing body of neurophysiological research (Bechara, 2005; Camerer, Loewenstein, & Prelec, 2005; DeMartino, Kumaran, Seymour & Dolan, 2006; Frank, Cohen, & Sanfey, 2009; Goel & Dolan, 2003; Greene, Nystrom, Engell, Darley, & Cohen, 2004; Lieberman, 2003; McClure, Laibson, Loewenstein & Cohen, 2004; Prado & Noveck, 2007; Sanfey, 2007; Toates, 2005, 2006; Westen, Blagov, Kilts, & Hamann, 2006). Dual-process computational architectures have been implemented as computer models that mimic human data patterns. For example, Schneider and Chein (2003) describe one such architecture involving a modular connectionist structure that reflects automatic processing in the brain. It is monitored by a symbolic control system "whose signals alter functional connectivity within the architecture, thereby enabling a wide variety of cognitive operations" (p. 534).
7 On the dual-process view implicit within the heuristics and biases approach, *see* Kahneman (2003), Kahneman and Frederick (2002, 2005), and Kahneman and Tversky (1982a, 1996).

TABLE 1.1   Some Alternative Terms for Type 1 and Type 2 Processing Used by Various Theorists

Theorist	Type 1	Type 2
Bargh & Chartrand (1999)	automatic processing	conscious processing
Bazerman, Tenbrunsel, & Wade-Benzoni, (1998)	want self	should self
Bickerton (1995)	online thinking	offline thinking
Brainerd & Reyna (2001)	gist processing	analytic processing
Chaiken et al. (1989)	heuristic processing	systematic processing
Evans (1984, 1989)	heuristic processing	analytic processing
Evans & Over (1996)	tacit thought processes	explicit thought processes
Evans & Wason (1976; Wason & Evans, 1975)	type 1 processes	type 2 processes
Fodor (1983)	modular processes	central processes
Gawronski & Bodenhausen (2006)	associative processes	propositional processes
Haidt (2001)	intuitive system	reasoning system
Johnson-Laird (1983)	implicit inferences	explicit inferences
Kahneman & Frederick (2002, 2005)	intuition	reasoning
Lieberman (2003)	reflexive system	reflective system
Loewenstein (1996)	visceral factors	tastes
Metcalfe & Mischel (1999)	hot system	cool system
Norman & Shallice (1986)	contention scheduling	supervisory attentional system
Pollock (1991)	quick & inflexible modules	intellection
Posner & Snyder (1975)	automatic activation	conscious processing
Reber (1993)	implicit cognition	explicit learning
Shiffrin & Schneider (1977)	automatic processing	controlled processing
Sloman (1996)	associative system	rule-based system
Smith & DeCoster (2000)	associative processing	rule-based processing
Strack & Deutsch (2004)	impulsive system	reflective system
Thaler & Shefrin (1981)	doer	planner
Toates (2006)	stimulus-bound	higher order
Wilson (2002)	adaptive unconscious	conscious

of nearly identical theories, I suggested the more generic terms *System* 1 and *System* 2 in a previous book (Stanovich, 1999). Although these terms have become popular, there is an infelicitousness to the System 1/System 2 terminology. Such terminology seems to connote that the two processes in dual-process theory map explicitly to two distinct brain systems.

This is a stronger assumption than most theorists wish to make. Additionally, both Evans (2006b) and Stanovich (2004) have discussed how terms such as System 1 or heuristic *system* are really misnomers because they imply that what is being referred to is a singular system. In actuality, the term used should be plural because it refers to a *set* of systems in the brain that operate autonomously in response to their own triggering stimuli and are not under higher-level cognitive control. I have suggested (Stanovich, 2004) the acronym TASS (The Autonomous Set of Systems) to describe what is in actuality a heterogeneous set.

Using the acronym TASS was a step forward in clearing up some of the confusions surrounding autonomous processes. For similar reasons, Evans (2008, 2009; *see also* Samuels, 2009) has suggested a terminology of Type 1 processing versus Type 2 processing to mark autonomous versus nonautonomous processing. The Type 1 terminology signals that autonomous processing might result from the operations of a variety of different subsystems. The Type 1/Type 2 terminology captures better than previous terminology that a dual-*process* theory is not necessarily a dual-*system* theory (*see* Evans, 2008, 2009, for an extensive discussion). For these reasons, I will rely most heavily on the Type 1/Type 2 terminology in this volume. An even earlier terminology resulting from Evans (1984, 1989)—heuristic versus analytic processing—will also be employed on occasions when it is felicitous.

Properties of Type 1 and Type 2 Processing

In my view, the defining feature of Type 1 processing is its autonomy— the execution of Type 1 processes is mandatory when their triggering stimuli are encountered, and they do not depend on input from high-level control systems. Autonomous processes have other correlated features—their execution is rapid, they do not put a heavy load on central processing capacity, they tend to operate in parallel without interfering with themselves or with Type 2 processing—but these other correlated features are not defining. Autonomous processes would include behavioral regulation by the emotions; the encapsulated modules for solving specific adaptive problems that have been posited by evolutionary psychologists; processes of implicit learning; and the automatic firing of overlearned associations. Type 1 processes conjoin the properties of automaticity, quasi-modularity, and heuristic processing, as these constructs have been variously discussed in cognitive science[8].

It is important to emphasize that Type 1 processing is not limited to modular subprocesses that meet all of the classic Fodorian (1983) criteria. Type 1 processing encompasses processes of unconscious implicit learning and conditioning. Also, many rules, stimulus discriminations, and decision-making principles that have been practiced to automaticity (e.g., Kahneman & Klein, 2009; Shiffrin & Schneider, 1977) are processed in a Type 1 manner. This learned information can sometimes be just as much a threat to rational behavior as are evolutionary modules that fire inappropriately in a modern environment. Rules learned to automaticity can be overgeneralized—they can autonomously trigger behavior when the situation is an exception to the class of events they are meant to cover (Arkes & Ayton, 1999; Hsee & Hastie, 2006).

Type 2 processing is nonautonomous. Type 2 processing contrasts with Type 1 processing on each of the correlated properties that define the latter. It is relatively slow and computationally expensive. Many Type 1 processes can operate at once in parallel, but Type 2 processing is largely serial. Type 2 processing is often language-based, but it is not necessarily so. One of the most critical functions of Type 2 processing is to override Type 1 processing. This is sometimes necessary because autonomous processing has heuristic qualities. It is designed to get the response into the right ballpark when solving a problem or making a decision, but it is not designed for the type of fine-grained analysis called for in situations of unusual importance (financial decisions, fairness judgments, employment decisions, legal judgments, etc.). Heuristics depend on

---

8 There has been much research on each of the different kinds of Type 1 processing (e.g., Atran, 1998; Aunger & Curtis, 2008; Brase, 2004; Buss, 2005; Carruthers, 2006; Evans, 2003, 2006a; Ferguson & Zayas, 2009; Fodor, 1983; Kahneman & Klein, 2009; Lieberman, 2000, 2003; Oatley, 1992; Ohman & Mineka, 2001; Pinker, 1997; Smith, Patalino, & Jonides, 1998; Willingham, 1998, 1999). Likewise, there is a large literature on the concepts of modularity and automaticity in cognitive science (e.g., Bargh & Chartrand, 1999; Barrett & Kurzban, 2006; Carruthers, 2006; Coltheart, 1999; Evans, 1984, 2006b, 2008, 2009; Samuels, 2005, 2009; Shiffrin & Schneider, 1977; Sperber, 1994).

benign environments. In hostile environments, they can be costly (*see* Hilton, 2003; Over, 2000; Stanovich, 2004, 2009b). A benign environment means one that contains useful (i.e., diagnostic) cues that can be exploited by various heuristics (e.g., affect-triggering cues, vivid and salient stimulus components, convenient anchors). Additionally, for an environment to be classified as benign, it also must contain no other individuals who will adjust their behavior to exploit those relying only on heuristics. In contrast, a hostile environment for heuristics is one in which there are few cues that are usable by heuristic processes or there are misleading cues (Kahneman & Klein, 2009). Another way that an environment can turn hostile for a heuristic processor is if other agents discern the simple cues being used and the other agents start to arrange the cues for their own advantage (e.g., advertisements, or the deliberate design of supermarket floorspace to maximize revenue).

All of the different kinds of Type 1 processing (processes of emotional regulation, Darwinian modules, associative and implicit learning processes) can produce responses that are irrational in a particular context if not overridden. For example, often humans act as cognitive misers (*see* Stanovich, 2009b) by engaging in attribute substitution (Kahneman & Frederick, 2002)—the substitution of an easy-to-evaluate characteristic for a harder one, even if the easier one is less accurate. For example, the cognitive miser will substitute the less effortful attributes of vividness or affect for the more effortful retrieval of relevant facts (Kahneman, 2003; Li & Chapman, 2009; Slovic & Peters, 2006; Wang, 2009). But when we are evaluating important risks—such as the risk of certain activities and environments for our children—we do not want to substitute vividness for careful thought about the situation. In such situations, we want to employ Type 2 override processing to block the attribute substitution of the cognitive miser.

To override Type 1 processing, Type 2 processing must display at least two related capabilities. One is the capability of interrupting Type 1 processing and suppressing its response tendencies. Type 2 processing thus involves inhibitory mechanisms of the type that have been the focus of work on executive functioning (Aron, 2008; Best, Miller, & Jones, 2009; Hasher, Lustig, & Zacks, 2007; Miyake et al., 2000; Zelazo, 2004). But the ability to suppress Type 1 processing gets the job only half done. Suppressing one response is not helpful unless there is a better response available to substitute for it. Where do these better responses come from? One answer is that they come from processes of hypothetical reasoning and cognitive simulation that are a unique aspect of Type 2 processing. When we reason hypothetically, we create temporary models of the world and test out actions (or alternative causes) in that simulated world. However, to reason hypothetically, we must have one critical cognitive capability—we must be able to prevent our representations of the real world from becoming confused with representations of imaginary situations. The so-called "cognitive decoupling operations" that make this possible have implications for how we conceptualize both intelligence and rationality, and they will be the focus of several chapters of this book.

Dual-Process Theory and Human Goals: Implications for the Rationality Debate

The findings on individual differences that I discussed briefly above can be used to reconcile the positions in the Great Rationality Debate. My proposal (*see* Stanovich, 2004), is that the statistical distributions of the types of goals being pursued by Type 1 and Type 2 processing are different and that important consequences for human self-fulfillment follow from this fact. The greater evolutionary age of *some* of the mechanisms underlying Type 1 processing accounts for why it more closely tracks ancient evolutionary goals (i.e., the genes' goals), whereas Type 2 processing instantiates a more flexible goal hierarchy that is oriented toward maximizing overall goal satisfaction at the level of the whole organism[9].

---

9 It is also possible that humans pursue goals that are neither in their genes' interests nor in their interests as a person. There are two ways this might occur. One is that the modern world has shifted from the contingencies present in the environment of evolutionary adaptation, rendering evolutionarily instantiated goal structures neither fitness-enhancing nor helpful to the vehicle. This is what gene-culture co-evolution theorists Richerson and Boyd (2005) term the "big mistake." Another way that humans can end up with goals serving neither vehicle nor genes' interests is when a parasitic cultural replicator has infected a host, yielding goal-directed behavior that duplicates the cultural replicator but that is not fitness enhancing nor efficacious for the host (Blackmore, 1999; Dawkins, 1993; Dennett, 1991, 1995, 2006; Distin, 2005; Hull, 2000; Laland & Brown, 2002; Lynch, 1996; Mesoudi, Whiten, &

Because Type 2 processing is more attuned to the person's needs as a coherent organism than is Type processing 1, in the minority of cases where the outputs of the two systems conflict, people will often be better served by executing a system override of the Type 1-triggered output (the full argument is contained in Stanovich, 2004).

From within this framework, I have previously criticized some work in evolutionary psychology and adaptive modeling for implicitly under-valuing instrumental rationality by defending nonnormative responses made by many subjects in reasoning experiments. Many such instances occur when there is a conflict between the responses primed by Type 1 and Type 2 processing and the former dominates. Such situations are interpreted within the framework I have outlined as reflecting conflicts between two different types of optimization—fitness maximization at the subpersonal genetic level and utility maximization at the personal level. Evolutionarily adaptive behavior is not the same as rational behavior. Evolutionary psychologists obscure this by sometimes imply-ing that if a behavior is adaptive, then it is rational. Such a conflation represents a fundamental error of much import for human affairs. Definitions of rationality must be kept consistent with the entity whose optimization is at issue. To maintain this consistency, the different "interests" of the replicators and the vehicle must be explicitly recognized (Dawkins, 1976/1989; Dennett, 1995).

A failure to differentiate these interests is at the heart of the disputes between researchers working in the heuristics and biases tradition and their critics in the evolutionary psychology camp. In several much-cited papers, the empirical demonstrations of a gap between descriptive and normative models of reasoning have been reinterpreted by vari-ous evolutionary psychologists, adaptationist modelers, and ecological theorists[10]. These theorists have reinterpreted the modal response in most of the classic heuristics and biases experiments as indicating an optimal

---

Laland, 2006; Stanovich, 2004). In Chapter 6, this situation will be discussed as one category in a taxonomy of thinking errors.

10 This strand of the Great Rationality Debate is represented by several influential papers and summaries (e.g., Chater & Oaxford, 2001; Cosmides & Tooby, 1992, 1996, 2005; Gigerenzer, 2007, 2008; Oaxford & Chater, 1994, 2007; Todd & Gigerenzer, 2000, 2007; Todd, Hertwig, & Hoffrage, 2005).

information processing adaptation on the part of the subjects. In the extreme, these investigators have argued that the research in the heuristics and biases tradition has not demonstrated *any* human irrationality at all.

First, it certainly must be said that the evolutionary psychologists are on to something with respect to the tasks they have analyzed, because in each case the adaptive response is the *modal* response in the task—the one most subjects give. However, work from my research lab has been triangulating a data pattern relevant to this discussion—an analysis of patterns of covariation and individual differences across these tasks. We have found, as I discussed previously, a very interesting data pattern that holds across many tasks in this dispute: cognitive ability often (but not always) dissociates from the response deemed adaptive on an evolutionary analysis. For example, it is to the credit of the Oaksford and Chater (1994) model of optimal data selection that it predicts the modal PQ response in the Wason four-card selection task. But we are left with the seemingly puzzling finding (*see* Stanovich & West, 1998a, 1998c, 2008b; West et al., 2008) that the response deemed *optimal* under such an analysis (P and Q) is given by subjects of lower general intelligence than the minority giving the response originally deemed correct by Peter Wason (i.e., P and not Q).

A similar puzzle surrounds findings on the Linda conjunction problem, covariation detection paradigm, probability learning paradigm, and belief bias effect in argument evaluation tasks[11]. We have found the same pattern in all of these tasks—the response that is consistent with many evolutionary analyses (optimal foraging and so forth) is the modal response, but the most cognitively able subjects give the response that has traditionally been considered instrumentally rational. Thus, there are two basic patterns that must be reconciled—the modal pattern and the pattern of individual differences—and I have argued that dual-process theories do this if it is assumed that individuals of higher cognitive ability have a higher probability of successfully overriding the Type 1 response.

---

11 This research from my own lab is reported in a variety of publications (Kokis, Macpherson, Toplak, West, & Stanovich, 2002; Sá, West, & Stanovich, 1999; Stanovich & West, 1997, 1998b, 1998c, 1998d, 1999, 2008b; West & Stanovich, 2003; West et al., 2008).

In the model to be presented in this book, I will explain why this is the case.

The evolutionary psychologists are probably correct that most Type 1 processing is evolutionarily adaptive. Nevertheless, their evolutionary interpretations do not impeach the position of the heuristics and biases researchers that the alternative response given by the minority of subjects is rational at the level of the individual. Subjects of higher analytic intelligence are simply more prone to override Type 1 processing and to use Type 2 processing to produce responses that are epistemically and instrumentally rational. This rapprochement between the two camps that my colleague Richard West and I have championed in several papers (e.g., Stanovich & West, 2000) has also been advocated in several articles by Samuels and Stich (Samuels & Stich, 2004; Samuels, Stich, & Bishop, 2002; Samuels, Stich, & Tremoulet, 1999), who have argued for a similar synthesis.

The Rest of This Book: Complications in Dual-Process Theory and Their Implications for the Concepts of Rationality and Intelligence

Given the multifarious nature of human rationality, no one would expect the rapprochement described above to completely end the Great Rationality Debate. It, of course, is a tentative synthesis conceptualized at a fairly gross level of analysis. In an attempt to further understand the source of human rational and irrational behavior, I will introduce several complications to this basic dual-process model in subsequent chapters. These complications will be driven by the need to accommodate findings related to individual differences generated by my lab and several others. I will end up defending a tripartite model of mind that derives from fractionating the notion of Type 2 processing. This alteration in dual-process theory has strong implications for how we understand the overarching constructs of intelligence and human rationality. My purpose is not to sketch a comprehensive theory of the architecture of cognition (in the manner of Carruthers, 2006), but instead to focus on those aspects of a revised tripartite theory that explicate the concept of intelligence and that of human rationality.

In Chapter 2 I argue that it is useful to distinguish the algorithmic level of processing from the reflective level when discussing Type 2 processing. Individual differences in the former reflect the efficiency of the functional cognitive machinery that carries out mental tasks. Individual differences at the reflective level result from variance in higher-level goal states and epistemic thinking dispositions. Measures of intelligence index individual differences at the algorithmic level. Measures of cognitive styles and thinking dispositions index individual differences at the reflective level. In this chapter, I summarize empirical evidence indicating that thinking dispositions and intelligence predict independent variance in performance on various measures of rational thinking.

In Chapter 3, I identify the key operations of the algorithmic mind and the reflective mind that support human rationality. The key function of the algorithmic mind is to sustain the processing of decoupled secondary representations. Secondary representations are copies of primary representations that are not directly connected to input processes or output processes. It is argued in this chapter that measures of fluid intelligence are in part indicating the ability to sustain such offline representations. The ability to sustain decoupled representations is critical to human rationality because it underlies hypothetical thinking—the simulation activities we use to synthesize a response that is better than the response primed by the autonomous mind. The reflective mind, in contrast, sends out the call to begin these types of activities—to interrupt autonomous processing and to begin simulation activities that will result in a response better than that computed by Type 1 autonomous mechanisms.

In Chapter 4, the full tri-process model (autonomous level, algorithmic level, and reflective level) of the mind is fleshed out. Fully decoupled cognitive simulation is distinguished from another type of Type 2 cognition termed serial associative cognition. Three different types of cognitive decoupling are also distinguished. In the override case, decoupling involves taking offline the connection between a primary representation and response programming. In the second case—the case of comprehensive simulation—decoupling involves segregating simulated models of the world from primary representations. A third type of decoupling involves interrupting serial associative cognition—that is, decoupling from the next step in an associative sequence that would otherwise direct thought. Chapter 5 contains speculations on the evolutionary origins of Type 2 processing and describes what I have termed the *Master Rationality Motive* and its origins.

Chapter 6 uses the tri-process model and other distinctions introduced in the book to develop a taxonomy of rational thinking errors that have been revealed in the heuristics and biases literature. The taxonomy is used to classify a large number of tasks and effects from the literature on judgment and decision making. This chapter also stresses the importance of knowledge bases (so-called "mindware") in determining the rationality of beliefs and actions. Chapter 7 contains a comprehensive review of what is known about the connections between intelligence and the reasoning biases related to human rationality. Overall, the associations are surprisingly modest. There is great variability, however. Some well-known thinking biases are virtually independent of cognitive ability. Others do show modest associations. Chapter 7 presents a model of performance on heuristics and biases tasks that explains why some tasks associate with intelligence and others do not.

Having sketched out a model of how and when cognitive ability associates with heuristics and biases tasks in Chapters 6 and 7, in Chapter 8 I use the model to summarize the empirical findings on the nature of the relationship between intelligence and rational thought. It is argued that the relative dissociation between intelligence and rationality is consistent with the tri-process model sketched in earlier chapters and reinforces the usefulness of that framework. This chapter revisits the Great Rationality Debate in cognitive science in light of the findings on individual differences discussed in previous chapters.

Chapter 9 explores the social consequences of the modest association between rational thinking and intelligence. It is argued that an understanding of the implications of the modest association helps to check the imperialism of the intelligence concept in folk psychology. Extant IQ tests do not measure rational thought, but instead are good indicators (in their fluid g component) of algorithmic-level decoupling ability. We should thus not fold rationality into the concept of intelligence, because the most notable operational indicators of the latter do not begin to index the former. That is indeed the thrust of the data discussed in Chapters 7 and 8. Simply put, those data indicate that knowledge of a person's intelligence does very little to predict how they will do on measures of rational thinking.

The data presented in this book indicate that the rankings of individuals on assessments of rational thinking would be different from rankings on intelligence. At present, of course, there is no IQ-type test for rationality—that is, a test of one's RQ (rationality quotient). In Chapter 10, we argue that it is time to start talking about such a thing. We argue that assessing rationality more explicitly is what is needed to draw more attention toward rational thinking skills and to highlight the limitations of what intelligence tests assess. In Chapter 10, we defend the proposition that there is nothing conceptually or theoretically preventing us from developing such a assessment device. In fact, we know the types of thinking processes that would be assessed in such an instrument, and we have in hand prototypes of the kinds of tasks that would be used in the domains of both instrumental rationality and epistemic rationality. We demonstrate this in Chapter 10 by laying out a framework for the assessment of rational thought complete with examples.

2

Differentiating the Algorithmic Mind and the Reflective Mind

A major theme throughout the past 40 years of research in psychology and cognitive science is that humans are cognitive misers (Dawes, 1976; Simon, 1955, 1956; Taylor, 1981; Tversky and Kahneman, 1974). When approaching any problem, our brains have available various computational mechanisms for dealing with the situation. These mechanisms embody a tradeoff, however. The tradeoff is between power and expense. Some mechanisms have great computational power—they can solve a large number of problems and solve them with great accuracy. However, this power comes with a cost. These mechanisms take up a great deal of attention, tend to be slow, tend to interfere with other thoughts and actions we are carrying out, and they require great concentration that is often experienced as aversive. They represent Type 2 processing. In contrast, other brain mechanisms are low in computational power but have the advantage that they are low in cost. These mechanisms do not permit fine-grained accuracy, but they are fast-acting, do not interfere with other ongoing cognition, require little concentration and are not experienced as aversive. They are the Type 1 processes discussed in the previous chapter, which are sometimes also termed heuristic processes.

Humans are cognitive misers because their basic tendency is to default to Type 1 processing mechanisms of low computational expense. Using less computational capacity for one task means there is more left over for another task if they both must be completed simultaneously. This would seem to be adaptive. Nevertheless, this strong bias to default to the simplest cognitive mechanism—to be a cognitive miser—means that humans are often less than rational. Increasingly in the modern world, we are presented with decisions and problems that require more accurate responses than those generated by heuristic processing. Type 1 processes often provide a quick solution that is a first approximation to an optimal response. But modern life often requires more precise thought than this. Modern technological societies are in fact hostile environments for people reliant on only the most easily computed automatic response. Think of the multimillion-dollar advertising industry that has been designed to exploit just this tendency. Modern society keeps proliferating such situations where shallow processing is not sufficient for maximizing personal happiness—precisely because many structures of market-based societies have been designed explicitly to *exploit* such tendencies. Being cognitive misers will seriously impede people from achieving their goals.

In this discussion, I do not mean to imply that using such shortcuts is always wrong. To the contrary, there is a rich literature in psychology showing that in many situations, such heuristic processing is quite useful. In fact, they are so useful that one group of influential psychologists has been led to extol their advantages even to the extent of minimizing the usefulness of the formal rules of rationality[1]. Nevertheless, although clearly acknowledging the usefulness of heuristics, my emphasis in this book will be the opposite—to highlight the dangers of using these heuristics in too many situations, including those that modern society has deliberately designed to trap cognitive misers. When we are over-reliant on heuristic processing we lose personal autonomy. We give up our thinking to those who manipulate our environments, and we let our actions be determined by those who can create the stimuli that best trigger our shallow automatic processing tendencies.

The number of situations where the use of heuristics will lead us astray may not be large, but such situations may be of unusual importance. The importance of a thinking strategy is not assessed by simply counting the number of instances in which it is engaged. We cannot

---

1 Gigerenzer is an influential champion of this view (Gigerenzer, 2002, 2007; Brandstatter, Gigerenzer, & Hertwig, 2006; Gigerenzer & Brighton, 2009; Todd and Gigerenzer, 2000, 2007; *see also* Juslin, Nilsson, & Winman, 2009). His view is controversial, however (in rebuttal, *see* Broder & Newell, 2008; Dougherty, Franco-Watkins, & Thomas, 2008; Evans, 2007; Evans & Over, 2009; Hilbig & Pohl, 2008; Kahneman & Tversky, 1996; Newell, 2005; Oppenheimer, 2003; Over, 2000; Stanovich, 2004). It is important to note that it is doubtful whether many of the heuristics studied by the Gigerenzer group fit the category of Type 1 processes (*see* Broder & Newell, 2008; Evans, 2007a; Evans & Over, 2010; Kahneman & Frederick, 2002; Kahneman & Klein, 2009).

dismiss Type 2 thinking by saying that heuristics will get a "close enough" answer 98% of the time, because the 2% of the instances where heuristics lead us seriously astray may be critical to our lives. A small subset of all the decisions we will make in our life might end up being the dominating factors in determining our life satisfaction. Deciding what occupation to pursue, what specific job to take, who to marry, how to invest, where to locate, how to house ourselves, and whether to have children may, when we look back on our lives decades later, turn out to have determined everything. Yet, in terms of raw numbers, these might represent only 20 to 30 decisions out of thousands that we have made throughout our lives. The 20 to 30 decisions may also be quite unique, and this may render heuristics unhelpful for two reasons. Events that are small in number and not recurring give Type 1 implicit learning mechanisms no chance to abstract information that could be used heuristically. Second, if they are unique, they are probably unprecedented from an evolutionary point of view, and thus there is no chance that Type 1 processing resulting from evolutionary adaptations could help us. For both of these reasons, it is doubtful that relying solely on Type 1 processing will be adequate. The "quick and dirty" answers that heuristics are likely to provide could lead us seriously astray.

Unpacking Type 2 Functioning Using Individual Differences

We know from over three decades of work in the heuristics and biases tradition that exclusive reliance on the heuristic processing tendencies of Type 1 sometimes results in suboptimal responding[2]. The thinking

---

2 There is voluminous evidence that exclusive reliance on the heuristic processing tendencies of Type 1 sometimes results in suboptimal responding (Baron, 2008; Evans, 2007a; Gilovich, Griffin, & Kahneman, 2002; Johnson-Laird, 2006; Kahneman & Tversky, 1973, 1996, 2000; Koehler & Harvey, 2004; Nickerson, 2004, 2008; Nisbett & Ross, 1980; Tversky & Kahneman, 1974, 1983, 1986) and that such thinking errors are not limited to the laboratory (Ariely, 2008; Åstebro, Jeffrey, & Adomdza, 2007; Baron, 1998; Baron, Bazerman, & Shonk, 2006; Belsky & Gilovich, 1999; Berner & Graber, 2008; Camerer, 2000; Chapman & Elstein, 2000; Croskerry, 2009a, 2009b; Dawes, 2001; Hilton, 2003; Kahneman & Tversky, 2000;

errors resulting from Type 1 processing are not limited to the laboratory. These errors have been shown to occur in such important domains as financial planning, medical decision making, career decisions, family planning, resource allocation, tax policy, and insurance purchases. Thus, one of the most important capabilities of Type 2 processing is the ability to interrupt and override the autonomous processing of Type 1 subsystems. One of the primary arguments of this book is that the logic of the override of autonomous subsystems needs to be understood in terms of two levels of processing. The reason for this is described in the following paragraphs.

The autonomous set of systems (TASS) will implement their short-leashed goals unless overridden by mechanisms implementing more global goals of p\ersonal well-being. But override itself is initiated by higher-level control—that is, the algorithmic level of the analytic system (Newell, 1982; Stanovich, 1999) is conceptualized as subordinate to higher-level goal states and epistemic thinking dispositions, some of which have been studied empirically[3]. These goal states and epistemic dispositions exist at what might be termed the reflective level of processing—a level containing control states that regulate behavior at a high level of generality. Such high-level goal states are common in the intelligent agents built by artificial intelligence (AI) researchers (Franklin, 1995; Pollock, 1995; A. Sloman, 1993; A. Sloman & Chrisley, 2003).

My attempt to differentiate the levels of control involved in Type 2 processing actually creates a kind of tripartite theory of mind. Figure 2–1 presents the tripartite proposal in a simple form. In the spirit of Dennett's (1996) book, *Kinds of Minds*, I have labeled the traditional TASS (the source of Type 1 processing) as the autonomous mind, the algorithmic level of Type 2 processing the algorithmic mind, and the reflective level

Lichtenstein & Slovic, 2006; Lilienfeld, Ammirati, & Landfield, 2009; Myers, 2002; Prentice, 2003; Reyna et al., 2009; Stewart, 2009; Sunstein, 2002, 2005; Taleb, 2001, 2007; Tavris & Aronson, 2007; Tetlock, 2005; Thaler & Sunstein, 2008; Ubel, 2000).

3 Thinking dispositions will be discussed later in this chapter, but the literature on the type of disposition I am referring to here is growing (e.g., Cacioppo, Petty, Feinstein, & Jarvis, 1996; Duckworth & Seligman, 2005; Kruglanski & Webster, 1996; Sá, Kelley, Ho, & Stanovich, 2005; Stanovich & West, 1997, 1998c, 2007; West et al., 2008).

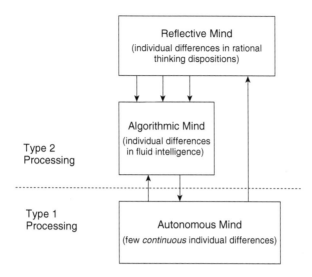

FIGURE 2.1.   The Tripartite Structure and the Locus of Individual Differences.

of Type 2 processing the reflective mind. Dennett's "kinds of minds" terminology helps to mark the distinction I would like to emphasize in this book and should do no harm as long as we respect the caveat that it refers to hierarchies of control rather than separate systems, with all the additional theoretical baggage that the "systems" terminology sometimes carries.

My position on these terminology and definitional issues in dual-process theory is well-captured in a statement by Gilbert (1999):

> "Few of the psychologists whose chapters appear in this volume would claim that the dual processes in their models necessarily correspond to the activity of two distinct brain structures . . . . Psychologists who champion dual-process models are not usually stuck on two. Few would come undone if their models were recast in terms of three processes, or four, or even five. Indeed, the only number they would not happily accept is one, because claims about dual processes in psychology are not so much claims about how many processes there are, but claims about how many processes there aren't. And the claim is this: There aren't one." (pp. 3–4)

These preliminaries aside, what might motivate a tripartite model? First, it might be noted that researchers in AI take the possibility of a tripartite structure quite seriously (*see* A. Sloman & Chrisley, 2003; Samuels, 2005). It thus has precedent in at least some subdisciplines of cognitive science. However, are there any other reasons, aside from the precedent in AI research, for accepting this alternative structure? First, it must be acknowledged that there is no way that the distinctions between the algorithmic and reflective mind will cleave as nicely as those that have traditionally differentiated Type 1 and 2 processing (the dashed line in Fig. 2–1 signals this) because the algorithmic and reflective mind will both share properties (e.g., capacity-limited serial processing) that differentiate them from the autonomous mind.

Nonetheless, there are reasons for giving the algorithmic/reflective distinction some consideration. The empirical work on individual differences in rational thought that was discussed in the previous chapter provides one such rationale. This relatively unique focus on individual differences has motivated our attempt to separate aspects of Type 2 processing that had heretofore been conflated. I call this emphasis on individual differences unique only in the context of the heuristics and biases research tradition. Of course, psychology as a whole—with its subfield of psychometrics—is no stranger to individual differences. But that perspective was largely missing from the Great Rationality Debate and from most early dual-process theorizing.

So what have we found? First, we have found that individual differences in some very important critical thinking pitfalls such as the tendency toward myside thinking and the tendency toward one-sided thinking are relatively independent of intelligence (Stanovich & West, 2007, 2008a). We take this to indicate that the critical thinking skills necessary to avoid myside bias and one-side bias are instantiated at the reflective level of the mind as opposed to the algorithmic level. Second, across a variety of tasks from the heuristics and biases literature, it has consistently been found that rational thinking dispositions will predict variance in these tasks after the effects of general intelligence have been controlled[4]. In these empirical studies, the rational thinking dispositions

---

4 This evidence is substantial and growing (Bruine de Bruin et al., 2007; Klaczynski, Gordon, & Fauth, 1997; Klaczynski & Lavallee, 2005; Klaczynski & Robinson, 2000;

examined have encompassed assessments of epistemic regulation such as actively open-minded thinking and dogmatism (Stanovich & West, 1997, 2007), assessments of response regulation such as the Matching Familiar Figures Test (Kagan, Rosman, Day, Albert, & Philips, 1964), and assessments of cognitive regulation such as need for cognition (Cacioppo et al., 1996). That thinking dispositions and cognitive ability both explain unique variance in rational thinking is one of the foundational data patterns supporting the fractionation of Type 2 processing that is proposed in the tripartite model of this book.

Cognitive Ability and Thinking Dispositions Partition the Algorithmic and the Reflective Mind

The difference between the algorithmic mind and the reflective mind is captured in the well-established distinction in the measurement of individual differences between cognitive ability and thinking dispositions. The former are measures of the efficiency of the algorithmic mind. In contrast, thinking dispositions (sometimes termed cognitive styles) are measures of the functioning of the reflective mind. Many thinking dispositions concern beliefs, belief structure, and, importantly, attitudes toward forming and changing beliefs. Other thinking dispositions that have been identified concern a person's goals and goal hierarchy. Examples of some thinking dispositions that have been investigated by psychologists are: actively open-minded thinking, need for cognition (the tendency to think a lot), consideration of future consequences, typical intellectual engagement, need for closure, superstitious thinking, and dogmatism.

The literature on these types of thinking dispositions is vast[5], and my purpose is not to review that literature here. It is only necessary to note

---

Kokis et al., 2002; Ku & Ho, 2010; Newstead, Handley, Harley, Wright, & Farrelly, 2004; Macpherson & Stanovich, 2007; Parker & Fischhoff, 2005; Sá & Stanovich, 2001; Stanovich & West, 1997, 1998c, 2000; Toplak & Stanovich, 2002; Toplak, Liu, Macpherson, Toneatto, & Stanovich, 2007; West et al., 2008).

5 Many publications review parts of the literature on thinking dispositions (e.g., Ackerman & Heggestad, 1997; Baron, 1985, 2008; Cacioppo et al., 1996; Dole & Sinatra, 1998; Kruglanski & Webster, 1996; Norris & Ennis, 1989; Perkins, 1995;

that the types of cognitive propensities that these thinking disposition measures reflect are: the tendency to collect information before making up one's mind, the tendency to seek various points of view before coming to a conclusion, the disposition to think extensively about a problem before responding, the tendency to calibrate the degree of strength of one's opinion to the degree of evidence available, the tendency to think about future consequences before taking action, the tendency to explicitly weigh pluses and minuses of situations before making a decision, and the tendency to seek nuance and avoid absolutism. In short, individual differences in thinking dispositions are assessing variation in people's goal management, epistemic values, and epistemic self-regulation—differences in the operation of the reflective mind.

The cognitive abilities assessed on intelligence tests are not of this type. They are not about high-level personal goals and their regulation, or about the tendency to change beliefs in the face of contrary evidence, or about how knowledge acquisition is internally regulated when not externally directed. Theorists have indeed come up with *definitions* of intelligence that encompass such things. For example, intelligence is sometimes defined in ways that encompass rational action and belief (Stanovich, 2009b). However, despite the popularity of such theoretical stipulations, the actual measures of intelligence in use assess only algorithmic-level cognitive capacity. No current intelligence test that is even moderately used in practice assesses rational thought or behavior.

Thinking disposition measures are telling us about the individual's goals and epistemic values—and they are indexing broad tendencies of pragmatic and epistemic self-regulation at a high level of cognitive control. The empirical studies cited in Footnote 4 indicate that these different types of cognitive predictors are tapping separable variance, and the reason that this is to be expected is because cognitive capacity measures (like intelligence tests) and thinking dispositions map on to different levels of analysis in cognitive theory. Figure 2–1 reflects this theoretical conjecture (Stanovich, 2002, 2009a, 2009b). It is proposed that variation in fluid intelligence largely indexes individual differences

Schommer, 1990; Stanovich, 1999; Sternberg, 1997c, 2003; Sternberg & Grigorenko, 1997; Strathman, Gleicher, Boninger, & Edwards, 1994).

in the efficiency of processing of the algorithmic mind. In contrast, thinking dispositions index individual differences in the reflective mind.

One further reason for endorsing a tripartite structure is that break-downs in cognitive functioning in the three kinds of minds manifest very differently. For example, disruptions in algorithmic-level functioning are apparent in general impairments in intellectual ability of the type that cause mental retardation (Anderson, 1998, 2005). And these disruptions vary quite continuously. Disruptions to the autonomous mind, in con-trast, often reflect damage to cognitive modules that result in very dis-continuous cognitive dysfunction such as autism or the agnosias and alexias[6]. Importantly, Bermudez (2001; *see also* Murphy & Stich, 2000) notes that they are traditionally explained by recourse to subpersonal functions (*see* Davies, 2000, Frankish, 2009, for discussions of personal and subpersonal constructs). In complete contrast are many psychiatric disorders (particularly those such as delusions), which implicate func-tioning in what I here call the reflective mind. Bermudez (2001) argues that the

> "impairments in which they manifest themselves are of the sort
> that would standardly be explained at the personal level, rather
> than at the subpersonal level. In the terms of Fodor's dichotomy,
> psychiatric disorders seem to be disorders of central processing
> rather than peripheral modules . . .. Many of the symptoms of
> psychiatric disorders involve impairments of rationality—and
> consequently that the norms of rationality must be taken to
> play a vital role in the understanding of psychiatric disorders."
> (pp. 460–461)

Thus, there is an important sense in which rationality is a more encompassing construct than intelligence. The reason is that rationality is an organismic-level concept. It concerns the actions of an entity in its environment that serve its goals. It concerns both levels of analysis—the algorithmic and the reflective levels. To be rational, an organism must have well-calibrated beliefs (reflective level) and must act appropriately

---

6 Several empirical and theoretical papers discuss individual differences in the autonomous mind (Anderson, 2005; Kanazawa, 2004; Reber, 1992, 1993; Saffran, Aslin, & Newport, 1996; Vinter & Detable, 2003; Zacks, Hasher, & Sanft, 1982).

on those beliefs to achieve its goals (reflective level). The organism must, of course, have the algorithmic-level machinery that enables it to carry out the actions and to process the environment in a way that enables the correct beliefs to be fixed and the correct actions to be taken.

Thus, individual differences in rational thought and action can arise because of individual differences in intelligence (an algorithmic-level construct) or because of individual differences in thinking dispositions (a reflective-level construct). To put it simply, the concept of rationality encompasses two things (thinking dispositions and algorithmic-level capacity), whereas the concept of intelligence—at least as it is commonly operationalized—is largely confined to algorithmic-level capacity. Thus, it is clear from Figure 2–1 why rationality and intelligence can come apart. As long as variation in thinking dispositions is not perfectly correlated with intelligence, then there is the statistical possibility of dissociations between rationality and intelligence. Substantial empirical evidence indicates that individual differences in thinking dispositions and intelligence are far from perfectly correlated. Many different studies involving thousands of subjects (Ackerman & Heggestad, 1997; Bates & Shieles, 2003; Cacioppo et al., 1996; Fleischhauer et al., 2010; Goff & Ackerman, 1992; Noftle & Robins, 2007) have indicated that measures of intelligence display only moderate to weak correlations (usually less than 0.30) with some thinking dispositions (e.g., actively open-minded thinking, need for cognition) and near zero correlations with others (e.g., conscientiousness, curiosity, diligence).

It is important to note that the thinking dispositions of the reflective mind are the psychological mechanisms that underlie rational thought. Maximizing these dispositions is *not* the criterion of rational thought itself. Rationality involves instead the maximization of goal achievement via judicious decision making and optimizing the fit of belief to evidence. The thinking dispositions of the reflective mind are a means to these ends. Certainly high levels of such commonly studied dispositions as reflectivity and belief flexibility are needed for rational thought and action. But the highest levels of such thinking dispositions are not necessarily the maximal levels. One does not maximize the reflectivity dimension, for example, because such a person might get lost in interminable pondering and never make a decision. Similarly, one does not maximize the thinking disposition of belief flexibility either, because such a person might end up with a pathologically unstable personality. Reflectivity and belief flexibility are "good" cognitive styles (in that most people are not high enough on these dimensions, so that "more" would be better), but they are not meant to be maximized.

Intelligence Tests and Critical Thinking Tests Partition the Algorithmic from the Reflective Mind

The difference between the reflective mind and the algorithmic mind is captured operationally in the distinction that psychologists make between tests of intelligence and tests of critical thinking. To a layperson, the tasks on tests of cognitive capacities (intelligence tests or other aptitude measures) might seem superficially similar to those on tests of critical thinking (in the educational literature, the term *critical thinking* is often used to cover tasks and mental operations that a cognitive scientist would term indicators of rational thought). An outsider to psychometrics or cognitive science might deem the classification of tasks into one category or the other somewhat arbitrary. In fact, it is far from arbitrary and actually reflects the distinction between the reflective mind and the algorithmic mind.

Psychometricians have long distinguished typical performance situations from optimal (sometimes termed *maximal*) performance situations (Ackerman, 1994, 1996; Ackerman & Kanfer, 2004; Cronbach, 1949; Matthews, Zeidner, & Roberts, 2002). Typical performance situations are unconstrained in that no overt instructions to maximize performance are given, and the task interpretation is determined to some extent by the participant. The goals to be pursued in the task are left somewhat open. Typical performance measures are measures of the reflective mind—they assess, in part, goal prioritization and epistemic regulation. In contrast, optimal performance situations are those where the task interpretation is determined externally (not left to the participant) and the participant is instructed to maximize performance and is told how to do so. Duckworth (2009) has discussed the surprisingly weak relation between typical and maximal performance across a variety of domains. For example, Sackett, Zedeck, and Fogli, (1988) found that there were very low correlations between the maximal item processing efficiency

that supermarket cashiers could attain and the typical processing efficiency that they usually attained.

All tests of intelligence or cognitive aptitude are optimal performance assessments, whereas measures of critical or rational thinking are
often assessed under typical performance conditions. This means that
tests of intelligence are constrained at the reflective level (an attempt is
made to specify the task demands so explicitly that variation in high-
level thinking dispositions are minimally influential). In contrast, tests
of critical or rational thinking are not constrained at the reflective level
(or at least are much less constrained). Tasks of the latter, but not the
former, type allow high-level personal goals (and epistemic goals) to
become implicated in performance.

Consider the type of syllogistic reasoning item usually examined by
cognitive psychologists studying belief bias effects (*see* Evans, Barston, &
Pollard, 1983; Evans & Curtis-Holmes, 2005; Evans, Newstead, Allen, &
Pollard, 1994):

Premise 1: All living things need water.
Premise 2: Roses need water.
Therefore, Roses are living things.

Approximately 70% of the university students who have been given
this problem incorrectly think that the conclusion is valid (Markovits &
Nantel, 1989; Sá, West, & Stanovich, 1999; Stanovich & West, 1998c).
Clearly, the believability of the conclusion is interfering with the assessment of logical validity.

The important point for the present discussion is that it would not
be surprising to see an item such as the "rose" syllogism (i.e., an item
that pitted prior belief against logical validity) on a critical thinking test.
Such tests do not constrain high-level thinking dispositions and, in fact,
attempt to probe and assess the nature of such cognitive tendencies to
bias judgments in the direction of prior belief or to trump prior belief
with new evidence. Thus, for example, an exercise on the *Watson-Glaser
Critical Thinking Appraisal* (Watson & Glaser, 1980) requires that respon-
dents reason regarding the proposition: Groups in this country who are
opposed to some of our government's policies should be permitted
unrestricted freedom of press and speech. Obviously, this is an issue on
which prior opinion might be strong. However, to do well on a test such

as this, one has to set aside prior opinion because one must evaluate whether arguments relevant to the proposition are strong or weak, independent of prior belief. When such tests are well-designed, strong and weak arguments are presented supporting both the "pro" side of the proposition and the "anti" side of the proposition. Regardless of prior opinion, on some items the respondent is presented with a conflict between prior opinion and argument strength. Thus, the respondent must regulate how much to weigh the structure of the argument versus the prior belief. The test directly taps reflective-level epistemic regulation.

In using items with such content, critical thinking tests such as the Watson-Glaser create (even if the instructions attempt to clarify) ambiguity about what feature of the problem to rely upon—ambiguity that is resolved differently by individuals with different epistemic dispositions. The point is that on an intelligence test, there would be no epistemic ambiguity created in the first place. Such tests attempt to constrain reflective-level functioning to isolate processing abilities at the algorithmic level of analysis. It is the efficiency of computational abilities under optimal (not typical) conditions that is the focus of IQ tests. Variation in high-level thinking dispositions would contaminate this algorithmic-level assessment.

I do not wish to argue that intelligence tests are entirely successful in this respect—that they entirely eliminate reflective-level factors; I argue only that the constructors of the tests *attempt* to do so. Additionally, it is certainly the case that some strategic control is exercised on intelligence test items, but this tends to be a type of micro-level control rather than the activation of macro-strategies that are engaged by critical thinking tests. For example, on multiple-choice IQ-test items, the respondent is certainly engaging in a variety of control processes such as suppressing responses to identified distracter items. Nonetheless, if the test is properly designed, then they are not engaging in the type of macro-level strategizing that is common on critical thinking tests—for example, deciding how to construe the task or how to allocate effort across differing construals.

Thus, you will not find an item like the "rose" syllogism on an intelligence test (or any aptitude measure or cognitive capacity measure). Instead, on a cognitive ability test, a syllogistic reasoning item would be stripped of content (all As are Bs, etc.) to remove any possible belief bias component. In complete contrast, in the reasoning and rational thinking literature, conflict between knowledge and validity is often deliberately *created* to study belief bias. Thus, cognitive ability tests eliminate the conflict between epistemic tendencies to preserve logical validity and the tendency to project prior knowledge. In contrast, critical thinking tasks deliberately leave reflective-level strategic decisions unconstrained, because it is precisely such epistemic regulation that they wish to assess. Of course, this is why debates about the normative response on rational thinking measures have been prolonged in a way that has not characterized IQ tests[7]. The more a measure taps the reflective-level psychology of rationality, the more it will implicate normative issues that are largely moot when measuring algorithmic-level efficiency.

Critical thinking skills of the type that underlie the unbiased processing of evidence have repeatedly shown a connection to thinking dispositions independent of intelligence. For example, Schommer (1990) found that a measure of the disposition to believe that knowledge is certain predicted the tendency to draw one-sided conclusions from ambiguous evidence even after verbal ability was controlled. Kardash and Scholes (1996) found that the tendency to properly draw inconclusive inferences from mixed evidence was negatively related to belief in certain knowledge and positively related to a measure of need for cognition (Cacioppo et al., 1996). Furthermore, these relationships were not mediated by verbal ability because a vocabulary measure was essentially unrelated to evidence evaluation. Likewise, Klaczynski (1997; *see also* Klaczynski & Gordon, 1996; Klaczynski et al., 1997; Klaczynski & Lavallee, 2005; Klaczynski & Robinson, 2000) found that the degree to which participants criticized belief-inconsistent evidence more than belief-consistent evidence was unrelated to cognitive ability.

---

7 Again, see the literature on the Great Rationality Debate mentioned in the previous chapter (e.g., Bagassi & Macchi, 2006; Cohen, 1981; Gigerenzer, 1996; Kahneman & Tversky, 1996; Keys & Schwartz, 2007; Koehler, 1996; Kuhberger, 2002; Lopes, 1991; Manktelow, 2004; Margolis, 1987; Nickerson, 2008; Over, 2002, 2004; Prentice, 2003; Samuels & Stich, 2004; Samuels, Stich, & Bishop, 2002; Shafir & LeBoeuf, 2002; Stanovich, 1999, 2004; Stein, 1996; Tetlock & Mellers, 2002; Vranas, 2000).

Results from my own laboratory have converged with those of Schommer (1990) and Kardash and Scholes (1996) in indicating that thinking dispositions can predict argument evaluation skill once cognitive ability is partialled out. We have developed an argument evaluation task in which we derive an index of the degree to which argument evaluation is associated with argument quality independent of prior belief (*see* Stanovich & West, 1997, 1998c; Sá et al., 1999). We have consistently found that even after controlling for cognitive ability, individual differences on our index of argument-driven processing can be predicted by measures of dogmatism and absolutism (Rokeach, 1960), categorical thinking (Epstein & Meier, 1989), openness (Costa & McCrae, 1992), flexible thinking (Stanovich & West, 1997), belief identification (Sá et al., 1999), counterfactual thinking, superstitious thinking (Stanovich, 1989; Tobacyk & Milford, 1983), and actively open-minded thinking (Sá et al., 2005; Stanovich & West, 1997).

Thinking Dispositions as Independent Predictors of Rational Thought

Thus, to fully understand variation in tests of unbiased reasoning (the basic skill on many critical thinking tests), we need to consider variation at the reflective level as well as at the algorithmic level of cognitive analysis. Indeed, this seems to be true for many other tasks in the heuristics and biases literature as well. For example, we have linked various measures of thinking dispositions to statistical reasoning tasks of various types (Kokis et al., 2002; Stanovich, 1999; Stanovich & West, 1998c, 1999, 2000). One such task derives from the work of Nisbett and Ross (1980), who studied the tendency of human judgment to be overinfluenced by vivid but unrepresentative personal and testimonial evidence and to be underinfluenced by more representative and diagnostic statistical evidence. Studying the variation in this response tendency is important because, as Griffin and Tversky (1992) argue, "the tendency to prefer an individual or 'inside' view rather than a statistical or 'outside' view represents one of the major departures of intuitive judgment from normative theory" (pp. 431–432). The quintessential problem (*see* Fong, Krantz, & Nisbett, 1986) involves choosing between contradictory car purchase recommendations—one from a large-sample survey of car buyers and the other the heartfelt and emotional testimony of a single friend. Fong et al. (1986) and Jepson, Krantz, and Nisbett (1983) have studied a variety of such problems and we have examined a number of them in our own research. We have consistently found that dispositions toward actively open-minded thinking are consistently associated with reliance on the statistical evidence rather than the testimonial evidence. Furthermore, this association remains even after cognitive ability has been controlled.

We have examined a variety of other critical and rational thinking tasks and have consistently found the same pattern. For example, we have examined the phenomenon of outcome bias in decision evaluation (Baron & Hershey, 1988)—the tendency to rate decision quality according to the outcome of the decision even when the outcome provides no cues to the information available to the decision maker. We again found that the ability to avoid outcome bias was associated with dispositions toward actively open-minded thinking and that this tendency did not solely result from differences in cognitive ability. Similar results were found for a variety of other hypothesis testing and reasoning tasks (Bruine de Bruin et al., 2007; Kokis et al., 2002; Stanovich, 1999, 2009b; Stanovich & West, 1998c, 2000; Toplak & Stanovich, 2002; West et al., 2008). I have argued elsewhere that the thinking dispositions that serve as good independent predictors in these studies tend to be those that reflect a tendency toward cognitive decontextualization—the tendency to strip unnecessary context from problems (Stanovich, 1999, 2003, 2004). Such dispositions serve to counter one aspect of what I have termed the *fundamental computational bias of human cognition*. That aspect is the tendency to contextualize a problem with as much prior knowledge as is easily accessible. This fundamental computational bias was useful in our evolutionary history, but modern bureaucratic societies often require that this bias be overridden. Many tasks in the heuristics and biases literature tap the ease with which we recognize this necessity.

In summary, throughout several of our studies, normative responding on a variety of problems from the heuristics and biases literature was moderately correlated with cognitive ability. Nevertheless, the magnitude of the associations with cognitive ability left considerable room for the possibility that the remaining reliable variance might index systematic variation in reflective-level psychological tendencies. In fact, it was rarely the case that once capacity limitations had been controlled, the remaining variations from normative responding were unpredictable (which would have indicated that the residual variance consisted largely of random error). First, in several studies, we have shown that there was significant covariance among the scores from a variety of tasks in the heuristics and biases literature after they had been residualized on measures of cognitive ability (Stanovich, 1999; *see also* Bruine de Bruin et al., 2007; Parker & Fischhoff, 2005; West et al., 2008). Second, in the studies just reviewed, the residual variance (after partialling cognitive ability) was also systematically associated with cognitive styles relating to epistemic regulation. Both of these findings are indications that the residual variance is systematic.

Finally, not only are aspects of rational thought predicted by thinking dispositions after intelligence is controlled, but the *outcomes* of rational thought are likewise predicted by variation in characteristics of the reflective mind. For example, Bruine de Bruin, Parker, and Fischhoff (2007) recruited a sample of 360 citizens who resembled the demographics of the 2000 U.S Census for their area and administered a battery of rational thinking tasks. They then formed a composite score reflecting overall rational thinking skill and found that it was correlated (negatively) with a composite measure of poor decision-making outcomes (e.g., bouncing checks, having been arrested, losing driving privileges, credit card debt, eviction). Importantly, Bruine de Bruin et al. (2007) found that variance in their decision outcome measure was predicted by rational thinking skill after the variance associated with cognitive ability had been removed.

Duckworth and Seligman (2005) found that the grade point averages of a group of eighth graders was predicted by measures of self-discipline after the variance associated with intelligence was partialled out. A longitudinal analysis showed that self-discipline was a better predictor of changes in grade point average across the school year than intelligence. A converging finding is that the personality variable of conscientiousness—which taps the higher-level regulatory properties of the reflective mind—has been shown to predict (independent of intelligence) academic performance and measures of performance in the workplace (Goff & Ackerman, 1992; Higgins, Peterson, Pihl, & Lee, 2007).

Finally, Tetlock (2005) studied expert political forecasters, all of whom had doctoral degrees (and hence were presumably of high intelligence), and found that overconfidence was related to thinking dispositions that tapped epistemic regulation.

In short, there is a substantial amount of research indicating the psychometric separability of the aspects of rational thought connected to intelligence from the rational thinking tendencies linked to thinking dispositions of the reflective mind.

3

The Key Functions of the Reflective Mind and the Algorithmic Mind that Support Human Rationality

The reflective mind and the algorithmic mind both have a key function that serves to support human rationality. Both functions operate to create an aspect of reasoning that has received considerable attention in parts of the dual-process literature—hypothetical thinking (Evans, 2003, 2006b, 2007a; Evans & Over, 1996, 2004). Evans (2006b) has made the important argument that "the analytic system is involved whenever hypothetical thought is required" (p. 379). Stated in the form of a conditional, Evans' assertion is: If hypothetical thought is required, then the analytic system is involved. Such a formulation preserves an important point I will make later—not all Type 2 thought involves hypothetical thinking.

Hypothetical thinking is the foundation of rationality because it is tightly connected to the notion of autonomous system override (*see* Stanovich, 2004). Type 2 processing must be able to take early response tendencies triggered by TASS offline and be able to substitute better responses. But from where do these better responses come? One answer is that they come from a process of cognitive simulation[1]. In Chapter 1, I explained why responses that have survived a selective process during simulation are often better choices than responses triggered by the autonomous mind.

So the key mechanism of the *reflective* mind that supports human rationality is the mechanism that sends out a call to begin cognitive

---

1 There is a large and growing literature on cognitive simulation (e.g., Atance & Jackson, 2009; Barrett, Henzi, & Dunbar, 2003; Beck, Riggs, & Gorniak, 2009; Buckner & Carroll, 2007; Byrne, 2005; Currie & Ravenscroft, 2002; Decety & Grezes, 2006; Dougherty, Gettys, & Thomas, 1997; Evans, 2007a; Evans & Over, 2004; Goldman, 2006; Kahneman & Tversky, 1982b; Nichols & Stich, 2003; Oatley, 1999; Roese, 1997; Schacter & Addis, 2007; Sterelny, 2001; Suddendorf & Corballis, 2007; Suddendorf & Whiten, 2001).

simulation or hypothetical reasoning more generally. Individual differences in the operation of this mechanism contribute to differences in
rational thinking. Correspondingly, there is a key operation of the algorithmic mind that supports hypothetical thinking and is characterized by
large individual differences. Cognitive simulation and hypothetical reasoning depend on the operation of cognitive decoupling carried out by
the algorithmic mind. Cognitive decoupling has been discussed in related
and somewhat differing ways by a large number of different investigators
coming from a variety of different perspectives, not limited to: developmental psychology, evolutionary psychology, artificial intelligence, and
philosophy of mind[2]. I shall emphasize the origins of the concept in
developmental psychology because of a useful theoretical link to important models of the origins of Type 2 processing (*see* Chapter 5).

To reason hypothetically, we must be able to prevent our representations of the real world from becoming confused with representations of
imaginary situations. For example, when considering a goal state that is
different from the one we currently have, we must be able to represent
our current goal and the alternative goal and keep straight which is
which. Likewise, we need to be able to differentiate the representation of
an action about to be taken from representations of potential *alternative*
actions we are trying out in cognitive simulations. Otherwise, we would
confuse the action about to be taken with alternatives that we were just
simulating.

The potential for confusion among representational states (sometimes termed representational abuse) has been a major issue for developmental psychologists trying to understand the emergence of pretense
and pretend play in children (e.g., a child saying "this banana is a phone").
Playing with the banana as a phone must take place without actual
representations of banana and phone in the mind becoming confused or
indistinct. In a much-cited article in the early theory of mind literature,

---

2 Cognitive decoupling has been discussed in many different disciplines, although
not always under that name (Atance & O'Neill, 2001; Carruthers, 2000, 2006; Clark
& Karmiloff-Smith, 1993; Corballis, 2003; Cosmides & Tooby, 2000; Dennett, 1984;
Dienes & Perner, 1999; Evans & Over, 1999; Glenberg, 1997; Jackendoff, 1996;
Lillard, 2001; Nichols & Stich, 2003; Perner, 1991, 1998; Sperber, 2000; Sterelny, 2001;
Suddendorf, 1999; Suddendorf & Corballis, 2007; M. Wilson, 2002).

Leslie (1987) provided a model of pretence that made use of the concept of cognitive decoupling. Leslie's (1987) model can best be understood by adopting a terminology later used by Perner (1991). In the latter's view, a primary representation is one that is used to directly map the world and/or is also rather directly connected to a response. Leslie (1987) modeled pretense by positing a so-called "secondary representation" (to use Perner's [1991] terms) that was a copy of the primary representation but that was decoupled from the world so that it could be manipulated— that is, be a mechanism for simulation (*see* Fig. 3–1). Nichols and Stich (2003) model this cognitive decoupling as a separate "Possible Worlds Box" (PWB) in which the simulations are carried out without contaminating the relationship between the world and primary representation.

For Leslie (1987), the decoupled secondary representation is necessary to avoid representational abuse—the possibility of confusing our simulations with our primary representations of the world as it actually is. The cognitive operation of decoupling, or what Nichols and Stich (2003) term *cognitive quarantine*, prevents our representations of the real world from becoming confused with representations of imaginary situations. To engage in exercises of hypothetical thinking and high-level cognitive control, one has to explicitly represent a psychological attitude toward the state of affairs as well as the state of affairs itself

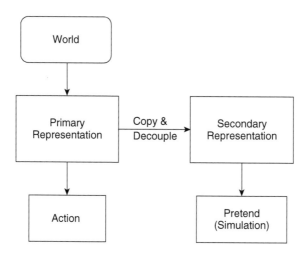

FIGURE 3.1.   Cognitive Decoupling (Based on Leslie, 1987).

(Dienes & Perner, 1999; Evans & Over, 1999). Thus, decoupled representations of actions about to be taken become representations of potential actions, but the latter must not infect the former while the mental simulation is being carried out.

As Leslie (1987) notes, the ongoing simulation leaves intact the tracking of the world by the primary representation: "Meanwhile the original primary representation, a copy of which was raised to a second order, continues with its definite and literal reference, truth, and existence relations. It is free to continue exerting whatever influence it would have on ongoing processes" (p. 417). Nonetheless, dealing with secondary representations—keeping them decoupled—is costly in terms of cognitive capacity. Evolution has guaranteed the high cost of decoupling for a very good reason. As we were becoming the first creatures to rely strongly on cognitive simulation, it was especially important that we not become "unhooked" from the world too much of the time. Thus, dealing with primary representations of the world always has a special salience. Glenberg (1997) argues that an indication of the difficulty of decoupling is a behavior such as closing one's eyes while engaged in deep thought—or looking up at the sky or averting one's gaze (*see* Doherty-Sneddon, Phelps, & Clark, 2007). Such behaviors are attempts to prevent changes in our primary representations of the world from disrupting ongoing simulation—that is, the transformation of a secondary representation.

Decoupling operations must be continually in force during any ongoing simulations, and I have conjectured (Stanovich, 2001, 2004, 2009a) that the raw ability to sustain such mental simulations while keeping the relevant representations decoupled is likely the key aspect of the brain's computational power that is being assessed by measures of fluid intelligence (on fluid intelligence, *see* Carroll, 1993; Horn & Cattell, 1967; Horn & Noll, 1997; Kane & Engle, 2002; Unsworth & Engle, 2005). Decoupling—outside of certain domains such as behavioral prediction (so-called "theory of mind")—is a cognitively demanding operation. Language appears to be one mental tool that can aid this computationally expensive process. Language provides the discrete representational medium that greatly enables hypothetical thinking to flourish as a culturally acquired mode of thought (*see* Flynn, 2007). For example, hypothetical thought involves representing assumptions, and linguistic forms such as conditionals provide a medium for such representations (Carruthers, 2006; Evans, 2007a; Evans & Over, 2004).

Decoupling skills vary in their recursiveness and complexity. The skills discussed thus far are those that are necessary for creating what Perner (1991) calls *secondary representations*—the decoupled representations that are the multiple models of the world that enable hypothetical thought. At a certain level of development, decoupling becomes used for so-called "metarepresentation"—thinking about thinking itself[3]. Decoupling processes enable one to distance oneself from representations of the world so that they can be reflected upon and potentially improved. The use of metarepresentational abilities in such a program of cognitive reform would be an example of what has been termed the quest for broad rationality (Elster, 1983)—the cognitive critique of the beliefs and desires that are input into the implicit calculations that result in instrumental rationality (*see* Stanovich, 2004).

The level of cognitive decoupling ability also has implications for everyday functioning in real life. For example, Kane et al. (2007) used an experience-sampling method to study 124 undergraduates over a 7-day period—signaling them eight times daily to see if their minds were currently wandering from their present activity. Subjects with lower working memory capacity reported more instances of mind wandering. This study provides a real-life example of how sustained decoupling ability cashes out in the real world. People with more ability to sustain decoupling (conjectured here to be indicated by measures such as working memory that load heavily on fluid intelligence) are less likely to have their ongoing cognitive simulations degenerate into serial associative cognition. In a related study of the real-world consequences of sustained decoupling ability, Pronk et al. (2010) found that measures of sustained decoupling (a variety of executive functioning measures) predicted the disposition of forgiveness as well as the development of forgiveness over a 5-week period. People with more ability to sustain decoupling displayed more forgiveness. Those higher in executive functioning

---

3 There are many subtleties surrounding the concept of metarepresentation (*see* Dennett, 1984; Nichols & Stich, 2003; Perner, 1991; Sperber 2000; Sterelny, 2003; Suddendorf & Whiten, 2001; Whiten, 2001).

were found to be better at suppressing negative rumination about the transgression.

In summary, the reflective mind initiates the call to interrupt Type 1 processing and it signals the need to decouple representations to begin simulation operations. Both of these high-level control operations serve the dictates of human rationality. As discussed in the first two chapters, Type 1 processing will, if unimpeded, sometimes result in non-normative responding, as the heuristics and biases literature amply demonstrates. However, the generation of a superior response often necessitates running cognitive simulations, and the signal to decouple representations for this purpose is a function of the reflective mind.

In contrast, sustaining the decoupling operations over time is the key function of the algorithmic mind that supports human rationality, and it is the operation that accounts for several other features of Type 2 processing—particularly its seriality and most importantly its computational expense. In short, we are beginning to understand the key computational function of the algorithmic mind that supports human rationality—taking representations offline and sustaining them offline (Bickerton, 1995; Toates, 2005, 2006). I have discussed here two such types of cognitive decoupling. The first involves taking Type 1 processing offline and holding the response representation that it has primed in abeyance. The second involves the type of cognitive decoupling illustrated in Figure 3–1 and discussed by Leslie (1987)—the copying of a primary representation and its use in cognitive simulation.

I have argued that individual differences in fluid intelligence are a key indicator of the variability across individuals in the ability to sustain decoupling operations (Stanovich, 2001, 2009b). For this conceptualization, I rely on the Cattell/Horn/Carroll (CHC) theory of intelligence (Carroll, 1993; Cattell, 1963, 1998; Horn & Cattell, 1967). Sometimes termed the theory of fluid and crystallized intelligence (symbolized Gf/Gc theory), this theory posits that tests of mental ability tap, in addition to a general factor, a small number of broad factors, of which two are dominant[4]. Fluid intelligence (Gf) reflects reasoning abilities

4 There is a large literature on the theory and on the processing correlates of Gf and Gc (*see* Daniel, 2000; Duncan et al., 2008; Geary, 2005; Gignac, 2005; Horn & Noll, 1997; Kane & Engle, 2002; Mackintosh & Bennett, 2003; McArdle, et al., 2002;

operating across of variety of domains—particularly novel ones. It is measured by tasks of abstract reasoning such as figural analogies, Raven Matrices, and series completion. Crystallized intelligence (Gc) reflects declarative knowledge acquired from acculturated learning experiences. It is measured by vocabulary tasks, verbal comprehension, and general knowledge measures. Ackerman (1996) discusses how the two dominant factors in the CHC theory reflect a long history of considering two aspects of intelligence: intelligence-as-process (Gf) and intelligence-as-knowledge (Gc).

It is becoming increasingly apparent that one of the critical mental operations being tapped by measures of fluid intelligence is the cognitive decoupling operation I have discussed in this chapter. This is becoming clear from converging work on executive function and working memory[5]. First, there is a startling degree of overlap in individual differences on working memory tasks and individual differences in measures of fluid intelligence. Second, it is becoming clear that working memory tasks are only incidentally about memory. Or, as Engle (2002) puts it:

> "WM capacity is just as important in retention of a single
> representation, such as the representation of a goal or of the status
> of a changing variable, as it is in determining how many

McGrew, 1997; McGrew & Woodcock, 2001; Taub & McGrew, 2004). In addition to Gf and Gc, other broad factors at the level termed *stratum II* are things like memory and learning, auditory perception, and processing speed (*see* Carroll, 1993, for a full account).

5 Executive function tasks all seem to involve some type of cognitive decoupling, and they have substantial correlations with fluid intelligence (Baddeley, 1992; Baddeley, Chincotta, & Adlam, 2001; Duncan, et al., 2000; Duncan, et al., 2008; Fuster, 1990; Gernsbacher & Faust, 1991; Goldman-Rakic, 1992; Gray, Chabris, & Braver, 2003; Hasher, Zacks, & May, 1999; Kane, 2003; Kane & Engle, 2002; Salthouse, Atkinson, & Berish, 2003; Salthouse & Davis, 2006). Working memory tasks show substantial correlations with fluid intelligence (Colom, Rebollo, Palacios, Juan-Espinosa, & Kyllonen, 2004; Conway, Cowan, Bunting, Therriault, & Minkoff, 2002; Conway, Kane, & Engle, 2003; Engle, 2002; Engle, Tuholski, Laughlin, & Conway, 1999; Geary, 2005; Jaeggi, Buschkuehl, Jonides, & Perrig, 2008; Kane, Bleckley, Conway, & Engle, 2001; Kane & Engle, 2003; Kane, Hambrick, & Conway, 2005; Kane, Hambrick, Tuholski, Wilhelm, Payne, & Engle, 2004; Lepine, Barrouillet, & Camos, 2005; Salthouse & Pink, 2008; Sub et al., 2002; Unsworth & Engle, 2007).

representations can be maintained. WM capacity is not directly about memory—it is about using attention to maintain or suppress information. WM capacity is about memory only indirectly. Greater WM capacity does mean that more items can be maintained as active, but this is a result of greater ability to control attention, not a larger memory store" (p. 20).

Hasher, Lustig, and Zacks (2007) concur with this view when they conclude that "our evidence raises the possibility that what most working memory span tasks measure is inhibitory control, not something like the size of operating capacity." (p. 231)

In a parallel argument, it has been proposed that the reaction time tasks that have been found to correlate with fluid intelligence (see Deary, 2000; Neubauer & Fink, 2005) do so not because they tap into some factor of "neural speed" but instead because they make attentional demands that are similar to those of some working memory tasks (see Conway et al., 2002). Such an interpretation is suggested by the evidence in favor of the so-called "worst performance rule"—that the slowest trials on a reaction time task correlate more strongly with intelligence than does the mean reaction time or the fastest reaction time trials (Coyle, 2003). Schmiedek, Oberauer, Wilhelm, Sub, and Wittmann (2007) have confirmed the worst performance rule most elegantly by showing that a latent working memory factor was more highly correlated with the parameter reflecting the tail of the distribution (the exponential parameter) than with the parameters reflecting the Gaussian part of the distribution. On the present view, the tail of the distribution is disproportionately made up of trials on which goals have momentarily deactivated because of partially failed decoupling, and such failures are more likely in those of lower fluid intelligence.

Lepine, Barrouillet, and Camos, (2005) report an experiment showing that working memory tasks with simple processing components are actually better predictors of high-level cognitive performance than are working memory tasks with complex processing requirements—as long as the former are rapidly paced to lock up attention. Likewise, Salthouse and Pink (2008) found that the very simplest versions of working memory tasks did not show attenuated correlations with fluid intelligence and that the correlation with fluid intelligence did not increase over trials.

They argued that their results suggest that "the relation between working memory and fluid intelligence is not dependent on the amount of information that must be maintained, or on processes that occur over the course of performing the tasks" (p. 364).

Research outcomes such as these are consistent with Engle's (2002) review of evidence indicating that working memory tasks really tap the preservation of internal representations in the presence of distraction or, as I have termed it, the ability to decouple a secondary representation (or metarepresentation) from a primary representation and to manipulate the former. For example, he describes an experiment using the so-called "antisaccade task." Subjects must look at the middle of a computer screen and respond to a target stimulus that will appear on the left or right of the screen. Before the target appears, a cue is flashed on the opposite side of the screen. Subjects must resist the attention-capturing cue and respond to the target on the opposite side when it appears. Subjects scoring low on working memory tasks were more likely to make an eye movement (saccade) in the direction of the distracting cue than were subjects who scored high on working memory task.

That the antisaccade task has very little to do with memory is an indication of why investigators have reconceptualized the individual difference variables that working memory tasks are tapping. Individual differences on such tasks are now described with a variety of different terms (attentional control, resistance to distraction, executive control), but the critical operation needed to succeed in them—and the reason they are a prime indicator of fluid intelligence—is that they reflect the ability to sustain decoupled representations. Such decoupling is an important aspect of behavioral control that is related to rationality[6].

---

6 Consistent with my argument are the findings of a study of children ages 3 to 5 years by Atance and Jackson (2009). They found some relations between different tasks that were viewed as measures of future thinking: delay of gratification, mental time travel, planning, and prospective memory. The tasks were correlated with each other, but the associations disappeared once age and a proxy measure of cognitive ability were partialled from the correlations. I would argue that what the age and cognitive ability measure were partialling was the ability to sustain cognitive decoupling, which is the common component of all future-oriented thinking.

My view of individual differences in cognitive decoupling as the key operation assessed by measures of fluid intelligence was anticipated by Thurstone (1927), who also stressed the idea that intelligence was related to inhibition of automatic responses:

"Intelligence is therefore the capacity of abstraction, which is an inhibitory process. In the intelligent moment the impulse is inhibited while it is still only partially specified, while it is still only loosely organized . . ..The trial-and-error choice and elimination, in intelligent conduct, is carried out with alternatives that are so incomplete and so loosely organized that they point only toward types of behaviour without specifying the behaviour in detail." (p. 159)

So-Called "Executive Functioning" Measures Tap the Algorithmic Mind and Not the Reflective Mind

One interesting implication that follows from the distinction between the algorithmic mind and reflective mind is that the measures of so-called "executive functioning" in the neuropsychological literature actually measure nothing of the sort. The term *executive* implies that these tasks assess the most strategic (often deemed the "highest") level of cognitive functioning—the reflective level. However, a consideration of the tasks most commonly used in the neuropsychological literature to assess executive functioning (*see* Jurado & Rosselli, 2007; Pennington & Ozonoff, 1996; Salthouse, Atkinson, & Berish, 2003) reveals that almost without exception they are optimal performance tasks and not typical performance tasks and that most of them rather severely constrain reflective-level functioning. Thus, because reflective-level functioning is constrained, such tasks are largely assessing individual differences in algorithmic-level functioning. This is the reason why several studies have shown very strong correlations between executive functioning and fluid intelligence[7].

---

7 Strong correlations between executive functioning and fluid intelligence have been found in many studies (Buehner, Krumm, & Pick, 2005; Colom et al., 2004;

Consider some of the classic tasks in the neuropsychological literature on executive function (*see* Pennington & Ozonoff, 1996; Salthouse
et al., 2003). In the critical part of the Trailmaking Test, the subject must,
in the shortest time possible, connect with a line a series of numbered
and lettered circles going from 1 to A to 2 to B to 3 to C, and so forth.
The rule is specified in advance, and there is no ambiguity about what
constitutes optimal performance. There is no task interpretation required
of the subject. Cognitive decoupling is required, however, to keep the
right sequence in mind and not revert to number sequencing alone or
letter sequencing alone. Thus, the task does require algorithmic-level
decoupling in order to suppress TASS from disrupting performance by
defaulting to an overlearned rule. But the task does not require reflective
control in the sense that I have defined it here (or it does in only the
most basic sense by requiring a decision to comply with the tester or
experimenter).

The situation is similar regarding another test of executive functioning from the neuropsychological literature, the Stroop Test. The subject is
explicitly told to name the color and not read the word, and optimal
performance is clearly defined as going as fast as possible. Algorithmic-
level decoupling is needed to suppress the automatic response from
TASS to read the word. But strategic-level reflective control never enters
the picture. The response requirements of the task are very basic and the
task set is dictated externally. It is a test of suppression via algorithmic-
level decoupling pure and simple.

Fluency tasks are also commonly used to measure executive functioning (Jurado & Rosselli, 2007; Salthouse et al., 2003). Here, the subject
simply articulates as many words as they can from a specified category
(words beginning with the letter F, names of red things, etc.). Again, in
such a task there is no reflective choice about what rule to use. The task
requirements are entirely specified in advance, and the assessment concerns merely the efficiency of execution.

Conway et al., 2003; Engle et al., 1999; Friedman, Miyake, Young, DeFries, Corley,
& Hewitt, 2008; Gray et al., 2003; Kane et al., 2005; Kane et al., 2004; Kyllonen &
Christal, 1990; Miyake, Friedman, Rettinger, Shah, & Hegarty, 2001; Salthouse
et al., 2003; Unsworth & Engle, 2005, 2007).

A widely used measure of executive functioning, the Wisconsin Card Sorting Test (Heaton, Chelune, Talley, Kay, & Curtiss, 1993; Rhodes, 2004), does begin to tap more reflective processes, although variance in suppression via decoupling is still probably the dominant individual difference component that it taps. In the WCST, the subject sees a set of target cards containing shapes varying in color, form, and number. The instructions are to correctly sort new cards in a deck by grouping them with the correct target card. The subject must discover the dimension (color, form, or number) that should be the basis of the sort, and at predetermined points, the correct dimension of sort is changed on the subject without warning. Although the basic task structure is set by the examiner, there may well be some reflective involvement in the rule discovery stages of the task. Nevertheless, once the rule is switched, suppression of the tendency to sort by the previous rule is probably the dominant influence on performance. This suppression is carried out by algorithmic-level decoupling abilities and is probably why the task is correlated with fluid intelligence (Salthouse et al., 2003).

The tasks I have discussed so far come from the neuropsychological literature. However, more precise experimental tasks have been used in the literature of cognitive psychology to measure exactly the same construct as the neuropsychological executive function measures. These more precise tasks—stop signal paradigms, working memory paradigms, time sharing paradigms, inhibition paradigms of various types (*see* Salthouse et al., 2003)—are all subject to exactly the same arguments just made regarding the neuropsychological measures. The more precise experimental measures are optimal performance tasks (not typical performance tasks), and they severely constrain reflective-level functioning. All measure algorithmic-level decoupling power, which is why they display a considerable degree of overlap with fluid intelligence (Gray et al., 2003; Kane & Engle, 2002; Hasher et al., 2007; Salthouse et al., 2003; Salthouse & Davis, 2006; Salthouse & Pink, 2008). Individual differences in the reflective mind are only tangentially implicated. This is because tapping reflective processes requires measures of typical performance, and tasks whose instructions leave the reflective level unconstrained so that individual differences in epistemic regulation and cognitive allocation (e.g., need for cognition) become implicated in performance beyond simply the computational power to sustain decoupling operations.

This point about the laboratory measures has been made before by Salthouse et al. (2003): "The role of executive functioning may also be rather limited in many laboratory tasks because much of the organization or structure of the tasks is provided by the experimenter and does not need to be discovered or created by the research participant" (p. 569). Jurado and Rosselli (2007) credit Lezak (1983) with the observation that executive function tasks are problematic "in that goal setting, structuring and decision making are behaviors which need to be assessed, yet their assessment is highly structured within the examination. The examiner is the one usually determining when and how the task must be executed" (p. 219).

In short, my argument is that executive processes are misnamed in the psychological literature. Executive functioning measures are nothing of the kind—at least as most people would understand the word "executive." These tasks might instead be better termed *measures of supervisory* processes. They assess the ability to carry out the rules instantiated not by internal regulation (*true* executive control) but by an external authority that explicitly sets the rules and tells the subject what constitutes maximal performance. The subject does not set the agenda in these tasks (as is the case in many tasks in the rational thinking and critical thinking literatures) but instead attempts to optimize criteria explicitly given to them. The processes assessed by such tasks do involve algorithmic-level decoupling (which is why they are so highly related to fluid intelligence), but they are supervisory in nature—decoupling is used to screen out distracting stimuli and make sure the externally provided rule remains the goal state.

In contrast, processes of the reflective mind operate to set the goal agenda or they operate in the service of epistemic regulation (i.e., to direct the sequence of information pickup). Such processes that set and regulate the goal and epistemic agendas are little engaged by so-called "executive function tasks." The term *executive* thus can lead to theoretical confusion in the literature. More importantly, it contributes to the tendency to overlook the importance of measuring variation in the reflective mind. The term *executive* mistakenly implies that everything "higher up" has been taken care of or that there is no level higher than what these executive functioning tasks measure.

4

The Tri-Process Model and Serial Associative Cognition

The current tripartite view of the mind has begun to look somewhat like that displayed in Figure 4–1. Previous dual-process theories have emphasized the importance of the override function—the ability of Type 2 processing to take early response tendencies triggered by Type 1 processing offline and to substitute better responses. This override capacity is a property of the algorithmic mind and it is indicated by the arrow labeled A in Figure 4–1. However, previous dual-process theories have tended to ignore the higher-level cognitive function that *initiates* override in the first place. This is a dispositional property of the reflective mind that is related to rationality. In the model in Figure 4–1, it is represented by arrow B, which represents, in machine intelligence terms, the call to the algorithmic mind to override the Type 1 response by taking it offline. This is a different mental function than the override function itself (arrow A), and in Chapter 2, I have presented evidence indicating that the two functions are indexed by different types of individual differences—the ability to sustain the inhibition of the Type 1 response is indexed by measures of fluid intelligence, and the tendency to initiate override operations is indexed by thinking dispositions such as reflectiveness and need for cognition.

Figure 4–1 represents another aspect of cognition that is somewhat neglected by previous dual-process theories. Specifically, the override function has loomed large in dual-process theory but less so the simulation process that computes the alternative response that makes the override worthwhile. Figure 4–1 explicitly represents the simulation function as well as the fact that the call to initiate simulation originates in the reflective mind. The decoupling operation (indicated by arrow C) is carried out by the algorithmic mind and the call to initiate simulation (indicated by arrow D) by the reflective mind. Again, two different types of individual differences are associated with the initiation call and the

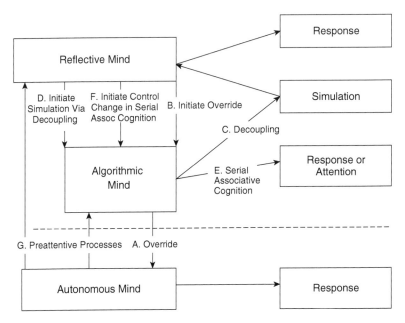

FIGURE 4.1.   A More Complete Model of the Tripartite Structure.

decoupling operator—specifically, rational thinking dispositions with the former and fluid intelligence with the latter. Finally, Type 2 processing operations receive inputs from the computations of the autonomous mind via so-called "preattentive processes" (arrows labeled **G**). Particularly good discussions of the importance of these preattentive processes in fixing the content of Type 2 processing have been presented by Evans (2006b, 2007a, 2008, 2009).

The model in Figure 4–1 defines a third critical function for the algorithmic mind in addition to Type 1 processing override and enabling simulation via decoupling. The third is a function that is termed serial associative cognition in Figure 4–1 (arrow labeled E). This function is there to remind us that not all Type 2 processing involves strongly decoupled cognitive simulation. There are types of slow, serial cognition that do not involve simulating alternative worlds and exploring them exhaustively. Their existence points up the reason for my earlier statement (in Chapter 3): All hypothetical thinking involves the analytic system (Evans & Over, 2004), but not all Type 2 processing involves hypothetical thinking. Serial associative cognition represents this latter category.

There are less expensive kinds of Type 2 processing that we tend to fall back on when Type 1 mechanisms are not available for solving the problem. Recall that the category of Type 1 processes is composed of affective responses; previously learned responses that have been practiced to automaticity; conditioned responses; and adaptive modules that have been shaped by our evolutionary history. These cover many situations indeed, but modern life still creates many problems for which none of these mechanisms are suited. Consider Wason's (1966) four-card selection task, which has generated a vast literature (e.g., Evans, Newstead, & Byrne, 1993; Evans & Over, 2004). There have been many theories proposed to explain why subjects respond to it as they do[1]. The abstract version of the problem is often presented as follows. Imagine four rectangles, each representing a card lying on a table. Each one of the cards has a letter on one side and a number on the other side. Here is a rule: If a card has a vowel on its letter side, then it has an even number on its number side. Two of the cards are letter-side up, and two of the cards are number-side up. Your task is to decide which card or cards must be turned over to find out whether the rule is true or false. Indicate which cards must be turned over. The four cards confronting the subject have the stimuli K, A, 8, and 5 showing.

The correct answer is A and 5 (the only two cards that could show the rule to be false), but the majority of subjects answer (incorrectly) A and 8 (showing a so-called "matching bias"). Evans (2006b) has pointed out that the previous emphasis on the matching bias (Evans, 1972, 1998; Evans & Lynch, 1973) might have led some investigators to infer that Type 2 processing is not occurring in the task. In fact, matching bias

---

1 The literature on the various different proposals is large (Evans, 1972, 1996, 1998, 2006b, 2007a; Girotto & Tentori, 2008; Hardman, 1998; Johnson-Laird, 1999, 2006; Klauer, Stahl, & Erdfelder, 2007; Liberman & Klar, 1996; Margolis, 1987; Newstead & Evans, 1995; Oaksford & Chater, 1994, 2007; Osman, 2007; Osman & Laming, 2001; Sperber, Cara & Girotto, 1995; Stanovich, 1999; Stanovich & West, 1998a; Stenning & van Lambalgen, 2004a, 2004b). On the many suggestions that little thinking goes on in the task, *see* Hardman (1998), Margolis (1987), Stanovich and West (1998a), and Tweney and Yachanin (1985).

might be viewed as just one of several such suggestions in the literature that only the shallowest of thinking occurs. In contrast, however, Evans (2006b) presents evidence indicating that there may be Type 2 processing occurring during the task—even on the part of the majority who do not give the normatively correct response (P and Q) but instead give the PQ response.

First, in discussing the card inspection paradigm (Evans, 1996) that he pioneered (see also Lucas & Ball, 2005; Roberts & Newton, 2001), Evans (2006b) notes that although subjects look disproportionately at the cards they will choose (the finding leading to the inference that heuristic, Type 1 processes were determining the responses), the lengthy amount of time they spend on those cards suggests that analytic Type 2-thought is occurring (if only to generate justification for the heuristically triggered choices). Second, in verbal protocol studies, subjects can justify their responses (indeed, can justify any set of responses they are told are correct; see Evans & Wason, 1976) with analytic arguments—arguments that sometimes refer to the hidden side of cards chosen.

I think it is correct to argue that Type 2 cognition is occurring in the task, but I also want to argue that it is not full-blown cognitive simulation of alternative world models. It is Type 2 processing of a shallower type. When think-aloud protocols were analyzed, it has seemed that most subjects were engaging in some slow, serial processing, but of a type that was simply incomplete. A typical protocol from a subject might go something like this: "Well, let's see, I'd turn the A to see if there is an even number on the back. Then I'd turn the 8 to make sure a vowel is in the back." Then the subject stops. Several things are apparent. First, it makes sense that subjects are engaging in some kind of Type 2 processing. Most Type 1 processes would be of no help on this problem. Affective processing is not engaged, so processes of emotional regulation are no help. Unless the subject is a philosophy major, there are no highly practiced procedures (logic) that have become automatized that would be of any help. Finally, the problem is evolutionarily unprecedented, so there will be no Darwinian modules that would be helpful.

The subject is left to rely on Type 2 processing, but I would argue that the processing is seriously incomplete in the example I have given. The subject has relied on serial associative cognition rather than exhaustive simulation of an alternative world—a world that includes situations in which the rule is false. The subject has not constructed the false case—a vowel with an odd number on the back. Nor have they gone systematically through the cards asking the question of whether that card could be a vowel/odd combination. Answer: K (no), A (yes), 8 (no), 5 (yes). Such a procedure yields the correct choice of A and 5. Instead, the subject with this protocol started from the model given—the rule as true—and then just worked through implications of what would be expected if the rule were true. A fully simulated world with all the possibilities—including the possibility of a false rule—was never constructed. The subject starts with the focal rule as given and then just generates associates that follow from that. The fact that they refer to hidden sides of the cards does not mean that they have constructed any alternative model of the situation beyond what was given to them by the experimenter and their own assumption that the rule is true.

Thus, it is correct to argue that Type 2 processing is occurring in this task, but I also want to argue that it is not full-blown cognitive simulation of alternative world models. It is thinking of a shallower type—cognition that is inflexibly locked into an associative mode that takes as its starting point a model of the world that is given to the subject. It is cognition that is not rapid and parallel (in the manner of the systems contained in the autonomous mind) but is nonetheless inflexibly locked into an associative mode that takes as its starting point the model of the world that is most easy to construct.

In fact, an exhaustive simulation of alternative worlds would guarantee correct responding in the task. Instead, in the selection task, subjects accept the rule as given, assume it is true, and simply describe how they would go about verifying it. They reason from a single focal model—systematically generating associations from this focal model but never constructing another model of the situation. This is what I would term *serial associative cognition with a focal bias*. It is how I would begin to operationalize the satisficing bias in Type 2 processing posited in several papers by Evans (2006b; Evans, Over, & Handley, 2003).

The Cognitive Miser and Focal Bias

One way to contextualize the idea of focal bias is as the second stage in a framework for thinking about human information processing discussed in Chapter 2—the idea of humans as cognitive misers. Humans are cognitive misers because their basic tendency is to default to processing mechanisms of low computational expense. Humorously, Hull (2001) has said that "the rule that human beings seem to follow is to engage the brain only when all else fails—and usually not even then" (p. 37). More seriously, Richerson and Boyd (2005) have put the same point in terms of its origins in evolution: "In effect, all animals are under stringent selection pressure to be as stupid as they can get away with" (p. 135).

There are, in fact, two aspects of cognitive miserliness. Dual-process theory has heretofore highlighted only Rule 1 of the Cognitive Miser: Default to Type 1 processing whenever possible. But defaulting to Type 1 processing is not always possible—particularly in novel situations where there are no stimuli available to domain-specific evolutionary modules nor, perhaps, any information with which to run overlearned and well-compiled procedures that the autonomous mind has acquired through practice. Type 2 processing procedures will be necessary, but a cognitive miser default is operating even there. Rule 2 of the Cognitive Miser is: When Type 2 processing is necessary, default to serial associative cognition with a focal bias (*not* fully decoupled cognitive simulation).

Evans (2006b) draws attention to Rule 2 of humans as cognitive misers by emphasizing a satisficing principle in his conception of Type 2 processing. The notion of focal bias is a way of conceiving of just what Type 2 satisficing is in terms of actual information processing mechanics. My proposal is, simply, that it amounts to a focal bias with an additional tendency *not* to interrupt serial associative cognition with a decoupling call from the reflective mind.

The notion of a focal bias conjoins several closely related ideas in the literature—Evans, Over and Handley's (2003) singularity principle, Johnson-Laird's (1999, 2005, 2006) principle of truth, focusing (Legrenzi, Girotto, & Johnson-Laird, 1993), the effect/effort issues discussed by Sperber, Cara, and Girotto (1995), and finally, the focalism (Wilson, Wheatley, Meyers, Gilbert, & Axsom, 2000) and belief acceptance (Gilbert, 1991) issues that have been prominent in the social psychological literature. My notion of focal bias conjoins many of these ideas under the overarching theme that they all have in common—that humans will find any way they can to ease the cognitive load and process less information. Focal bias combines all of these tendencies into the basic idea that the information processor is strongly disposed to deal only with the most easily constructed cognitive model.

So the focal model that will dominate processing—the only model that serial associative cognition deals with—is the most easily constructed model. The focal model tends to: represent only one state of affairs (the Evan et al., 2003, singularity idea), accept what is directly presented and models what is presented as true (e.g., Gilbert, 1991; Johnson-Laird, 1999), is a model that minimizes effort (Sperber et al., 1995), and ignores moderating factors (as the social psychological literature has demonstrated, e.g., Wilson et al., 2000)—probably because taking account of those factors would necessitate modeling several alternative worlds, and this is just what a focal processing allows us to avoid. And finally, given the voluminous literature in cognitive science on belief bias and the informal reasoning literature on myside bias, the easiest models to represent clearly appear to be those closest to what a person already believes in and has modeled previously (e.g., Evans, 2002; Evans & Feeney, 2004; Nickerson, 1998; Stanovich & West, 2007, 2008a).

Thus, serial associative cognition is defined by its reliance on a single focal model that triggers all subsequent thought. Framing effects, for instance, are a clear example of serial associative cognition with a focal bias. As Kahneman (2003) notes, "the basic principle of framing is the passive acceptance of the formulation given" (p. 703). The frame presented to the subject is taken as focal, and all subsequent thought derives from it rather than from alternative framings because the latter would necessitate more computationally expensive simulation operations.

In short, serial associative cognition is serial and analytic (as opposed to holistic) in style, but it relies on a single focal model that triggers all subsequent thought. Such a view is consistent with the aforementioned discussion of thinking during the selection task and the conclusion that Type 2 cognition does indeed occur even for the incorrect responders (*see* Evans, 2006b; Evans & Over, 2004). Incorrect responders are engaging in serial associative cognition with a focal bias, but reflective processes are not prone to send additional decoupling calls to explore alternative models to the focal one.

Consider an informal example of the difference between a full simulation with alternative worlds and serial association cognition. Here is a
fully fleshed out simulation of alternative worlds in everyday thinking:

> Imagine I take a day to work at home. It occurs to me that I will
> only have four such days the rest of this term, so I must plan
> carefully. I have many work projects that are commitments I must
> meet—commitments to students, colleagues, and to university
> administration. On the other hand, there are the projects that
> I am really passionate about. Sadly though, I realize two things:
> that my commitments have piled up quite a bit since my last free
> day, and that on my previous three free days I have chosen to
> work on my "passion projects" the entire day. Weighing these
> considerations, I find that I feel obligated to work on some of
> my commitments. In that arena, there are committee reports due,
> partially completed reviews that I owe to two journals, and one
> letter of recommendation I must write for a graduate student.
> The letter can be written during a normal working day, so that
> can eliminated. Regarding the committees, I remember the saying
> that "no one on their deathbed says that they regret not going to
> more committee meetings." Therefore I turn to a consideration
> of the partially completed reviews that I owe to two journals.
> Both are overdue about the same amount of time. One, however,
> is much closer to completion, so I shall work on it.

Although this is clearly informal thought, it has many of the characteristics of fully disjunctive reasoning—a fleshed out simulation of alternative worlds. Instead of branching out into irrelevant concerns, it
concentrates on drilling down and making sure all of the alternatives at
each level of analysis are covered. Two alternatives are fleshed out originally: passion projects versus commitments. Reasons are given to rule
out the former. Regarding commitments, three are identified: commit-
tee reports due, two partially completed reviews, and one letter of rec-
ommendation. These are then, in turn, narrowed down. The point is that
at each stage, some semblance of an exhaustive set of possibilities is considered—and the possibilities are all relevant to the problem at hand, to
the central problem situation, the key alternative world, that is relevant to

solving the problem. These are all characteristics of offline simulation (Fig. 4–1, arrow C).

Now consider another example of informal thought, taking place via serial associative cognition (arrow E):

> Let's see, I'm going downtown tomorrow. What should I do? I was reading *Money* magazine last night and it looks like I haven't been saving enough for retirement. I'll go see my broker, that's what I'll do. If I go to his place I'll take the bus. Oh, I just remembered that there is a great sandwich shop next to the bus station. I'll arrange to go in about lunchtime then and have that special mozzarella, tomato, and basil on foccacia bread that I saw on the board there once. I really do love foccacia. I think I'll bring some home. I'd like to have sandwiches on foccacia all week. I know a good bakery on the east side that I bet would have great foccacia. Let's see though, bakery items sell out early in the day. I better get down there early. I'll take the first bus in the morning. . . .

This second example is as different as can be from the previous example of informal thinking. Note, however, that the second example still represents Type 2 thinking—it is serial and relatively slow (at least compared to Type 1 processing), and it is conscious rather than unconscious thought. Nevertheless, it is different in important ways. The thinker is driven forward in his/her thinking simply by the most salient association in the current mental model being considered. At each stage in the process, the thinker does not explore all of the options. The thinking is only about the current objective that has popped into consciousness via an associative process. Notice also how the models being considered become "unclamped." The issue of what to do downtown was quickly transformed into the issue of saving for retirement but before any options other than one ("go see your broker") for achieving *this* option was considered, the thinker was on to a different issue (having a sandwich by taking a noontime bus for lunch), and within a second *this* goal was lost (to the goal of going downtown early to get some bread). In serial associative cognition, models do not stay clamped long enough for all the possibilities surrounding them to be fleshed out. The thinking sequence shifts to anything that temporarily becomes focal (because of vividness, salience, availability, or recentness) and generates primary associates from that focal model.

Differentiating serial associative cognition from fully decoupled simulation contributes to the understanding of the phenomenon of mind wandering that Smallwood and Schooler (2006) have analyzed. They conceive of mind wandering as "a shift of attention away from a primary task toward internal information, such as memories" (p. 946). If we assume that the primary task to which they refer was necessitating fully explicit cognitive simulation, we can conceive of mind wandering as a switch from decoupled simulation to (the less cognitively demanding) serial associative cognition. This is consistent with Smallwood and Schooler's (2006) description of mind wandering as sharing "certain similarities with standard views of controlled processing, however, there is an important difference. Controlled processing is generally associated with the intentional pursuit of a goal. Mind wandering, however, often occurs without intention….mind wandering involves executive control yet seems to lack deliberate intent" (p. 946). I would argue that what Smallwood and Schooler are struggling to portray here are two different kinds of Type 2 processing. One is an attempt to exhaustively model an imaginary world that would facilitate the primary task. The other is a less computationally expensive type of cognition that proceeds successively through the most convenient and salient associate of a single (often incomplete) focal model. When the costly fully decoupled cognition of the former type fails, cognition reverts to the less costly (and often irrelevant to the task) second type of processing, and when this happens we report that "my mind has wandered."

Smallwood and Schooler (2006) see paradoxes in the phenomenon of mind wandering that are not apparent when it is viewed from the current tripartite view. First, they note: that "the central challenge for incorporating mind wandering into executive models of attention is that our mind often wanders in the absence of explicit intention. Generally, deliberate intent is considered a hallmark of controlled processing, so the apparent absence of intent from mind wandering challenges the suggestion that both mind wandering and controlled processing share working-memory resources" (p. 947). Second, they speculate (*see* p. 956) on the adaptive value of mind wandering. The latter, in the present view, is simply the result of a mind structured with natural defaults toward the least computationally expensive cognition—defaults that occasionally will trigger inefficaciously when more computationally expensive cognition is underway. The former also presents no paradox because it is not mind wandering (defaulting to serial associative cognition) that requires intentionality, but instead it is intentional goal pursuit that sustains the more cognitively demanding (and perhaps aversive, *see* Gailliot & Baumeister, 2007; Navon, 1989) simulation of alternative worlds. The deactivation of that goal results in the default to serial associative cognition that we often call mind wandering.

Having introduced the idea of serial associative cognition, we can now return to Figure 4–1 and identify a third function of the reflective mind—initiating an interrupt of serial associative cognition (arrow F). This interrupt signal alters the next step in a serial associative sequence that would otherwise direct thought. This interrupt signal might stop serial associative cognition altogether to initiate a comprehensive simulation (arrow C). Alternatively, it might start a new serial associative chain (arrow E) from a different starting point by altering the temporary focal model that is the source of a current associative chain.

The preceding discussion identifies three different functions of cognitive decoupling. In the override case, decoupling involves taking offline the connection between a primary representation and response programming in the autonomous mind (arrow A). In the second case, the case of comprehensive simulation, it involves segregating from representational abuse multiple models undergoing simultaneous evaluation and transformation (arrow C). Of course, these two are related—autonomous responses are often decoupled pending a comprehensive simulation that determines whether there is a better response. A third type of decoupling involves interrupting serial associative cognition (arrow E)—that is, decoupling from the next step in an associative sequence that would otherwise direct thought. This third type of decoupling might shunt the processor to comprehensive simulation or simply start a new associative chain from a different starting point. In all three cases, sustaining a decoupling operation is a function of the algorithmic mind. The autonomous mind does not decouple representations except when evolutionary adaptation has created dedicated mental machinery for such decoupling in a specific domain (e.g., the theory of mind module for behavioral prediction of other agents).

Converging Evidence in the Dual-Process Literature

The general tri-process model illustrated in Figure 4–1 meshes well with other ongoing theoretical developments in dual-process theory (*see* Evans, 2007a, 2008, 2009). Evans (2009), for example, now sees the need to distinguish Type 3 processes from Type 2 and Type 1. Type 3 processes, in his view, are concerned with issues of control, conflict resolution, and resource allocation. The Type 3 processes in his discussion correspond, in the present tri-process theory, to the signals from the reflective mind for the algorithmic mind to begin decoupling operations.

Theoretical speculations about the genetics of individual differences have supported the distinction between thinking dispositions and cognitive ability (computational capacity) that underlies the differentiation of the algorithmic from the reflective mind. For many years, evolutionary psychology had little to say about individual differences because the field had as a foundational assumption that natural selection would eliminate heritable differences because heritable traits would be driven to fixation (Buss, 2009). Recently however, evolutionary psychologists have attempted to explain the contrary evidence that virtually all cognitive and personality traits that have been measured have heritabilities hovering around 50%. Penke, Denissen, and Miller (2007) have proposed a theory that explains these individual differences. Interestingly, the theory accounts for heritable cognitive ability differences in a different way than it accounts for heritable thinking dispositions and personality variables. The basis of their theory is a distinction that I will be stressing throughout this book—that between typical performance indicators and optimal performance indicators.

Penke et al. (2007) argue that "the classical distinction between cognitive abilities and personality traits is much more than just a historical convention or a methodological matter of different measurement approaches (Cronbach, 1949), and instead reflects different kinds of selection pressures that have shaped distinctive genetic architectures for these two classes" (p. 550) of individual differences. On their view, personality traits and thinking dispositions (reflective-level individual differences) represent preserved, heritable variability that is maintained by different biological processes than intelligence (algorithmic-level individual differences). Thinking dispositions and personality traits are maintained by balanced selection, most probably frequency-dependent selection (Buss, 2009). The most famous example of the latter is cheater-based personality traits that flourish when they are rare but become less adaptive as the proportion of cheaters in the population rises (as cheaters begin to cheat each other), finally reaching an equilibrium.

In contrast, variability in intelligence is thought to be maintained by constant changes in mutation load (Buss, 2009; Penke et al., 2007). As Pinker (2009) notes:

> "new mutations creep into the genome faster than natural selection can weed them out. At any given moment, the population is laden with a portfolio of recent mutations, each of whose days are numbered. This Sisyphean struggle between selection and mutation is common with traits that depend on many genes, because there are so many things that can go wrong . . .. Unlike personality, where it takes all kinds to make a world, with intelligence, smarter is simply better, so balancing selection is unlikely. But intelligence depends on a large network of brain areas, and it thrives in a body that is properly nourished and free of diseases and defects . . . . Mutations in general are far more likely to be harmful than helpful, and the large, helpful ones were low-hanging fruit that were picked long ago in our evolutionary history and entrenched in the species . . . . But as the barrel gets closer to the target, smaller and smaller tweaks are needed to bring any further improvement . . . . Though we know that genes for intelligence must exist, each is likely to be small in effect, found in only a few people, or both . . . . The hunt for personality genes, though not yet Nobel-worthy, has had better fortunes. Several associations have been found between personality traits and genes that govern the breakdown, recycling or detection of neurotransmitters." (p. 46)

Thus, according to the theory of Penke et al. (2007), the evolutionary processes that sustain variability in thinking dispositions and traits at the reflective level are different from those that sustain variability in cognitive capacities at the algorithmic level.

In addition to the theoretical commonalities discussed so far, there are a number of further convergences that can be discerned in the literature. For example, the three different decoupling operations just discussed in the previous section map conceptually onto three of the most important operations that have been discussed in the literature on executive functioning[2]: inhibition, updating, and set shifting. In the executive functioning literature, inhibition is measured with tasks such as the Stroop test, the stop-signal paradigm (Logan, 1994), and the antisaccade task where subjects must resist the tendency to look in a cued direction and instead look in the opposite direction. Updating is measured by working memory tasks such as the n-back task and the keeping track task where subjects must remember the last instance of several target categories. Set shifting is measured with tasks such the Wisconsin Card Sorting Test (Heaton et al., 1993) and the Trailmaking Test (Pennington & Ozonoff, 1996; Reitan, 1955, 1958). In the latter, the subject must, in the shortest time possible, connect with a line a series of numbered and lettered circles going from 1 to A to 2 to B to 3 to C, and so forth.

These three different aspects of executive functioning correspond to the three types of decoupling operation discussed previously. Inhibition is most similar to the use of decoupling to suppress a response triggered by the autonomous mind. Updating in the executive functioning literature indexes the ability to sustain comprehensive simulation by segregating from representational abuse a secondary representation as it undergoes evaluation and transformation. Set shifting indexes the ability to interrupt serial associative cognition—that is, to decouple from the next step in an associative sequence that would otherwise direct thought.

This parsing of executive functioning maps well onto discussions of that construct in the literature on attention deficit hyperactivity disorder (ADHD). Executive functioning deficits have been linked with ADHD in several different theoretical accounts (Barkley, 1998; Nigg, 2000, 2001; Pennington & Ozonoff, 1996; Sonuga-Barke, 2002, 2003). The inhibitory function of executive tasks has been singled out by theorists as a particular locus of processing difficulty in ADHD (Barkley, 1998; Nigg, 2001). Friedman et al. (2007) tested this directly by giving measures of

---

2 Inhibition, updating, and set shifting are discussed in many publications on executive functioning (Aron, 2008; Best et al., 2009; Friedman, Haberstick, Willcutt, Miyake, Young, Corley, & Hewitt, 2007; Friedman, Miyake, Corley, Young, DeFries, & Hewitt, 2006; Friedman et al., 2008; Miyake, Friedman, Emerson, & Witzki, 2000; Pennington & Ozonoff, 1996; Salthouse et al., 2003).

inhibition, updating, and set shifting (measured as latent variables) to a large sample of late adolescents (ages 16–17). Teacher-rated attentional problems at earlier ages were most strongly related to the latent construct of inhibition and least related to the latent construct of set shifting. This finding would seem to indicate that childhood attentional problems are most closely associated with the decoupling operation that involves taking offline the connection between a primary representation and response programming in the autonomous mind. In a study of 10-year-old children, Handley et al. (2004) observed that measures of inhibition became particularly important in reasoning tasks where the use of logic was necessary to trump prior belief.

Many findings in cognitive neuroscience[3] converge nicely with some of the distinctions displayed in Figure 4–1. For example, Botvinick, Cohen, and Carter (2004) and MacDonald, Cohen, Stenger, and Carter (2000) describe a model of the function of the anterior cingulate cortex (ACC) and the dorsolateral prefrontal cortex (DLPFC) that maps nicely onto the framework presented here. In their model, the ACC registers conflict during information processing and triggers strategic adjustments in cognitive control. Those adjustments in cognitive control are largely implemented by the DLPFC. The ACC, according to Botvinick et al. (2004), "detects internal states signaling a need to intensify or redirect attention or control" (p. 539). As such, it maps onto Figure 4–1 as one of the mechanisms of the reflective mind that triggers the onset of cognitive decoupling. The sustained decoupling itself is carried out by the DLPFC. The model of Botvinick et al. (2004) maps into contemporary theories of self-control that distinguish between the process of goal–conflict recognition and goal–conflict resolution (Myrseth & Fishbach, 2009).

Studies employing the Stroop task have supported the model of Botvinick et al. (2004). They cite research indicating that after an interference trial on which there was strong ACC activity, relatively low interference was observed on a subsequent trial and that subsequent trial

---

3 The convergence can be seen in a literature that grows daily (e.g., Camerer, Loewenstein, & Prelec, 2005; DeMartino, Kumaran, Seymour, & Dolan, 2006; Frank, Cohen, & Sanfey, 2009; Goel & Dolan, 2003; Greene, 2005; Prado & Noveck, 2007; Sanfey, Loewenstein, McClure, & Cohen, 2006; van Veen & Carter, 2006).

tended to have stronger DLPFC activity. This pattern suggests that "the ACC response to conflict triggers strategic adjustments in cognitive control, which serve to reduce conflict in subsequent performance" (Botvinick et al., 2004, p. 544). Mitchell et al. (2007) tested this model of the ACC as a transient indicator of the need for a change in control and the DLPFC as the mechanism sustaining attentional focus on the new goal or belief state. They measured brain activity in these areas during a thought suppression task ("do not think of a white bear," see Wegner, 1994, 2002) and found that the temporal scopes of ACC and DLPFC activity were different. ACC activity was transiently involved subsequent to the occurrence of unwanted thoughts. DLPFC activity was present on a more sustained basis during successful attempts at thought suppression.

The findings of Mitchell et al. (2007) are again consistent with the notion that DLPFC is indicating the operation of sustained decoupling and that ACC is an indicator of signals from the reflective mind that trigger the onset of decoupling operations. Also consistent is research by De Neys, Vartanian, and Goel (2008), who studied noncausal baserate problems where the baserate conflicted with the indicant information. DLPFC activity increased when subjects chose the baserate response over the stereotype-based response, indicating that this brain region was involved in inhibiting the stereotype-based response. The ACC showed increased activity regardless of which response the subject chose (baserate response or stereotype-based response), indicating that the ACC was involved in detecting the conflict but not in the sustained decoupling necessary to suppress the stereotype-based response lodged in the autonomous mind.

Geary's (2005) model of ACC and DLPFC functioning fits nicely with the model in Figure 4–1. First, he believes that both areas are heavily involved when heuristic processing does not yield a definitive answer to a problem. The ACC in his model signals novelty or conflict. Second, the ACC activation initiates DLPFC activity that signals the "explicit, controlled problem solving needed to cope with the novel situation or resolve the conflict" (p. 215). In the terms of my framework, the DLPFC carries out the ongoing decoupling operations that are necessary for sustained simulation and evaluation of alternative responses to be carried out. The ACC is the part of the reflective mind that detects situations where decoupling operations may be needed. Geary (2005) interprets the model of Botvinick et al. (2004) as eliminating the homunculus problem that has bedeviled discussions of controlled processing: "Novelty and conflict result in automatic attentional shifts and activation of executive functions is important, because it addresses the homunculus question. The central executive does not activate itself, but rather is automatically activated when heuristic-based processes are not sufficient for dealing with current information patterns or tasks" (Geary, 2005, p. 215).

Consistent with this mapping of brain structures, in his review of work in social cognitive neuroscience, Lieberman (2007) locates the DLPFC in his C-system (i.e., reflective system) along with medial prefrontal cortex, lateral parietal cortex, medial parietal cortex, medial temporal lobe, and rostral ACC (rACC). Lieberman, however, locates the dorsal ACC (dACC) with his X-system (i.e., reflexive system), along with the amygdala, basal ganglia, and ventromedial prefrontal cortex, and lateral temporal cortex. Nonetheless, Lieberman (2007) admits that the classification of the rACC and dACC is complex and confusing. Satpute and Lieberman (2006) cite evidence supporting the differentiation of these structures. For example, they note that the rACC seems to differentially respond to symbolic conflict and the dACC to nonsymbolic conflict. However, this difference is probably not sufficient to justify allocating the different structures to totally different systems (reflexive and reflective in Lieberman's terms).

What might tempt a theorist into classifying the dACC as part of the reflexive system is that it is associated with transient processing—the sending of transient signals to begin the more sustained process of cognitive decoupling. As Lieberman (2007) notes:

> "a number of neuroimaging studies have examined the process whereby individuals intentionally override a prepotent response or impulse. The two brain regions that have consistently been associated with this process are dACC and DLPFC (MacDonald et al. 2000). A number of studies have implicated the dACC in detecting the conflict between a current goal and the prepotent response rather than in the process of exerting top-down control to facilitate the appropriate response or inhibit the inappropriate response (Botvinick et al. 2004). Alternatively, LPFC has been more

closely tied to maintaining the current goal in working memory
and to implementing the top-down control needed to produce
appropriate responses . . .. Similar LPFC activations are present
when individuals must inhibit beliefs in order to reason
correctly." (p. 269)

I would stress, however, that the transient nature of the dACC
functioning is, alone, probably not enough to classify it as part of the
reflexive system. The conceptual level of the types of conflicts that it
detects should probably be a more determining factor.

Evans' (2009) distinction among Type 1, Type 2, and Type 3 processing is useful here. Lieberman (2007) is correct that dACC activity is not
indicating sustained decoupling activity (which instead is most clearly
indicated by DLPFC activity). However, from this correct inference, it
does not follow that dACC activity is indicating Type 1 processing. Evans'
call for a third category of process distinctions applies in this case. The
conflict detection and control switching indicated by dACC activities
falls more clearly within Type 3 processing in the Evans' (2009) framework. It is an indicator of activity of the reflective mind in the present
tripartite view.

Such an interpretation of the findings does highlight, however, that
higher-level control processes do not necessarily operate in a sustained
manner—that control may be redirected based on fairly rapid processing.
Decisions to redirect control might be based on a variety of different
cues that have different time-courses. Detection of conflict as a cue to
intensify decoupling operations might have a brief time-course. More
sustained metacognitive judgments that result in control changes (*see*
Thompson, 2009) may tend to be more extended in time. For example,
Alter, Oppenheimer, Epley, and Eyre (2007) found that sustained experiences of dysfluency increased Type 2 processing. For example, reading a
degraded font or performing under conditions suggesting dysfluency
resulted in better performance in syllogistic reasoning, better performance
on Frederick's (2005) cognitive reflection test, and fewer probability judgments based on representativeness (*see also* Alter & Oppenheimer, 2009;
Song & Schwarz, 2009).

That conflict detection can have varying time-courses highlights the
important point that the reflective mind is defined in reference to *levels*

of control, not in terms of time. The term reflective mind is defined in terms of cognition involving high-level control change, not in terms of dictionary definitions of the term reflective (thoughtfulness, contemplation, etc.). As such, the term may be a bit of a misnomer. High-level control change *will* often be extended in time, but not always. For instance, consider Thompson's (2009) argument that the monitoring (and potential override) of Type 1 processing is triggered (or not triggered) by an initial feeling of rightness (FOR) that is processed along with the content of the Type 1 processing. The feeling of rightness leads to a judgment of rightness at the reflective level. The lower the judgment of rightness, the greater the probability of Type 2 intervention.

The important point for our present discussion is that Thompson's (2009) posited judgment of rightness is a reflective-level operation regardless of the amount of time it takes. In some cases, a strong feeling of rightness might very automatically yield shallow monitoring of the Type 1 response. However, Thompson (2009) notes "although in most cases, the strength of the FOR should be a sufficient basis for judgment, there will be circumstances in which the FOR may be explicitly discounted. For example, if participants are given an alternative explanation for the basis of their metacognitive experience, they are less likely to rely on fluency of retrieval as a cue" (p. 181). The discounting process might take time and thus result in a much more extended judgment of rightness process than the case where a very high FOR is registered immediately with no discounting context. In short, the reflective level is about cognitive control, not time. Likewise, at the end of her chapter, Thompson (2009) speculates about the relationship between consciousness and judgments of rightness. Consciousness will tend to be correlated with the time such judgments take but, in my view, neither are defining features of reflective-level processing—which is defined in terms of levels of control, not consciousness or time.

There is some evidence that ACC activity is most strongly involved in situations of response conflict as opposed to mere thought conflict, although it occurs in the latter as well (*see* Mitchell et al., 2007). To the extent that it is associated with response conflict, such a connection would suggest that ACC activity is primarily associated with a reflective-level signal to decouple for inhibitory purposes (Fig. 4–1, arrow B)—to take offline the connection between a primary representation and response programming in an autonomous system. Such a view would be consistent with the model of Schneider and Chein (2003), who view the ACC monitoring function as coming into play "when performance is error prone and when prepotent automatic responses must be overcome" (p. 550). In contrast, Schneider and Chein (2003) view monitoring for frequent attentional shifts as taking place in the posterior parietal cortex (PPC). Thus, in their view, the initiation signal indicated by arrow F in Figure 4–1 has its source in a different area (the PPC) than the initiation signal to begin response override (arrow B), which has as its source the ACC. Regardless of how that specific controversy in cognitive neuroscience is resolved, the data, at a more macro-level of analysis, are pointing to a differentiation between the reflective level and the algorithmic level of processing—between initiation signals to begin cognitive decoupling and the ability to sustain decoupling itself.

5

The Master Rationality Motive and the Origins of the Nonautonomous Mind

In this book, I have focused on the nature of Type 2 processing in dual-process models. Both the reflective level and algorithmic level of processing are nonautonomous, as I defined it in Chapter 1. In this chapter, I will elaborate on some of the uniquely human functionality of the nonautonomous minds and speculate on the evolutionary origins of Type 2 processing.

Although I have argued for the theoretical usefulness of differentiating two levels within Type 2 processing in this volume, there is no question that the distinction between the reflective mind and the algorithmic mind is going to be harder to draw experimentally than the more traditional distinction in dual-process theory—that between TASS and nonautonomous processing. Nonetheless, in Chapter 2, I argued that research deriving from an individual differences perspective has attempted to separate the former two by showing that measures of thinking dispositions can predict aspects of rational thought unaccounted for by measures of algorithmic processing capacity.

The central *evolutionary* question, however, is no doubt the origins of Type 2 processing itself. The algorithmic and reflective mind might be linked in this evolutionary story. My own speculations involve conjoining a concept much discussed in the literature with one of my own invention. The more well-known concept is that of metarepresentation, and the new concept is something I term the *Master Rationality Motive*.

Metarepresentation and Higher-Order Preferences

All multiple-process models of mind capture a phenomenal aspect of human decision making that is of profound importance—that humans often feel alienated from their choices. We display what folk psychology and philosophers term *weakness of will*[1]. For example, we continue to smoke when we know that it is a harmful habit. We order a sweet after a large meal, merely an hour after pledging to ourselves that we would not. In fact, we display alienation from our responses even in situations that do not involve weakness of will—we find ourselves recoiling from the sight of a disfigured person even after a lifetime of dedication to diversity and inclusion.

This feeling of alienation—although emotionally discomfiting when it occurs—is actually a reflection of a unique aspect of human cognition: the use of Type 2 metarepresentational abilities to enable a cognitive critique of our beliefs and our desires. Beliefs about how well we are forming beliefs become possible because of such metarepresentation, as does the ability to evaluate one's own desires—to desire to desire differently[2]. Humans alone appear to be able to represent a model not only of the actual preference structure currently acted upon but also of a model of an idealized preference structure. There are two mental capacities that enable thinking about higher-level preferences. The first, cognitive decoupling, is an algorithmic-level construct that has been discussed extensively in this book. The second construct, which I will explore in this chapter, is more of a thinking disposition at the reflective level.

In all hypothetical reasoning, a person must be able to represent a belief as separate from the world it is representing. As has been discussed, decoupling skills prevent our representations of the real world from

---

1 On being alienated from one's choices, *see* Ainslie (2001, 2005). There is a large literature on so-called "akrasia (weakness of the will)" in philosophy (Davidson, 1980; Stroud & Tappolet, 2003) and an equally large literature on problems of self-control in psychology, economics, and neurophysiology (Ainslie, 1992, 2001; Baumeister & Vohs, 2003, 2007; Berridge, 2003; Hofmann, Friese, & Strack, 2009; Loewenstein, Read, & Baumeister, 2003; Milkman, Rogers, & Bazerman, 2008; Mischel, Shoda, & Rodriguez, 1989; O'Donoghue & Rabin, 2000; Rachlin, 1995, 2000).

2 As noted in Chapter 3, many different disciplines deal with the issue of metarepresentation (Dennett, 1984; Dienes & Perner, 1999; Jackendoff, 1996; Sperber, 2000; Nichols & Stich, 2003; Stanovich, 2004). It is not uncontroversial to say that humans alone appear to be able to metarepresent, but the literature favoring this conclusion is growing (*see* Kaminski, Call, & Tomasello, 2008; Penn, Holyoak, & Povinelli, 2008, 2009; Povinelli & Bering, 2002; Povinelli & Giambrone, 2001; Suddendorf & Corballis, 2007).

becoming confused with representations of imaginary situations (simulations) that we create on a temporary basis to predict the effects of future actions or to think of the consequences of pursuing alternative goals and desires. Metarepresentation occurs when a representational relationship itself becomes decoupled (*see* Perner, 1991). Several theorists have emphasized how the metarepresentational abilities of the analytic system make possible a cognitive critique of our own beliefs and desires (e.g., Carruthers, 2002; Dennett, 1984; Stanovich, 2004). Decoupling for this type of cognitive critique may be one of the most important aspects of the analytic minds (algorithmic and reflective) that relate to rationality. It may be even more important—and perhaps even more computationally expensive[3]—than decoupling for the purposes of redirecting serial associative thought or for the purposes of inhibiting an infelicitous TASS response that has been primed.

Cognitive decoupling underlies the *ability* to reason about alternative preferences and to form higher-order preferences. However, it is not in itself the motive for forming higher-level preferences. There must be a motivational mechanism that creates the need for such self-evaluation. In this chapter, I will speculate about the nature of this motive and argue that it is a dispositional variable at a high level of generality that is, nonetheless, potentially measurable.

A metarepresentationally based critique of one's beliefs is important in epistemic calibration, and this operation has been emphasized in the memetics literature (Dawkins, 1993; Stanovich, 2004). Here, however, I would like to discuss cognitive critique in the domain of desires. There is a philosophical literature on the notion of higher-order evaluation of desires[4], and it is one that is of potential theoretical interest for decision scientists (*see* Flanagan, 1996, for an insightful discussion that is informed by cognitive science). For example, in a classic paper on second-order desires, Frankfurt (1971) speculated that only humans have such

3 Friedman et al. (2006) found that measures of fluid intelligence were more highly related to the updating component of so-called "executive functioning measures" than to the inhibition or set shifting components (*see also* Friedman et al., 2008).
4 Many philosophers have discussed the conceptual status of higher-order desires (Bratman, 2003; Dworkin, 1988; Harman, 1995 Lehrer, 1990, 1997; Lewis, 1989; Maher, 1993; Nozick, 1993; Taylor, 1989; Watson, 1975).

metarepresentational states. He evocatively termed creatures without second-order desires (other animals, human babies) *wantons*. To say that a wanton does not form second-order desires does not mean that they are heedless or careless about their first-order desires. Wantons can be rational in the purely instrumental sense. Wantons may well act in their environments to fulfill their goals with optimal efficiency. A wanton simply does not reflect on his/her goals. Wantons want—but they do not *care* what they want.

Nonwantons, however, can represent a model of an idealized preference structure—perhaps, for example, a model based on a superordinate judgment of long-term lifespan considerations (or what Gauthier, 1986, calls considered preferences). So a human can say: I would prefer to prefer not to smoke. This second-order preference can then become a motivational competitor to the first-order preference. At the level of second-order preferences, I prefer to prefer to not smoke; nevertheless, as a first-order preference, I prefer to smoke. The resulting conflict signals that I lack what Nozick (1993) terms *rational integration* in my preference structures. Such a mismatched first-/second-order preference structure is one reason why humans are often less rational than bees in an axiomatic sense (*see* Stanovich, 2004, pp. 243–247). This is because the struggle to achieve rational integration can destabilize first-order preferences in ways that make them more prone to the context effects that lead to the violation of the basic axioms of utility theory (*see* Lee, Amir, & Ariely, 2009).

The struggle for rational integration is also what contributes to the feeling of alienation that people in the modern world often feel when contemplating the choices that they have made. People easily detect when their high-order preferences conflict with the choices actually made.

Of course, there is no limit to the hierarchy of higher-order desires that might be constructed. But the representational abilities of humans may set some limits—certainly three levels seems a realistic limit for most people in the nonsocial domain (Dworkin, 1988). However, third-order judgments can be called upon to help achieve rational integration at lower levels. So, for example, imagine that John is a smoker. He might realize the following when he probes his feelings: He prefers his preference to prefer not to smoke over his preference for smoking.

We might in this case say that John's third-order judgment has ratified his second-order evaluation. Presumably this ratification of his second-order judgment adds to the cognitive pressure to change the first-order preference by taking behavioral measures that will make change more likely (entering a smoking secession program, consulting his physician, staying out of smoky bars, etc.).

On the other hand, a third-order judgment might undermine the second-order preference by failing to ratify it: John might prefer to smoke more than he prefers his preference to prefer not to smoke.

In this case, although John wishes he did not want to smoke, the preference for this preference is not as strong as his preference for smoking itself. We might suspect that this third-order judgment might not only prevent John from taking strong behavioral steps to rid himself of his addiction, but that over time it might erode his conviction in his second-order preference itself, thus bringing rational integration to all three levels.

Typically, philosophers have tended to bias their analyses toward the highest level desire that is constructed—privileging the highest point in the regress of higher-order evaluations, using that as the foundation, and defining it as the true self. Modern cognitive science would suggest instead a Neurathian project in which no level of analysis is uniquely privileged. Philosopher Otto Neurath (1932/33; *see* Quine, 1960, pp. 3–4) employed the metaphor of a boat having some rotten planks. The best way to repair the planks would be to bring the boat ashore, stand on firm ground, and replace the planks. But what if the boat could not be brought ashore? Actually, the boat could still be repaired but at some risk. We could repair the planks at sea by standing on some of the planks while repairing others. The project could work—we could repair the boat without being on the firm foundation of ground. The Neurathian project is not guaranteed, however, because we might choose to stand on a rotten plank. For example, nothing in Frankfurt's (1971) notion of higher-order desires guarantees against higher-order judgments being infected by memes (units of cultural transmission, *see* Chapter 8) that are personally damaging.

Many philosophers have thought that unless we had a level of cognitive analysis (preferably the highest one) that was foundational, something that we value about ourselves (various candidates in the philosophical literature have been personhood, autonomy, identity, and free will) would be put in jeopardy. Hurley (1989), in contrast, endorses a Neurathian view in which there does not exist either a "highest platform" or a so-called true-self, outside of the interlocking nexus of desires. She argues that "the exercise of autonomy involves depending on certain of our values as a basis for criticizing and revising others, but not detachment from all of them, and that autonomy does not depend on a regress into higher and higher order attitudes, but on the first step" (p. 364). In short, the uniquely human project of self-definition begins at the first step, when an individual begins to climb the ladder of hierarchical values—when a person has, for the first time, a problem of rational integration.

What Motivates the Search for Rational Integration?

But how do we know that a person is engaging deeply in such a process of self-definition and rational integration? Interestingly, perhaps the best indicator is when we detect a mismatch between a person's first- and second-order desires with which the person is struggling: The person avows a certain set of values that imply that they should prefer to do something other than they do. In fact, they will often tell you that they are struggling to find rational integration (without using those terms, of course).

No dual-process theorist would posit that rational integration is an automatic process. It is more likely an effortful process that needs motivational force to initiate. An important philosophical paper by Velleman (1992) provides guidance to psychologists in modeling and measuring the mechanisms involved in the process of rational integration. Velleman (1992) attempts to unpack Frankfurt's (1971) idea that "the agent's role is to adjudicate conflicts of motives" (p. 476). Under Frankfurt's view, Velleman notes, the role of adjudicator cannot be taken up by a higher-order attitude itself, because these will be always subject to review.

Velleman (1992) asks us to get used to that idea that practical thought itself (Manktelow, 2004; Millgram, 2001; Over, 2004) is propelled by a distinctive motive. For Velleman, that motive is: "your desire to act in accordance with reasons, a desire that produces behavior, in your name, by adding its motivational force to that of whichever motives appear to provide the strongest reasons for acting" (p. 479). This attitude, for Velleman, performs the function of agency.

I would contend that what Velleman (1992) has identified is a motive at such a high level of generality that I have termed it the *Master Rationality Motive* (MRM; Stanovich, 2008). It is the motive that drives the search for rational integration across our preference hierarchies. Importantly, Nozick (1993) has argued that it is not a particular algorithm for rational integration that is rational. Instead, what is rational is the *felt need* for rational integration. The need for rational integration is probably a function of the strength of the MRM, and individual differences in the former probably arise because of individual differences in the latter. Thus, the MRM is what sustains the search for rational integration.

The Master Rationality Motive as a Psychological Construct

The psychological literature on individual differences in rational thought does contain some attempts to measure constructs similar to the MRM. Epstein's Head-Over-Heart scale (a precursor to his rational-experiential inventory; *see* Epstein, Pacini, Heier, & Denes-Raj, 1995; Epstein et al., 1996) is perhaps the measure with the most overlap with the MRM[5]. Our own actively open-minded thinking scale (Stanovich & West, 2007) taps a partially overlapping construct. Recently, however, we have tried to be more systematic and have compiled items from a variety of existing scales and have tested new ones in an attempt to measure the MRM in questionnaire form. Table 5–1 presents a proposed MRM scale.

My conjecture is that the MRM scale will tap an individual difference characteristic different from cognitive ability (intelligence). Thus, it is proposed that it is a scale that could capture unique variance in rational thinking after cognitive ability has been partialled out. One reason for making this conjecture is that there are already empirical indications that more micro-thinking dispositions can predict variance in reasoning tasks.

---

5 There has been a reasonable amount of work on the rational-experiential inventory (*see* Bartels, 2006; Klaczynski & Lavallee, 2005; Newstead, Handley, Harley, Wright, & Farrelly, 2004; Pacini & Epstein, 1999).

TABLE 5.1   Items on the Master Rationality Motive Scale

Item	Source
Intuition is the best guide in making decisions. (R)	Stanovich & West (1997)
Certain beliefs are just too important to abandon, no matter how good a case can be made against them. (R)	Sá, West, & Stanovich (1999)
I am only confident of decisions that are made after careful analysis of all available information.	Leary, Shepperd, McNeil, Jenkins, & Barnes (1986)
I do not like to be too objective in the way I look at things. (R)	Leary, Shepperd, McNeil, Jenkins, & Barnes (1986)
After I make a decision, it is often difficult for me to give logical reasons for it. (R)	Leary, Shepperd, McNeil, Jenkins, & Barnes (1986)
I believe in following my heart more than my head. (R)	Epstein, Pacini, Heier, & Denes-Raj (1995)
It is more important to me than to most people to behave in a logical way.	Epstein, Pacini, Heier, & Denes-Raj (1995)
I like to gather many different types of evidence before I decide what to do.	New item
I don't feel I have to have reasons for what I do. (R)	New item
I like to think that my actions are motivated by sound reasons.	New item
I like to have reasons for what I do.	New item
I don't like to have to justify my actions. (R)	New item
If a belief suits me and I am comfortable, it really doesn't matter if the belief is true. (R)	New item
Item #2 from Facet 6 (Deliberation) of the Conscientious domain of the NEO PI-R	Costa & McCrae (1992)
Item #4 from Facet 6 (Deliberation) of the Conscientious domain of the NEO PI-R	Costa & McCrae (1992)

R = item reversed scored

For example, various thinking dispositions such as need for cognition and actively open-minded thinking have been found to predict (sometimes after control for cognitive ability) performance on a host of tasks from the heuristics and biases literature[6].

6 This literature is growing (Bartels, 2006; Chatterjee et al., 2000; Klaczynski & Lavallee, 2005; Kokis et al., 2002; Ku & Ho, 2010; McElroy & Seta, 2003; Newstead et al., 2004; Pacini & Epstein, 1999; Parker & Fischhoff, 2005; Perkins & Ritchhart, 2004; Shiloh, Salton, & Sharabi, 2002; Simon, Fagley, & Halleran, 2004; Smith

This previous literature differs, however, from what I am proposing here in two ways. First, the thinking dispositions that have been studied are at a lower level of generality than the MRM (Perkins & Ritchhart, 2004). Second, the criterion variables have been limited to aspects of instrumental rationality—for example, how well people satisfy the choice axioms of utility theory or the strictures of Bayesian belief updating. As such, the criterion variables have reflected aspects of what has been termed a thin theory of rationality (*see* Elster, 1983; Chapter 8 of Stanovich, 2004) . Thin theories define rationality in terms of current beliefs and desires. However, it is a broad notion of rationality (one that critiques current beliefs and first-order desires) that is most likely to have a unique connection to the MRM.

Of course, I do not wish to paint the MRM in too essentialist a fashion before investigation has even begun. The extent to which it is a generic motive is yet to be determined. There may well be a good degree of domain specificity in the extent to which people strive to achieve rational integration. Nonetheless, some degree of domain specificity might not necessarily be antithetical to the MRM construct. The logic of memetics has suggested that there are individual differences not only among people but also among the beliefs that they host. Importantly, beliefs differ in the extent of their so-called adversarial properties (Blackmore, 1999; Dawkins, 1993; Lynch, 1996)—how strongly they are structured to repel competing ideas. Thus, how much the beliefs that are the source of higher-order evaluations encourage or repel the process of rational integration may be quite variable. This implies that domain specificity in rational integration could well exist without domain specificity in the MRM construct itself. Issues such as this are the type of question about the MRM that future research will need to answer.

Human thinking is not just confined to the pursuit of instrumental rationality. Humans also are concerned about issues of broad rationality. They attempt to critique current desires and goals using their metarepresentational abilities. It is conjectured here that the critique itself— and the consistency issues it raises—is driven by a distinctive thinking

& Levin, 1996; Stanovich & West, 1998c, 1999, 2000; Toplak & Stanovich, 2002; Verplanken, 1993).

disposition at a high level of generality, the MRM. Preliminary research on related constructs encourages the view that this construct is measurable.

Evolutionary Origins of the Master Rational Motive and Type 2 Processing

How did the MRM get lodged in the reflective mind? This issue is a small part of the larger question of how Type 2 processing, in general, arose. There are currently several related proposals for answering both questions floating around in the literature, and these proposals have enough similarity that I will attempt a synthesis here.

Nozick (1993) has argued that in prehistory, when mechanisms for revealing what is true about the world were few, a crude route to reliable knowledge might have been just to demand reasons for assertions by conspecifics. True propositions might have been supported by more reasons and by reasons of better quality. In a related proposal, Sperber (2000) posits that we have a logico-argumentative module that is an evolutionary adaptation for checking the consistency of the statements of other people to enable us to develop "the proper calibration of trust" (p. 135). These reason-checking procedures might bootstrap metarepresentational abilities into existence because they encourage self-evaluation for purposes of internal consistency assessment. In short, applying the MRM to the thoughts of the self might be a cognitive (as well as cultural) achievement that follows the development of consistency-checking procedures applied to others (*see also* Carruthers, 2009).

Dennett (1996, pp. 126–127) has argued that the need to respond to the justification queries of other conspecifics helped shape the internal mental inquiry processes in the direction of discrete categories—categories that mesh well with the properties of language-based thought. These discrete categories fostered by language then become an ideal medium for representing one's own thoughts to oneself (*see* Carruthers, 2006). Some years ago, philosopher Allan Gibbard (1990) anticipated all of these proposals with his emphasis on consistency checking among conspecifics—"the need to work through normative commitments in community" (p. 74)—and his view that "to prepare oneself to meet demands for consistency may require a strong imaginative life. A person will engage in imaginative rehearsal for actual normative discussion; he practices by holding himself to consistency" (p. 74). All of these views are, despite subtle differences between them, sketching the gene/cultural co-evolutionary history (*see* Richerson & Boyd, 2005) of the MRM—the desire to have reasons behind our cognitive evaluations. This is, I conjecture, the master motive that provides the motivational press to engage in internal cognitive reform.

What about the evolution of Type 2 processing more generally? My view is in no way original but is instead a synthesis of the views of a variety of scholars (e.g., Carruthers, 2002, 2006; Mithen, 1996, 2000, 2002; Sterelny, 2001, 2003). Sterelny (2001), like many other theorists, links the development of early simulation ability to the social intelligence hypothesis—the idea that our ancient social life was the selection pressure for the development of simulation abilities[7]. I follow a plethora of such social intelligence proposals in assuming that the root of hypothetical thinking is in the development of the at least quasi-modular theory of mind (ToM) module. In the domain of behavioral prediction, we were first able to track what Sterelny (2001, 2003; *see also* Clark, 1997 pp. 167–168) calls *robust representations*—representations that map very abstractly (i.e., theoretically) to a large variety of contingent and context-dependent cues.

I follow Mithen (1996) in thinking that language helped to break down an evolutionarily older modular mind by delivering nonsocial information to the social module, or perhaps exapting the modular social mind for hypothetical representation of the nonsocial world. Carruthers' (2000, 2002, 2006) notion of language as a mediating representational system that serves to integrate the modular mind would also serve here just as well. The end result is a story similar to Mithen's (1996):

"As soon as language acted as a vehicle for delivering information into the mind (whether one's own or that of another person),

---

7 The literature on aspects of the social intelligence hypothesis is huge (e.g., Baldwin, 2000; Cummins, 1996, 2002; Dunbar, 1998; Gibbard, 1990; Goldman, 2006; Goody, 1995; Herrmann, Call, Hernandez-Lloreda, Hare, & Tomasello, 2007; Humphrey, 1976, 1986; Kummer, Daston, Gigerenzer, & Silk, 1997; Levinson, 1995; Mithen, 1996, 2000, 2002; Tomasello, 1998, 1999; Whiten & Byrne, 1997).

carrying with it snippets of nonsocial information, a transformation in the nature of the mind began. . . . language switched from a social to a general-purpose function, consciousness from a means to predict other individuals' behavior to managing a mental database of information relating to all domains of behavior" (p. 209).

Whatever the exact mechanism, we have a discontinuity between social and nonsocial representation of hypotheticals. Overcoming focal bias to construct hypothetical worlds in the social domain is effortless because of the dedicated mental machinery (the ToM module) that supports decoupling in that domain. Decoupling to represent alternative worlds in other domains is effortful because it is a derivative ability, evolutionarily late to the table.

On the issue of the origins of the nonautonomous systems, perhaps even more can be said. For example, Sterelny (2001, p. 237) argues that simulation may be more developmentally fundamental and evolution- arily basic than metarepresentation. Following Goldman (1995), he argues that taking the agent's decision mechanisms offline in the service of conditional planning solves the "trajectory" problem. The trajectory problem is the issue of how, in its very early stages of evolution, a very basic simulator could have helped. Simulating the self comes first in this view, because simulating others "involves much more radical shifts from the agent's current state than does conditional planning" (p. 238).

There is a family resemblance in all of these proposals. For example, analogous to how Mithen (1996) argues that modules dedicated to social information processing were recruited for other tasks, Sterelny (2001) argues that these initial conditional planning abilities and modeling of the minds of others via simulation abilities then became recruited for other nonsocial hypothetical reasoning tasks.

Alternatively, one could depict the evolutionary development in terms of the boxology models employed by Nichols and Stich (2003) in their book on ToM abilities. They depict the dedicated mindreading system as including a mindreading coordinator to update beliefs about agents and most importantly a Possible Worlds Box (PWB), which embodies what I have been calling decoupling operations—in essence, the mechanism that prevents representation abuse in Leslie's (1987) terms (*see* Chapter 3). The Mithen/Sterelny idea of simulation abilities becoming recruited for other nonsocial hypothetical reasoning tasks can be portrayed within the Nichols/Stich model. It amounts to positing that the PWB eventually comes to exist as a general mechanism (unattached to the theory of mind apparatus) that is available to receive input from any domain. In other domains, there would be no dedicated mindreading coordinator, and perhaps this would account, in some as yet unspecified way, for the fact that decoupling for hypothetical thinking—that is, dealing with robust representations—is so much harder in nonsocial domains.

One of the most complex activities that can take place in the PWB is to manipulate and evaluate metarepresentations—representations of one's own representations. Metarepresentation is involved when we evaluate whether we are satisfied with our own preference structures and when we critique our own beliefs (*see* Stanovich, 2004). It is a function that might have been borrowed from ToM abilities (again, in the manner of Mithen's model of the nonsocial thought infecting the social).

It should be noted, however, that my conception of this is not how Nichols and Stich (2003) see it, because their model is just the opposite. They (*see* p. 65) view the PWB (a general hypothetical reasoning device) being exapted for use in behavior prediction and mindreading. I join many other theorists however (e.g., Mithen, 1996, 2002; Tomasello, 1998, 1999) in seeing the causal direction running the other way—from ToM to hypothetical reasoning abilities. This follows from the idea that forming robust representations (*see* Clark, 1997; Sterelny, 2001) and developing robust prediction abilities probably originated in the social domain of predicting the complex behaviors of others who were potentially hostile (*see* Sterelny, 2003). Robust representation was probably necessary in this social domain and developed in innate—if not modular—mental machinery. This machinery was then used more abstractly (in the manner of the PWB) for hypothetical reasoning more generally. The decoupling abilities of the algorithmic mind and the calls for decoupling from the reflective mind are the modern remnants of this evolutionary history.

Whatever specific evolutionary explanation is true, the MRM serves to reinforce the distinctions in the tripartite cognitive model presented in this volume. The MRM is a high-level control state that resides in the reflective mind. It is, indirectly, a sign that we *need* to posit the reflective mind. It also demonstrates some of the important ways that IQ tests are incomplete—an important theme in the remaining chapters of this book. Nothing like the MRM is assessed on IQ tests. Such tests assess algorithmic-level functioning only—crystallized knowledge (Gc) plus decoupling abilities (Gf). Variation in the "desire to act in accordance with reasons" is a thinking disposition that needs to be assessed under typical, not maximal, conditions. It is more related to rationality than to intelligence. In fact, it is only one of a myriad of rational thinking skills that go unassessed on IQ tests. The relationship between intelligence and rational thought has remained unexplored for many years. My research lab's program on individual differences in performance on heuristics and biases tasks has been in an ideal position to explore this issue.

In the next chapters, an attempt is made to organize the literature on rational thinking errors and biases and to look at the data on the associations between these errors and intelligence. A model for predicting which rational thinking tasks will be associated with intelligence and which will not is developed. The rational thinking skills that are missed by intelligence tests will be highlighted by this model and it will provide a framework for the development of formal procedures to assess individual differences in rational thought that are discussed in Chapter 10.

6

A Taxonomy of Rational Thinking Problems

(Keith E. Stanovich and Richard F. West)

The concepts introduced so far in this book provide the foundation for a taxonomy of rational thinking problems that can be used to organize the heuristics and biases literature. We need just one additional concept—but it is an important one because it is often overlooked.

Dual-Process Theory and Knowledge Structures

An aspect of dual-process theory that has been relatively neglected is that successful Type 2 override operations require both procedural and declarative knowledge. Although taking the Type 1 response priming offline might itself be procedural, the process of synthesizing an alternative response often utilizes stored knowledge of various types. During the simulation process, declarative knowledge and strategic rules (linguistically coded strategies) are used to transform a decoupled representation. In the previous dual-process literature, override has been treated as a somewhat disembodied process. The knowledge bases and strategies that are brought to bear on the secondary representations during the simulation process have been given little attention.

In fact, each of the levels in the tripartite model has to access knowledge to carry out its operations (*see* Fig. 6–1). The reflective mind not only accesses general knowledge structures but, importantly, accesses the person's opinions, beliefs, and reflectively acquired goal structure (considered preferences, *see* Gauthier, 1986). The algorithmic mind accesses micro-strategies for cognitive operations and production system rules for sequencing behaviors and thoughts. Finally, the autonomous mind accesses not only evolutionarily compiled encapsulated knowledge bases but also retrieves information that has become tightly compiled and automatically activated because of overlearning and practice.

It is important to note that what is displayed in Figure 6–1 are the knowledge bases that are *unique* to each mind. Algorithmic- and reflective-level processes also receive inputs from the computations of the autonomous mind (*see* the G arrows in Fig. 4–1, which indicate the influence of preattentive processes). The knowledge structures available for retrieval—particularly those available to the reflective mind—represent crystallized intelligence (Gc; intelligence-as-knowledge) in the Cattell/Horn/Carroll theory of intelligence mentioned in Chapter 3. Recall that fluid intelligence (Gf; intelligence-as-process) is already represented in the figure. It is the general computational power of the algorithmic mind—importantly exemplified by the ability to sustain cognitive decoupling.

Because the Gf/Gc theory is one of the most comprehensively validated theories of intelligence available, it is important to see how both of its major components miss critical aspects of rational thought. Fluid intelligence will, of course, have some relation to rationality because it

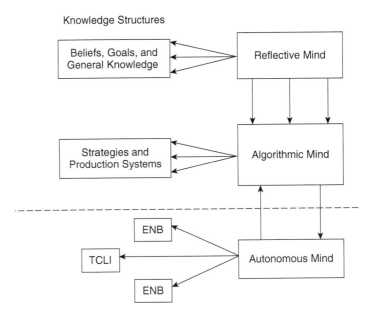

ENB = Encapsulated Knowledge Base
TCLI = Tightly Compiled Learned Information

FIGURE 6.1.   Knowledge Structures in the Tripartite Framework.

indexes the computational power of the algorithmic mind to sustain decoupling. Because override and simulation are important operations for rational thought, Gf will definitely facilitate rational action in some situations. Nevertheless, the tendency to initiate override (arrow B in Fig. 4–1) and to initiate simulation activities (arrow D in Fig. 4–1) are both aspects of the reflective mind unassessed by intelligence tests, so the tests will miss these components of rationality. These propensities are instead indexed by measures of typical performance (cognitive styles and thinking dispositions) as opposed to measures of maximal performance such as IQ tests.

The situation with respect to Gc is a little different. Rational thought depends critically on the acquisition of certain types of knowledge. That knowledge would, in the abstract, be classified as crystallized intelligence. But is it the kind of crystallized knowledge that is assessed on actual tests of intelligence? The answer is no. The knowledge structures that support rational thought are specialized (they cluster in the domains of probabilistic reasoning, causal reasoning, and scientific reasoning). In contrast, the crystallized knowledge assessed on IQ tests is deliberately designed to be nonspecialized. The designers of the tests, to make sure the sampling of vocabulary and knowledge is fair and unbiased, explicitly attempt to *broadly* sample vocabulary, verbal comprehension domains, and general knowledge. In short, Gc, as traditionally measured, does not assess individual differences in rationality, and Gf will do so only indirectly and to a mild extent.

The knowledge, rules, procedures, and strategies that can be retrieved and used to transform decoupled representations have been referred to as mindware, a term coined by David Perkins in a 1995 book (Clark, 2001, uses it in a slightly different way from Perkins' original coinage). The mindware available for use during cognitive simulation is in part the product of past learning experiences. This means that there will be individual differences in the ability to simulate better alternatives to a TASS-based response. Indeed, if one is going to trump a TASS-primed response with conflicting information or a learned rule, one must have previously learned the information or the rule. If, in fact, the relevant mindware is not available because it has not been learned, then we have a case of missing mindware rather than a TASS-override failure. This distinction in fact represents the beginning of a taxonomy of the causes of cognitive failure related to rational behavior that we are currently using to organize the heuristics and biases literature and to classify various practical problems of rational thinking—for example, to understand the thinking problems of pathological gamblers (Toplak et al., 2007).

With mindware problems established as a possible cause of rational thinking problems, we are now in a position to lay out a taxonomy of thinking errors that captures most of the effects studied in the heuristics and biases literature[1]. We will see that the taxonomy captures the distinction between rationality as process and rationality as content in a manner similar to the way that process and content are partitioned in the fluid/crystallized (Gf/Gc) theory of intelligence.

The Preliminary Taxonomy

A preliminary attempt at such a taxonomy is displayed in Figure 6–2. Presented at the top of the figure are three classes of rational thinking error that result from the human tendency to process information as a cognitive miser. The three classes are listed in order of relative cognitive engagement. The characteristic of the cognitive miser that is presented first is the tendency to default to the response options primed by the autonomous mind. It represents the shallowest kind of processing because no Type 2 processing is done at all. In the dual-process literature, this type of processing default has sometimes been termed a failure to override TASS processing. However, in the taxonomy we are presenting here, for something to be considered a TASS override failure, Type 2 processing must lose out to Type 1 processing in a conflict of discrepant outputs. If Type 2 processing is not engaged at all, then it is not considered an override failure in our view.

In fact, the early heuristics and biases researchers were clearer on this point than many later dual-process theorists. The distinction between impressions and judgments in the early heuristics and biases work (*see*

---

1 Other taxonomies have been introduced into the literature, but they are not based on the type of dual-process model that is the inspiration for our framework (e.g., Arkes, 1991; Oreg & Bayazit, 2009; Reyna, Lloyd, & Brainerd, 2003; Shah & Oppenheimer, 2008).

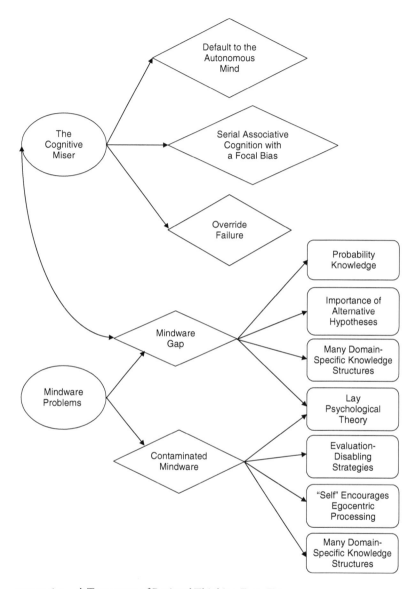

FIGURE 6.2.   A Taxonomy of Rational Thinking Error Types.

Kahneman, 2003; Kahneman & Frederick, 2002, 2005, for a discussion) made it clearer that non-normative responses often resulted not from a Type 2/Type 1 struggle but from intuitive impressions that are left uncorrected by the rules and strategies that Type 2 processing can recruit. In fact, in many cases that have been called override failure in the literature, the subject probably does not even consider overriding the TASS-based response (even when the mindware to do so is readily available and well learned). In such cases, the subject does not recognize the need for override or chooses not to sustain the necessary decoupling and simulation with alternative mindware that would make override possible.

The second type of processing tendency of the cognitive miser that is represented in Figure 6–2 is to engage in serial associative cognition with a focal bias. This characteristic represents a tendency to over-economize during Type 2 processing—specifically, to fail to engage in the full-blown simulation of alternative worlds or to engage in fully disjunctive reasoning (Shafir, 1994; Toplak & Stanovich, 2002).

The third category is that of override failure—which represents the least miserly tendency because, here, Type 2 cognitive decoupling is engaged. Inhibitory Type 2 processes try to take the Type 1 processing of the autonomous mind offline in these cases, but they fail. So in override failure, cognitive decoupling does occur, but it fails to suppress the Type 1 processing of the autonomous mind. Override failure in this taxonomy encompasses what folk theory would call problems of willpower or the problem of multiple minds (see Ainslie, 2001, 2005, for a nuanced discussion of the folk concept of willpower in light of modern cognitive science). Psychologists and economists often term these situations as reflecting problems of self-control[2].

However, there are more than just willpower and self-control issues in this category. For some subjects, heuristics and biases tasks can also trigger override problems because of an architecture of multiple minds. Sloman (1996) points out that at least for some subjects, the Linda conjunction problem (see Tversky & Kahneman, 1983) is the quintessence of dual-process conflict. He quotes Stephen Gould's introspection that "I know the [conjunction] is least probable, yet a little homunculus in my head continues to jump up and down, shouting at me—'but she can't be a bank teller; read the description'" (Gould, 1991, p. 469). For sophisticated subjects such as Gould, resolving the Linda problem clearly

---

2 Some of the literature on self-control was cited in the previous chapter (see Baumeister & Vohs, 2003, 2007; Gailliot & Baumeister, 2007; Loewenstein, Read, & Baumeister, 2003; Mischel, Shoda, & Rodriguez, 1989; O'Donoghue & Rabin, 2000; Rachlin, 1995, 2000).

involves a Type 1/Type 2 processing conflict, and in his case, a conjunction error on the task would represent a true case of override failure. However, for the majority of subjects in this task, there may well be no conscious introspection going on—Type 2 processing is either not engaged or engaged so little that there is no awareness of a cognitive struggle. Instead, TASS-based heuristics such as representativeness or conversational pragmatics trigger the response. The detailed controversies about the Linda task are beyond our scope here[3]. The algorithmic and reflective minds (that carry out Type 2 processing) have not lost a struggle when they have not been called into the battle. For such subjects, committing the conjunction error in the Linda problem represents a case of defaulting to the processing of the autonomous mind (the first category in Fig. 6–2).

The next two categories of rational thinking error in Figure 6–2 concern mindware problems. The first is termed a *mindware gap*—missing knowledge of the rules and strategies of rational thought. In Figure 6–2, the curved rectangles are meant to represent these missing knowledge bases. The figure is not meant to represent an exhaustive set of knowledge partitionings—to the contrary, only a minimal sampling of a potentially large set of coherent knowledge bases is represented. Many domains of knowledge in the areas of probabilistic reasoning, causal reasoning, logic, and scientific thinking could result in irrational thought or behavior if they are not available during simulation operations. The two represented in Figure 6–2 are mindware categories that have been implicated in research in the heuristics and biases tradition: missing knowledge about probability and probabilistic reasoning strategies and ignoring alternative hypotheses when evaluating hypotheses. The study of pathological gambling behavior, for example, has focused on a class of missing mindware of particular relevance to that condition: knowledge and procedures for dealing with probability and probabilistic events (Keren, 1994; Rogers, 1998; Toneatto, 1999; Toplak et al., 2007; Wagenaar, 1988). Many studies of such gamblers now administer measures of knowledge

---

3 There is a large literature on alternative interpretations of responses on the Linda task (see Adler, 1984, 1991; Dulany & Hilton, 1991; Girotto, 2004; Hertwig, Benz, & Krauss, 2008; Hilton, 1995; Lee, 2006; Mellers, Hertwig, & Kahneman, 2001; Politzer & Macchi, 2000; Politzer & Noveck, 1991).

of regression to the mean, outcome bias, the gambler's fallacy, probability matching, baserate neglect, Bayesian probabilistic updating, and covariation detection. However, these are just a few of many mindware gaps that have been suggested in the literature on behavioral decision making. There are many others, and the box labeled "Many Domain-Specific Knowledge Structures" indicates this.

Note that the curved, double-headed arrow in this figure, indicating an important relationship between the mindware gap category and miserly processing. Most previous discussions in the dual-process literature have simply assumed that mindware was available to Type 2 to allow it to synthesize a response superior to that primed by Type 1 processing. If, in fact, the mindware is not available because it has not been learned or at least not learned to the requisite level to sustain override, then in this taxonomy it is considered a mindware gap rather than any type of miserly processing.

One interesting implication of the relation between miserly processing and mindware gaps is that the fewer gaps one has, the more likely that an error may be attributable to miserly processing. In contrast, errors made by someone with little relevant mindware installed are less likely to result from miserly processing than to mindware gaps. Of course, the two categories trade off in a continuous manner with a fuzzy boundary between them. For example, a well-learned rule that is not strongly enough applied might be seen as a case of override failure. When a rule is less well-instantiated, there is a point where it is so poorly compiled that it is not an alternative to the Type 1 response, and thus the processing error becomes a mindware gap.

Although mindware gaps may lead to suboptimal reasoning, the next category in the taxonomy is designed to draw attention to the fact that not all mindware is helpful—either to goal attainment or to epistemic accuracy. In fact, some acquired mindware can be the direct cause of irrational actions that thwart our goals. Such effects thus define the last category in the taxonomy of thinking errors displayed in Figure 6–2: contaminated mindware[4]. The curved rectangles represent problematic

---

4 Many theorists speculating on the properties of cultural replication would allow for the possibility of mindware that not only does not help support rational thought and behavior but is itself a direct cause of irrational action (Aunger, 2000, 2002;

knowledge and strategies. Again, they do not represent an exhaustive partitioning (the mindware-related categories are too diverse for that) but instead represent some of the mechanisms that have received some discussion in the literature. One is a subcategory of contaminated mindware that is much discussed in the literature—mindware that contains evaluation-disabling properties. Some of the evaluation-disabling properties that help keep some mindware lodged in their hosts are: the promise of punishment if the mindware is questioned; the promise of rewards for unquestioning faith in the mindware; or the thwarting of evaluation attempts by rendering the mindware unfalsifiable.

Another subcategory of contaminated mindware that has been discussed by several theorists is a concept of "self" that serves to encourage egocentric thinking (Blackmore, 1999; Dennett, 1991, 1995). The self, according to these theorists, is a mechanism that fosters one characteristic of focal bias: that we tend to build models of the world from a single myside perspective. The egocentrism of the self was, of course, evolutionarily adaptive. However, for many of the same reasons that the heuristics of the autonomous mind are sometimes nonoptimal in a technological environment different from the environment of evolutionary adaptation, the decontextualizing demands of modernity increasingly require such characteristics. Consider, for example, such modern social/psychological requirements: fairness, rule-following despite context, even-handedness, sanctioning of nepotism, unbiasedness, universalism, inclusiveness, contractually mandated equal treatment, and discouragement of familial, racial, and religious discrimination. These requirements are difficult ones, probably because they override processing defaults related to the self.

Finally, the last subcategory of contaminated mindware pictured in Figure 6–2 is meant to represent what is actually a whole set of categories: mindware representing specific categories of maladaptive information. Similarly to the missing mindware category, there may be many clusters of misinformation that would support irrational thought and behavior. For example, the gambler's fallacy and many of the other misunderstandings of probability that have been studied in the heuristics and

Blackmore, 1999, 2005; Dawkins, 1993; Dennett, 1991, 2006; Distin, 2005; Hull, 2000; Laland & Brown, 2002; McKay & Dennett, 2010; Mesoudi, Whiten, & Laland, 2006; Richerson & Boyd, 2005; Stanovich, 2004).

biases literature would fit here (Ayton & Fischer, 2004; Burns & Corpus, 2004; Croson & Sundali, 2005; Nickerson, 2004; Roney & Trick, 2009). Of course, the line between missing mindware and contaminated mindware might get fuzzy in some cases, and the domain of probabilistic thinking is probably one such case.

Lay psychological theory is represented as the potential locus of contaminated mindware and as the potential locus of a mindware gap in Figure 6–2. Lay psychological theories are the theories that people have about their own minds. Mindware gaps in this domain would be represented by the many things about our own minds that we do not know—for example, how quickly we will adapt to both fortunate and unfortunate events (Gilbert, 2006; Kahneman, 1999; Wilson & Gilbert, 2005). Other things we think we know about our own minds are wrong. These misconceptions represent contaminated mindware. An example would be the folk belief that we accurately know our own minds, what philosophers of mind call the incorrigibility of introspection (Churchland, 1988). This contaminated mindware leads people to incorrectly believe that they always know the causes of their own actions (Nisbett & Wilson, 1977) and to think that although others display thinking biases, they themselves have special immunity from the very same biases (Ehrlinger, Gilovich, & Ross, 2005; Pronin, 2006; Pronin, Berger, & Molouki, 2007).

Heuristics and Biases Tasks in Terms of the Taxonomy

Table 6–1 illustrates how various well-known effects in the heuristics and biases literature fit into the taxonomy. This again is not an exhaustive list but instead reflects some of the effects that have received the most attention in the literature. The first three Xs in the first column signify defaults to the autonomous mind: vividness effects (Nisbett & Ross, 1980), affect substitution (Slovic et al., 2002; Slovic & Peters, 2006), and impulsively associative thinking. Defaulting to the most vivid or salient stimulus is a common way that the cognitive miser avoids Type 2 processing. Likewise, defaulting to affective valence is often used in situations with emotional salience. Affect substitution is a specific form of a more generic trick of the cognitive miser discussed by Kahneman and Frederick (2002): attribute substitution—the substitution of an easy-to-evaluate characteristic for a harder one, even if the easier one is less accurate.

TABLE 6.1. Classification of Several Tasks, Effects, and Processing Styles in Terms of a Taxonomy of Rational Thinking Errors

Tasks, Effects, and Processing Styles	The Cognitive Miser			Mindware Gaps (MG)		MG & CM	Contaminated Mindware (CM)	
	Default to the Autonomous Mind	Focal Bias	Override Failure	Probability Knowledge	Alternative Thinking	Lay Psychological Theory	Evaluation Disabling Strategies	Self and Egocentric Processing
Vividness effects	X							
Affect substitution	X							
Impulsively associative thinking	X							
Framing effects		X						
Anchoring effects		X						
Belief bias			X					
Denominator neglect			X					
Outcome bias			X					
Hindsight bias ("curse of knowledge" effects)			X					
Self-control problems			X					
Gambler's fallacy				X				
Noncausal baserates				X				
Bias blind spot						X		
Causal baserates			X	X				
Conjunction errors	X			X				
Four card selection task	X	X			X			
Myside processing		X						X

(Continued)

TABLE 6.1. Classification of Several Tasks, Effects, and Processing Styles in Terms of a Taxonomy of Rational Thinking Errors (*Cont'd*)

| Tasks, Effects, and Processing Styles | The Cognitive Miser | | | Mindware Gaps (MG) | | MG & CM | Contaminated Mindware (CM) |
	Default to the Autonomous Mind	Focal Bias	Override Failure	Probability Knowledge	Alternative Thinking	Lay Psychological Theory	Evaluation Disabling Strategies	Self and Egocentric Processing
Affective forecasting errors		X				X		
Ignoring P(D/~H)		X			X			
Confirmation bias		X			X		X	
Overconfidence effects		X						X
Probability matching		X		X				
Pseudoscientific beliefs					X		X	
Evaluability effects		X				X		

The effect in the next row of Table 6–1 is an example of a form of intellectual laziness that we term *impulsively associative thinking*. Consider the following problem, taken from the work of Levesque (1986, 1989) and studied by our research group (*see* Toplak & Stanovich, 2002): Jack is looking at Anne, but Anne is looking at George. Jack is married, but George is not. Is a married person looking at an unmarried person? A) Yes, B) No, C) Cannot be determined.

The vast majority of people answer C (cannot be determined), when in fact the correct answer to this problem is A (yes). To answer correctly, both possibilities for Anne's marital status (married and unmarried) must be considered to determine whether a conclusion can be drawn. If Anne is married, then the answer is "Yes" because she would be looking at George, who is unmarried. If Anne is not married, then the answer is still "Yes" because Jack, who is married, would be looking at Anne. Considering all the possibilities (the fully disjunctive reasoning strategy) reveals that a married person is looking at an unmarried person, whether Anne is married or not. The fact that the problem does not *reveal* whether Anne is married immediately suggests to people that nothing can be determined. Impulsively associative thinking results in the preponderance of "cannot be determined" responses to this problem because the subject tends not to look for all the information that can be inferred. Many people make the easiest (incorrect) inference from the information given and do not proceed with the more difficult (but correct) inference that follows from fully disjunctive reasoning. Subjects look for any simple association that will prevent them from having to engage in Type 2 thought (in this case, associating Anne's unknown status with the response "cannot be determined").

Another example of impulsively associative thinking is described in a chapter by Kahneman and Frederick (2002). They describe a simple experiment in which people were asked to consider the following puzzle: A bat and a ball cost $1.10 in total. The bat costs $1 more than the ball. How much does the ball cost?

Many people emit the response that first comes to mind—10¢—without thinking further and realizing that this cannot be right. The bat would then have to cost $1.10, and the total cost would then be $1.20 rather than the required $1.10. People often do not think deeply enough to make this simple correction, however, and many students at very selective universities will answer incorrectly and move on to the next problem without realizing that impulsively associative thinking has led them to make an error. Frederick (2005) has found that when given this and other similar problems, large numbers of students at MIT, Princeton, and Harvard display such impulsively associative thinking.

The second default of the cognitive miser is to utilize serial associative cognition with a focal bias. Framing effects represent the classic example of this default in the heuristics and biases literature[5]. For example,

---

[5] The literature on framing effects is vast (see Epley, Mak, & Chen Idson, 2006; Kahneman & Tversky, 1984, 2000; Kuhberger, 1998; Levin, Gaeth, Schreiber, &

in discussing the mechanisms causing framing effects, Kahneman has stated that "the basic principle of framing is the passive acceptance of the formulation given" (2003, p. 703). The frame presented to the subject is taken as focal, and all subsequent thought derives from it rather than from alternative framings because the latter would require more thought. One of the most compelling framing demonstrations is from the early work of Tversky and Kahneman (1981):

Decision 1. Imagine that the United States is preparing for the outbreak of an unusual disease, which is expected to kill 600 people. Two alternative programs to combat the disease have been proposed. Assume that the exact scientific estimates of the consequences of the programs are as follows: If Program A is adopted, 200 people will be saved. If Program B is adopted, there is a one-third probability that 600 people will be saved and a two-thirds probability that no people will be saved. Which of the two programs would you favor, Program A or Program B?

When given this problem, most people prefer Program A—the one that saves 200 lives for sure. There is nothing wrong with this choice taken alone. However, inconsistent responses to another problem define a framing effect:

Decision 2. Imagine that the United States is preparing for the outbreak of an unusual disease, which is expected to kill 600 people. Two alternative programs to combat the disease have been proposed. Assume that the exact scientific estimates of the consequences of the programs are as follows: If Program C is adopted, 400 people will die. If Program D is adopted, there is a one-third probability that nobody will die and a two-thirds probability that 600 people will die. Which of the two programs would you favor, Program C or Program D?

When presented with Decision 2, most people prefer Program D. Thus, across the two problems, the most popular choices are Program A and Program D. The problem here is that Decision 1 and Decision 2 are really the same decision—they are merely redescriptions of the same situation. Program A and C are the same—that 400 will die in Program

Lauriola, 2002; Maule & Villejoubert, 2007; Schneider et al., 2005; Whitney, Rinehart, & Hinson, 2008).

C implies that 200 will be saved, which is precisely the same number saved (200) in Program A. Likewise, the two-thirds chance that 600 will die in Program D is the same two-thirds chance that 600 will die ("no people will be saved") in Program B. Many people show inconsistent preferences—their choice switches depending on the phrasing of the question. This is an example of a problem with very transparent equivalence. When presented with both versions of the problem together, most people agree that the problems are identical and that the alternative phrasing should not have made a difference. Such a lack of so-called "descriptive invariance" is a very fundamental violation of some of the simplest strictures of rational thought (*see* Tversky & Kahneman, 1981, 1986).

Anchoring effects are listed next in Table 6–1 and, of course, refer to the *inappropriate* anchoring and insufficient adjustment that have been reported in the literature (Epley & Gilovich, 2006; Stewart, 2009). For example, in a classic experiment, Tversky and Kahneman (1974) demonstrated that the anchoring tendency is much too mindless—that it does not bother to assess for relevance. They had subjects watch a spinning wheel, and when the pointer landed on a number (rigged to be the number 65) they were asked whether the percentage of African countries in the United Nations was higher or lower than this percentage. After answering higher or lower to this question, the subjects then had to give their best estimate of the percentage of African countries in the United Nations. Another group of subjects had it arranged so that their pointer landed on the number 10. They were also asked to make the higher or lower judgment and then to estimate the percentage of African countries in the United Nations. Now it is clear that because a spinning wheel was used, the number involved in the first question was totally irrelevant to the task of answering second question. Yet the number that came up on the spinning wheel affected the answer to the second question. The mean estimate of the first group (the group where the spinning wheel stopped at 65) turned out to be significantly larger (45) compared to the mean estimate (25) for the second group. Both groups are using the anchoring and adjustment heuristic—the high anchor group adjusting down and the low group adjusting up—but their adjustments are "sticky." They are not adjusting enough because they have failed to fully take into account that the anchor is determined in a totally random manner. The anchoring and adjustment heuristic reveals the operation of an inappropriate focal bias.

Override failure (the third category of thinking errors presented in the columns of Table 6–1) is illustrated by a variety of effects: belief bias effects, denominator neglect, outcome bias, hindsight bias, and self-control problems such as the inability to delay gratification. Belief bias occurs when people have difficulty evaluating conclusions that conflict with what they think they know about the world (Evans et al., 1983). It is most often assessed with syllogistic reasoning tasks in which the believability of the conclusion conflicts with logical validity (discussed in Chapter 2). Belief bias provides a classic example of the failure of sustained decoupling. In a syllogism such as: All living things need water; Roses need water; Therefore, Roses are living things; subjects must suppress the tendency to endorse a valid response because of the "naturalness" (*see* Kahneman, 2003) of the conclusion—roses are flowers.

Another phenomenon from the heuristics and biases literature that illustrates the failure of sustained decoupling is the phenomenon of denominator neglect. Epstein and colleagues (Denes-Raj & Epstein, 1994; Kirkpatrick & Epstein, 1992; Pacini & Epstein, 1999) demonstrated that it can result in a startling failure of rational judgment. Adults in several of his experiments were presented with two bowls that each contained clearly identified numbers of jelly beans. The first held 9 white jelly beans and 1 red jelly bean. The second held 92 white jelly beans and 8 red. A random draw was to be made from one of the two bowls, and if the red jelly bean was picked, the participant would receive a dollar. The participant could choose which bowl to draw from. Although the two bowls clearly represent a 10% and an 8% chance of winning a dollar, a number of subjects chose the 100 bean bowl, thus reducing their chance of winning. The majority did pick the 10% bowl, but a healthy minority (30%–40% of the participants) picked the 8% bowl. Although most of these participants in the minority were aware that the large bowl was statistically a worse bet, that bowl also contained more enticing winning beans—the 8 red ones. In short, the tendency to respond to the absolute number of winners, for these participants, trumped the formal rule (pick the one with the best percentage of reds) that they knew was the better choice. That many subjects were aware of the poorer probability but failed to resist picking the large bowl is indicated by comments from some of them, such as the following: "I picked the one with more red jelly beans because it looked like there were more ways to get a winner, even though I knew there were also more whites, and that the percents were against me" (Denes-Raj & Epstein, 1994, p. 823).

Override failures thus often have a different phenomenology than the errors in the other two categories of miser errors (defaulting to the autonomous mind and displaying a focal bias). In the case of override failure, but not in the other two, the subject is often aware of a cognitive struggle—that is, the subject is conscious of being an organism with multiple minds. When our thinking is affected by vividness (or any aspect of accessibility) or when we substitute affect for a more difficult judgment, we are often unaware of alternative ways of thinking. Similarly, when a person is presented with a problem, they are often not even aware that there is an alternative framing. They are not aware that they are failing to think as much as they could. When people are engaged in myside thinking (which derives in part from focal bias, *see* Table 6–1), they often are not aware of alternative ways of processing information. In contrast, even those who chose the 10% bowl in the Epstein jelly bean task were probably tempted by the larger number of "winners" in the 8% bowl.

Likewise, in self-control situations, people have no trouble at all realizing that they are made up of multiple minds and that an override of the autonomous mind is necessary. In fact, they are all too aware of it. The struggle between minds is, in fact, almost the defining feature of these situations. They are situations where we have to resist temptation: where we have to get up and make breakfast despite wanting to sleep; have to resist an extra $3 coffee in the afternoon because we know the budget is tight this month; or are on a diet and know that our snack should be carrots and not chips. Here, the internal struggle is palpably real. It is only too apparent to us in these instances that there are parts of our brains at war with each other. Our natural language even has a term to designate these instances: *willpower*. Willpower is a folk term, but in the last two decades, cognitive researchers have begun to understand it scientifically[6].

---

6 Our colloquial notion of willpower usually refers to the ability to delay gratification or to override visceral responses prompting us to make a choice that is not in our long-term interests. This inability to properly value immediate and delayed

Table 6–1 portrays two examples of mindware gaps: the gambler's fallacy (Roney & Trick, 2009) and missing probability knowledge that leads to the failure to appreciate the importance of noncausal baserates (Bar-Hillel, 1980; Kahneman & Tversky, 1972, 1973; Koehler, 1996; Sloman, Over, Slovak, & Stibel, 2003; Tversky & Kahneman, 1982). Listed next is the effect known as the bias blind spot—the fact that people view other people as more biased than themselves (Pronin, 2006). The bias blind spot is thought to arise because people have incorrect lay psychological theories. They think, incorrectly, that biased thinking on their part would be detectable by conscious introspection. In fact, most social and cognitive biases operate unconsciously. The incorrect lay theory that they do not might be viewed as either contaminated mindware or the result of a mindware gap.

Multiply-Determined Problems of Rational Thought

Several of the remaining tasks and effects illustrated in Table 6–1 represent irrational thought problems that are hybrids. That is, they are codetermined by several different cognitive difficulties. It is no surprise that some of the most complex tasks are those that are among the most contentious in the heuristics and biases literature. Thus, the taxonomy argues indirectly that non-normative responding on some of these tasks is overdetermined. For example, conjunction errors on tasks such as the Linda problem could result from attribute substitution in the manner that

---

rewards is a source of irrationality that keeps many people from maximizing their goal fulfillment. The logic of many addictions, such as alcoholism, overeating, and credit card shopping, illustrate this point. From a long-term perspective, a person definitely prefers sobriety, dieting, and keeping his credit card debt low. However, when immediately confronted with a stimulus that challenges this preference—a drink, a dessert, an item on sale—the long-term preference is trumped by the short-term desire. Psychologists have studied these situations using delayed-reward paradigms in which people have been shown to display intertemporal preference reversal (Ainslie, 2001, 2005; Baumeister & Vohs, 2003, 2007; Green & Myerson, 2004; Herrnstein, 1990; Kirby & Herrnstein, 1995; Kirby, Winston, & Santiesteban, 2005; Loewenstein et al., 2003; McClure et al., 2004; Milkman, Rogers, & Bazerman, 2008; Rachlin, 1995, 2000).

Tversky and Kahneman (1983) originally argued; from conversational defaults of the type discussed by a host of theorists (e.g., Girotto, 2004; Hilton, 1995; Politzer & Macchi, 2000); and/or from missing mindware—that is, inadequately instantiated probabilistic mindware that impairs not just probabilistic calculations but also the tendency to see a problem in probabilistic terms.

It is similar with the four-card selection task. Table 6–1 reflects the conjecture that focal bias (usually termed *matching bias* in the context of this task, *see* Evans, 1972, 1998; Evans & Lynch, 1973) is implicated in selection task performance, as are the interpretational defaults emphasized by many theorists[7]. But Table 6–1 also captures the way that the task was often treated in the earliest years of research on it—as a proxy for Popperian falsifiability tendencies (*see* Stenning & van Lambalgen, 2004b). From this latter standpoint, problems in dealing with the task might be analyzed as a missing mindware problem. Certainly training programs in the critical thinking literature consider the generation of alternative hypotheses and falsification strategies as learnable mindware (Nickerson, 2004; Nisbett, 1993; Ritchhart & Perkins, 2005).

Another thinking error with multiple determinants is myside processing[8]. Excessive myside thinking is no doubt fostered by contaminated mindware—our notion of "self" makes us egocentrically think that the world revolves around ourselves. But a form of focal bias may be contributing to this error as well—the bias to base processing on the mental model that is the easiest to construct. What easier model is there to construct than a model based on our own previous beliefs and experiences? Such a focal bias is different from the egocentric mindware of the self. The focal bias is not egocentric in the motivational sense that we want to build our self-esteem or sense of self-worth. The focal bias is simply concerned with conserving computational capacity, and it does so in

---

7 I have previously cited the arguments for differing interpretational defaults in this task (e.g., Gebauer & Laming, 1997; Klauer et al., 2007; Margolis, 1987; Oaksford & Chater, 1994; Osman, 2007; Sperber et al., 1995; Stenning & van Lambalgen, 2004a, 2004b).

8 Various paradigms have been used to demonstrate myside processing (Baron, 1995; Greenhoot, Semb, Colombo, & Schreiber, 2004; Klaczynski & Lavallee, 2005; Perkins, 1985, 1995; Stanovich & West, 2007, 2008a; Wolfe & Britt, 2008).

most cases by encouraging reliance on a model from a myside perspective. Both motivationally driven "self" mindware and computationally driven focal biases might be contributing to myside processing, making it another multiply-determined bias.

Errors in affective forecasting are likewise multiply-determined. Affective forecasting refers to our ability to predict what will make us happy in the future, and people turn out to be surprisingly poor at such predictions (Gilbert, 2006; Hsee & Hastie, 2006; Kahneman, Krueger, Schkade, Schwarz, & Stone, 2006; Kahneman, Diener, & Schwarz, 1999; Wilson et al., 2000; Wilson & Gilbert, 2005). People often make choices that reduce their happiness because they find it hard to predict what will make them happy. For example, they underestimate how quickly they will adapt to both fortunate and unfortunate events. One reason that people overestimate how unhappy they will be after a negative event is that they have something missing from their lay psychological theories—the personal theories they use to explain their own behavior. They fail to take into account the rationalization and emotion-dampening protective thought they will engage in after the negative event ("I really didn't want the job anyway," "colleagues told me he was biased against older employees"). People's lay theories of their own psychology do not give enough weight to these factors, and thus they fail to predict how much their own psychological mechanisms will damp down any unhappiness about the negative event.

Another important source of affective forecasting errors is focal bias. Researchers in the affective forecasting literature have theorized specifically about focalism interfering with hedonic predictions ("predictors pay too much attention to the central event and overlook context events," p. 31, Hsee & Hastie, 2006). For example, a sports fan overestimates how happy the victory of the home team will make him 2 days after the event. When making the prediction, he fixates on the salient focal event (winning the game), simulates the emotion he will feel in response to the event, and projects that same emotion 2 days into the future. What does not enter into his model—because such models are not easy to construct in imagination (hence too effortful for the cognitive miser)—is the myriad other events that will be happening 2 days after his game and that will then impinge on his happiness in various ways (it is the case that most of these other events will not be as happiness-inducing as was winning the game). In a much-cited study, Schkade and Kahneman (1998) found that subjects from the Midwest and California were about equal in life satisfaction. However, when predicting the satisfaction of the other, both the Midwestern and California subjects thought that California subjects would be more satisfied with life. The *comparative* judgment made focal an aspect of life, the weather, that in fact was not one of the most important dimensions in life satisfaction (job prospects, financial considerations, social life, and five other factors ranked higher). As Schkade and Kahneman (1998) have argued, "'nothing that you focus on will make as much difference as you think'" (p. 345). Thus, as Table 6–1 indicates, errors in affective forecasting are a complex mix of focal bias and gaps in lay psychological theories.

Finally, Table 6–1 lists several other effects in the heuristics and biases literature that are multiply-determined. For example, the much debated concept of confirmation bias (Evans, 1989, 2007a; Klayman & Ha, 1987; Nickerson, 1998) is listed. Depending on how it is defined, it could result from focal bias or from a failure to have instantiated the thinking mindware that prompts a consideration of alternative hypotheses. In more motivationally based accounts, however, confirmation bias might arise because of evaluation-disabling strategies embodied in contaminated mindware.

Of course, Table 6–1 is not meant to be exhaustive. It is very much a preliminary sketch, and it is not meant to be the final word on many definitional/conceptual issues. The taxonomy is meant to serve an organizing function, to provoke research on the conjectures implicit within it, and to demonstrate how a framework deriving from dual-process theory might bring some order to the unwieldy heuristics and biases literature.

Missing Input from the Autonomous Mind

In subsequent chapters, we will discuss the linkage between each of the major categories in Table 6–1 and intelligence. However, for completeness, another category needs to be introduced here. It was not included earlier because it is not a fully *cognitive* category.

If override failure is characterized as arising from too much output from the autonomous mind, an additional category of cognitive dysfunction might be characterized as arising from too little—that is, missing—output from the autonomous mind. Cognitive neuroscientists have uncovered cases of mental pathology that are characterized by inadequate behavioral regulation from the emotion subsystems in the autonomous mind—for example, Damasio's (1994, 1996; Bechara, Damasio, Damasio, & Anderson, 1994; Eslinger & Damasio, 1985) well-known studies of patients with damage in the ventromedial prefrontal cortex. These individuals have severe difficulties in real-life decision making but do not display the impairments in sustained attention and executive control that are characteristic of individuals with damage in dorsolateral frontal regions[9]. Instead, they are thought to lack the emotions that constrain the combinatorial explosion of possible actions to a manageable number based on somatic markers stored from similar situations in the past.

The key insight here is that there are two ways in which the behavioral regulation involving the autonomous mind can go wrong. The override failures discussed previously are one way. In these situations, the signals shaping behavior from the autonomous mind are too pervasive and are not trumped by Type 2 processing. The second way that behavioral regulation involving the autonomous mind can go awry has the opposite properties. In this case, the automatic regulation of goals by the autonomous mind is absent and Type 2 processing is faced with a combinatorial explosion of possibilities because the constraining function of autonomous modules such as emotions is missing. Behavioral regulation is not aided by crude but effective autonomous signals that help to prioritize goals for subsequent action.

There is empirical evidence for rationality failures of the two different types. Dorsolateral prefrontal damage has been associated with executive functioning difficulties (and/or working memory difficulties) that can be interpreted as the failure to override automatized processes.

---

9 The difficulties and strengths of patients with damage in the ventromedial prefrontal cortex and dorsolateral frontal regions have been well-documented (e.g., Bechara, 2005; Duncan et al., 1996; Kimberg, D'Esposito, & Farah, 1998; McCarthy & Warrington, 1990).

In contrast, ventromedial damage to the prefrontal cortex has been associated with problems in behavioral regulation that are accompanied by affective disruption. Difficulties of the former, but not the latter, kind are associated with lowered intelligence (*see* Bechara et al., 1998; Duncan et al., 1996; Harnishfeger & Bjorklund, 1994; Kimberg et al., 1998; Shallice, 1988).

A laboratory marker for the type of problem that Damasio had observed was developed by Bechara, Damasio, Damasio, and Anderson (1994). In their task (Iowa Gambling Task), the participant sat facing four decks of cards (labeled A, B, C, and D), was given $2000 of play money, and was told to choose cards from any deck. Two decks (A and B) contained high rewards on the back but had enough intermittent high penalties on them that the expected values of the decks were negative. Two other decks (C and D) contained low rewards but low enough penalties so that they had positive expected values.

Bechara et al. (1994) found that normal subjects began by sampling all of the decks with perhaps a slight bias toward the "bad" decks A and B but by the final 50 trials had migrated away from the low-expected-values decks A and B and ended up making most of their final choices from "good" decks C and D (the high-expected-value decks). Patients with ventromedial prefrontal damage also begin by sampling all the decks, but their preference for the high-reward A and B decks did not diminish throughout the testing period. Despite being conscious of rewards and penalties in their environments (when queried, the patients say they know that decks A and B are risky and generally bad), they consistently repeated acts that were inefficacious.

Damasio (1994) argued that individuals with ventromedial prefrontal damage seem to lack emotional systems that mark positive and negative outcomes with evaluative valence and that regenerate these valences the next time a similar situation arises. Damasio's famous case of Elliot is an instance of what we will call here the Mr. Spock problem, naming it after the *Star Trek* character depicted as having attenuated emotions. Elliot had a problem in decision making because of a lack of regulatory signals from emotion subsystems in the autonomous mind.

There is increasing evidence that the Mr. Spock form of rational thinking problem may extend beyond extreme clinical cases such as that of

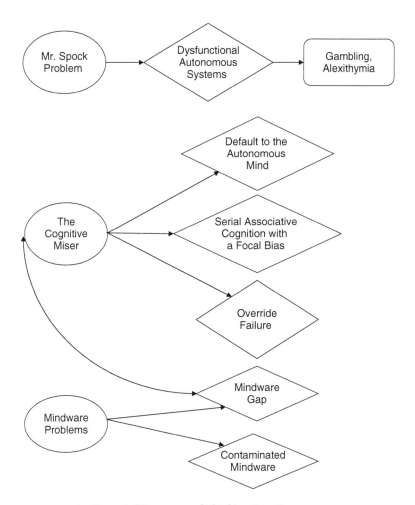

FIGURE 6.3.   An Expanded Taxonomy of Thinking Error Types.

Elliot (with measurable ventromedial prefrontal damage). Several groups of people with problems of behavioral regulation perform poorly on the Iowa Gambling Task despite having near normal intelligence[10].

---

10 It is important to emphasize that the Iowa Gambling Task is deliberately designed so that the large rewards in decks A and B will be overwhelmed by infrequent, but large, penalties (thus resulting in negative expected value). As Loewenstein, Weber, Hsee, and Welch, (2001) point out, it would be easy to design an experiment with

For example, Petry, Bickel, and Arnett (1998) found that heroin addicts also displayed more disadvantageous choices in the Iowa Gambling Task than controls of equal intelligence. Stanovich, Grunewald, and West (2003) examined the performance of a nonclinical sample of adolescents who were experiencing problems of behavioral adjustment (multiple school suspensions) on the Iowa Gambling Task (this time playing for real money). Like Damasio's (1994) patients, our participants with suspensions did not differ from their controls in general intelligence. The students with multiple suspensions in our study made significantly more choices from "bad" decks A and B. Other studies of subjects without overt brain damage have also shown subpar performance on the Iowa Gambling Task—for example, pathological gamblers (Cavedini, Riboldi, Keller, D'Annucci, & Bellodi, 2002; Toplak et al., 2007), criminal offenders (Yechiam et al., 2008), patients with neurological disorders (Labudda et al., 2009; Sinz et al., 2008), and patients with psychiatric disorders (Nakamura et al., 2008). Likewise, neuropsychological research has demonstrated a variety of mental disabilities—for example, alexithymia (difficulty in identifying feelings) and schizophrenia—that implicate defects in various types of autonomous monitoring activities that are independent of intelligence (Bechara, 2005 Bermudez, 2001; Coltheart & Davies, 2000; Mealey, 1995; Murphy & Stich, 2000; Nichols & Stich, 2003; Weller, Levin, Shiv, & Bechara, 2007).

With the introduction of the Mr. Spock problem, we can now present a fuller taxonomy of the categories of rational thinking error, and it is illustrated in Figure 6–3. Each of the six categories represents a separate explanation of why human thought and action are sometimes irrational. Next, we will examine, both empirically and theoretically, the relation between each type of rational thinking error and intelligence.

---

the opposite payoff structure—where the risky choices had a higher payoff (Shiv, Loewenstein, Bechara, Damasio, & Damasio, 2005). Indeed, there are real-world examples of just this structure. If one is investing for the long-term, stocks—riskier on a short-term basis—tend to outperform bonds. It is an open question which structure (positive expected value being associated with large variance or negative expected value being associated with large variance) is more common in the real world.

7

Intelligence as a Predictor of Performance on Heuristics and Biases Tasks

(Keith E. Stanovich and Richard F. West)

In Chapter 2 it was stressed that rationality is a more encompassing construct than intelligence because rationality is an organismic-level concept. Variation in instrumental rationality, for example, reflects variation in how well the actions of an organism serve its goals. Intelligence, in contrast, reflects the information processing efficiency of algorithmic-level processing—it is an indicator of processing at a subpersonal level.

Although rationality is a more encompassing construct than intelligence, we would expect the two to be related because rationality requires the algorithmic-level machinery that enables the correct beliefs to be fixed (epistemic rationality) and that enables the correct actions to be taken (instrumental rationality). To provide a visual reminder of the situation, Figure 7–1 duplicates Figure 2–1 of Chapter 2. It is clear from the Figure that individual differences in rational thought and action can arise because of individual differences in intelligence (an algorithmic-level construct) or because of individual differences in thinking dispositions (a reflective-level construct).

Given the large role that intelligence plays in public discourse, it is disconcerting to realize that it is a more restricted concept than rationality. Although it is true that some definitions of intelligence are broad and encompass aspects of rational thought, this is not reflected at all in how intelligence is measured in laboratories and in applied settings such as hospitals and schools. The implications of adopting definitions of intelligence that do not reflect how the construct is actually measured in psychology will be discussed in Chapter 9 (*see also* Stanovich, 2009b). For now, it is sufficient to note that in psychology and among the lay public alike, assessments of intelligence and tests of cognitive ability are taken to be the sine qua non of good thinking. Critics of these instruments often

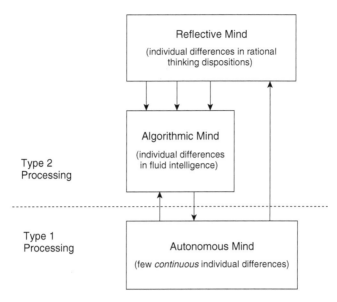

FIGURE 7.1. The Tripartite Structure and the Locus of Individual Differences.

point out that IQ tests fail to assess many domains of psychological functioning that are essential. For example, it is often noted that many largely noncognitive domains such as socioemotional abilities, creativity, empathy, and interpersonal skills are not assessed by tests of cognitive ability. However, even these standard critiques of intelligence tests often contain the unstated assumption that although intelligence tests miss certain key noncognitive areas, they encompass most of what is important cognitively. One of the goals of this chapter and those that follow is to show that this unstated assumption is unwarranted. Intelligence tests ignore important aspects of thinking itself—tendencies toward rational thought.

As reviewed in Chapters 1 and 2, many tasks in the heuristics and biases literature show moderate, but far from perfect, correlations with intelligence. There are, in fact, reasons for expecting some degree of relationship between cognitive ability and individual differences in the operation of thinking biases, even if the latter are not directly assessed on intelligence tests. This follows from the fact that theorizing in the heuristics and biases literature has emphasized dual-process models of the type that were discussed in Chapters 1 and 2. Such models embody the assumption that thinking biases result from tendencies toward miserly processing[1]. Nonetheless, although the presence of thinking biases might be universal, their ability to result in non-normative choices varies from individual to individual because they are sometimes overridden. The computational power needed to override a computationally inexpensive but inefficacious response might be related to intelligence, thus creating a (negative) relationship between biased responding and cognitive ability even though thinking biases are not directly assessed on IQ tests[2].

There has been some research indicating that cognitive ability is modestly related to performance on several tasks from the heuristics and biases literature. Stanovich and West (1997, 1998c, 1998d, 1999, 2000; *see also* Kokis et al., 2002; Sá, West, & Stanovich, 1999; Toplak & Stanovich, 2002; West & Stanovich, 2003; West et al., 2008) found correlations

---

1 The earlier versions of these models contained the assumption that this miserly processing always involved defaulting to the autonomous mind. More contemporary models (*see* Evans, 2007a; Stanovich, 2009a; Chapter 4 of the present volume) have allowed for the possibility of miserly Type 2 processing.

2 We reiterate here Evans' (2008) point that it is wrong to equate Type 2 processing with normatively correct responding and Type 1 processing with normatively incorrect processing. First, *both* types of processing are most often normatively correct. It is also possible for a situation to trigger a Type 1 response that is normatively correct and a Type 2 response that is normatively incorrect. The only claim that most dual-process theorists make is that the converse is statistically more likely. Evans' (2008) point illustrates why certain terms for the two processes in dual-process theory are infelicitous. For example, Epstein's (1994) terminology (experiential system and rational system) mistakenly implies that Type 2 processing always yields a response that is normatively rational (and perhaps pragmatically that the experiential system does not). Gibbard's (1990) labeling of Type 2 processing as emanating from a "normative control system" mistakenly implies the same thing (that Type 2 processing is always normative), as does Klein's (1998) labeling of Type 2 strategies as "rational choice strategies." Rationality is an organismic-level concept and should never be used to label a subpersonal process. Our face recognition systems are not rational or irrational. They are, instead, either efficient or inefficient.

A second point is that intelligence might associate with unbiased responding for two different reasons—first, that individuals higher in cognitive ability are more likely to compute the correct response given that they have engaged Type 2 processing (what Evans [2007b] calls the quality hypothesis regarding cognitive ability). The second (what Evans [2007b] calls the quantity hypothesis) is that individuals higher in cognitive ability are more likely to see the need for Type 2 processing.

with cognitive ability to be roughly (in absolute magnitude): 0.35 to 0.45 for belief bias in syllogistic reasoning, in the range of 0.25 to 0.35 for various probabilistic reasoning tasks, in the range of 0.20 to 0.25 for various covariation detection and hypothesis testing tasks, 0.25 to 0.35 on informal reasoning tasks, 0.15 to 0.20 with outcome bias measured within-subjects, 0.20 to 0.40 with performance in the four-card selection task, 0.10 to 0.20 with performance in various disjunctive reasoning tasks, 0.15 to 0.25 with hindsight bias, 0.25 to 0.30 with denominator neglect, and 0.05 to 0.20 with various indices of Bayesian reasoning. All correlations were in the expected direction. Other investigators have found relationships of a similar effect size between cognitive ability and a variety of tasks in the heuristics and biases literature[3].

In a commentary on this research on individual differences, Kahneman (2000) pointed out that the correlations observed may well have been inflated because most of the relevant studies used within-subjects designs containing cues signaling the necessity of overriding Type 1 processing (Bartels, 2006; Fischhoff, Slovic, & Lichtenstein, 1979; Frisch, 1993; Kahneman & Tversky, 1982a; however, see Lambdin & Shaffer, 2009). He has argued that a between-subjects test of the coherence of responses represents a much stricter criterion and perhaps a more appropriate one because "much of life resembles a between-subjects experiment" (p. 682, Kahneman, 2000). Shafir (1998) makes a similar argument when speculating about why people's behavior is often at variance with their own normative intuitions. He argues that this discrepancy "mirrors a discrepancy between the nature of people's everyday experiences and the conditions that yield philosophical intuitions. In life, people typically experience and evaluate things one at a time, as in a between-subjects design, whereas many of the relevant intuitions result from concurrent, within-subject introspections" (p. 72).

That the mental factors operative in within-subjects designs might be different from those operative in between-subjects designs suggests

---

3 Some of this literature was cited in earlier chapters (e.g., Bruine de Bruin, Parker, & Fischhoff, 2007; De Neys, 2006b; DeShon, Smith, Chan, & Schmitt, 1998; Handley, Capon, Beveridge, Dennis, & Evans, 2004; Klaczynski & Lavallee, 2005; Newstead et al., 2004; Parker & Fischhoff, 2005; Perkins & Ritchhart, 2004; Peters et al. 2006; Valentine, 1975).

that the individual difference factors associated with biased processing in the two different paradigms might also vary. LeBoeuf and Shafir (2003) have produced some data indicating that biases that are assessed within-subjects display different relationships with individual difference variables than biases assessed between-subjects. They found that various framing effects were associated with the need for cognition thinking disposition (*see* Cacioppo et al., 1996) when evaluated on a within-subjects basis but were independent of need for cognition when framing was assessed between-subjects.

Kahneman's (2000; *see also* Kahneman & Frederick, 2002) conjecture is that these less transparent designs would reduce the observed relationships between cognitive ability and the judgmental biases. Much less is known about the relation between cognitive ability and the tendency to make coherent judgments in between-subjects situations. Thus, in a series of studies, Stanovich and West (2008a, 2008b) attempted to examine a variety of effects from the heuristics and biases literature to determine whether cognitive ability was associated with these biases as they are displayed in between-subjects paradigms. In this series of experiments, we found that, to a surprising degree, cognitive ability was independent of the tendency to show a variety of rational thinking biases. We shall present here a selection of representative findings from our laboratory that illustrate this trend.

Intelligence and Classic Heuristics and Biases Effects

In one experiment, we examined some biases and effects that are among the oldest in the literature (Kahneman & Tversky, 1972, 1973; Tversky & Kahneman, 1973, 1974, 1983): base-rate neglect, framing effects, conjunction effects, outcome bias, and anchoring biases. The participants were 434 undergraduate students, and they were partitioned into high- and low-cognitive-ability (intelligence) groups based on their Total SAT scores[4]. Subjects completed either Form A or Form B—that is, Form was

---

4 The majority of our studies employed university students as participants. There is thus a restriction of range in our samples. The higher and lower SAT groupings are partitionings of the upper half and lower half of the sample. The low SAT group

a between-subjects variable. The analyses then examined whether the magnitude of the effect or bias demonstrated by the task was moderated by cognitive ability. One such analysis, for example, examines whether, in an analysis of variance (ANOVA) context, the effect of form interacted with SAT group.

The tasks, many of them classics in the literature, were as follows below.

Baserate Problem. Kahneman and Tversky's (1973) much-studied lawyer/engineer problem was employed as a probe of the degree of baserate usage. The two versions were identical except that the baserates given for the engineers and lawyers were switched as a between-subjects variable (30 engineers and 70 lawyers in Form A and 70 engineers and 30 lawyers in Form B). In Form A, the problem was as follows:

A panel of psychologists has interviewed and administered personality tests to 30 engineers and 70 lawyers, all successful in their respective fields. On the basis of this information, thumbnail descriptions of the 30 engineers and 70 lawyers have been written. One of the descriptions is below. After reading the description, please indicate, on a scale from 0 to 100, what you think the probability is that the person described is an engineer. Here is the description:

Jack is a 45-year-old man. He is married and has four children. He is generally conservative, careful, and ambitious. He shows no interest in political and social issues and spends most of his free time on his many hobbies, which include home carpentry, sailing, and mathematical puzzles.

The probability that Jack is one of the 30 engineers in the sample of 100 is _____ percent.

---

is not low in an absolute sense; they simply are of lower cognitive ability relative to their counterparts in that particular study. Certainly, it is true that individuals with average and above average cognitive ability are over-represented in samples composed entirely of university students. Thus, the magnitude of the correlations involving SAT obtained in these studies is undoubtedly attenuated because of restriction of range. However, the fact that the range of the samples studied is somewhat restricted, makes many of the findings (of near zero correlations between cognitive ability and many aspects of rational thought) no less startling. It is quite unexpected that across even the range of ability in a university population there would be so little relation between rational thought and cognitive ability.

Disease Framing Problem. This was the famous Asian disease problem introduced by Tversky and Kahneman's (1981) that was discussed in the previous chapter.

Conjunction Problem. This problem was based on Tversky and Kahneman's (1983) much-studied Linda problem. Participants read the following:

Linda is 31 years old, single, outspoken, and very bright. She majored in philosophy. As a student, she was deeply concerned with issues of discrimination and social justice and also participated in antinuclear demonstrations.

Participants then used a 6-point scale (i.e., 1 = extremely improbable; 2 = very improbable; 3 = somewhat probable; 4 = moderately probable; 5 = very probable; 6 = extremely probable) to indicate the relative probability of three statements that described Linda. The first two statements were identical for the two groups of participants:

(1) It is _____ that Linda is a teacher in an elementary school.
(2) It is _____ that Linda works in a bookstore and takes Yoga classes.

Each group then read one of two statements that differed in whether they did or did not contain a conjunction of two descriptions. Participants getting Form A read:

(3) It is _____ that Linda is a bank teller and is active in the feminist movement.

Participants getting Form B read:

(4) It is _____ that Linda is a bank teller.

Outcome Bias. Our measure of outcome bias derived from a problem investigated by Baron and Hershey (1988). Participants receiving Form A read the positive outcome version: A 55-year-old man had a heart condition. He had to stop working because of chest pain. He enjoyed his work and did not want to stop. His pain also interfered with other things, such as travel and recreation. A successful bypass operation would relieve his pain and increase his life expectancy from age 65 to age 70. However, 8% of the people who have this operation die as a result of the operation itself. His physician decided to go ahead with the operation. The operation succeeded. Evaluate the physician's decision to go ahead with the operation. (1) incorrect, a very bad decision; (2) incorrect, all things considered; (3) incorrect, but not unreasonable; (4) the decision and its opposite are equally good; (5) correct, but the opposite would be reasonable too; (6) correct, all things considered; or (7) clearly correct, an excellent decision.

Participants receiving Form B (negative outcome) evaluated a medical decision that was designed to be objectively better than the first: 2% chance of death rather than 8%; 10-year increase in life expectancy versus 5-year, and so forth. However, it had an unfortunate negative outcome—death of the patient.

Anchoring and Adjustment Problems. The two problems used here were adapted from an anchoring and adjustment problem in Tversky and Kahneman (1974) and one used by Epley and Gilovich (2004). Prior to making an estimation of a particular value, participants answered a question containing a small or large anchor value. The Form A version is given, with the Form B value in brackets:

1. Do you think there are more or less than 65 [12] African countries in the United Nations? (a = more; b = less); How many African countries do you think are in the United Nations? _____

2. Is the tallest redwood tree in the world more that 85 [1000] feet tall? (a = more; b = less); How tall do you think the tallest redwood tree in the world is? _____

Table 7–1 displays, for each of the experimental tasks, the mean response as a function of Form (A vs. B) and cognitive ability group (low vs. high SAT). Table 7–1 also contains, for each of the experimental tasks, an analysis that examines whether the magnitude of the effect or bias demonstrated by the task was moderated by cognitive ability. This was done by examining, in an ANOVA context, whether the effect of Form interacted with SAT group.

The first analysis indicates that there was a significant baserate effect on the engineer/lawyer problem ($F[1,430] = 35.93$, MSE = 472.2, $p < .001$). The mean probability that Jack was one of the engineers was lower in the 30% baserate condition (60.8% for the entire sample) than the mean probability that Jack was one of the engineers in the 70% baserate condition (73.4% for the entire sample). However, the effect of

TABLE 7.1 ANOVA (Form x SAT) and Mean Scores as a Function of Form
(A vs. B) and SAT; Results From a Parallel Regression Analysis are Also Indicated

Source				Mean (*SD* in Cell)	
	$F(1,430)$	η_p^2		Form A	Form B
Baserate problem (Engineer/Lawyer problem)					
Form	35.93★★★	0.077		30 Engineers	70 Engineers
SAT	4.47★	0.010	Low SAT	57.4 (25.6)	72.3 (18.2)
Form x SAT	1.30	0.003	High SAT	64.2 (26.5)	74.3 (14.6)
Form x SAT interaction in regression: F = 1.43, R^2 change for interaction = 0.003					
Framing problem (Asian Disease)					
Form	50.98★★★	0.106		Gain Frame	Loss Frame
SAT	4.81★	0.011	Low SAT	3.00 (1.24)	3.67 (1.13)
Form x SAT	1.48	0.003	High SAT	3.11 (1.16)	4.05 (1.16)
Form x SAT interaction in regression: F = 0.08, R^2 change for interaction = 0.001					
Conjunction problem (Linda problem)					
Form	120.5★★★	0.219		Bank teller	Feminist bank teller
SAT	0.24	0.001	Low SAT	2.53 (1.03)	3.46 (1.13)
Form x SAT	4.66★	0.011	High SAT	2.36 (0.98)	3.73 (1.19)
Form x SAT interaction in regression: F = 4.15★, R^2 change for interaction = 0.008					
Outcome Bias					
Form	20.50★★★	0.045		Positive Outcome	Negative Outcome
SAT	10.09★★	0.023	Low SAT	5.79 (1.07)	5.12 (1.26)
Form x SAT	3.88★	0.009	High SAT	5.91 (0.87)	5.65 (1.04)
Form x SAT interaction in regression: F = 4.34★, R^2 change for interaction = 0.009					
Anchoring (African Countries)					
Form	219.1★★★	0.338		Large anchor	Small anchor
SAT	1.37	0.003	Low SAT	45.2 (26.4)	14.4 (14.4)
Form x SAT	2.53	0.006	High SAT	40.0 (22.7)	15.2 (11.0)
Form x SAT interaction in regression: F = 3.82, R^2 change for interaction = 0.006					
Anchoring (Redwoods)					
Form	461.0★★★	0.520		Small anchor	Large anchor
SAT	0.09	0.000	Low SAT	126.1 (88.4)	977.4 (580.4)
Form x SAT	0.05	0.000	High SAT	128.6 (77.3)	998.5 (580.6)
Form x SAT interaction in regression: F = 0.19, R^2 change for interaction = 0.001					

Note: η_p^2 = partial eta squared; df on Redwoods is 426 ★$p < .05$, ★★$p < .01$, ★★★$p < .001$

baserate failed to interact with cognitive ability, as the Form by SAT group interaction was not significant ($F[1,430] = 1.30$, MSE = 472.2). To the extent there is any hint of an interaction in the means, it is in the opposite direction from the expected finding. The low SAT group was slightly more sensitive to baserates than the high SAT group.

The next task displayed in Table 7–1 is the disease framing task, and it is clear that both groups displayed the expected framing effect on this problem—the loss frame (Form B) resulted in a greater preference for the risky option. The main effect of frame type (Form) was significant, but the effect of frame type failed to interact with cognitive ability, as the Form by SAT group interaction was not significant. To the extent there is any hint of an interaction in the means, it is again in the opposite direction from the expected finding. The high SAT group displayed a slightly larger framing effect.

The next task displayed in Table 7–1 is the conjunction problem (Linda problem). The means of both groups displayed the expected conjunction fallacy—Linda was judged more probably a feminist bank teller than a bank teller. The main effect of Form was highly significant and there was a significant Form by cognitive ability interaction ($F[1,430] = 4.66$, MSE = 1.18, $p < .05$) although the size of the effect was small ($\eta_p^2 = .011$). Additionally, the interaction was in the opposite direction from the expected finding—the high SAT group was more susceptible to the conjunction fallacy.

The next task displayed in Table 7–1 is the outcome bias problem. The means of both groups displayed the expected outcome bias—the decision with the positive outcome was rated as a better decision than the decision with the negative outcome, despite the fact that the latter was objectively better. The main effect of outcome (Form) was highly significant, and there was a significant Form by cognitive ability interaction ($F[1,430] = 3.88$, MSE = 1.13, $p < 0.05$), although the size of the effect was small ($\eta_p^2 = 0.009$). This interaction was in the expected direction—the low SAT group displayed more outcome bias.

The remaining two analyses in Table 7–1 concern the two anchoring and adjustment problems. In the African countries item, it is clear that both groups displayed the expected anchoring effect—the large anchor resulted in higher estimates of the number of African countries in the United Nations (mean for the entire sample = 42.6) than did the small anchor (mean for the entire sample = 14.9). The number of African countries in the United Nations is actually 53. The main effect of anchor magnitude (Form) was highly significant ($p < .001$). However, the effect of anchor magnitude failed to interact with cognitive ability, as the Form by SAT group interaction was not significant.

Results were similar for the redwoods problem. Both groups displayed the expected anchoring effect—the large anchor resulted in higher estimates of the height of the tallest redwood (mean for the entire sample = 989.0 feet) than did the small anchor (mean for the entire sample = 127.4 feet). The tallest redwood tree is actually 370 feet high. The main effect of anchor magnitude (Form) was highly significant ($p < .001$). However, the effect of anchor magnitude failed to interact with cognitive ability, as the Form by SAT group interaction was not significant.

Thus, across all of the ANOVAs, only two of the six interactions between Form and cognitive ability were statistically significant, and only one of these (that for outcome bias) was in the direction of reduced judgmental bias on the part of the group higher in cognitive ability. Of course, some information is lost—and power reduced—by dichotomizing on the cognitive ability variable (SAT). Thus, Table 7–1 also presents the results of a continuous analysis for each task in which the significance of the Form by cognitive ability interaction was tested in a regression analysis in which SAT was used as a continuous variable rather than as a dichotomous variable. Immediately below the ANOVA in Table 7–1 is presented the F ratio for the test of the interaction: the Form by SAT cross-product when entered third in the equation predicting item response after Form and SAT. In addition to the F ratio, the R^2 change for the interaction is presented.

The regression analyses converged completely with the results from the ANOVAs. Only two of the six interaction terms reached statistical significance and only one of those, that for outcome bias, was in the expected direction—the degree of outcome bias was larger for the group lower on the SAT. The significant interaction term for the Linda problem indicated a data pattern in the opposite direction—the conjunction fallacy was displayed to a greater extent by the group with higher SAT scores.

In summary, this experiment produced very little evidence indicating that cognitive ability was related to judgmental biases when the latter were assessed in between-subjects designs. In six comparisons involving five different classic effects from the heuristics and biases literature, only one comparison provided any indication that cognitive ability attenuated a judgmental bias. Even in that case (outcome bias) the effect was extremely modest. The variance associated with the interaction effect was less than 1% in both the ANOVA and in the regression analysis. We shall summarize results in the remainder of this chapter rather than provide statistics. More detailed statistics are available in the published papers.

We have studied many more such effects from the heuristics and biases literature and have found data patterns that are largely converging—many between-subjects biases are remarkably dissociated from intelligence. This was true when we tested so-called "less-is-more" effects in decision making. Much empirical work has gone into determining whether humans adhere to the axioms of choice[5] (transitivity, independence, reduction of compound lotteries, etc.). However, a between-subjects comparison makes it possible to test an even simpler requirement of rational choice—that people prefer more to less (e.g., prefer $6 to $5). Of course, one would not bother testing such a proposition in a within-subjects situation. Nonetheless, it has been shown that given the proper context, in between-subjects comparisons, people sometimes prefer less to more. For example, Slovic, Finucane, Peters, and MacGregor (2002; see also Bateman, Dent, Peters, Slovic, & Starmer, 2007) found that people rated a gamble with 7 in 36 chance to win $9 and 29 in 36 to lose 5¢ more favorably than a gamble with 7 in 36 chance to win $9 and 29 in 36 chance to win nothing. Indeed, they reported that the latter gamble was even rated less desirable than a gamble having a 7 in 36 chance to win $9 and 29 in 36 to lose 25¢. Presumably, in a

---

5 The model of rational judgment used by decision scientists is one in which a person chooses options based on which option has the highest expected utility (Baron, 1993, 1999; Dawes, 1998; Fishburn, 1981, 1999; Gauthier, 1975; Kahneman, 1994; Kleindorfer, Kunreuther, & Schoemaker, 1993; McFadden, 1999; Pratt, Raiffa & Schlaifer, 1995). It has been proven through several formal analyses that if people's preferences follow certain logical patterns (the so-called "axioms of choice"), then they are behaving as if they are maximizing utility (Edwards, 1954; Jeffrey, 1983; Luce & Raiffa, 1957; Savage, 1954; von Neumann & Morgenstern, 1944).

between-subjects design, the representation of the numerically small loss highlights the magnitude and desirability of the $9 to be won.

Likewise, the phenomenon of proportion dominance can result in people preferring less to more in a between-subjects design. Slovic et al. (2002) reported a study in which people rated a safety measure that would save 150 lives less favorably than a safety measure that would save 98% of 150 lives at risk (*see also* Bartels, 2006; Slovic & Peters, 2006). Their explanation of this "less-is-more" effect exhibited in a between-subjects design is that saving 150 lives is more diffusely good than saving 98% of some target figure because the 98% is more evaluable (see Bartels, 2006; Hsee, 1996; Hsee, Loewenstein, Blount, & Bazerman, 1999; Hsee & Zhang, 2004)—it is close to the upper bound on a percentage scale. We (Stanovich & West, 2008b) have found that all of these "less-is-more" effects are largely independent of intelligence.

In another experiment involving 729 university students, we examined the non-normative economic behavior of honoring sunk costs—the tendency to persist in a negative expected value activity because a significant investment has already been made (Arkes & Ayton, 1999; Arkes & Blumer, 1985). Additionally, we examined the economically inefficient tendency to pursue the maximum *relative* savings rather than the maximum *absolute* savings (Thaler, 1980; Tversky & Kahneman, 1981). Using between-subjects designs, we found that neither of these thinking errors were related to intelligence.

Slovic et al. (2002; Slovic & Peters, 2006) have suggested that judgments about the risks and benefits of various activities and technologies derive not from separable knowledge sources relevant to risk and benefit but instead derive from a common source: affect. Evidence for this conjecture derives from the finding that ratings of risk and reward are negatively correlated (Finucane, Alhakami, Slovic, & Johnson, 2000; Slovic & Peters, 2006), both across activities within participants and across participants within activities. When something is rated as having high benefits it tends to be seen as having low risk, and when something is rated as having high risk, it is seen as having low benefits. Finucane et al. (2000) argued that such a finding is non-normative because the risk/benefit relationship is most likely positive in a natural ecology. Their argument is that of the four cells in a high/low partitioning of risk and benefit, one of the cells—that for activities of high risk and low benefit—must be vastly underpopulated. This is because activities of this type are usually not adopted, and they are often proscribed by authorities even when they are. If the high-risk, low-benefit quadrant is under-populated, then the overall risk/benefit of activities in the actual world must be positively correlated.

In a study involving 458 participants, we investigated whether the non-normative tendency to view risk and reward as negatively corre-lated was attenuated in individuals high in cognitive ability. The non-normative tendency to view risk and reward as negatively correlated was not attenuated by high cognitive ability within the range that we studied. In fact, each of the four negative correlations was higher in the high-SAT group than in the low-SAT group.

Omission bias is the tendency to avoid actions that carry some risk but that would prevent a larger risk (Baron, 1998; Baron & Ritov, 2004; Bazerman, Baron, & Shonk, 2001). People often do not realize that by failing to act they often subject themselves and others to greater risk. Our research group examined whether the extent of omission bias was attenuated by cognitive ability and, as with so many of the between-subjects effects we have examined, it was not.

The theory of reference-dependent preferences (Bateman, Munro, Rhodes, Starmer, & Sugden, 1997; Kahneman & Tversky, 1979, 1984; Tversky & Kahneman, 1991) predicts a large difference in willingness-to-accept (WTA) and willingness-to-pay (WTP) valuations. Stanovich and West (2008b) examined individual differences in WTA/WTP dis-crepancies and another effect predicted by prospect theory (Kahneman & Tversky, 1979): the certainty effect. Prospect theory predicts that people overweight probability differences that make an outcome certain over similar probability differences that do not (a violation of the standard assumptions of utility theory). Neither of these non-normative tendencies were moderated by intelligence.

One of the broadest cognitive biases is known as the "bias blind spot" (Pronin, Lin, & Ross, 2002). Bias is relatively easy to recognize in the decisions of others but often difficult to detect in our own judg-ments. We found that across a wide range of cognitive biases, the ten-dency to magnify the biases of others and minimize our own was not attenuated by high intelligence (Meserve, West, & Stanovich, 2008). If anything, the tendency was increased by high intelligence, not because the more intelligent subjects were in fact less biased but instead because they tended to assume that they would be less biased.

Belief Bias and Myside Bias

Critical thinking is often thought to entail the ability to decouple prior beliefs and opinions from the evaluation of evidence and arguments[6]. The literature on Bayesian reasoning (e.g., de Finetti, 1989; Earman, 1992; Fischhoff & Beyth-Marom, 1983; Howson & Urbach, 1993) provides justification for the emphasis on unbiased evidence evaluation in the critical thinking literature. The key reasoning principle captured by Bayes' theorem is that the evaluation of the diagnosticity of the evidence (the likelihood ratio) should be conducted *independently* of the assessment of the prior odds favoring the focal hypothesis. The point is *not* that prior beliefs should not affect the posterior probability of the hypothesis. They most certainly should. A Bayesian analysis is an explicit procedure for factoring in such prior beliefs. The point is that they should not be factored in *twice*. Prior beliefs are encompassed in one of two multiplicative terms that define the posterior probability, but the diagnosticity of the evidence should be assessed separately from the prior belief.

Thus, the concern in the critical thinking literature for segregating prior belief from evidence evaluation receives support from the Bayesian literature: "The interpretation of new evidence may be affected by previous beliefs, thereby subverting the independence of the likelihood ratio and priors" (Fischhoff & Beyth-Marom, 1983, p. 247). Nevertheless, people often fall short of this rational ideal by displaying both *belief bias* and *myside bias*. Belief bias occurs when people have difficulty evaluating conclusions that conflict with what they think they know about the world. It is most often assessed with syllogistic reasoning tasks in which the believability of the conclusion conflicts with logical validity (*see* Chapter 2). Similarly, people display myside bias when they evaluate

---

6 See the literature on decoupling opinion from evaluation (Baltes & Staudinger, 2000; Baron, 1991, 2000; Evans, 2002; Kuhn, 1991, 2001; Johnson-Laird, 2006; Nickerson, 1998; Perkins, 1995, 2002; Stanovich, 1999, 2004; Sternberg, 1997c, 2001, 2003).

evidence, generate evidence, and test hypotheses in a manner biased toward their own opinions. The degree of belief bias has been found to be negatively associated with cognitive ability[7]. Myside bias, in contrast, seems to be much less strongly associated with cognitive ability, particularly when it is assessed in a between-subjects format (Stanovich & West, 2007, 2008a).

The theory outlined in Chapter 2 explains this pattern of results regarding individual differences. Syllogistic reasoning tasks with validity/ knowledge conflict are still quite constrained at the reflective level because the instructions for such tasks often explicitly direct the subject to ignore prior knowledge and focus on validity. Thus, although the validity/belief conflict in such tasks appears to create room for individual differences in interpretation and goal priority, the instructions constrain the variability in such factors by heavily biasing task interpretation and goal choice. However, other tasks in the literature have much less constraint. For example, Klaczynski and colleagues (Klaczynski & Gordon, 1996; Klaczynski & Lavallee, 2005; Klaczynski & Robinson, 2000) presented participants with flawed hypothetical experiments that led to either opinion-consistent or -inconsistent conclusions. Participants critiqued the flaws in the experiments, and they evaluated the strength of the conclusion that could be drawn from each experiment without any explicit instruction to set aside their prior opinions. Interestingly, in this paradigm, the myside bias observed (the tendency to rate the opinion-consistent experiment higher than the opinion-inconsistent experiment)

---

7 There are substantial literatures on both belief bias (Evans, 2002; Evans, Barston, & Pollard, 1983; Evans, Newstead, Allen, & Pollard, 1994; Klauer, Musch, & Naumer, 2000) and myside bias (Baron, 1991; Greenhoot, Semb, Colombo, & Schreiber, 2004; Klaczynski & Lavallee, 2005; Klaczynski & Robinson, 2000; Nussbaum & Kardash, 2005; Perkins, 1985; Perkins, Farady, & Bushey, 1991; Sá, Kelley, Ho, & Stanovich, 2005; Toplak & Stanovich, 2003). The moderate correlation of the former with intelligence (Gilinsky & Judd, 1994; Handley, Capon, Beveridge, Dennis, & Evans, 2004; Kokis et al., 2002; Macpherson & Stanovich, 2007; Sá, West, & Stanovich, 1999; Simoneau & Markovits, 2003; Stanovich & West, 1997, 1998c; however, see Torrens, Thompson, & Cramer, 1999) and the lack of correlation of the latter with intelligence are reasonably well-documented (Klaczynski & Gordon, 1996; Klaczynski & Lavallee, 2005; Klaczynski & Robinson, 2000; Macpherson & Stanovich, 2007; Sá et al., 2005; Toplak & Stanovich, 2003)

displayed extremely modest associations with measures of cognitive ability (the majority of such correlations in the Klaczynski experiments were nonsignificant).

The lack of explicit instructions to detach prior opinion from experiment evaluation in the Klaczynski (1997) paradigm probably left reflective-level functioning relatively unconstrained and decreased the association between myside bias and algorithmic-level functioning. However, even this paradigm contains cues that might help participants interpret what the experimenter might deem optimal performance (in this case, a lack of myside bias). The experiments are run within subjects—that is, each participant evaluates both opinion-consistent and -inconsistent experiments. Such designs provide an important cue that part of the experimental demand is to avoid bias.

Thus, a between-subjects design, in not containing cues to the variable of interest, might even further reduce the relationship between myside bias and individual difference variables. This was found in several paradigms that Stanovich and West (2007, 2008a, 2008b) introduced to study so-called "natural myside bias." Natural myside bias is the tendency to evaluate propositions from within one's own perspective when given no instructions to avoid doing so and when there are no implicit cues (such as within-subjects conditions) to avoid doing so. An example of one of our experiments (Stanovich & West, 2008b) illustrates a between-subjects myside paradigm. Subjects (458 university students) were randomly assigned to either a myside group (Ford Explorer condition) or an otherside group (German car condition). In the Ford Explorer condition[8], the group read the following problem:

> According to a comprehensive study by the U.S. Department of Transportation, Ford Explorers are 8 times more likely than a typical family car to kill occupants of another car in a crash.
> The Department of Transportation in Germany is considering

---

8 These were the relevant crash statistics for the Ford Explorer at the time the study was conducted, see *Vehicle design versus aggressivity*, National Highway Traffic Safety Administration, U.S. Department of Transportation (DOT HS 809 194), Retrieved February 23, 2002, from NHTSA website http://www-nrd.nhtsa.dot.gov/pdf/nrd-11/DOT_HS_809194.pdf.

recommending a ban on the sale of the Ford Explorer in Germany. Do you think that Germany should ban the sale of the Ford Explorer? Subjects answered on the following scale: definitely yes (scored as 6), yes (scored as 5), probably yes (scored as 4), probably no (scored as 3), no (scored as 2), definitely no (scored as 1). Participants were also asked: Should the Ford Explorer be allowed on German streets, just like other cars? They answered on the same scale as the previous question.

The German Car group read the following problem:

According to a comprehensive study by the U.S. Department of Transportation, a particular German car is 8 times more likely than a typical family car to kill occupants of another car in a crash. The U.S. Department of Transportation is considering recommending a ban on the sale of this German car. Subjects answered the following two questions on the scale presented above: (1) Do you think that the United States should ban the sale of this car? (2) Do you think that this car should be allowed on U.S. streets, just like other cars?

The paradigm used in this experiment was successful in creating a myside bias effect. On the ban-the-car question, the mean for the Ford Explorer (myside) condition was significantly lower (3.61, SD = 1.23) than the mean for the German car (otherside) condition (4.34, SD = 1.23; t[456] = −6.33, p < .001, Cohen's d = .593). Subjects were more likely to think that the German car should be banned in the United States than they were to think that the Ford Explorer should be banned in Germany. Correspondingly, on the "allowed on the streets like other cars" question, the mean for the Ford Explorer (myside) condition was significantly higher (3.82, SD = 1.19) than the mean for the German car (otherside) condition (2.86, SD = 1.20; t[456], = 8.59, p < 0.001, Cohen's d = 0.805). Subjects were more likely to think that the Ford Explorer should be allowed on German streets like other cars than they were to think that the German car should be allowed on U.S. streets like other cars. However, both cognitive ability groups displayed myside bias effects of roughly equal magnitude. The bias toward the rights of the Ford Explorer in Germany and against the rights of the German car in the United States was not attenuated by cognitive ability in the range studied in this sample.

Why Thinking Biases Do and Do Not Associate with Cognitive Ability

The myside effect thus represents another cognitive bias that is not strongly attenuated by cognitive ability. In several of the experiments discussed in this chapter, we have shown that a wide variety of cognitive biases are surprisingly dissociated from cognitive ability. We say surprisingly because ever since Spearman (1904) first discovered positive manifold, intelligence indicators have correlated with a plethora of cognitive abilities and thinking skills that are almost too large to enumerate[9]. However, we do not mean to imply that effects from the heuristics and biases literature are invariably independent of intelligence. To the contrary, at the beginning of the chapter, several thinking biases were mentioned that display correlations in the range of 0.15 to 0.45 with intelligence. This raises the obvious question of why certain thinking biases correlate with cognitive ability and others do not. In the remainder of this chapter, we will present a framework that helps to explain when we should expect correlations between cognitive ability and thinking biases and when we should not.

Table 7–2 presents a selection of effects and biases from the literature that have failed to correlate with cognitive ability and a selection of those that do[10]. Kahneman (2000) offers the beginning of an explanation of why certain rational thinking tasks might show associations with cognitive ability and others may not. He begins his argument by making a distinction between coherence rationality and reasoning rationality. Reasoning rationality "requires an ability to reason correctly about the information currently at hand without demanding perfect consistency among beliefs that are not simultaneously evoked" (Kahneman & Frederick, 2005, p. 277). In contrast, "coherence is much stricter . . . coherence requires choices and beliefs to be immune to variations

---

9 A large number of cognitive abilities correlate with intelligence (e.g., Ackerman, Kyllonen, & Richards, 1999; Carroll, 1993; Deary, 2000, 2001; Deary, Whiteman, Starr, Whalley, & Fox, 2004; Lubinski, 2000, 2004; Lubinski & Humphreys, 1997).

10 We would reiterate here the warning that there is a restriction of range in our samples because our studies employed university students as participants.

TABLE 7.2   Thinking Heuristics, Biases, and Effects Classified in Terms of Their Associations with Cognitive Ability

Tasks/Effects that fail to correlate with cognitive ability	Tasks/Effects that correlate with cognitive ability
Noncausal baserate usage (Stanovich & West, 1998c, 1999, 2008b)	Causal baserate usage (Kokis et al., 2002; Stanovich & West, 1998c, 1998d)
Conjunction fallacy between-subjects (Stanovich & West, 2008b)	Outcome bias between- and within-subjects (Stanovich & West, 1998c, 2008b)
Framing between-subjects (Stanovich & West, 2008b)	Framing within-subjects (Bruine de Bruin, et al. 2007; Frederick, 2005; Parker & Fischhoff, 2005; Stanovich & West, 1998b, 1999)
Anchoring effect (Stanovich & West, 2008b)	Denominator neglect (Kokis et al., 2002; Stanovich & West, 2008b)
Evaluability Less is More Effect (Stanovich & West, 2008b)	Probability matching (Stanovich & West, 2008b; West & Stanovich, 2003)
Proportion dominance effect (Stanovich & West, 2008b)	Hindsight bias (Stanovich & West, 1998c)
Sunk-cost effect (Stanovich & West, 2008b; Parker & Fischhoff, 2005)	Ignoring P(D/NH) (Stanovich & West, 1998d, 1999)
Risk/Benefit confounding (Stanovich & West, 2008b)	Covariation detection (Stanovich & West, 1998c, 1998d; Sa et al., 1999)
Omission bias (Stanovich & West, 2008b)	Belief bias in syllogistic reasoning (Macpherson & Stanovich, 2007; Stanovich & West, 1998c, 2008b)
One-side bias, within-subjects (Stanovich & West, 2008a)	Belief bias in modus ponens (Stanovich & West, 2008b)
Certainty effect (Stanovich & West, 2008b)	Informal argument evaluation (Stanovich & West, 1997, 2008b)
Willingness to pay/Willingness to accept difference (Stanovich & West, 2008b)	Four-card selection task (Stanovich & West, 1998a, 2008b; Toplak & Stanovich, 2002; Valentine, 1975)
Myside bias: between and within-S (Klaczynski & Lavallee, 2005; Klaczynski & Robinson, 2000; Sá, Kelley, Ho, & Stanovich, 2005; Stanovich & West, 2007, 2008a, 2008b; Toplak & Stanovich, 2003)	EV maximization in gambles (Benjamin & Shapiro, 2005; Frederick, 2005)
Newcomb's problem (Stanovich & West, 1999; Toplak & Stanovich, 2002)	Overconfidence effect (Bruine de Bruin et al., 2007; Stanovich & West, 1998c)

of framing and context. This is a lot to ask for, but an inability to pass between-subjects tests of coherence is indeed a significant flaw" (Kahneman, 2000, p. 682). Kahneman and Frederick (2002; *see* Kahneman, 2000), utilizing a dual-process framework, argue that correlations with cognitive ability will occur only in the intermediate range of difficulty. There, they argue:

> "intelligent people are more likely to possess the relevant logical rules and also to recognize the applicability of these rules in particular situations. In the terms of the present analysis, high-IQ respondents benefit from relatively efficient System 2 operations that enable them to overcome erroneous intuitions when adequate information is available. When a problem is too difficult for everyone, however, the correlation is likely to reverse" (Kahneman & Frederick, 2002, p. 68).

The phrase "possess the relevant logical rules and also to recognize the applicability of these rules in particular situations" suggests two conditions that have to be fulfilled for a heuristically-based response to be overridden by Type 2 processing (Evans, 2003, 2006b, 2007a; Kahneman & Frederick, 2002; Stanovich, 1999). These two conditions are actually the two sources of judgmental error that Kahneman and Tversky (1982a), two-decades ago, labeled as errors of application and errors of comprehension. The latter refers to errors that occur because people do not recognize the validity of a norm that they have violated. The former occurs when a person fails to apply a rule that he/she has learned.

In the remainder of this chapter, we use two slightly different terms for the loci of these problems. An *error of comprehension* corresponds to a mindware gap as discussed in Chapter 6. In contrast, errors of application can only occur when the relevant mindware has been learned and is available for use in the override process. Errors of application occur when people fail to detect the situational cues, indicating that the heuristically primed response needs to be overridden. We give this requirement the label override detection (detecting the necessity for heuristic override). When it fails, it represents, in the taxonomy of Chapter 6 (*see* Fig. 6–2), the first two categories of thinking error that result from miserly processing—defaulting to the autonomous mind or to serial associative cognition.

The above quote from Kahneman and Frederick (2002) suggests that cognitive ability differences only arise when the experimental task allows for variation in the presence of the relevant mindware and in the override detection process. It will be argued here that this analysis ignores another cause of non-normative responding that might be an even more important source of individual differences—what in the taxonomy of Chapter 6 (*see* Fig. 6–2) is called override failure.

Most of the tasks in the heuristics and biases literature were deliberately designed to pit a heuristically triggered response against a normative response generated by Type 2 processing[11]. However, this means that even after the necessity for override has been detected and the relevant mindware is available, the conflict has to be resolved. Resolving the conflict in favor of the Type 2 response may require cognitive capacity, especially if cognitive decoupling must take place for a considerable period of time. Cognitive decoupling is involved in inhibiting the heuristic response and in simulating alternative responses (*see* Chapters 3 and 4). Recent work on inhibition and executive functioning has indicated that such cognitive decoupling is very capacity-demanding and that it is strongly related to individual differences in fluid intelligence[12].

It will be argued here that this third factor present in some heuristics and biases tasks—the necessity for sustained cognitive decoupling—is the major source of the variability in the association between cognitive ability and task performance that is displayed in Table 7–2. Building on

---

11 For ease of communication, we are using the term *heuristic response* to refer to responses that emanate from the autonomous mind or responses based on serial associative cognition (*see* Evans, 2007a). It should be stressed again that the connection between normative responding and Type 2 processing is not invariable (*see* Evans, 2008). Rational responses can, and often do, originate from the autonomous mind and irrational responses from contaminated mindware substituted by Type 2 processing. The only assumption that most dual-process theorists make is the weak assumption that in cases of conflict between the two, the response generated by Type 2 processing is a statistically better bet.

12 We have previously cited the work on decoupling and fluid intelligence (e.g., Conway et al., 2001; Conway et al., 2003; Duncan et al., 1996; Duncan et al., 2008; Engle, 2002; Friedman et al., 2008; Geary, 2005; Gray et al., 2003; Kane & Engle, 2002, 2003; Salthouse et al., 2003; Salthouse & Davis, 2006; Unsworth & Engle, 2005, 2007).

the conjectures of Kahneman (2000) and Kahneman and Frederick (2002), our framework for conceptualizing individual differences on heuristics and biases tasks is displayed in Figure 7–2. The question addressed in the first stage of the framework is whether, for a given task, the mindware is available to carry out override (whether the procedures and declarative knowledge are available to substitute an analytic response for a heuristic one). If the relevant mindware is not available, then the person must, of necessity, respond heuristically. It is immaterial whether the person detects the necessity for override or has the capacity to sustain override if the normatively appropriate response is simply not available. If the relevant mindware (probabilistic thinking skills, falsifiability tendencies, sensitivity to contradiction, etc.) is not present, then subjects will end up at what has been termed in Figure 7–2 as path #1 to a heuristic

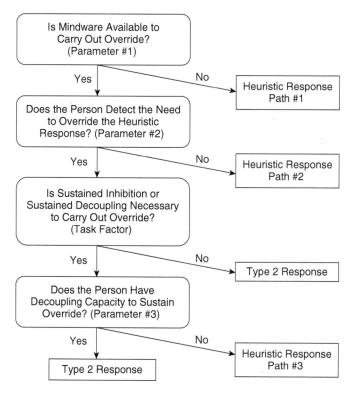

FIGURE 7.2.   A Framework for Conceptualizing Individual Differences on Heuristics and Biases Tasks.

response[13]. Because of a mindware gap, they will fail to give the normative response.

If the relevant mindware is available, then the next question that becomes operative is whether the person detects the need to override the heuristic response. Even if the relevant mindware is present, if the subject does not detect any reason to override the heuristic response, then it will be emitted (this is path #2 to a heuristic response as labeled in Fig. 7–2). Many heuristics and biases tasks lead people down this path. People do not detect the need to override the response that comes naturally (Kahneman, 2003) even though, in retrospect, they would endorse the norm that the heuristic response violated.

The next choice point in Figure 7–2 concerns the task rather than the participant. If the relevant mindware is present and if the need for override has been noted, the question then becomes whether or not the task requires sustained inhibition (cognitive decoupling) to carry out the override of the heuristic response. If not (or if the capacity required is low—this of course may not be an all or nothing issue), then the Type 2 response will be substituted for the heuristic response. In contrast, if the task requires sustained decoupling to carry out override, then we must ask whether the subject has the cognitive capacity that will be necessary. If so, then the Type 2 response will be given. If not, then the heuristic response will be given (path #3 to the heuristic response in Fig. 7–2), despite the availability of the relevant mindware and the recognition of the need to use it.

For cognitive ability to associate with a bias, there must be differences correlated with cognitive ability at some of the choice points in the framework—that is, in some of the person parameters that branch toward or away from heuristic paths. As Kahneman (2000) notes, "a task will be too difficult if (1) System 1 favors an incorrect answer, and (2) System 2 is incapable of applying the correct rule, either because the rule is unknown [mindware gap] or because the cues that would evoke it are absent [no override detection]" (p. 682). Performance on such a task will be floored and will show no association with cognitive ability.

---

13 The reader is reminded again that for ease of communication, we are using the term *heuristic response* to refer to responses that emanate from the autonomous mind or responses based on serial associative cognition.

Some of the tasks in Table 7–2 are no doubt of this type (between-subjects conjunction effects for example). However, several of the tasks in Table 7–2 without associations with cognitive ability cannot be viewed as displaying floor effects. For a cognitive ability difference to be observed, there must be differential cleaving by intelligence at some of the critical nodes in Figure 7–2—that is, there must be a correlation between intelligence and at least one of the person parameters. It is also important to realize that the partitioning of cognitive ability groups at each of the nodes might vary from task to task. We will advance here, however, a generic conjecture about the source of associations with cognitive ability. The conjecture is that the primary source of associations with cognitive ability in heuristics and biases tasks is the way that people are partitioned by person parameter #3 ("Does the person have the decoupling capacity to sustain override?").

Cognitive Decoupling, Mindware Gaps, and Override Detection in Heuristics and Biases Tasks

As discussed in Chapter 3, there is evidence in the literature indicating that tests of fluid intelligence (*see* Carroll, 1993; Horn & Cattell, 1967; Horn & Noll, 1997) directly tap the ability to sustain the decoupling of representations from the world so that cognitive simulations can be run that test the outcomes of imaginary actions. Thus, there is probably a substantial differential in the cleaving at node #3 based on cognitive ability (Duncan et al., 2008; Kane & Engle, 2002; Salthouse et al., 2003). In contrast, we conjecture that for many tasks in the heuristics and biases literature, the other two parameters show only modest differential partitioning based on cognitive ability.

Regarding parameter #1 and the availability of mindware, it is true that the rules, knowledge, and strategies available to the analytic system to use in heuristic system overrides are partly the product of past learning experiences. One might expect that people with more cognitive ability would profit more from learning experiences. However, the relevant mindware for our present discussion is not just generic procedural knowledge, nor is it the hodge-podge of declarative knowledge that is often used to assess crystallized intelligence on ability tests. Instead, it is a very special subset of knowledge related to how one views probability and chance; whether one has the tools to think scientifically and the propensity to do so; the tendency to think logically; and knowledge of some special rules of formal reasoning and good argumentation. At least among the restricted range of the university students typically tested in these studies, acquiring these sets of skills and knowledge bases might be, experientially, very haphazard. Thus, the correlation between this parameter and intelligence, although certainly positive, might be lower in magnitude than we might think.

Although it is true that more intelligent individuals learn more things than the less intelligent, much information relevant to rationality is acquired rather late in life, and the explicit teaching of this mindware is very spotty and inconsistent. For example, the tendency to think of alternative explanations for a phenomenon leads to the ability to more accurately infer causal models of events. Such principles are taught very inconsistently (by either explicit or implicit means). Or take, for example, the conjunction rule of probability, the violation of which is illustrated in the Linda problem. Kahneman and Tversky (1982a) report that tests of rule endorsement and argument endorsement conducted after participants had made the conjunction error revealed that statistically sophisticated psychology graduate students did endorse the rule they had violated (they possessed the relevant mindware but did not detect the necessity for override). However, a majority of statistically naïve *undergraduate* students failed to endorse the conjunction rule—they lacked the relevant mindware ("much to our surprise, naive subjects did not have a solid grasp of the conjunction rule," p. 127, Kahneman & Tversky, 1982a). The lack of uniform teaching and learning conditions for the acquisition of this mindware might attenuate any natural correlation with intelligence that there would be if it were taught under uniform conditions.

Turning next to override detection (parameter #2), it would seem to be as much a thinking disposition as it is an aspect of cognitive capacity. Overrride detection should relate to constructs like need for cognition, for instance (*see* Cacioppo et al., 1996). As such, it seems as much an aspect of the reflective level of processing as an aspect of the algorithmic level. Consistent with this interpretation, individual differences in override detection become apparent in typical performance situations rather than optimal performance situations (Ackerman, 1994, 1996). That is, they become apparent in performance situations that are unconstrained in that no overt instructions to maximize performance are given, and the task interpretation is determined to some extent by the participant. Because override detection parses, in terms of the structure of cognitive abilities, at least partially with thinking dispositions, we think that person parameter #2 in the framework is less the source of associations with cognitive ability than is parameter #3 (which is more exclusively a function of the algorithmic level).

Additionally, it should be noted that there are two ways that the influence of parameter #2, as a generator of individual differences, becomes attenuated: essentially by floor effects (as Kahneman [2000] argues) but also by ceiling effects. Certain tasks in between-subjects designs (perhaps anchoring problems or the Linda problem) give so few cues to the possibility of heuristic/analytic conflict that this parameter is probably floored for most subjects. Conversely, the instructions in other tasks (e.g., belief bias assessed with syllogisms) and some situations in real life ("the salesperson is trying to sell you—don't forget") are so explicit in calling attention to heuristic/analytic conflict that this parameter is probably near ceiling.

The case of belief bias in syllogistic reasoning is probably a good illustration of our argument that it is parameter #3 (the decoupling capacity parameter) that is the primary generator of associations with cognitive ability in rational thinking tasks (*see* De Neys, 2006a, 2006b). The mindware available to reason logically on these simple categorical syllogisms (parameter #1) is probably pretty uniformly present in the samples of university students examined in most studies in the reasoning literature. The procedures needed to reason through the syllogisms used in these studies (e.g., the invalid syllogism: all A are B, all C are B, therefore all C are A) are within the mindware of the vast majority of the students in research studies. In one study (Stanovich & West, 2008b), the percentage correct in the neutral condition (84.1%) was almost as high as the percentage correct in the consistent condition (85.0%), where belief and validity were in alignment.

Additionally, as just mentioned, the instructions on this task probably ceiling out parameter #2—override detection. Recall that the instructions sensitize the participants to potential conflict (between argument validity and the truth of argument components). Thus, parameters #1 and #2 probably leave little room for any individual difference variable to associate with performance.

In contrast, the syllogistic reasoning task does require sustained cognitive decoupling (De Neys, 2006b). For example, in the "rose" syllogism (All flowers have petals; roses have petals; therefore, roses are flowers—which is invalid), subjects must suppress the tendency to endorse a valid response because of the "naturalness" of the conclusion—roses are flowers. This response must be held in abeyance while reasoning procedures work through the partially overlapping set logic indicating that the conclusion does not necessarily follow and that the syllogism is thus invalid. The reasoning process may take several seconds of perhaps somewhat aversive concentration (*see* Botvinick et al., 2004; Glenberg, 1997; Kahneman, 1973; Navon, 1989)—seconds during which the urge to foreclose the conflict by acceding to the natural tendency to affirm "roses are flowers" (by responding "valid") must be suppressed. Such response suppression during reasoning is closely related to the inhibitory and conflict resolution processes being studied by investigators examining the construct of executive functioning (e.g., Botvinick et al., 2004; Salthouse et al., 2003). Individual differences in such inhibitory processes have been found to be strongly associated with individual differences in fluid intelligence.

Our conjecture here amounts to an endorsement of what Evans (2007b) calls the quality hypothesis regarding cognitive ability: individuals higher in cognitive ability are more likely to compute the correct response *given* that they have engaged in Type 2 processing. The alternative hypothesis—the quantity hypothesis—is that individuals higher in cognitive ability are more likely to engage in Type 2 processing. Our hypothesis is that the effect of cognitive ability is more qualitative than quantitative, to use Evans' terms: individuals higher in cognitive ability are more likely to compute the correct response *given* that they have engaged in Type 2 processing, but they are not much more likely to actually engage in Type 2 processing. Cognitive ability is more related to maximal/optimal processing (which stresses the algorithmic mind) than it is to typical performance (which more closely tracks the reflective mind).

We conjecture that many of the other tasks that do show associations with cognitive ability (second column of Table 7–2) are tasks that involve some type of inhibition and/or sustained cognitive decoupling. For example, in within-subjects tests of outcome bias (Stanovich & West, 1998c), the appearance of the second item gives a pretty clear signal to the subject that there is an issue of consistency in their responses to the two different forms—that is, the within-subjects design probably puts parameter #2 at ceiling, thus ensuring that it is not the source of any associations with cognitive ability that are obtained. Detecting the need for consistency is not the issue. Instead, the difficulty comes from the necessity of inhibiting the tendency to downgrade the decision in the negative outcome condition, despite its having a better rationale than the positive outcome decision. Even in the between-subjects version of this task, one group of participants—those getting the negative outcome version—is alerted to the potential conflict between the seemingly good reasons to have the operation and the shockingly bad outcome. Subjects must suppress the desire to sanction the decision, decouple their knowledge of the outcome, and simulate what they would have thought had they not known the outcome. Indeed, this condition creates a situation similar to those of various "curse of knowledge" paradigms[14]. Note that the two cognitive ability groups show no difference in mean ratings in the positive outcome condition (*see* Table 7–1), which does not necessitate heuristic system override. The difference is entirely in the negative outcome condition in which sustained suppression is required.

The "curse of knowledge" logic of the negative item in the outcome bias task is similar to that in hindsight bias paradigms (e.g., Christiansen-Szalanski & Williams, 1991; Fischhoff, 1975; Pohl, 2004), which have also shown associations with cognitive ability (Stanovich & West, 1998c). In hindsight paradigms, the marking of the correct response sensitizes every respondent to the potential conflict involved—between what you know now and what you would have known without the correct response being indicated. Thus again, parameter #2 must be at ceiling. However, there is a need for sustained decoupling in the task, so whatever association between bias and cognitive ability exists on the task

---

14 There are many different "curse of knowledge" paradigms (*see* Birch, 2005; Camerer, Loewenstein, & Weber, 1989; Gilovich, Medvec, & Sativsky, 1998; Keysar & Barr, 2002; Royzman, Cassidy, & Baron, 2003).

(a modest one; *see* Stanovich & West, 1998c) is likely generated by individual differences in parameter #3.

Within-subjects framing paradigms probably have a similar logic. The appearance of the second problem surely signals that an issue of consistency is at stake (putting parameter #2 at ceiling) and virtually all of the university students in these studies have acquired the value of consistency (parameter #1 is also at ceiling). The modest cognitive ability associations that are generated by this task probably derive from lower cognitive ability participants who cannot suppress the attractiveness of an alternative response despite the threat to consistent responding that it represents—in short, from variation in parameter #3. In contrast, between-subjects framing situations probably drive parameter #2 to a very low value (few people recognize that there is a conflict to be resolved between a potentially different response to an alternative framing), thus eliminating associations with individual differences (in the manner suggested by Kahneman, 2000).

The logic of the Linda problem is similar. Transparent, within-subjects versions are easier because they signal the conflict involved and the necessity for override. Such versions create at least modest associations with cognitive ability. In the between-subjects version, however, individual differences are eliminated entirely because this design obscures the heuristic/analytic conflict and puts parameter #2 at floor.

As a final example, consider the difference between causal and non-causal baserates[15] illustrated in Table 6–2. Noncausal baserate problems

---

15 Baserates that have a causal relationship to the criterion behavior (Ajzen, 1977; Bar-Hillel, 1980, 1990; Tversky & Kahneman, 1979) are often distinguished from noncausal baserate problems—those involving base rates with no obvious causal relationship to the criterion behavior. A famous noncausal problem is the well-known cab problem (*see* Bar-Hillel, 1980; Lyon & Slovic, 1976; Tversky & Kahneman, 1982): "A cab was involved in a hit-and-run accident at night. Two cab companies, the Green and the Blue, operate in the city in which the accident occurred. You are given the following facts: 85 percent of the cabs in the city are Green and 15 percent are Blue. A witness identified the cab as Blue. The court tested the reliability of the witness under the same circumstances that existed on the night of the accident and concluded that the witness correctly identified each of the two colors 80 percent of the time. What is the probability that the cab involved in the accident was Blue?" (Amalgamating the baserate and the indicant according to Bayes' rule yields .41 as the

trigger conflict detection in so few participants that parameter #2 is floored and hence cognitive ability differences are eliminated. In contrast, in a classic causal baserate problem such as the Volvo versus Saab problem (*see* Footnote 15)—where clearly relevant aggregate information is pitted against indicant information—the aggregate information has a causal relationship to the criterion behavior and thus clearly signals that there are two pieces of information in conflict. Parameter #2 is near ceiling, and individual differences are determined largely by parameter #3 (the sustained decoupling parameter), which is, we conjecture, linked to individual differences in cognitive ability. Thus, causal—but not noncausal—baserate problems show cognitive ability differences.

It is important to note that this interpretation does not contradict the results of De Neys (De Neys & Franssens, 2009; De Neys & Glumicic, 2008; De Neys, Moyens, & Vansteenwegen, 2010; De Neys et al., 2008; Franssens & De Neys, 2009), who demonstrated that various implicit measures of performance on noncausal baserate problems (decision latencies, unannounced recall, brain activation, autonomic arousal) indicated that conflict between baserate and indicant information was detected and that when indicant information was overridden, inhibition areas of the brain were activated (lateral prefrontal cortex). Unlike the

---

posterior probability of the cab being blue.) The causal variant of the same problem substitutes for the first fact the phrase "Although the two companies are roughly equal in size, 85% of cab accidents in the city involve Green cabs and 15% involve Blue cabs" (p. 157, Tversky & Kahneman, 1982).

Another type of causal baserate problem is structured so that the participant has to make an inductive inference in a simulation of a real-life decision. The information relevant to the decision is conflicting and of two different types. One type of evidence is statistical: either probabilistic or aggregate base-rate information that favors one of the bipolar decisions. The other evidence is a concrete case or personal experience that points in the opposite direction. The classic Volvo versus Saab item (*see* p. 285 of Fong, Krantz, & Nisbett, 1986) provides an example. In this problem, a couple is deciding to buy one of two otherwise equal cars. Consumer surveys, statistics on repair records, and polls of experts favor the Volvo over the Saab. However, a friend reports experiencing a severe mechanical problem with the Volvo he owns. The participant is asked to provide advice to the couple. Preference for the Volvo indicates a tendency to rely on the large-sample information in spite of salient personal testimony. A preference for the Saab indicates reliance on the personal testimony over the opinion of experts and the large-sample information.

classic 70/30 lawyer/engineer problem of Kahneman and Tversky (1973), very extreme baserates were used in the De Neys work, for example: "In a study 1000 people were tested. Among the participants there were 5 engineers and 995 lawyers." These extreme numbers serve to draw attention to the baserate and move parameter #2 to ceiling from its relatively low level in the traditional 70/30 version of the problem. The problem is turned from one where the pitfall is override detection to one where the central task is to inhibit the stereotype that is automatically triggered and replace it with reliance on the extreme baserate. Thus, individual differences in these extreme baserate problems would be determined largely by parameter #3 (the sustained decoupling parameter), and it is thus to be expected that inhibition areas of the brain would be activated on trials where successful override is achieved. Likewise, because this version of the paradigm results in a moderate-to-high value of parameter #2, it is expected under our model that various implicit measures (including brain activation) would indicate that conflict between baserate and indicant information was detected.

Of course, with this discussion of what creates associations between biases and cognitive ability, we do not mean to draw attention away from the left side of Table 7–2. There, it is apparent that a startlingly wide range of rational thinking tendencies appear to be independent of intelligence within the range existing in a university sample. These include many tasks that test some very basic strictures of rational thought. For example, the absence of framing and context effects are performance patterns that ensure that people's choices are utility maximizing. The failure to adhere to these strictures leads to descriptive models of human rationality that have profound public policy implications (Camerer et al., 2003; Lilienfeld et al., 2009; Milkman, Chugh, & Bazerman, 2009; Mitchell, 2005; Prentice, 2003; Thaler & Sunstein, 2008). But adherence to these strictures of utility maximization were unrelated to cognitive ability in our sample. Within the range of intelligence that we studied, individuals of the highest cognitive capacity were no less likely to display baserate neglect, the conjunction fallacy, myside bias, anchoring effects, the sunk cost effect, proportion dominance, and a host of other cognitive biases.

The framework in Figure 7–2 illustrates why rationality will not be uniformly related to intelligence. Instead, that relationship will depend on the degree that rational responding requires sustained cognitive decoupling. When the heart of the task is recognizing the need for heuristic override, and the override operation itself is easily accomplished, no sustained decoupling is necessary and rational thinking will depend more on the operations of the reflective mind than on those of the algorithmic mind (*see* Chapter 2 and Stanovich, 2009a, 2009b). Thus, relationships with intelligence will be attenuated. Additionally, as Kahneman (2000) has argued, when detecting the necessity for override is very difficult (parameter #2 is low), performance overall will be quite low and no relationships with cognitive ability will be evident.

Conversely, however, highly intelligent people will display fewer reasoning biases when you tell them what the bias is and what they need to do to avoid it. That is, when parameters #1 and #2 are ceilinged and considerable cognitive capacity is needed to sustain decoupling while the correct response is computed, then highly intelligent people will do better in a rational thinking task. However, if there is no advance warning that biased processing must be avoided (as is the case in many between-subjects designs), then more intelligent individuals are not much more likely to perform any better on the task. Another way to phrase this is to say that often, people of higher cognitive ability are no more likely to recognize the *need* for a normative principle than are individuals of lower cognitive ability. When the former believe that nothing normative is at stake, they behave remarkably like other people (equally likely for example to be "anchored" into responding that redwoods are almost 1000 feet tall!; *see* Table 7–1). If told, however, that they are in a situation of normative conflict and if resolving the conflict requires holding a prepotent response in abeyance, then the individual of high cognitive ability will show less of many different cognitive biases.

An important caveat to the model presented in Figure 7–2 is that which rational thinking tasks yield a conflict between heuristic and analytic responses is not fixed but instead is a function of the individual's history of mindware acquisition. Early in developmental history, the relevant mindware will not be present and the heuristic response will be inevitable—no conflict will even be detected. Someone with no training in thinking probabilistically—or, for that matter, logically in terms of subset and superset—may experience no conflict in the Linda problem. As experience with statistical and probabilistic thinking grows, a person will begin to experience more of a conflict because relevant mindware is available for use in the simulation of an alternative response. The final developmental stage in this sequence might well be that the mindware used in simulation becomes so tightly compiled that it is triggered in the manner of a natural heuristic response. Some statistics instructors, for example, become unable to empathize with their students for whom the basic probability axioms are not transparent. The instructor can no longer remember when these axioms were not primary intuitions. This final stage of processing is perhaps captured by developmental models of heuristic versus analytic processing that trace a trajectory where fluent performance looks very heuristic[16].

Under the view presented here, there turn out to be numerous circumstances under which rational thought will dissociate from cognitive ability. First, cues to the necessity for override might be missing, thus leading most individuals to respond heuristically regardless of cognitive ability. Second, cues to the need for override might be present, but the disposition to respond to such cues may not be correlated with algorithmic capacity. If this is the case, there will be no association with cognitive ability as long as there is no need for sustained decoupling. The disposition to spot a heuristic/analytic conflict is not necessarily related to the computational power needed (in some situations) to resolve the conflict in favor of the analytic response. Thinking dispositions that relate to override cue detection are not assessed on intelligence tests (*see* Stanovich, 2009b) and are thus not part of the intelligence construct. In the next chapter, we will explore more thoroughly the conditions that lead to a dissociation between intelligence and rational thinking.

---

16 There are many models of cognitive abilities that view the endpoint of the performance trajectory as reflecting properties of autonomous processing (Ericsson & Charness, 1994; Kahneman & Klein, 2009; Klein, 1998; Reyna, Lloyd, & Brainerd, 2003; Reyna et al., 2005; Shiffrin & Schneider, 1977).

8

Rationality and Intelligence: Empirical and Theoretical Relationships and Implications for the Great Rationality Debate

Having sketched out a model of how and when cognitive ability associates with heuristics and biases tasks in Chapter 7, this chapter will use the taxonomy of Chapter 6 to summarize the empirical findings on the nature of the relationship between intelligence and rational thought. Each of the major categories displayed in Figure 8–1 (which recapitulates Fig. 6–3) represents a separate explanation of why human thought and action are sometimes irrational.

Intelligence and Rationality Associations in Terms of the Taxonomy

The Mr. Spock problem represents the most clear-cut category because it is likely to be as prevalent in high-IQ individuals as in low-IQ individuals. The reason is that these problems result from inadequate (or incorrect) input from the autonomous mind (e.g., from modules of emotional regulation). Variation in the subprocesses of the autonomous mind tend to be independent of intelligence[1]. Thus, the Mr. Spock prob-

---

1 Subprocesses of the autonomous mind might not be totally independent from intelligence, but they tend to be considerably dissociated (Anderson, 2005; Baron-Cohen, 1995; Kanazawa, 2004; Reber, 1992, 1993; Reber, Walkenfeld, & Hernstadt, 1991; Saffran, Aslin, & Newport, 1996; Toplak, Sorge, Benoit, West, & Stanovich, 2010; Vinter & Detable, 2003; Vinter & Perruchet, 2000; Zacks, Hasher, & Sanft, 1982). It is important to understand that intelligence tests assess only those aspects of cognitive functioning on which people tend to show large differences. What this means is that intelligence tests will not routinely assess *all* aspects of cognitive functioning—only those on which people tend to show large individual differences. There are many kinds of Type 1 processing that are important for us as a species but

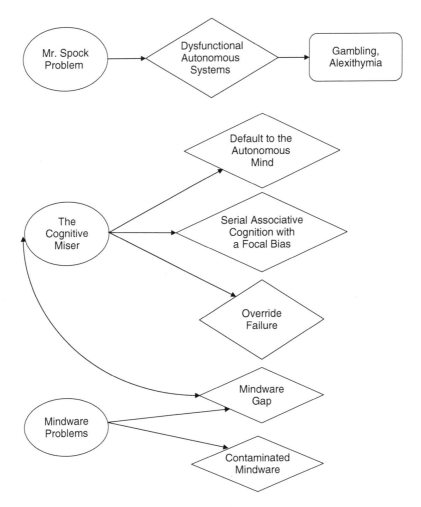

FIGURE 8.1.   An Expanded Taxonomy of Thinking Errors.

lem is just as likely to occur in individuals of high intelligence as in individuals of lower intelligence.

The next category (defaulting to the autonomous mind and not engaging at all in Type 2 processing) is the most shallow processing

on which there tend not to be large differences *between* people in the efficiency of functioning. Face recognition, syntactic processing, gaze direction detection, and kin recognition provide four examples of such domains.

tendency of the cognitive miser. Although the ability to sustain Type 2 cognitive decoupling is, of course, related to intelligence, the *tendency* to engage in such processing or to default to autonomous processes is a property of the reflective mind that is not assessed on IQ tests. Consider the Levesque (1986, 1989) problem mentioned in Chapter 6 (e.g., "Jack is looking at Anne but Anne is looking at George") as an example of avoiding Type 2 processing. The subjects who answer this problem correctly are no higher in intelligence than those that do not, at least in our sample of university students (Toplak & Stanovich, 2002). In unpublished work with other versions of tasks sharing the logic of this problem, we have found statistically significant associations with intelligence, but the associations were small in absolute magnitude.

Disjunctive reasoning problems such as the Levesque problem (*see* Shafir, 1994) require the decoupling of cognitive representations and the computation of possible worlds with the decoupled representations—one of the central operations of algorithmic mind discussed in Chapter 3 (and one of the processes at the heart of fluid intelligence). But clearly one has to discern the necessity of disjunctive reasoning in this situation to answer correctly. One has to avoid the heuristic reaction: "Oh, since we don't know whether Anne is married or not we cannot determine anything." And with respect at least to this particular problem, Toplak and Stanovich (2002) observed that individuals of high intelligence were no more likely to do so. The reflective-level cognition of individuals of high intelligence is no more likely to send instructions to engage in decoupling operations to the algorithmic level. No doubt, were they sent, the decoupled operations would be more reliably sustained by people of higher intelligence (they differ on parameter #3 in the model presented in Fig. 7–2). But intelligence is of no use in this task unless the instruction is sent to engage in the modeling of possible worlds.

There is, however, one theoretical reason why one might expect a positive correlation between intelligence and the tendency of the reflective mind to initiate Type 2 processing. The reason is that it might be assumed that those of high intelligence would be more optimistic about the potential efficacy of Type 2 processing and thus be more likely to engage in it. Indeed, some tasks designed to trap the cognitive miser do show a positive correlation with intelligence. One is the task studied by Frederick (2005) and mentioned in Chapter 6: A bat and a ball cost

$1.10 in total. The bat costs $1 more than the ball. How much does the ball cost? Frederick (2005) found that the correlation between intelligence and a set of such similar items is in the range of 0.43 to 0.46. Gilhooly and Murphy (2005; Gilhooly & Fioratou, 2009) found that the correlations between performance on a set of insight problems somewhat different than those[2] used by Frederick (2005) and various measures of sustained decoupling ability (i.e., measures of fluid intelligence) were in the range of 0.20 to 0.45. Correlations with disjunctive reasoning tasks were lower in the Toplak and Stanovich (2002) study. Correlations of this magnitude leave plenty of room for dissociations between rationality and intelligence. That is, the scatterplot of such a relationship would contain many cases of poor rational thought despite substantial intelligence, and numerous cases of highly rational thought conjoined with lower-than-average intelligence. Of course, the correlations observed in all of these investigations are attenuated somewhat by restriction of range in the university samples.

A somewhat more demanding strategy of the cognitive miser displayed in Figure 8–1 is to rely on serial associative processing with a focal bias. It is a more demanding strategy in that it does involve Type 2 processing. It is still a strategy of the miser, however, in that it does not involve fully fleshed-out mental simulation (*see* Evans, 2006b, 2007a, 2009, on satisficing in Type 2 processing). Framing effects (*see* Chapters 6 and 7) provide examples of the focal bias in the processing of the cognitive miser. When between-subjects framing effects are examined, the tendency to display this type of bias is virtually independent of intelligence. When examined within-subjects, the tendency to avoid framing does show a very small correlation with intelligence (for individual

---

2 Not all insight problems are of the type used by Frederick to reveal the tendency to default to the cognitive miser's response. The key aspect of the problems in Frederick's (2005) Cognitive Reflection Test is that they strongly prime a heuristic response that must be overridden. Some classic insight problems are difficult because the correct answer is not obvious, but they do not prime a contradictory heuristic response. Such insight problems would not be candidates for Frederick's (2005) Cognitive Reflection Test because they require no Type 1 processing override because an alternative response need not be inhibited. Also, such problems would not be the best measures of miserly processing.

differences work on framing using both types of designs, *see* Bruine de Bruin et al., 2007; Parker & Fischhoff, 2005; Stanovich & West, 1998b, 1999, 2008b). Within a university sample, individuals of the highest intelligence are almost as likely to display irrational framing effects as those of lower intelligence. The same is true with anchoring effects (*see* Table 7–1). Among a university sample, anchoring biases are virtually independent of cognitive ability.

The next category of thinking error in Figure 8–1 is override failure. In this case, inhibitory processes try to take the processing of the autonomous mind offline to substitute an alternative response, but the decoupling operations fail to suppress the Type 1 response (or fail to sustain decoupling long enough for an alternative response to be computed). We would expect that this category of cognitive failure would have the highest (negative) correlation with intelligence. This is because intelligence indexes the computational power of the algorithmic mind that can be used for the decoupling operation. Theoretically, however, we should still expect the correlation to be somewhat less than perfect. The reflective mind must first trigger override operations before any individual differences in decoupling can become apparent.

In dealing with the data involving override failure, we might begin by distinguishing so-called "hot override" from so-called "cold override." The former refers to the override of emotions, visceral drives, or short-term temptations (by analogy to what has been called "hot" cognition in the literature; *see* Abelson, 1963). The latter refers to the override of over-practiced rules, Darwinian modules, or tendencies of the autonomous mind that are not necessarily linked to visceral systems (by analogy to what has been called "cold" cognition in the literature).

In the domain of hot override, we know most about delay of gratification situations. Mischel (Ayduk & Mischel, 2002; Mischel & Ebbesen, 1970; Mischel, Shoda, & Rodriguez, 1989) pioneered the study of the delay of gratification paradigm with children. The paradigm has many variants, but the essence of the procedure is as follows. Age-appropriate rewards (e.g., toys, desirable snacks) are established, and the child is told that he/she will receive a small reward (e.g., one marshmallow) or a larger reward (e.g., two marshmallows). The child receives the larger reward if, after the experimenter leaves the room, the child waits until the experimenter returns and does not recall the experimenter by ringing a bell.

If the bell is rung before the experimenter returns, the child receives only the smaller reward. The dependent variable is the amount of time that child waits before ringing the bell[3].

Rodriguez, Mischel, and Shoda (1989) observed a correlation of 0.39 between measured intelligence and delay in the Mischel paradigm. Likewise, in a similar study of young children, Funder and Block (1989) observed a correlation of 0.34 between intelligence and delay. Consistent with the idea that this paradigm involves the reflective mind as well as the algorithmic mind, Funder and Block found that personality measures predicted delay after the variance associated with intelligence had been partialled out.

Data from adults converge with these findings (Kirby, Winston, & Santiesteban, 2005). There is a large literature on the extent to which adults discount monetary amounts into the future. Many different paradigms have been used to assess how people compare a smaller reward immediately over a larger reward in the future and how much larger the future reward has to be to tip the preference (Green & Myerson, 2004; Loewenstein, Read, & Baumeister, 2003; McClure, Laibson, Loewenstein, & Cohen, 2004). Higher intelligence is associated with a greater tendency to wait for the larger monetary reward. However, Shamosh and Gray (2008) meta-analyzed this literature and found that across 24 different studies, the correlation between the tendency to wait for delayed larger rewards and intelligence averaged 0.23.

Delayed-discounting paradigms are laboratory tasks. Real-life override failures in adults correlate with intelligence too. The correlations are modest, however. For example, the control of addictive behaviors such as smoking, gambling, and drug use are often analyzed in terms of override failure (Ainslie, 2001, 2005). Thus, it is interesting that Austin and Deary (2002) report analyses of the longitudinal Edinburgh Artery Study looking at whether intelligence might be a long-term protective

---

3 It should be noted that other investigators interpret the failure to delay in the Mischel paradigm not as a failure of the override function but instead as indicating flawed reward and reward-discounting mechanisms in the autonomous mind (e.g., Sonuga-Barke, 2002, 2003). If this alternative interpretation is correct, then it reclassifies failure in the Mischel paradigm as an instance of the Mr. Spock problem rather than failure of override.

factor against both smoking and drinking (presumably through the greater ability to sustain inhibition of the autonomous mind). They found no evidence at all that longitudinally, intelligence served as a protective against problem drinking. There was a very small but significant longitudinal link between intelligence and smoking.

The correlations in the studies of Rodriguez et al., (1989), Funder and Block (1989), and Austin and Deary (2002) and in the data of Shamosh & Gray (2008) were statistically significant, but they are, by all estimates, moderate in absolute magnitude. They leave plenty of room for dissociations between intelligence and successful override of autonomous systems.

A very similar story plays out when we look at the relationship between intelligence and "cold" override failure. Two cold override tasks discussed in Chapter 6 provide examples: belief bias tasks ("roses are living things") and denominator neglect (pick from bowl with 1 of 10 red vs. 8 of 100 red; see Denes-Raj & Epstein, 1994; Kirkpatrick & Epstein, 1992; Pacini & Epstein, 1999). Successful override correlates with intelligence in the range of 0.35 to 0.45 for belief bias task and in the range of 0.25 to 0.30 for the Epstein task (Kokis et al., 2002; Macpherson & Stanovich, 2007; Stanovich & West, 1998c, 2008a, 2008b). Two other examples of override failure (see Table 6–1) are outcome bias and hindsight bias, and both show significant, but small, correlations with cognitive ability. Both are examples of "curse of knowledge" effects that demand sustained decoupling (Birch, 2005; Keysar & Barr, 2002; Royzman et al., 2003). Outcome bias shows correlations of from 0.15 to 0.25 with intelligence (Stanovich & West, 1998c, 2008b). Likewise, hindsight bias displays a correlation of 0.25 with intelligence (Stanovich & West, 1998c).

Continuing down in the taxonomy in Figure 8–1, we see that irrational behavior can occur for a fifth reason: the right mindware (cognitive rules, strategies, knowledge, and belief systems) is not available to use in decision making. We would expect to see a correlation with intelligence here because mindware gaps most often arise from lack of education or experience. However, as argued in Chapter 7, this correlation, although certainly positive, might be smaller in magnitude than is commonly thought. Although it is true that more intelligent individuals learn more things than less intelligent individuals, much knowledge relevant to rationality (and many thinking dispositions) are picked up rather late in life. Explicit teaching of this mindware is not uniform in the school curriculum at any level. Because principles are taught very inconsistently, some intelligent people may fail to learn these important aspects of critical thinking. Correlations with cognitive ability have been found to be roughly (in absolute magnitude) in the range of 0.25 to 0.35 for various probabilistic reasoning tasks, 0.20 to 0.25 for various covariation detection and hypothesis testing tasks, and 0.05 to 0.20 for various indices of Bayesian reasoning—again relationships allowing for substantial discrepancies between intelligence and the presence of the mindware necessary for rational thought. These correlations are derived from a variety of investigations (Bruine de Bruin et al., 2007; Kokis et al., 2002; Parker & Fischhoff, 2005; Peters et al., 2006; Sá et al., 1999; Stanovich & West, 1998c, 1998d, 1999, 2000, 2008b; Toplak & Stanovich, 2002; West & Stanovich, 2003). Some of these data are from studies of children spanning a wide range of ability. The adult samples employ mostly range-restricted university samples.

Regarding the sixth category in Figure 8–1—contaminated mindware—we would of course expect more intelligent individuals to acquire more mindware of all types based on their superior learning abilities. This would result in them acquiring more mindware that fosters rational thought. However, this superior learning ability would not preclude more intelligent individuals from acquiring contaminated mindware—that is, mindware that literally causes irrationality. Many parasitic belief systems are conceptually somewhat complex. Examples of complex parasitic mindware would be Holocaust denial (Lipstadt, 1994; Shermer, 1997) and many financial get-rich-quick schemes as well as bogus tax evasion schemes. Such complex mindware might even require a certain level of intelligence to be enticing to the host. George Orwell conjectured in this vein when discussing political attitudes in the World War II era: "There is no limit to the follies that can be swallowed if one is under the influence of feelings of this kind. . . . One has to belong to the intelligentsia to believe things like that: no ordinary man could be such a fool" (1968, p. 379).

This conjecture is supported by the results of a study commissioned by the National Association of Securities Dealers (Consumer Fraud Research Group, 2006). The study found that the investment fraud victims had significantly more education than a comparison group—68.6% of the investment fraud victims group had at least a BA degree compared to just 37.2% in the control group. Finally, surveys show that pseudoscientific beliefs have a quite high prevalence among those of high intelligence (Chatillon, 1989). Also suggestive is a study reported by Zagorsky (2007) in which a regression analysis showed a positive beta weight for intelligence as a predictor of income but a negative beta weight for intelligence as a predictor of wealth and financial distress (debt problems, bankruptcy, etc.). Income is more dependent on IQ-type selection devices used by selective schools, corporations, and the military (SAT, GRE, LSAT, GMAT, ASVAB, etc.). In contrast, wealth management and personal financial decision making involve much more the rational thinking skills that go largely unassessed by conventional IQ tests and intelligence test proxies such as the SAT.

Summary of the Relationships

In the aggregate, across the different categories of thinking error displayed in Figure 8–1, the correlations between intelligence and the various types of thinking error seem to be remarkably modest. The Mr. Spock problem is largely independent of intelligence. The various ways that the cognitive miser avoids computationally expensive information appear to correlate in the range of 0.25 to 0.40 with intelligence at the highest—that is, when they correlate with intelligence at all. However, there are many effects and biases that result from miserly processing tendencies that show virtually no correlation at all with intelligence in university samples—for example, myside bias, anchoring effects, and between-subjects framing effects framing. Mindware gaps show correlations with intelligence in the range of 0.20 to 0.40. Correlations involving contaminated mindware are largely unknown but are unlikely to be larger than this in university samples. The bias blind spot, arising because of a mindware gap and contaminated mindware, is at least as robust among the highly intelligent (Meserve et al., 2008). It certainly shows no positive correlation with intelligence.

Collapsing across all of these categories of cognitive error, it must be said that the correlations with intelligence are surprisingly modest.

The context for such a statement is the general esteem with which intelligence is held in folk psychology. In psychology and among the lay public alike, assessments of intelligence and tests of cognitive ability are taken to be the sine qua non of good thinking. It is surprising when they are so little correlated with cognitive tasks that measure processes that are so important. In 2002, Daniel Kahneman won the Nobel Prize in Economics for work done with his longtime collaborator Amos Tversky (who died in 1996). Their work inaugurated the so-called "heuristics and bias research program," one of the most successful intellectual projects in all of cognitive science. It is a profound historical irony of the behavioral sciences that the Nobel Prize was awarded for studies of cognitive characteristics that are entirely missing from the most well-known mental assessment device in the behavioral sciences—the intelligence test (and its many proxies, such as the SAT). This might not be such an important omission if it were the case that intelligence was a strong *predictor* of rational thinking, but as we have seen, it is not.

In Chapters 2 and 3, the concepts of rationality and intelligence were theoretically differentiated. In Chapter 7 and 8, it was shown that the concepts separate in actual human performance—they are empirically separable as well. This theoretical and empirical separation has implications for the Great Rationality Debate that was discussed at beginning of this book. It also has profound social implications. In the remainder of this chapter, I discuss how the relative dissociation has implications for the Great Rationality Debate. In the remaining chapters, we will explore the social implications of the modest correlation between the two.

Individual Differences, the Reflective Mind, and the Great Rationality Debate

In previous chapters, I have established that rationality requires three different classes of mental characteristic. First, algorithmic-level cognitive capacity is needed for override and simulation activities to be sustained. Second, the reflective mind must be characterized by the tendency to initiate the override of suboptimal responses generated by the autonomous mind and to initiate simulation activities that will result in a better response. Finally, the mindware that allows the computation of rational responses needs to be available and accessible during simulation activities.

Because there are individual differences in each of these three domains, there will be individual differences in rational thought and action. The Panglossian position in the Great Rationality Debate has obscured the existence of individual differences in rational thought and its underlying components. In particular, Panglossian philosophers have obscured the importance of the reflective mind. Philosophical treatments of rationality by Panglossians tend to have a common structure. Such treatments tend to stress the importance of the competence/performance distinction and then proceed to allocate all of the truly important psychological mechanisms to the competence side of the dichotomy.

For example, Rescher (1988) argues that "to construe the data of these interesting experimental studies [of probabilistic reasoning] to mean that people are systematically programmed to fallacious processes of reasoning—rather than merely that they are inclined to a variety of (occasionally questionable) substantive suppositions—is a very questionable step. . . .While all (normal) people are to be credited with the capacity to reason, they frequently do not exercise it well" (p. 196). There are two parts to Rescher's (1988) point here: the "systematically programmed" part and the "inclination toward questionable suppositions" part (or, as Rips [1994] puts it, whether incorrect reasoning is "systematically programmed or just a peccadillo," p. 394). Rescher's (1988) focus (like that of many who have dealt with the philosophical implications of the idea of human irrationality) is on the issue of how humans are "systematically programmed." "Inclinations toward questionable suppositions" are only of interest to those in the philosophical debates as mechanisms that allow one to drive a wedge between competence and performance—thus maintaining a theory of near-optimal human rational competence in the face of a host of responses that seemingly defy explanation in terms of standard normative models.

Analogously to Rescher, Cohen (1982) argues that there really are only two factors affecting performance on rational thinking tasks: "normatively correct mechanisms on the one side, and adventitious causes of error on the other" (p. 252). Not surprisingly given such a conceptualization, the processes contributing to error ("adventitious causes") are of little interest to Cohen (1981, 1982). In his view, human performance arises from an intrinsic human competence that is impeccably rational, but responses occasionally deviate from normative correctness due to inattention, memory lapses, lack of motivation, and other fluctuating but basically unimportant causes (in Cohen's view). There is nothing in such a conception that would motivate any interest in patterns of errors or individual differences in such errors.

One of the goals of this volume is to reverse the figure and ground in the rationality debate, which has tended to be dominated by the particular way that philosophers frame the competence/performance distinction. From a psychological standpoint, there may be important implications in precisely the aspects of performance that have been back-grounded in this controversy ("adventitious causes," "peccadillos"). That is, whatever the outcome of the disputes about how humans are "systematically programmed," variation in the "inclination toward questionable suppositions" is of psychological interest as a topic of study in its own right. The experiments discussed in this volume provide at least tentative indications that the "inclination toward questionable suppositions" has some degree of domain generality and that it is predicted by thinking dispositions that concern the epistemic and pragmatic goals of the individual and that are part of the reflective mind.

Johnson-Laird and Byrne (1993; *see* Johnson-Laird, 2006) articulate a view of rational thought that parses the competence/performance distinction much differently from that of Cohen (1981, 1982, 1986). It is a view that highlights the importance of the reflective mind and leaves room for individual differences in important components of cognition. At the heart of the rational competence that Johnson-Laird and Byrne (1993) attribute to humans is not perfect rationality but instead just one meta-principle: People are programmed to accept inferences as valid provided that they have constructed no mental model of the premises that contradict the inference. Inferences are categorized as false when a mental model is discovered that is contradictory. However, the search for contradictory models is "not governed by any systematic or comprehensive principles" (p. 178).

The key point in Johnson-Laird and Byrne's (1993) account is that once an individual constructs a mental model from the premises, once the individual draws a new conclusion from the model, and once the individual begins the search for an alternative model of the premises that contradicts the conclusion, the individual "lacks any systematic method to make this search for counter-examples" (p. 205). Here is where Johnson-Laird and Byrne's (1993) model could be modified to allow for the influence of thinking styles in ways that the impeccable competence view of Cohen (1981) does not. In this passage, Johnson-Laird and Byrne seem to be arguing that there are no systematic control features of the search process. But epistemically related thinking dispositions may in fact be reflecting just such control features. Individual differences in the extensiveness of the search for contradictory models could arise from a variety of cognitive factors that, although they may not be completely systematic, may be far from "adventitious"—factors such as dispositions toward premature closure, cognitive confidence, reflectivity, dispositions toward confirmation bias, and ideational generativity.

In Chapter 2, I mentioned the conjecture that many thinking disposition measures were good predictors of rational thought because they tapped the propensity toward decontextualization that commonly results when Type 1 processes are overridden by Type 2 processing. The decontextualizing requirement of many heuristics and biases tasks is a feature that is emphasized by many *critics* of that literature who, nevertheless, fail to see it as implying a research program for differential psychology. For example, I have argued that to contextualize a problem is such a ubiquitous reasoning style of human beings that it is one of a very few so-called Fundamental Computational Biases of information processing (Stanovich, 2003, 2004). Thus, it is not surprising that many people respond incorrectly when attempting a psychological task that is explicitly designed to require a decontextualized reasoning style (contrary-to-fact syllogisms, argument evaluation, etc.). But recall the empirically demonstrated variability on all of these tasks. The fact that some people *do* give the decontextualized response means that at least some people have available a larger repertoire of reasoning styles (they can flexibly reason so as to override Fundamental Computational Biases if the situation requires).

Many Panglossian philosophers ignore this variability (*see* Stanovich, 1999, for a fuller discussion of this tendency). For example, Rescher (1988) defends responses that exhibit the gambler's fallacy on the grounds that people assume a model of saturation that is valid in other domains (e.g., food ingestion, sleep) and that "the issue may well be one of a mistaken factual supposition rather than one of fallacious reasoning" (pp. 195–196). His argument stresses the enthymematic character of much human reasoning. But, again, the fact remains that many people do *not* reason enthymematically in this or other reasoning problems and instead give the normative response, and this means that at least some people have available a larger repertoire of reasoning styles (they can flexibly reason enthymematically and nonenthymematically as the task requires). Or, at the very least, it means that certain people are more easily shifted out of their natural enthymematic reasoning style.

My argument here rests on two empirical findings discussed extensively in this volume: *(1)* there is substantial variance in responding on most rational thinking tasks; *(2)* thinking disposition measures can predict that variance even after cognitive ability has been controlled. Another way of framing my argument is in terms of Dennett's (1987) so-called "intentional stance," which he marries to an assumption of idealized rationality. Dennett (1988) argues that we use the intentional stance for humans and dogs but not for lecterns because for the latter "there is no predictive leverage gained by adopting the intentional stance" (p. 496). However, in several experiments discussed in this volume, it has been shown that there is additional predictive leverage to be gained by relaxing the idealized rationality assumption of Dennett's (1987, 1988) intentional stance and by positing measurable and systematic variation in intentional-level psychologies (i.e., in the reflective mind). Knowledge about such individual differences in people's intentional-level psychologies can be used to predict variance in the normative/descriptive gap displayed on many reasoning tasks. Consistent with the Meliorist conclusion that there can be individual differences in human rationality, the results show that there is variability in reasoning that cannot be accommodated within a model of perfect rational competence operating in the presence of performance errors and computational limitations.

The idea that humans have computational limitations that keep them from being fully rational has spawned another position in the Great Rationality Debate that Stanovich (1999) termed *the Apologist position*.

Like the Meliorist, the Apologist accepts the empirical reality and non-spuriousness of normative/descriptive gaps, but the Apologist is much more hesitant to term them instances of irrationality. This is because the Apologist takes very seriously the stricture that to characterize a suboptimal behavior as irrational, it must be the case that the normative model is computable by the individual. If there are computational limitations affecting task performance, then the normative model may not be prescriptive, at least for individuals of low algorithmic capacity. Prescriptive models are usually viewed as specifying how processes of belief formation and decision making should be carried out, given the limitations of the human cognitive apparatus and the situational constraints (e.g., time pressure) with which the decision maker must deal (Baron, 2008). From the Apologist's perspective, the descriptive model is quite close to the prescriptive model and the descriptive/normative gap is attributed to a computational limitation. Although the Apologist admits that performance is suboptimal from the standpoint of the normative model, it is not irrational because there is no prescriptive/descriptive gap.

However, as demonstrated in Chapter 7, the Apologist stratagem will not work for all of the irrational tendencies that have been uncovered in the heuristics and biases literature. First, some cognitive biases are completely independent of intelligence (algorithmic capacity)—for example, myside bias. Others are, in fact, correlated with cognitive capacity, but the magnitude of the correlations (0.25–0.45) leaves ample opportunity for rational thinking and cognitive ability to dissociate, so that there will be plenty of people with high cognitive ability thinking irrationally, and plenty with modest cognitive abilities who are responding normatively. Finally, there is the finding that there is reliable variance in rational thinking after cognitive ability is controlled and that the reliable variance is associated with thinking dispositions in theoretically predictable ways. These thinking dispositions reflect control features of the reflective mind that can lead to responses that are more or less rational. They are one of the main sources of the individual differences in rational thought that I have been exploring in this volume. Such thinking dispositions vary systematically from individual to individual and are the source of what Meliorists consider the variance in the irrationalities in human cognition. Unlike the Panglossian, who assumes uniform rationality, the Meliorist is accepting of variability in rational thought.

Skepticism About Mindware-Caused Irrationalities

In the Great Rationality Debate, there is considerable contention surrounding one particular type of human irrationality—that caused by contaminated mindware. This aspect of the rationality debate borders on the disputes in the memetics literature about the possibility of truly nonfunctional mindware (Blackmore, 1999, 2005; Dawkins, 1993; Dennett, 1991, 2006; Distin, 2005; Hull, 2000; Stanovich, 2004). I will argue that those who dispute the idea of irrationality causing contaminated mindware are making what I term a *grain-size error*. A grain-size error occurs when theorists focus on mindware content that is too broad and complex. For example, Dawkins (1993) and Blackmore (2000) have famously claimed that most religions are essentially "copy-me" memeplexes, "backed up with threats, promises, and ways of preventing their claims from being tested" (Blackmore, 2000, pp. 35–36). Their arguments have spawned a series of rebuttals by investigators who study the psychology of religion (Atran, 2002; Barrett, 2004; Bering, 2006; Bloom, 2004; Boyer, 2001, 2003; Wilson, 2002). These critics of the Dawkins/Blackmore argument differ among themselves. Some believe that religion is an evolved adaptation. Others think it is a byproduct of a series of cognitive modules that evolved for other purposes (agent detection, theory of mind, etc.). All of them see the ubiquitous presence of religious belief as grounded in biology. Regardless of whether the theorist takes an adaptationist or a byproduct stance toward religion, they oppose the Dawkins/Blackmore position that religion is a meme virus—a "copy-me" instruction that not only is not functional for the human host but may actually be deleterious.

I would argue that *all* of these theorists—Dawkins and Blackmore as well as their critics—are focused on the wrong grain-size. The debate should not be about whether *religion* itself is contaminated mindware but about the specific content that tends to go into the "slots" created by the confluence of cognitive modules that support religion, according to some theorists (*see* Atran, 2002; Bloom, 2004; Boyer, 2001; Hood, 2009). As one commentator on these debates stated, "the bottom line, according to byproduct theorists, is that children are born with a tendency to believe in omniscience, invisible minds, immaterial souls—and then they grow up in cultures that fill their minds, hard-wired for belief, with specifics" (p. 8, Henig, 2007). The model here is analogous to those of language. Memetics can accept much of this model without dispute. The fundamental insight behind my grain-size argument is simply that the "specifics" matter. It matters whether the content going into the hard-wired "slots" serves the hosts interest (for indeed, it is well-accepted that vehicle interests can diverge from replicator interests; *see* Dawkins, 1982; Stanovich, 2004). In the case of religion, it matters whether the "specifics" are slaughtering infidels or whether the specifics are ministering to the poor in Calcutta. The specifics that go into the slots can be more or less rational for the individual.

Atran (2002), for example, produces an example of the grain-size error in making the argument that cultural knowledge is constrained. He describes a study of people interpreting a cartoon with a group of fish together and a single outlier fish on the outside of the group. Chinese participants interpret the lone fish as an outcast, whereas Americans interpret the lone fish as more daring and intelligent. Atran (2002) acknowledges that it seems that "such robust and systematic cultural differences actually reinforce the memeticist's claim" (p. 258). However, Atran (2002), aligning himself with the evolutionary psychologist's emphasis on evoked rather than transmitted culture, chooses to emphasize the cultural *constraints* in the situation rather than the variability. He calls on us to notice that "members of neither cultural group interpret the animated fish cartoon simply as changing patterns of illumination, as a lifeless screen, as a moving cluster and point, as a temporal sequence of clusters and point . . .. or any of the infinitely many other logically possible interpretations of the scene observed" (p. 258).

These are constraints surely, but I would argue that they are so loose that they demarcate only a belief structure of large grain size. More to the point is to ask whether these constraints limit the belief structures demarcated to only fitness-increasing or vehicle-enhancing beliefs. If not, then these biological constraints are at a large enough grain size that they leave untouched the fundamental memetic insight: that a belief may spread without necessarily being true or helping the human being who holds the belief in any way.

Cosmides and Tooby (1994), in an essay published in an economics journal to introduce economists to evolutionary psychology, provide a classic example of the grain-size problem. In a series of points laid out like a series of axioms, they argue that because "natural selection built the decision-making machinery in human minds" (p. 328) and because "this set of cognitive devices generates all economic behavior", "therefore . . . the design features of these devices define and constitute the human universal principles that guide economic decision making" (p. 328).

These postulates lead Cosmides and Tooby (1994) to the grandiose claim that "evolutionary psychology should be able to supply a list of human universal preferences, and of the procedures by which additional preferences are acquired or reordered" (p. 331). But to the extent that the claim is true, it is true only because the grain size of the predictions will be all wrong. The economics literature is not full of studies debating whether humans who are dying of thirst prefer water or shelter or whether men prefer 23-year-old females for mates rather than 75-year-old females. Instead, the literature is full of studies trying to determine the rationale for such fine-grained judgments as, for example, whether a poorly designed briefcase produced by an athletic shoe company will adversely affect the family brand name (Ahluwalia & Gurhan-Canli, 2000). Economists and psychologists are not debating the reasons for preferences among basic biological needs. Instead, they are debating the reasons for fine-grained preferences among highly symbolic products. Even after we grant evolutionary assumptions such as people using clothes purchases for some type of modern dominance or sexual display, we have not progressed very far in explaining how brand names wax and wane in the fashion world, how price-elastic such purchases will be, and/or what kind of substitutability there will be among these types of goods. The predictions that we can make from the postulates of evolutionary psychology are at too gross a level to be useful. As is the case with religion, all of the action is at the lower level of content specifics—precisely the area where memetic insights might be most useful.

Even a theorist as nuanced as Aunger (2000) makes a version of the grain-size error. He argues

"good indirect evidence for memes would consist of establishing that there is an independent dynamic to cultural change which cannot be assigned to the goal-directed activity of people. . . . This is why memes are commonly invoked to explain maladaptive cultural traits, why advocates often gravitate toward examples of memes which seem 'irrational' for individuals. . ... The problem is that—except for the odd trait here and there—culture is overwhelmingly adaptive for people, allowing our species to dominate our home planet in fairly spectacular fashion." (p. 208)

Yes, it is true that culture has allowed our species to dominate our home planet in a fairly spectacular fashion. But it is not the adaptiveness or self-replicating nature of culture *per se* that we are debating in the Great Rationality Debate—it is the *specific* cultural contents and whether they are nonfunctional for their human host (and thus are rightly classified as contaminated mindware). Aunger (2000) implicitly acknowledges this with his "odd trait here and there" comment (although I disagree with his quantitative assessment).

The debate over memes has indeed been contentious. There is, in fact, much hostility directed toward the meme concept. Certainly some of the professional hostility stems from territorial encroachment. Memetic theorists have come in with a new language and colonized areas previously occupied by disciplines that had claimed the study of cultural evolution for themselves such as anthropology and sociology. Aunger's quote here, in alluding to issues of rationality, reveals another source of hostility. Controversies over how to conceive human rationality—and over the existence of human irrationality—have loomed large in many academic disciplines, not restricted to economics, philosophy, psychology, and legal studies. Many important theories in these disciplines are committed to understanding humans from the standpoint of assumptions of optimality, rationality, and functionality. There are strong Panglossian default values built into the language of many of these disciplines. Panglossian theorists in these disciplines have also benefited from the default values built into folk language. For example, the term *belief*, both in folk language and in many areas of psychology, suggests something reflectively chosen or at least something that is characterized by an active commitment by the person's "true self." The very term *belief* directs attention away from the memetic insight—that you may be holding beliefs that are not true and that are not serving your goals in any way.

In any case, theorists using a grain size that is too large play into the hands of Panglossians who wish to deny the possibility of contaminated mindware. Of course, culture itself is functional. It is probably the case that religion itself has some functionality. But to move from these banalities to the assumption that there cannot be any *component* of these huge memeplexes that leads to irrational behavior is beyond what either evolutionary psychology or cultural anthropology has demonstrated.

9

The Social Implications of Separating the Concepts of Intelligence and Rationality

In psychology and among the lay public alike, assessments of intelligence and tests of cognitive ability are taken to be the sine qua non of good thinking. Of course, adhering to the strictures of instrumental and epistemic rationality is a prime example of "good thinking." Yet this type of good thinking appears to be surprisingly independent of intelligence. Of course, the extent to which it is surprising depends on our conceptualization of intelligence. Some conceptualizations of intelligence (*see* Matthews et al., 2002; Neisser et al., 1996; Sternberg & Detterman, 1986) define it as, at least in part, the ability to adapt to one's environment. But surely the tendency to make judicious decisions that serve one's goals is part of what we mean by adaptation to the environment. Such a definition conflates rationality and intelligence and makes it impossible for the two to dissociate. Yet the results just reviewed in Chapters 7 and 8 indicate considerable dissociation. So what is happening here?

Broad Versus Narrow Concepts of Intelligence

What is happening here is that we are bumping up against an old controversy in the study of cognitive ability—the distinction between broad and narrow theories of intelligence[1]. Broad theories include aspects of functioning that are captured by the vernacular term *intelligence* (adaptation to the environment, showing wisdom and creativity, etc.), whether or not these aspects are actually measured by existing tests of intelligence. Narrow theories, in contrast, confine the concept of intelligence to the

---

1 The distinction between broad and narrow theories of intelligence is discussed in a variety of sources (Baron, 1985; Gardner, 1983, 1999; Perkins, 1995, 2002; Stanovich, 2009b; Sternberg, 1997a, 1997b, 2000, 2003; Sternberg & Detterman, 1986; Sternberg & Kaufman, 1998).

set of mental abilities actually tested on extant IQ tests. Narrow theories adopt the operationalization of the term that is used in psychometric studies of intelligence, neurophysiological studies using brain imaging, and studies of brain disorder. This definition involves a statistical abstraction from performance on established tests and cognitive ability indicators. It yields a scientific concept of general intelligence usually symbolized by g or, in cases where the CHC (Carroll/Horn/Cattell) theory is adopted, fluid intelligence (Gf), crystallized intelligence (Gc), and other broad factors.

The finding of a considerable dissociation between intelligence and performance on heuristics and biases tasks would be surprising under two of three possible views of the rationality/intelligence relationship. Under a broad view of intelligence the findings are surprising because rationality is encompassed by intelligence and thus the two things are conceptually precluded from dissociating. The findings would also be surprising under a narrow concept of intelligence and an expectation of a strong positive manifold among adaptive thinking tendencies such as intelligence and rationality. It is only a narrow view of intelligence (restricted to what the tests actually measure) *without* the assumption that intelligence guarantees rationality (either causally or associatively) that can accommodate the results presented in the last two chapters.

In fact, the tripartite model of mind presented in Figure 2–1 represents exactly this third case. It provides a framework for understanding why intelligence sometimes dissociates from thinking biases related to rationality. In the view presented in this book, rationality is a more encompassing construct than intelligence. Rationality is an organismic-level concept. It concerns the actions of an entity in its environment that serve its goals. It is indexed by thinking dispositions tapping individual differences in the reflective mind as well as fluid intelligence, which taps individual differences in the algorithmic mind—especially the ability to sustain cognitive decoupling. By differentiating Type 2 processing into an algorithmic and reflective level of processing, it becomes easier to see that extant intelligence tests give short shrift to the reflective level of processing.

The findings reported here highlight the importance of recognizing rational thinking skills because they are not tapped by using intelligence tests as a proxy. In fact, broad theories of intelligence have implicitly

undervalued rational thinking by encompassing such skills under definitions of intelligence. The problem with such a stance is that it ignores
the fact that none of the most well-known intelligence tests measure
rational thinking in any way. In another book (Stanovich, 2009b) I have
argued that it is simply perverse for psychologists to adopt a definition
of intelligence that is not at all reflected in what is measured by the tests
most well-known to the public.

Such broad views of intelligence cause confusion, even among
leading intelligence theorists themselves. An example of the confusion
caused by broad definitions is illustrated in discussions of the so-called
"Flynn effect" in the study of intelligence. Flynn (1984, 1987; *see also*
Neisser, 1998) systematically documented what some restandardizations
of IQ tests had merely suggested—that IQs were rising over time. Overall
IQs seem to have risen about 3 points per decade since about 1930. The
gains are larger for Gf than for Gc. Neisser (1998) edited a book on
explanations for the Flynn effect (nutrition, urbanization, schooling,
television, preschool home environment, etc.). Interestingly, Flynn
(1998) himself favored none of these explanations. Instead, he believed
that the intelligence gains were in some sense not "real." In short, he
argued that there have been IQ gains but not intelligence gains, according to his definition. As evidence for his position, he pointed to the lack
of cultural flowering that he feels would result from a true intelligence
increase. For him, contrary trends are indicated by the fact that "the
number of inventions patented in fact showed a sharp decline over the
last generation" (p. 35) and that Who's Who books of eminent scientists
are not bursting at the seams.

But under a narrow definition of intelligence—in terms of what
cognitive ability tests actually measure—there is no puzzle in the fact
that rising IQs are not associated with the type of cultural achievements
mentioned by Flynn. The tests do not measure rationality or creativity—
things that might really lead to a cultural explosion of the type that Flynn
is looking for. Flynn has tacitly adopted some sort of environmental
adaptation definition of intelligence that departs from what the tests
actually measure. Thus, what some see as a paradox created by the Flynn
effect (that IQ gains over the past generation have not been paralleled
by concomitant societal achievements) is no paradox at all if we maintain
a narrow definition of intelligence. It is only puzzling because we find it

hard to keep in mind that although our folk concept of intelligence might include adaptation to the environment, the tests on which the gains have been shown do not measure that at all. The tests measure an important decoupling ability that is a critical mental skill, but one that, as I have shown in this book and elsewhere (Stanovich, 2004, 2009b), falls short of what is needed for fully rational thought and behavior.

My own view of the Flynn effect is that schooling and modernity in general have increased decontextualizing thinking styles and also the use of language as a decoupling tool (Evans & Over, 2004). These mechanisms represent mindware (like rehearsal strategies in short-term memory) that can increase algorithmic-level functioning—particularly the decoupling operation by making it less demanding of capacity and unnatural. Schooler (1998) explores a similar hypothesis in the Neisser volume (*see also* Greenfield, 1998; Williams, 1998). Interestingly, in a recent book, Flynn (2007) has altered his earlier position and now views the IQ gains as real—the result of the spread of scientific thinking making hypothetical thought more habitual.

Adopting a narrow view of intelligence—restricting it to what the tests actually measure—will make it easier emphasize cognitive processes and skills that go beyond the mechanisms of the algorithmic mind. These additional processes and skills will be separately named and measured and not merely subsumed under an imperialistic concept of intelligence—an imperialistic conception that is ultimately dishonest in not measuring the mechanisms within its proposed construct.

Intelligence Imperialism

In commenting on the history of his multiple intelligences theory, Howard Gardner relates that he considered other terms, such as skills or capacities, but then realized "that each of these words harbored pitfalls, I finally elected to take the bold step of appropriating a word from psychology and stretching it in new ways.... . I was proposing an expansion of the term intelligence so that it would encompass many capacities that had been considered outside its scope" (pp. 33, 34, 1999). Similarly, Robert Sternberg argues that "the time perhaps has come to expand our notion and everyone's notion of what it means to be intelligent" (p. 69, 2003).

Clearly one of the goals here is to emphasize that there are aspects of cognitive life that are important outside of narrow intelligence as measured by IQ tests. This is a goal that I share with many broad theorists.

However, it is important to note that the issue should not be framed dichotomously as broad theories of intelligence versus narrow theories. This is because, significantly, broad theorists do not agree among themselves. For example, Gardner (1999) warns that "Sternberg and I agree more on our criticism of standard intelligence theory than on the direction that new theoretical work should follow" (p. 101). Similarly, Gardner (1999) rejects the concepts of creative intelligence, moral intelligence, and emotional intelligence—types of "intelligences" that are quite popular with some other broad theorists. He goes on to warn that "we cannot hijack the word intelligence so that it becomes all things to all people—the psychometric equivalent of the Holy Grail" (p. 210). But, in fact, if we concatenate all of the broad theories that have been proposed by various theorists—with all of their different "intelligences"—under the umbrella term *intelligence*, we will have encompassed virtually all of mental life. Intelligence will be "everything the brain does"—a vacuous concept.

I do not see why everything in human nature, cognitively speaking, has to have the label intelligence, particularly when there are readily existing labels (both scientific labels and folk labels) for some of those things (rationality, creativity, wisdom, critical thinking, open-minded thinking, reflectivity, sensitivity to evidence). In fact, I feel that if we continue this tendency to label every positive cognitive trait with the term *intelligence*, that will just add to the inappropriate societal deification of IQ tests that Sternberg, Gardner, and I are united in deploring. Consider a thought experiment: Imagine that someone objected to the emphasis given to horsepower (engine power) when evaluating automobiles. They feel that horsepower looms too large in people's thinking. In an attempt to de-emphasize horsepower, they then begin to term the other features of the car things like "braking horsepower" and "cornering horsepower" and "comfort horsepower." Would such a strategy serve to make people less likely to look to engine power as an indicator of the "overall quality" of a car? I think not. I think it would instead serve to make more salient just the feature that the person wished to de-emphasize. Just as calling "all good car things" horsepower would serve to emphasize engine power, I would argue that calling "all good cognitive things" intelligence will contribute to the deification of IQ test scores[2].

Such a strategy will impede educational efforts to foster other cognitive characteristics. For example, critical thinking skills vanish under broad definitions of intelligence. All critical thinking or rationality assessments become part of intelligence if the latter is conceptualized broadly. And again, intelligence test producers gain from these broad definitions because people will continue to associate the broad concept of intelligence with these tests. How could they not? The tests carry the label "intelligence," and the producers of the tests are not eager to discourage the association with broad theories. For example, it took real chutzpah for David Wechsler to define intelligence in his book as "the aggregate or global capacity of the individual to act purposefully, to think rationally and to deal effectively with his environment" (p. 7, 1958), despite authoring an IQ test with his name on it that measured no such thing!

Broad views of intelligence that spread the term over a variety of other constructs are in part motivated by a desire to tame the valuation and prestige of IQ tests. The strategy seems to be to downplay the importance of IQ tests by broadening the definition of intelligence to make them only a small part of this larger concept—a strategy of dilution. But stretching the intelligence concept by dumping into it other positively valued things will not succeed in breaking the link with IQ tests for two reasons. The first reason is that the effects of the 100-year history of associating IQ tests with the concept intelligence are not going to be easily attenuated. Second, even in the expanded concept of the broad view, the IQ test component remains the easiest component to measure—and the most measurable component will always end up

---

2 Broad theorists might argue that there are higher correlations among the features of automobiles than there are among the intelligences they propose. I think the data on this conjecture is not in yet (Klein, 1997; Willingham, 2004), and even if a quantitative difference were obtained, I doubt that it would substantially reduce the force of the thought experiment. The point is that when Gardner (1999) states "I put forth the intelligences as a new definition of human nature, cognitively speaking" (p. 44), he is adding positive valence to the term intelligence and to its closest associates: IQ tests and scores.

dominating all other components, no matter how broad or encompassing the concept.

If I am right, then the strategy of the broad theorists ends up giving us the worst of all worlds—an intelligence concept more prestigious than ever (because all kinds of other good things have now been associated with it) and the value of IQ tests further inflated through its association with the new broadened view of intelligence! More importantly, short shrift is given to the concept of rationality because it is not separately named (but instead conflated with and lost within the intelligence concept). There is no imperative to actually assess rationality, because its semantic space has been gobbled up by the broadened view of intelligence. It will be even harder than it already is to stress that IQ -tests do not measure rational thinking. Although most people recognize that IQ tests do not encompass all of the important mental faculties, we often act (and talk) as if we have forgotten this fact. Where else does our surprise at smart people doing foolish things come from if not from the implicit assumption that rationality and intelligence should go together? Adopting a narrow view of intelligence (as I do in this book) will help to attenuate our surprise at this phenomenon and to create conceptual space in which we can value other abilities—specifically, the ability to form rational beliefs and to take rational action.

Professional psychologists will immediately recognize the relation of my stance to E. G. Boring's infamous dictum, and this recognition may cause some of them to balk at my proposal. Boring's dictum was that we should define intelligence as what the intelligence tests measure. However, what made Boring's suggestion objectionable was that neither he nor anyone else at the time (1923) knew what the tests measured. Because of this, Boring's definition of intelligence was truly circular. The situation now is totally different. We now know—from the standpoint of information processing and cognitive neuroscience—what the tests measure.

Unlike some critics of the traditional intelligence concept, I think there has been some justification in the inertia of the psychometric establishment regarding changes in IQ tests and in the (narrow) intelligence concept itself. Traditional intelligence research is a progressive research program in the sense that philosophers of science use that term. There is every indication that work in the traditional paradigm is carving nature at its joints. First, the field has a consensus model in the form of the CHC theory (Carroll, 1993). Much work has gone into uncovering the cognitive subcomponents of fluid intelligence. We now know that there is substantial overlap in the variance in Gf and the variance in measures of working memory capacity. The overlap is not 100%, but regression weights in structural equation models are on the order of 0.7 to 0.8 (Kane, Hambrick, & Conway, 2005). Importantly, the computational features of working memory have also been identified during the same period. The most critical insight has been that the central cognitive function tapped by working memory tasks is cognitive decoupling—the ability to manipulate secondary representations that do not track the world in one-to-one fashion as do primary representations.

Cognitive decoupling appears to be the central cognitive operation accounting for individual differences in Gf, and because of its role in simulation and hypothetical thinking, cognitive decoupling is a crucial mental capacity. Thus, traditional intelligence tests converge on something important in mental life. They represent the fruits of a scientific research program that is progressively carving nature at an appropriate and important joint. This conclusion is often obscured in introductory presentations of intelligence research to beginning students. Introductory psychology textbooks often present to students the broad versus narrow theory of intelligence controversy—usually with a bias toward the former, because it is easier to present nontechnically. Later in the same chapter, the textbook will often make reference to "how difficult it is to measure something as complex as intelligence." But, of course, there is a bias being displayed here. Intelligence is *not* difficult to measure on the narrow view. It is the broad view that causes the measurement problems. In addition to tests, we also have laboratory measures that index Gf and Gc pretty precisely in terms of information processing capabilities. It is a point in favor of the narrow concept that we have a reasonably stable construct of it and ways to reliably measure it.

Although I clearly do not wish to minimize the importance of cognitive decoupling, in this book I have emphasized that measuring it alone will provide an incomplete characterization of cognitive functioning. Decoupling operations are crucially important in hypothetical reasoning (Evans, 2007a). Nevertheless, cognitive decoupling as measured on these tests is still a property of the algorithmic mind that is assessed under maximal, rather than typical, conditions. Such measures do not assess how *typical* it is for a person to engage in decoupling operations. They do not assess the propensity of the reflective mind to use such decoupling abilities. They do not assess the *tendency* to engage in hypothetical thinking to aid problem solving. The *ability* to sustain cognitive decoupling does not guarantee rationality of behavior or thought. When we measure Gf, we measure a critical aspect of the engine of the brain but not the skill of the driver.

Intelligence Misidentified as Adaptation and the Deification of Intelligence

One type of broad definition of intelligence that has strong imperialist tendencies is represented by those definitions that emphasize intelligence as "adaptation to the environment," like that of Wechsler quoted previously. Such definitions appropriate large areas of instrumental rationality into the definition of intelligence. To define intelligence as adaptation to the environment when the best known tests of the construct do not assess any such thing creates tremendous potential for confusion. Such confusion was apparent in discussions of the Flynn effect in the study of intelligence discussed earlier in this chapter. That the Flynn effect is thought to present a puzzle shows how difficult it is not to deify intelligence by broadening the definition of it beyond what the tests measure.

Such deification of intelligence can have a truly perverse moral consequence that we often fail to recognize—the denigration of those who score low on conventional IQ tests. Such denigration goes back to the very beginnings of psychometrics as an enterprise. Sir Francis Galton would hardly concede that those low in IQ could feel pain:

> "The discriminative facility of idiots is curiously low; they hardly distinguish between heat and cold, and their sense of pain is so obtuse that some of the more idiotic seem hardly to know what it is. In their dull lives, such pain as can be excited in them may literally be accepted with a welcome surprise." (p. 28, 1883).

There is a historical tendency, as Robert Sternberg (2003) has noted, to "conflate scores on tests of intelligence with some kind of personal value" (p. 13). This tendency appears in modern life in many guises.

As Sternberg (2003) suggests, intelligence has come to signify something like one's personal essence—some indication of personal worth. The deification of IQ and the denigration of low intelligence are now so complete that people would rather have a high IQ than almost any other physical or mental quality. Note, for example, how the diagnosis of mental retardation has been reduced by almost half in the last three to four decades, accompanied by the explosion of the incidence of disabilities whose definitions—particularly those definitions aimed at parents— stress the presence of normal IQ[3] (e.g., learning disabilities, ADHD, Asperger's Syndrome). This shift is in part a function of social changes, consumerism infecting diagnostic categories, and ascertainment biases introduced by schools, clinicians, and parents. Many parents, for example, are much more accepting of diagnostic categories that do not have "low IQ" attached. But many people seem not to have appreciated an ironic implication of accepting a broad definition of intelligence. If a broad definition is accepted, particularly one that emphasizes the "adaptation to the environment" criterion, then all of the categories of disability that have exploded in recent years will have to be regarded in a new light. Many cases of emotional disorders, behavioral disorders, and ADHD would also now represent cases of low intelligence, because the primary features of these disabilities is that they represent poor adaptations to the environment.

It is fascinating to speculate about whether some of these categories of disability would have become so popular had the broad theorists won the day several decades ago. Imagine that the behavior of an ADHD child was routinely termed "low intelligence" in folk psychology.

---

3 Issues surrounding issues of prevalence can be complex (*see* Barbaresi et al., 2005; Friend, 2005; Gernsbacher, Dawson, & Goldsmith, 2005; Gordon, Lewandowski, & Keiser, 1999; Kelman & Lester, 1997; Lilienfeld & Arkowitz, 2007; Parsell, 2004). I would, however, insert a couple of additional caveats here. First, studies have indicated that ADHD is, in fact, associated with somewhat lower than normal intelligence (Barkley, 1998), but this empirical finding is not stressed at all on websites and informational packets directed to parents. Second, the tendency for information directed to the public to stress the high intelligence of individuals with learning disabilities is scientifically unjustified, because if learning disabilities were properly diagnosed, they would be just as prevalent in individuals with low IQs as in individuals with high IQs (Stanovich, 2005; Stuebing et al., 2009; Stuebing et al., 2002).

A response to the thought experiment might be that we would still notice "some difference" between an ADHD child (or even an emotionally disturbed child) and a child with intellectual disability. But it is important to recognize the implication of this response. Such a response means that we can notice and label Gf in folk psychology. As indicated earlier in this chapter, scientific evidence does converge on the conclusion that conventional IQ tests pick out a class of mental operations of considerable importance. The problem is just that folk psychology values those mental operations—and the tests used to measure them—too much. Gf is a mechanism, not a soul.

Strategies for Cutting Intelligence Down to Size

My strategy for taming the intelligence concept is different than that of the broad theorists. I have argued that we should adopt a narrow view of intelligence (it is what the tests measure) and restrict intelligence to that. We can tame intelligence in folk psychology by pointing out that there are legitimate scientific terms for the other valued parts of mentality and that some of these are measurable. This strategy uses to its advantage a fact of life that many critics of IQ test have lamented—that intelligence tests are not going to change any time soon. The tests have the label *intelligence*, and it is a mistake to ignore this fact.

My strategy is to open up some space for rationality in the lexicon of the mental and, in doing so, tame the intelligence concept. Thus, it is important to prevent intelligence from absorbing the concept of rationality by confining the former concept to what the tests actually measure—a practice having the not inconsiderable advantage of getting usage in line with the real world of measurement and testing. We have coherent and well-operationalized concepts of rational action and belief formation. We have a coherent and well-operationalized concept of intelligence, narrowly defined. No scientific purpose is served by fusing these concepts, because they are very different. To the contrary, scientific progress is made by *differentiating* concepts.

My argument is, essentially, that we would value IQ tests less if we would take care to label the things they do not assess (rationality) and not let the term *intelligence* incorporate those other things. I think that folk psychology does now differentiate rationality and intelligence somewhat but that folk psychology could be reformed to do this even more.

My feeling that folk psychology could be reformed to further mark the intelligence/rationality distinction is based on a study I conducted with my longtime colleague Richard West some years ago (*see* Chapter 4 in Stanovich, 2009b). We had subjects write, in a quite open-ended manner (and counterbalanced, of course), about what they thought that intelligence was, what they thought rationality was, and what they thought about the relationship between the two. Theories of intelligence were considerably less broad when the subjects had previously been asked to give their folk theories of rationality. Their responses seemed to indicate that folk psychology does distinguish between intelligence and rationality. Of course, this might have been more true in our experiment because previous questions drew attention to the concept of rationality and perhaps suggested the possibility of separating it from intelligence. But this is just my point: When they were given the term *rationality* (which they do not tend to think of spontaneously), our subjects had no trouble differentiating rationality from intelligence. In fact, in their responses they often described the possibility of intelligent people acting irrationally.

Referring to the title of this section of the chapter, we need to cut down to size our conceptualization of intelligence. We need to control the tendency to incorporate all important mental qualities into it or to append it to every valued mental quality that we wish to praise or highlight. Instead, we should conceptualize intelligence narrowly as what the tests measure. By constricting the term intelligence, we will create conceptual space for other qualities (rational thinking) that are currently given short shrift because they are not measured on IQ tests. Our culture's fixation on the intelligence concept has obscured other mental qualities that society needs at least as much. This is the case because, as we saw in Chapters 7 and 8, intelligence is no inoculation against irrational thought and behavior.

Society's Selection Mechanisms

The ability or inability to think rationally profoundly affects people's lives. Yet we fail to teach the tools of rational thinking in schools and refuse to focus our attention on them as a society. Instead, we keep using intelligence proxies as selection devices in a range of educational institutions from exclusive preschools to graduate schools. Corporations and the military are likewise excessively focused on IQ measures. Consider the example of Ivy League universities in the United States. These institutions are selecting society's future elite. What societal goals are served by the selection mechanisms (e.g., SAT tests) that they use? Social critics have argued that the tests serve only to maintain an economic elite. But the social critics seem to have missed a golden opportunity to critique current selection mechanisms by failing to ask the question "Why select for intelligence only and ignore rationality completely?"

In short, we have been valuing only the algorithmic mind and not the reflective mind. This is in part the result of historical accident. We had measures of algorithmic-level processing efficiency long before we had measures of rational thought and the operation of the reflective mind. The dominance and ubiquitousness of early IQ tests served to divert attention from any aspect of cognition except algorithmic-level efficiency. And then, because of this historical accident, we have been trying to back out of this mistake (overvaluing the algorithmic part of the mind) ever since.

The lavish attention devoted to intelligence (raising it, praising it, worrying when it is low, etc.) seems wasteful in light of the fact that we choose to virtually ignore another set of mental skills with just as much social consequence—rational thinking mindware and procedures. Popular books tell parents how to raise more intelligent children, educational psychology textbooks discuss the raising of students' intelligence, and we feel reassured when hearing that a particular disability does not impair intelligence. There is no corresponding concern on the part of parents that their children grow into rational beings, no corresponding concern on the part of schools that their students reason judiciously, and no corresponding recognition that intelligence is useless to a child unable to adapt to the world.

I simply do not think that society has weighed the consequences of its failure to focus on irrationality as a real social problem. Because of inadequately developed rational thinking abilities—because of the processing biases and mindware problems discussed in this book—physicians choose less effective medical treatments; people fail to accurately assess risks in their environment; information is misused in legal proceedings; millions of dollars are spent on unneeded projects by government and private industry; parents fail to vaccinate their children; unnecessary surgery is performed; animals are hunted to extinction; billions of dollars are wasted on fraudulent medical remedies; and costly financial misjudgments are made[4]. Distorted processes of belief formation are also implicated in various forms of ethnocentric, racist, sexist, and homophobic hatred.

It is thus clear that widespread societal effects result from inadequately developed rational thinking dispositions and knowledge. In the modern world, the impact of localized irrational thoughts and decisions can be propagated and magnified through globalized information technologies, thus affecting large numbers of people. That is, you may be affected by the irrational thinking of others even if you do not take irrational actions yourself. This is why, for example, the spread of pseudoscientific beliefs is everyone's concern. For example, police departments hire psychics to help with investigations, although research has shown that their use is not efficacious. Jurors have been caught making their decisions based on astrology. Major banks and several Fortune 500 companies employ graphologists for personnel decisions, although evidence indicates that graphology is useless.

Given the social consequences of rational versus irrational thinking, the practical relevance of this domain of skills cannot be questioned. Why, then, do the selection mechanisms used by society tap only algorithmic-level cognitive capacities and ignore rationality? It makes little sense to test for the narrow concept of intelligence and then confer rewards as if someone had been vetted on the larger, broader concept. There are moral and ethical issues raised by this sleight of hand that are almost never mentioned.

---

4 These examples are drawn from a variety of sources (Ariely, 2008; Arkes & Ayton, 1999; Baron, 1998, 2008; Bazerman, Baron, & Shonk, 2001; Camerer, 2000; Chapman & Elstein, 2000; Gigerenzer, 2002; Gilovich, 1991; Groopman, 2007; Hastie & Dawes, 2001; Hilton, 2003; Kahneman & Tversky, 2000; Lichtenstein & Slovic, 2006; Margolis, 1996; Myers, 2002; Reyna & Lloyd, 2006; Sunstein, 2002, 2005; Sunstein & Thaler, 2003; Taleb, 2001, 2007). On the study of hatred, *see* Sternberg (2005).

In fact, the issue of the differential privileging of some cognitive skills over others deserves more explicit public discussion. For example, some philosophers have found demonstrations of irrationality in the cognitive science literature implausible because, they say, the subjects— mostly college students—"will go on to become leading scientists, jurists, and civil servants" (Stich, 1990, p. 17). Actually, I do think that these philosophers have drawn our attention to something startling, but I derive a completely different moral from it. Most jurists and civil servants, in my experience, do seem to have adequate algorithmic-level cognitive capacities. However, despite this, their actions are often decidedly suboptimal. Their performance often fails to measure up, not because they lack working memory capacity or memory retrieval speed, but because their dispositions toward rationality are sometimes low. They may not lack intelligence, but they do lack some rational thinking skills.

The poor performance of the college students in the experiments in the literature on reasoning and decision making is not in the least paradoxical. The college students who fail laboratory tests of decision making and probabilistic reasoning are indeed the future jurists who, despite decent cognitive capacities, will reason badly. These students have never been specifically screened for rationality before entering the laboratory. And they will not be so assessed at any other time. If they are at elite state universities or elite private schools, they will continue up the academic, corporate, political, and economic ladders by passing SATs, GREs, placement tests, and performance simulations that primarily assess the algorithmic mind. Rationality assessment will never take place.

But what if it did? It is an interestingly open question, for example, whether race and social class differences on measures of rationality would be found to be as large as those displayed on intelligence tests. Suggestively, Sternberg (2004) finds that race and class differences on measures of practical intelligence (the aspect of his broad view of intelligence that is closest to rationality) are less than they are on IQ tests. The framework that I have outlined in this volume would at least predict that rankings of individuals on assessments of rational thinking would be different from rankings on intelligence. The reason is that rationality involves thinking dispositions of the reflective mind not assessed on intelligence tests.

Indeed, perhaps assessing rationality more explicitly is what is needed to draw more attention toward rational thinking skills and to highlight the limitations of what intelligence tests assess. At present, of course, there is no IQ-type test for rationality—that is, a test of one's rationality quotient (RQ). But it might at least help the debate to start talking about such a thing. I am not saying that an RQ test could be constructed tomorrow. Such instruments are not constructed on the back of an envelope. It would, of course, take an ETS-like effort, costing millions of dollars. But the point is that practically, in terms of the cognitive technology now in place, it is doable. Only issues of demand and cost prevent it.

Rather than debate the logistics of such an endeavor, the main point I wish to emphasize here is that there is nothing conceptually or theoretically preventing us from developing such a test. We know the types of thinking processes that would be assessed by such an instrument, and we have in hand prototypes of the kinds of tasks that would be used in the domains of both instrumental rationality and epistemic rationality. There is no limitation on constructing an RQ test that comes from the technology of ability surrounding rational thought. We will demonstrate this in Chapter 10 by laying out a framework for the assessment of rational thought.

IO

The Assessment of Rational Thought

(Keith E. Stanovich, Richard F. West, and Maggie E. Toplak)

To this point, we have established that rationality is a more encompassing construct than intelligence, narrowly defined. We have seen, from a conceptual standpoint, the components of rationality that IQ tests miss. What if we were to attempt to assess the larger concept—rational thought? As psychologists, we would turn to how the concept of rationality has been operationalized within cognitive science.

A Framework for the Assessment of Rational Thinking

Rationality is a multifarious concept—not a single mental quality. Cognitive scientists have developed ways to test both epistemic rationality and instrumental rationality as they were defined in Chapter 1. For example, psychologists have studied aspects of epistemic rationality such as the ability to avoid reasoning errors, including: the tendency toward overconfidence in knowledge judgments; the tendency to ignore base-rates; the tendency not to seek to falsify hypotheses; the tendency to try to explain chance events; the tendency toward self-serving personal judgments; the tendency to evaluate evidence with a myside bias; and the tendency to ignore the alternative hypothesis.

Additionally, psychologists have studied aspects of instrumental rationality such as the ability to avoid such reasoning errors as: the tendency to show inconsistent preferences because of framing effects; the tendency to show a default bias; the tendency to substitute affect for difficult evaluations; the tendency to overweight short-term rewards at the expense of long-term well-being; the tendency to have choices overly affected by vivid stimuli; and the tendency for decisions to be affected by irrelevant context.

In terms of concepts discussed in the tripartite model presented in this book, Figure 10–1 shows a conceptual structure for rational thought that could serve as a framework for assessment efforts. The first division in Figure 10–1 indicates that rational thought can be partitioned into fluid and crystallized components by analogy to the Gf and Gc of the

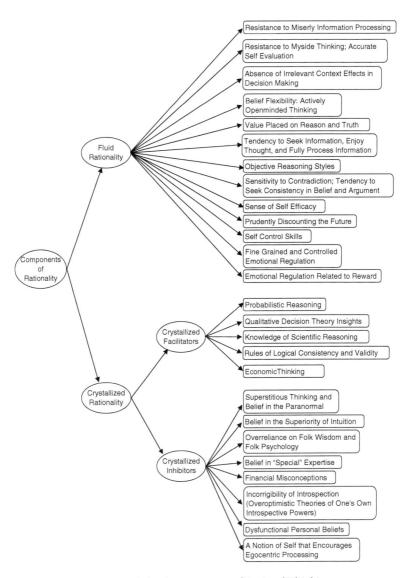

FIGURE 10.1.   A Framework for the Assessment of Rational Thinking.

Cattell/Horn/Carroll fluid-crystallized theory of intelligence (Carroll, 1993; Horn & Cattell, 1967). Fluid rationality encompasses the process part of rational thought—the thinking dispositions of the reflective mind that lead to rational thought and action. The top part of Figure 10–1 illustrates that unlike the case of fluid intelligence, fluid rationality is likely to be multifarious—composed of a variety of cognitive styles and dispositions. Some of these styles and dispositions will be related (e.g., actively open-minded thinking and objective reasoning styles) but others probably will not—research on the interrelationships among these thinking dispositions is in its infancy. As a multifarious concept, fluid rationality cannot be assessed with a single type of item in the manner that the homogeneous Raven Progressive Matrices, for example, provides a good measure of Gf.

Crystallized rationality is likewise multifarious. The bottom part of Figure 10–1 illustrates that the concept of crystallized rationality reflects the taxonomy that was developed in Chapter 6. That chapter illustrated how problems with rational thinking in the domain of mindware come in two types—mindware gaps and contaminated mindware. Mindware gaps occur because people lack declarative knowledge that can facilitate rational thought—they lack crystallized facilitators (as indicated in Fig. 10–1). A different type of mindware problem arises because not all mindware is helpful—either to attaining our goals (instrumental rationality) or to having accurate beliefs (epistemic rationality). It occurs when a person has acquired one (or more) of the crystallized inhibitors listed in Figure 10–1.

Figure 10–1 presents components of rationality that are of all three types—components of fluid rationality as well as some of the most common crystallized facilitators and crystallized inhibitors. Figure 10–1 should not be mistaken for the kind of list of "good thinking styles" that appears in textbooks on critical thinking, however. In terms of providing a basis for a system of rational thinking assessment, it goes considerably beyond such lists in a number of ways. First, unlike the many committee-like attempts to develop feature-lists of critical thinking skills (e.g., Facione, 1990), our conceptual components are grounded in paradigms that have been extensively researched within the literature of cognitive science. This will be illustrated more concretely when we discuss Table 10–1. Second, many textbook attempts at lists of "good thinking styles" deal only with aspects of fluid rationality and give short shrift to the crystallized knowledge bases that are necessary supports for rational thought and action. In contrast, our framework for rationality assessment emphasizes that crystallized knowledge underlies much rational responding (crystallized facilitators) and that crystallized knowledge can also be the direct cause of irrational behavior (crystallized inhibitors).

Even more important than these points, and unlike many such lists of thinking skills in textbooks, the conceptual components of the fluid characteristics and crystallized knowledge bases listed in Figure 10–1 are each grounded in a task or paradigm in the literature of cognitive science. That is, they are not just potentially measurable but, in fact, have been operationalized and measured at least once in the scientific literature—and in many cases (e.g., context effects in decision making; tendency to enjoy thought; probabilistic reasoning), they have generated enormous empirical literatures.

The components illustrated in Figure 10–1 reflect the tripartite model of mind described in previous chapters. Fluid rationality encompasses characteristics of both the reflective and the algorithmic mind. Many components of rational thought, such as actively open-minded thinking, the value placed on reason, and the tendency to seek information, are clearly dispositions of the reflective mind. Other components of fluid rationality such as self-control skills may require sustained decoupling and thus implicate the computational capacity of the algorithmic mind. Crystallized facilitators and inhibitors are mindware accessed by the reflective mind, as discussed in Chapter 6.

Operationalizing the Components of Rational Thought

Table 10–1 shows some of the paradigms that ground the component concepts and that could be used as the basis for constructing test items. Many of these are well-known to most cognitive psychologists. For example, there are many paradigms that have been used to measure the resistance to miserly information processing, the first major dimension of fluid rationality in Table 10–1. Many of these paradigms have been extensively investigated and have yielded tasks that could be used to devise assessment items. The study of belief bias—that people have difficulty

TABLE 10.1 Measurement Paradigms for the Major Dimensions of Rational Thought

Components of Rational Thought

Fluid Rationality

Major Dimensions	Measurement Paradigms	Source for Paradigm	Example Item
Resistance to miserly information processing	Belief bias paradigms	Evans, Barston, & Pollard (1983) or Markovits & Nantel (1989)	Decide if the conclusion follows logically from the premises, assuming the premises are absolutely true: All flowers have petals; roses have petals; therefore, roses are flowers.
	Attribute substitution (i.e., vividness substitution; affect substitution; denominator neglect)	Kahneman & Frederick (2002); Slovic et al. (2002); Denes-Raj & Epstein (1994)	Assume that you are presented with two trays of marbles that are spread in a single layer in each tray. You must draw out one marble (without peeking, of course) from either tray. If you draw a black marble, then you win $100. Consider a condition in which the small tray contains 1 black marble and 9 white marbles, and the large tray contains 8 black marbles and 92 white marbles. From which tray would you prefer to select a marble?
	Cognitive reflection test	Frederick (2005)	A bat and a ball cost $1.10 in total. The bat costs a dollar more than the ball. How much does the ball cost?
	Disjunctive reasoning tasks	Toplak & Stanovich (2002)	Jack is looking at Ann, but Ann is looking at George. Jack is married, but George is not. Is a married person looking at an unmarried person? A) Yes B) No C) Cannot be determined

(Continued)

TABLE 10.1 Measurement Paradigms for the Major Dimensions of Rational Thought (*Continued*)

Components of Rational Thought

Fluid Rationality

Major Dimensions	Measurement Paradigms	Source for Paradigm	Example Item
	Accurate perception of risks and benefits	Finucane, Alhakami, Slovic, & Johnson (2000)	Judgments of risks and benefits should be independent. For example, information about the benefits of nuclear energy should not reduce the risk estimate for this source of energy.
	Proper use of base-rates	Tversky & Kahneman (1982)	A cab was involved in a hit-and-run accident at night. Two cab companies, the Green and the Blue, operate in the city in which the accident occurred. You are given the following facts: 85% of the cabs in the city are green and 15% are blue. A witness reported that the cab in the accident was blue. The court tested the reliability of the witness under the same circumstances that existed on the night of the accident and concluded that the witness called about 80% of the blue cabs blue but called 20% of the blue cabs green. The witness also called about 80% of the green cabs green, but called 20% of the green cabs blue. What is the probability (expressed as a percentage ranging from 0 to 100%) that the cab involved in the accident was blue?

Outcome bias paradigms; status quo bias; endowment effects	Baron & Hershey (1988); Kahneman, Knetsch, & Thaler (1990, 1991)	A 55-year-old man had a heart condition. He had to stop working because of chest pain. He enjoyed his work and did not want to stop. His pain also interfered with other things, such as travel and recreation. A type of bypass operation would relieve his pain and increase his life expectancy by 5 [15] years. However, 8% [2%] of the people who have this operation die from the operation itself. His physician decided to go ahead with the operation. The operation succeeded [failed, and the man died]. Evaluate the physician's decision to go ahead with the operation.
Hindsight bias paradigms	Fischhoff (1975) or Pohl (2004)	An immigrant arriving at Ellis Island in 1900 was most likely to be from: (a) England or Ireland; (b) Scandinavia; (c) Latin America; ★(d) Eastern Europe The correct answer to the item is indicated by an asterisk. Please indicate on the scale provided the probability that you would have answered this item correctly.
Diagnostic hypothesis testing	(Stanovich (2010a)	Four-card selection task: If there is a vowel on one side of the card, then there is an even number on the other. Your task is to decide which card or cards must be turned over to find out whether the rule is true or false.
Accuracy of affective forecasting	Kermer, Driver-Linn, Wilson, & Gilbert (2006)	Part 1: How happy/sad do you think you will be if you win/lose this coin toss? Part 2: Now that you have won/lost the coin toss, how happy/sad are you right now?

(Continued)

TABLE 10.1 Measurement Paradigms for the Major Dimensions of Rational Thought (*Continued*)

Components of Rational Thought

Fluid Rationality

Major Dimensions	Measurement Paradigms	Source for Paradigm	Example Item
Resistance to myside thinking; accurate self-evaluation	Overconfidence paradigms; fairness paradigms; argument evaluation test	Fischhoff, Slovic, & Lichtenstein (1977); Messick & Sentis (1979); Stanovich & West (1997)	Select the correct answer: Absinthe is A) a precious stone or B) a liqueur. What is the probability that the alternative you selected is correct?
	Unbiased processing of evidence	Klaczynski (2000) or Taber & Lodge (2006)	In this part of the task, we will ask you to read a set of arguments on gun control and tell us how weak or strong you believe each argument is.
Absence of irrelevant context effects in decision making	Framing effects; preference reversals	Frisch (1993); Lichtenstein & Slovic (2006)	Decision 1. Imagine that the United States is preparing for the outbreak of a disease that is expected to kill 600 people. If Program A is adopted, 200 people will be saved. If Program B is adopted, there is a one-third probability that 600 people will be saved and a two-thirds probability that no people will be saved. Which of the two programs would you favor? Decision 2. Imagine that the United States is preparing for the outbreak of a disease that is expected to kill 600 people. If Program C is adopted, 400 people will die. If Program D is adopted, there is a one-third probability that nobody will die and a two-thirds probability that 600 people will die. Which of the two programs would you favor?

	Avoidance of irrelevant anchoring	Jacowitz & Kahneman (1995) or Epley & Gilovich (2004)	Is the length of the Mississippi River greater than 3000 [less than 200] miles? What is the length of the Mississippi River?
Belief flexibility: actively open-minded thinking	Actively Open-Minded Thinking Scale; need for closure; dogmatism; belief identification; epistemological understanding	Stanovich & West (2008a); Kruglanski & Webster (1996); Christie (1991); Sá, West, & Stanovich (1999); Kuhn et al. (2000)	Agree or disagree: Changing your mind is a sign of weakness (reflected item).
Value placed on reason and truth	The Master Rationality Motive Scale	Stanovich (2008)	Agree or disagree: I like to think that my actions are motivated by sound reasons.
Tendency to Seek Information, enjoy thought, and fully process information	Measures of need for cognition and typical intellectual engagement Disjunctive reasoning tasks	Cacioppo et al. (1996); Goff & Ackerman (1992) Toplak & Stanovich (2002)	Agree or disagree: I like the responsibility of handling a situation that requires a lot of thinking. There are five blocks in a stack pictured in the figure below. Block 1 is on the bottom and Block 5 is on the top. Block 4 (the second from the top) is green, and Block 2 (the second from the bottom) is not green. Is there a green block *directly* on top of a non-green block? A) Yes B) No C) Cannot be determined
Objective reasoning styles	Separating fact from opinion and theory from evidence; recognizing the validity and invalidity of informal arguments; argument evaluation test	Kuhn (1991); Watson & Glaser (1980) or Ricco (2007); Stanovich & West (1997)	Dale states: Seat belts should always be worn to make traveling by car safer; A critic's counter-argument is: There are times when your life may be saved by your being thrown free of a car during an accident (assume statement factually correct); Dale's rebuttal is: You are several times more likely to be killed if you are thrown from a car (assume statement factually correct). Indicate the strength of Dale's rebuttal to the critic's counter-argument.

(Continued)

TABLE 10.1 Measurement Paradigms for the Major Dimensions of Rational Thought (*Continued*)

Components of Rational Thought

Fluid Rationality

Major Dimensions	Measurement Paradigms	Source for Paradigm	Example Item
Sensitivity to contradiction; tendency to seek consistency in belief and argument	Informal reasoning and argument evaluation paradigms	Baron (1995) or Perkins (1985) or Toplak & Stanovich (2003) or Halpern (2008)	Subsequent to rating their level of agreement with positions expressed in a series of statements (e.g., The cost of gasoline should be doubled to discourage people from driving), participants were asked to write down arguments both for and against the position.
Sense of self-efficacy	Locus of Control Scales	Lefcourt (1991)	Agree or disagree: When bad things happen, they were just going to happen no matter what you did. (reflected)
Prudently discounting the future	Temporal discounting of reward	Kirby (2009); Shamosh et al. (2008)	Would you prefer $55 today, or $75 in 60 days?
Self-control skills	Delay of gratification paradigms; time preference; future orientation	Rodriguez, Mischel, & Shoda (1989); Steinberg et al. (2009); Strathman et al. (1994)	Which description best describes you: Some people would rather be happy today than take their chances on what might happen in the future, but other people will give up their happiness now so that they can get what they want in the future.
Fine-grained and controlled emotional regulation	Measures of Alexithymia	Bagby, Parker, & Taylor (1994)	Agree or disagree: I am often confused about what emotion I am feeling.

Major Dimensions	Measurement Paradigms	Source for Paradigm	Example Item
Emotional regulation related to reward	Iowa Gambling Task	Bechara, Damasio, Damasio, & Anderson, (1994)	Participants choose from four decks of cards, each of which is associated with a different potential payoff. They must learn to avoid decks that produce high immediate gains but larger future losses.

Crystallized Rationality: Crystallized Facilitators

Major Dimensions	Measurement Paradigms	Source for Paradigm	Example Item
Probabilistic reasoning	Importance of sample size	Tversky & Kahneman (1974) or Griffin & Tversky (1992) or Fong et al. (1986)	A certain town is served by two hospitals. In the larger hospital, about 45 babies are born each day, and in the smaller hospital about 15 babies are born each day. As you know, about 50% of all babies are boys. The exact percentage of baby boys, however, varies from day to day. Sometimes it may be higher than 50%, sometimes lower. For a period of 1 year, each hospital recorded the days on which more than 60% of the babies born were boys. Which hospital do you think recorded more such days? A) The larger hospital will have more days with more than 60% boys. B) The smaller hospital will have more days with more than 60% boys. C) About the same for both hospitals.

(Continued)

TABLE 10.1 Measurement Paradigms for the Major Dimensions of Rational Thought (*Continued*)

Components of Rational Thought

Crystallized Rationality: Crystallized Facilitators

Major Dimensions	Measurement Paradigms	Source for Paradigm	Example Item
	Consistent probability judgments	Bruine de Bruin et al. (2007); Peters et al. (2006)	In each time frame, some item pairs present nested subset and superset events (e.g., dying in a terrorist attack is a subset of the superset dying from any cause). To be scored as correct, the probability of a subset event should not exceed that of its superset event.
	Resistance to base-rate Neglect	Sloman et al. (2003); Jepson et al. (1983)	Imagine that disease X occurs in one in every 1000 people. A test has been developed to detect the disease. Every time the test is given to a person who has the disease, the test comes out positive. But sometimes the test also comes out positive when it is given to a person who is completely healthy. Specifically, 5% of all people who are perfectly healthy test positive for the disease. Imagine that we have given this test to a random sample of Americans. They were selected by a lottery. Those who conducted the lottery had no information about the health status of any of these people. What is the chance that a person found to have a positive result actually has the disease?

Resistance to gambler's fallacy	Ayton & Fischer (2004) or Burns & Corpus (2004) or Toplak et al., (2007)	When playing slot machines, people win something about 1 in every 10 times. Lori, however, has just won on her first three plays. What are her chances of winning the next time she plays?
Use of chance in explanatory frameworks; understanding random processes	Fenton-O'Creevy et al. (2003); Towse & Neil (1998)	Simulate the random outcome of tossing a fair coin 150 times in succession.
Understanding regression effects	Nisbett et al. (1983); Fong et al. (1986)	After the first 2 weeks of the major league baseball season, newspapers begin to print the top 10 batting averages. Typically, after 2 weeks, the leading batter often has an average of about .450. However, no batter in major league history has ever averaged .450 at the end of the season. Why do you think this is?
Recognizing biased and unbiased samples	Nisbett et al. (1983); Fong et al. (1986)	An economist was arguing in favor of a guaranteed minimum income for everyone. He cited a recent study of several hundred people in the United States with inherited wealth. Nearly 92% of those people, he said, worked at some job that provided earned income sufficient to provide at least a middle–class life style. The study showed, he said, that contrary to popular opinion, people will work in preference to being idle. Thus a guaranteed income policy would result in little or no increase in the number of people unwilling to work. Comment on the economist's reasoning.

(Continued)

TABLE 10.1 Measurement Paradigms for the Major Dimensions of Rational Thought (*Continued*)

Components of Rational Thought

Crystallized Rationality: Crystallized Facilitators

Major Dimensions	Measurement Paradigms	Source for Paradigm	Example Item
	Diagnostic hypothesis testing	Doherty & Mynatt (1990); Mynatt et al. (1993)	Imagine you are a doctor. A patient comes to you with a red rash on his fingers. What information would you want to diagnose whether the patient has the disease "Digirosa?" Which of the following pieces of information are necessary to make the diagnosis? A) percentage of people without Digirosa who have a red rash; B) percentage of people with Digirosa; C) percentage of people without Digirosa; and D) percentage of people with Digirosa who have a red rash
	Accurate perception of risks	Lichtenstein et al. (1978)	Consider all the people now living in the United States—children, adults, everyone. Which cause of death is more likely? A) dying in a tornado; B) dying of tuberculosis
Qualitative decision theory insights	Stable preferences; adherence to basic probability/utility trade-offs in SEU theory; preferences in line with SEU axioms	Moore (1999) or Lichtenstein & Slovic (1971, 1973); Frederick (2005) or Benjamin & Shapiro (2005); Birnbaum (1999)	Choose A or B: A) You get $0.40 for sure. B) If a die comes up 1, 2, or 3, you get $1.58. If a die comes up 4, 5, or 6, you get nothing.

Knowledge of scientific reasoning		
Scientific control concepts; causal variable isolation; control group necessity; understanding placebo and selection effects	Greenhoot et al. (2004); Tschirgi (1980); Lehman et al. (1988); Lehman & Nisbett (1990)	The city of Middletown has had an unpopular police chief for the past 2 years. He is a political appointee who is a crony of the mayor and he had little previous experience in police administration when he was appointed. The mayor has recently defended the police chief in public announcing that in the time since he took office, crime rates decreased by 12%. What evidence would most refute the mayor's claim and instead show that the police chief may not be doing a good job?
Avoidance of confirmation bias	Taber & Lodge (2006)	Search for pro or con information about a highly valenced issue (affirmative action, gun control, etc.)
Diagnostic covariation judgment	Wasserman, Dorner, & Kao (1990)	Imagine that you are a research chemist for a pharmaceutical company. You want to assess how well a certain experimental drug works on psoriasis, a severe skin rash. In your experiment, you will give some rats the drug and others a placebo, which is known to have no effect on psoriasis. After the experiment, there will be four types of rats: Those who did not receive the drug and whose psoriasis did not improve, and so forth. Was the treatment effective?
Covariation detection free of belief bias; avoidance of illusory correlations	Stanovich & West (1998d); Fiedler (2004)	As the cell above except for an issue with valence and/or prior belief, such as: Do couples who live together before marriage have more successful marriages?

(Continued)

TABLE 10.1 Measurement Paradigms for the Major Dimensions of Rational Thought (*Continued*)

Components of Rational Thought

Crystallized Rationality: Crystallized Facilitators

Major Dimensions	Measurement Paradigms	Source for Paradigm	Example Item
	Difference between correlation and causation; recognizing spurious correlation	Halpern (2008); Burns (1997)	A recent report in a magazine for parents and teachers showed that adolescents who smoke cigarettes also tend to get low grades in school. As the number of cigarettes smoked each day increased, grade point averages decreased. One suggestion made in this report was that we could improve school achievement by preventing adolescents from smoking. Based on this information, would you support this idea as a way of improving the school achievement of adolescents who smoke?
	Understanding falsifiability as a context for confirmation; thinking of the alternative hypothesis	Oswald & Grosjean (2004) or Gale & Ball (2006, 2009) or Tweney et al. (1980)	I have made up a rule for the construction of sequences of numbers. For instance, the three numbers 2-4-6 satisfy this rule. To find out what the rule is, you may construct other sets of three numbers to test your assumption about what the rule is. I will give you feedback about whether your set satisfies my rule or not. If you are sure you have the solution, you may stop testing and tell me what you believe the rule to be. [the rule is "increasing numbers"]

Differentiating theory from evidence	Kuhn (1991, 1992)	"How do you know that this is the cause?" "If you were trying to convince someone else that your view, [focal theory repeated here], is right, what evidence would you give to try to show this?"
Appreciation of converging evidence	Stanovich (2010b)	The principle of converging evidence urges us to base conclusions on data that arise from a number of slightly different experimental sources.
Appreciating the limits of Personal Observation, Testimonials, and Single-Case Evidence	Jepson et al. (1983) and Halpern (2008)	The Caldwells looked in Consumer Reports and there they found that the consensus of the experts was that the Volvo was superior to the Saab. Mr. Caldwell called up friends. One Volvo owner hated his car. Which car do you think the Caldwells should buy?
Logical validity judgment tasks	Evans, Handley, Harper, & Johnson-Laird (1999)	For "All A are B" evaluate logically: 1. No A are B 2. Some A are B 3. Some A are not B 4. All B are A 5. No B are A 6. Some B are A 7. Some B are not A Answer: conclusions 2 and 6 are necessary; 4 and 7 are possible (but not necessary); and 1, 3, and 5 are impossible.

(Continued)

Components of Rational Thought

Crystallized Rationality: Crystallized Facilitators

Major Dimensions	Measurement Paradigms	Source for Paradigm	Example Item
Economic thinking	Cost/Benefit reasoning; limited resource reasoning	Larrick, et al. (1993) or NCEE (2005); Larrick, et al. (1990)	When a person rents an apartment, who benefits from the transaction?
	Recognizing opportunity costs	Larrick, et al. (1990); Thaler (1985, 1987)	What are the costs involved in attending university. List all of the costs you can.
	Avoiding sunk costs	Arkes & Blumer (1985)	You are staying in a hotel room on vacation. You paid $6.95 to see a movie on pay TV. After 5 minutes, you are bored and the movie seems pretty bad. Would you continue to watch the movie or not?
	Understanding externalities	Heath (2001)	A customer walks in to a small convenience store and gives the store's owner $8 for a six-pack of beer. The owner of the store hands over the six- pack. After this transaction is complete, describe the gains and losses to everyone affected by this transaction.
	Awareness of the logic of exponential growth and compounding	Wagenaar & Sagaria (1975); Dorner (1996)	Pollution Index: 1970–3; 1971–7; 1972–20; 1973–55; 1974–148; 1975 –?
	Understanding commons dilemmas, zero-sum, and nonzero-sum games	Komorita & Parks (1994); Shafir & Tversky (1992)	Two players must choose to either cooperate or compete with the other player while being blind to the other's choice.

| Recognizing regression effects that encourage buying high and selling low | Nisbett et al. (1983) | Harold, a boys football coach says the following of his experience: "Every year we add 10–20 younger boys to the team on the basis of their performance at the try-out practice. Usually the staff and I are extremely excited about two or three of these kids—but they usually turn out to be no better than the rest." Why do you suppose that the coach usually has to revise downward his opinion of players that he originally thought were brilliant? |
| Appropriate mental accounting and understanding of fungibility | Thaler (1980, 1985, 1987) | Imagine that you go to purchase a calculator for $30. The salesperson informs you that the calculator you wish to buy is on sale for $20 at the other branch of the store which is ten minutes away by car. Would you drive to the other store? Option A: Yes, Option B: No Imagine that you go to purchase a jacket for $250. The salesperson informs you that the jacket you wish to buy is on sale for $240 at the other branch of the store which is ten minutes away by car. Would you drive to the other store? Option C: Yes, Option B: No |

(Continued)

TABLE 10.1 Measurement Paradigms for the Major Dimensions of Rational Thought (*Continued*)

Components of Rational Thought

Crystallized Rationality: Crystallized Facilitators

Major Dimensions	Measurement Paradigms	Source for Paradigm	Example Item
Superstitious thinking and belief in the paranormal	Paranormal, Superstitious Thinking, and Luck Scales; illusion of control	Stanovich (1989) or Tobacyk & Milford (1983); Fenton-O'Creevy et al. (2003) or Thompson (2004)	Agree or disagree: If you break a mirror, you will have bad luck.
Belief in the superiority of intuition	Faith in Intuition Scale	Epstein et al. (1996)	Agree or disagree: My initial impressions of people are almost always right.
Overreliance on folk wisdom and folk psychology	Bias Blind Spot Test	Pronin, Lin, & Ross (2002)	Psychologists have claimed that people show a "self-serving" tendency in that they take credit for success but deny responsibility for failure. Questions to participants: A) To what extent do you believe that *you* show this effect or tendency? B) To what extent do you believe the *average American* shows this effect or tendency?

	High value placed on nongrounded knowledge sources	Eckblad & Chapman (1983)	Agree or disagree: Horoscopes are right too often for it to be a coincidence.
Belief in "special" expertise			
Financial misconceptions	Financial Literacy/Illiteracy Scales	Chen & Volpe (1998); Mandell (2009); NCEE (2006)	What is the best way to minimize the dollar amount in finance charges on a credit card?
Incorrigibility of introspection (overoptimistic theories of one's own introspective powers)	Accuracy of affective forecasting	Kermer, Driver-Linn, Wilson, & Gilbert (2006)	Part 1: How happy/sad do you think you will be if you win/lose this coin toss? Part 2: Now that you have won/lost the coin toss, how happy/sad are you right now?
	Bias Blind Spot Test	Pronin, Lin, & Ross (2002)	Psychologists have shown that people tend not to trust media sources that contradict their views. Questions to participants: A) To what extent do you believe that *you* show this effect or tendency? B) To what extent do you believe the *average American* shows this effect or tendency?
Dysfunctional personal beliefs	Measures of irrational personal beliefs	Terjesen, Salhany, & Sciutto (2009) or Lindner et al. (1999)	Agree or disagree: If important people dislike me, it is because I am an unlikable, bad person.

(Continued)

TABLE 10.1 Measurement Paradigms for the Major Dimensions of Rational Thought (*Continued*)

Components of Rational Thought

Crystallized Rationality: Crystallized Facilitators

Major Dimensions	Measurement Paradigms	Source for Paradigm	Example Item
A notion of self that encourages egocentric processing	Unbiased processing of evidence	Klaczynski & Gordon (1996)	Belief-consistent conclusions were drawn from those experiments that yielded results that cast participants' religions in a positive light. Belief-inconsistent conclusions were drawn from research that yielded results casting participants' religions in a negative light. Unbiasedness is defined as rating the quality of the experiment independent of its level of belief consistency.
	Self-perception biases and unrealistic optimism	Weinstein (1980)	Compared to other students—same sex as you—what do you think are the chances that the following events will happen to you: You will get a good job before graduation.

processing data pointing toward conclusions that conflict with what they think they know about the world—has yielded many such items (e.g., Evans, Barston, & Pollard, 1983; Evans & Curtis-Holmes, 2005; Markovits & Nantel, 1989).

Good decision making is partly defined by decisions that are not unduly affected by irrelevant context (the third major dimension of fluid rationality in Table 10–1). Two paradigms that assess the latter tendency have each generated enormous literatures. Resistance to framing has been measured with countless tasks (e.g., Levin et al., 2002; Maule & Villejoubert, 2007), as has the resistance to irrelevant anchoring in decisions (e.g., Epley & Gilovich, 2004, 2006; Jacowitz & Kahneman, 1995).

As a final example of an area of rational thinking with a dense history of empirical research and with paradigms that could serve as assessment devices, consider the tendency to conform, qualitatively, to the insights of normative decision theory—the second major dimension of crystallized rationality facilitators in Table 10–1. Since the early 1950s (*see* Edwards, 1954), psychologists have studied the tendency to adhere to the axioms of expected utility theory with a variety of tasks and paradigms (e.g., Baron, 2008; Dawes, 1998; Kahneman & Tversky, 2000; Wu et al., 2004).

Not all of the concepts of rational thought listed in Table 10–1 have potential measurement paradigms with as much background research on them as those we have just singled out, but *most* of them do. For the reader not as conversant with the literature of cognitive psychology as the last several paragraphs have presumed, we have listed in Table 10–1 a source for each of the potential measurement paradigms. That is, Table 10–1 points the reader to specific studies or review papers in the research literature that contain examples of tasks that could be adapted to serve as actual test items. In most cases, the citations in Table 10–1 will allow the reader to uncover an extensive literature on such tasks (as in the examples in the previous paragraphs). At a minimum, the citations provide clear guidance on how such task items might be developed.

The citations in Table 10–1 are to papers that will lead the reader to empirical studies containing measurement paradigms that would make a good source of assessment items. The citation is *not* intended as a reference to the classic introduction of the effect, or to the paper with priority of discovery, or to the most historic or most cited paper. This is because often the best source for test items is not the paper in which the effect/task was introduced. For example, for framing effects, we have listed Frisch (1993) as the pointer citation because it contains a large number of framing items (we could equally have cited Levin et al., 1998, 2002) rather than the classic Tversky and Kahneman (1981) paper where framing was introduced with the now-famous Asian Disease problem.

The far right column of Table 10–1 presents an example of an item type from each of the measurement paradigms. The reader is warned that because of the size of Table 10–1 (i.e., number of different paradigms), many of these items have been truncated, abridged, or paraphrased so that they fit into a reasonable space. They are not meant to be literal exemplars that could be immediately inserted into a test but are there merely to give the reader unfamiliar with the measurement paradigm a flavor of what is being measured. Items of that type are explicated in detail in the citations given.

Some measurement paradigms appear in Table 10–1 more than once. For example, diagnostic hypothesis testing appears as a measure of resistance to miserly processing and as a measure of probabilistic reasoning. Likewise, the accuracy of affective forecasting appears as a measure of resistance to miserly processing and as a measure of contaminated mindware (belief in absolutely accurate introspection). These measurement paradigms are complex in this manner simply because some tasks tap more than one rationality dimension.

Table 10–1 illustrates the basis for our position that there is no *conceptual* barrier to creating a test of rational thinking. However, this does not mean that it would be *logistically* easy. Quite the contrary, we have stressed that both fluid and crystallized rationality are likely to be more multifarious than their analogous intelligence constructs. Likewise, we are not claiming that there exist comprehensive assessment devices for each of these components with adequate psychometric properties. However, in virtually every case, laboratory tasks that have appeared in the published literature give us, at a minimum, a hint at what comprehensive assessment of the particular component would look like. In fact, in some cases, there exist fully developed measures with adequate psychometric properties (e.g., measures of self- efficacy; *see* Lefcourt, 1991).

Nonetheless, there might be technical problems involved in measuring some of these constructs, particularly in the different domains of fluid rationality. Some may necessitate more naturalistic assessment techniques than those used to assess cognitive abilities. For the reasons discussed in Chapters 2 and 3, many of these domains must be assessed under typical rather than maximal performance conditions (*see* Duckworth, 2009). As such, were they to become actual assessment domains in real life, they might be subject to coaching effects. Several of the domains that are thinking dispositions measured by self-reports might be problematic in this respect, for example: actively open-minded thinking, the value placed on truth, and objective reasoning styles. However, many measures of other dimensions—such as the tendency toward miserly processing and to be affected by irrelevant context are less subject to this criticism. Assessing framing effects, base-rate neglect, and the accurate perception of risks would likewise be less subject to nonefficacious coaching effects.

The meaning of nonefficacious coaching effects needs to be explained, and we will do so by way of an analogy to the controversy about "teaching to the test" in education. The practice of "teaching to the test" is a bad thing when it raises test performance without truly affecting the larger construct being assessed. If a teacher learns that a statewide history assessment will contain many questions on the Great Depression and concentrates on that during class time to the exclusion of other important topics, then the teacher has perhaps increased the probability of a good score on this particular test but has not advanced more general historical knowledge. This is nonefficacious coaching. But in education, not all coaching in anticipation of assessments is of this type. Early reading skills provide the contrast to assessments of history knowledge. Imagine that teachers knew of the appearance of subtests measuring decoding skills on a statewide early reading test and "taught to" that test. In this case, the teachers would in fact be teaching the key generalizeable skills of early reading (*see* Stanovich, 2000; Vellutino, Fletcher, Snowling, & Scanlon, 2004). They would be teaching the most fundamental underpinning of the construct "early reading." This would be *efficacious* "teaching to the test."

The point here is that the coachability of a skill does not *necessarily* undermine the rationale for including the skill in an assessment. To put it colloquially, some "coaching" is little more than providing "tricks" that lift assessment scores without really changing the underlying skill, whereas other types of coaching result in changes in the underlying skill itself. There is no reason to consider the latter type of coaching a bad thing and thus no reason to consider an assessment domain to be necessarily problematic because it is coachable. Thus, it is important to realize that many rational thinking domains may be of the latter type—that is, amenable to what we might call virtuous coaching. If a person has been "coached" to always see the relevance of base-rates, to always explore all of the disjunctive possibilities, to routinely reframe decisions, to consider sample size, and to see event spaces and thus the relevance of probabilistic thinking—then one has increased rational thinking skills and tendencies. If the existence of assessment devices spawns such coaching then it seems that, for those of us arguing for the importance of rational and critical thinking in education, then this can be nothing but a good thing.

Thus, with these caveats in mind, Table 10–1 displays, in visual form, what we mean when we claim that the measurement of rational thought is conceptually possible with the use of currently available instruments. Nonetheless, the complexity of Table 10–1 illustrates that measuring rational thought could be logistically daunting. For example, the factor structure of Table 10–1 is still undetermined. We do not know the correlational relationships between the major dimensions or the measurement paradigms. This means that we do not know whether it might be possible to measure several features by measuring just a few with high multicollinearity.

Work on the structure of rational thought is nascent, but there are indications that there may be considerable separability in these components (Bruine de Bruin et al., 2007; Klaczynski, 2001; Parker & Fischhoff, 2005; Slugoski, Shields, & Dawson, 1993; Stanovich & West, 1998c, West et al., 2008). It may be that, to get reasonable coverage of the domains listed in Table 10–1, each of the domains would have to be assessed separately. It might be that a comprehensive assessment of rational thought could not be accomplished in a single sitting. Although this represents a logistical problem, a diffuse factor structure does not negate the importance of assessing individual differences in rational thought. Rational thought does not require a g-factor to justify its measurement. More important will be research linking these rational thinking tendencies to real-life decision making, and a reasonable amount of such research has already been conducted (Baron, Bazerman, & Shonk, 2006; Camerer, 2000; Fenton-O'Creevy et al., 2003; Groopman, 2007; Hilton, 2003; Milkman, Rogers, & Bazerman, 2008; Thaler & Sunstein, 2008).

Table 10–2 illustrates that these types of thinking skills have been linked to real-life outcomes. There, for each measurement paradigm listed in Table 10–1, an association with a real-life outcome is indicated. It is clear from the table that a large number of these assessment domains have been linked with important real-world outcomes. Not all the linkages in the table are of equal strength or empirical documentation. Although we have listed only one or two citations for each cell, there is often a much more voluminous literature documenting real-world associations. In other cases, the studies cited are virtually the only ones documenting an empirical connection to a real-world outcome. Regardless of this variability, it is impressive that there are documented real-world connections for all of these many components of rational thought.

With respect to Table 10–2, it is acknowledged that in the majority of cases, a causal connection has not yet been established by empirical research. We do not know, in most cases, whether the association between a rational thinking skill and an outcome would remain if intelligence were partialled out. In a few selected studies, however, it has been shown that rational thought makes an independent predictive contribution. For example, Bruine de Bruin et al. (2007) found that avoiding sunk costs, conjunction errors, and overconfidence was related to a Decision Outcomes Inventory of 41 negative outcomes (such as loan default, drunk driving, receiving parking tickets, and missing flights) and that this connection survived statistical control for cognitive ability. Clearly more work remains to be done on tracing the exact nature of the connections—that is, whether they are causal. The sheer number of real-world connections, however, serves to highlight the importance of the rational thinking skills in our framework. Panglossians sometimes attempt to devalue the heuristics and biases research tradition by claiming that the effects demonstrated there only obtain in laboratory tasks and not in real life. One of several purposes of Table 10–2 is to provide an easily accessible demonstration that such a claim is nonsense.

In short, the assessment of rational thought will be determined by the importance of the content domains listed in Table 10–1 and by the fact that they fit within extant conceptual models of reasoning and judgment.

TABLE 10.2   Association Between Aspects of Rational Thought and Real-World Outcomes

Components of Rational Thought

Fluid Rationality

Major Dimensions	Measurement Paradigms	Source for Association with Real-World Outcome	Association with Real-World Outcome
Resistance to miserly information processing	Belief bias paradigms	Hastie & Pennington (2000)	Jurors use prior knowledge in constructing narratives of a legal case even when instructed not to do so.
	Attribute substitution (i.e., vividness substitution; affect substitution; denominator neglect)	Wang (2009)	In the National Basketball Association, scoring performance (a vivid behavior) overpredicts salary and All-Star balloting compared with nonscoring statistics when the latter are equated for contribution to winning outcomes.
	Cognitive reflection	Toplak, Liu, Macpherson, Toneatto, & Stanovich (2007)	Problem gamblers are higher than control groups on measures of impulsivity and lower on measures of reflectivity.
	Disjunctive reasoning	Johnson, Hershey, Meszaros, & Kunreuther (2000)	Flight passengers mispriced insurance for component risks by not thinking disjunctively about the components.
	Accurate perception of risks and benefits	Sivak & Flannagan (2003); Gigerenzer (2006)	The relative risks of flying and driving shifted after September 11, 2001 in a manner that cost hundreds of lives.
	Resistance to base-rate neglect	Steen (1990); Gigerenzer, Hoffrage, & Ebert (1998)	Calls for mandatory AIDS testing ignore the implications of low base-rates; AIDS counseling likewise ignores the implications of base-rates.

	Outcome bias paradigms; status quo bias; endowment effects	Johnson et al. (2000); Samuelson & Zeckhauser (1988); Johnson & Goldstein (2006); Thaler & Benartzi (2004)	Insurance purchase decisions as well as utility purchases have been shown to be influenced by status quo biases; organ donations are higher in countries with presumed consent; default values strongly affect pension investment choices.
	Hindsight bias paradigms	Pohl (2004)	Hindsight bias is posited to lower the general motivation to learn because it is highest in those least knowledgeable in the domain.
	Diagnostic hypothesis testing	Kern & Doherty (1982)	Medical students failed to choose diagnostic symptoms when assessing diseases.
	Accuracy of affective forecasting	Kermer, Driver-Linn, Wilson, & Gilbert (2006)	Subjects mispredicted their level of happiness after actual monetary gains and losses.
Resistance to myside thinking; accurate self-evaluation	Overconfidence paradigms; fairness paradigms; argument evaluation test	Bruine de Bruin et al. (2007); Hilton (2003); Odean (1998)	Degree of overconfidence was related to a Decision Outcomes Inventory of 41 negative outcomes such as loan default and drunk driving; predictions of currency exchange rates by corporate treasurers are overconfident. Financial professionals are overconfident.
	Unbiased processing of evidence	Forsythe, Nelson, Neumann, & Wright (1992)	Investors in a political prediction stock market exchange made investment decisions that were influenced by which candidate they hoped would win.
Absence of irrelevant context effects in decision making	Framing effects; preference reversals	Hilton (2003); Camerer (2000)	Professional stock market traders overweight single-day losing positions; generally, traders sell losing positions too little and sell winning positions too much.
	Avoidance of irrelevant anchoring	Stewart (2009); Northcraft & Neale (1987)	The size of minimum payment requirements affects the size of the partial payment of credit card debt; the evaluation of home values by real estate agents is affected by the listing price.

(Continued)

TABLE 10.2 Association Between Aspects of Rational Thought and Real-World Outcomes (*Continued*)

Components of Rational Thought

Fluid Rationality

Major Dimensions	Measurement Paradigms	Source for Association with Real-World Outcome	Association with Real-World Outcome
Belief flexibility: actively open-minded thinking	Epistemological understanding	Sinatra & Pintrich (2003)	Epistemological beliefs are related to the efficiency of learning.
Value placed on reason and truth	The Master Rationality Motive Scale	Toplak, Liu, Macpherson, Toneatto, & Stanovich (2007)	Problem gamblers performed worse than controls on a measure of commitment to thought rather than intuition.
Tendency to seek information, enjoy thought, and fully process information	Measures of need for cognition and typical intellectual engagement	Cacioppo, Petty, Feinstein, & Jarvis (1996)	Moderate correlations with anxiety, neuroticism, and procrastination.
	Disjunctive reasoning	Redelmeier & Shafir (1995)	Making more treatment options available to a physician made it *more* likely, not less, that they would refer a patient to a specialist.
Objective reasoning styles	Recognizing the validity and invalidity of informal arguments	Watson & Glaser (2006)	Moderate correlations with job performance in a variety of occupations.
Tendency to seek consistency	Informal reasoning	Capon & Kuhn (1979)	Shoppers have difficulty comparison shopping among products of different sizes.
Sense of self-efficacy	Planning; Locus of Control Scales	Ameriks, Caplin, & Leahy (2003); Lefcourt (1991)	The propensity to plan has been linked to lifetime wealth accumulation; locus of control has been related to achievement in school and in sports, as well as to various health outcomes.
Prudently discounting the future	Temporal discounting of reward	Kirby, Petry, & Bickel (1999)	Research has revealed an association between future discount rates and heroin addiction.

	Measurement Paradigms	Source for Association with Real-World Outcome	Association with Real-World Outcome
Self-control skills	Delay of gratification paradigms; time preference; future orientation	Duckworth & Seligman (2005); Mischel, Shoda, & Rodriguez (1989)	Self-discipline measures predict school grades longitudinally, independent of intelligence. Delay of gratification measured at age 4 years predicted college entrance exam performance later in life.
Fine-grained and controlled emotional regulation	Measures of Alexithymia	Lumley & Roby (1995)	Problem gamblers performed worse than controls on measures of alexithymia.
Emotional regulation related to reward	Iowa Gambling Task	Yechiam, Kanz, Bechara, Stout, Busemeyer, Altmaier, & Paulsen (2008)	Criminal offenders performed worse than controls on the Iowa Gambling Task.
Crystallized Rationality: Crystallized Facilitators			
Major Dimensions	**Measurement Paradigms**	**Source for Association with Real-World Outcome**	**Association with Real-World Outcome**
Probabilistic reasoning	Importance of sample size	Tversky & Kahneman (1971)	Researchers run experiments of insufficient power because of the failure to fully appreciate the importance of sample size.
	Consistent probability judgments	Kramer & Gigerenzer (2005)	Newspapers regularly confuse p (outcome B/outcome A) with p (outcome A/outcome B)
	Proper use of base-rates	Koehler, Brenner, & Griffin (2002)	In studies of medical personnel, lawyers, stockbrokers, sportswriters, economists, and meteorologists, the authors concluded that the base rate likelihood was a "major predictor of miscalibration in experts' everyday judgments" (p. 714).
	Resistance to gambler's fallacy	Sundali & Croson (2006)	Actual gamblers videotaped in a casino displayed the gambler's fallacy.
	Use of chance in Explanatory frameworks; understanding random processes	Wagenaar (1988); Malkiel (2008)	Problem gamblers resist chance as an explanation of patterns they see in events; stock market investors mistakenly think that they can "beat the market" because they fail to appreciate the role of chance.

(Continued)

TABLE 10.2 Association Between Aspects of Rational Thought and Real-World Outcomes (*Continued*)

Components of Rational Thought

Crystallized Rationality: Crystallized Facilitators

Major Dimensions	Measurement Paradigms	Source for Association with Real-World Outcome	Association with Real-World Outcome
	Understanding regression effects	Toplak, Liu, Macpherson, Toneatto, & Stanovich (2007)	Problem gamblers were less able to recognize situations with the potential for regression effects.
	Recognizing biased and unbiased samples	Wainer (1993)	Failure to recognize the importance of selection effects leads media commentators to misinterpret the implications of SAT test scores.
	Diagnostic hypothesis testing	Groopman (2007); Croskerry (2009a); Lilienfeld (2007); Baker, McFall, & Shoham (2009)	Physicians and clinical psychologists fail to engage in diagnostic hypothesis testing.
	Accurate perception of risks	Sunstein (2002)	Hazard regulations reflect the mistaken human belief that the risks and benefits of various activities are negatively related.
Qualitative decision theory insights	Stable preferences; adherence to basic probability/utility trade-offs in SEU theory; preferences in line with SEU axioms	Bruine de Bruin et al. (2007)	Properly applying basic rules of choice was inversely related to a Decision Outcomes Inventory of 41 negative outcomes such as loan default and drunk driving.
Knowledge of scientific reasoning	Scientific control concepts; causal variable isolation; control group necessity; understanding placebo effects	Offit (2008); Pashler, McDaniel, Rohrer, & Bjork (2009)	Bogus autism treatments such as facilitated communication proliferated because of a failure to appreciate the necessity of scientific control; likewise, unproven educational fads such as "learning styles" persist because they are not subjected to test by true experimental control.

Avoidance of confirmation bias	Gibson, Sanbonmatsu, & Posavac (1997)	Basketball fans overestimated the chance that a team would win the championship when that team was made focal.
Diagnostic covariation judgment	Chapman & Chapman (1969)	Clinicians perceive connections between Rorschach responses and diagnoses that are not present.
Covariation detection free of belief bias; avoidance of illusory correlations	King & Koehler (2000); Gilovich & Savitsky (2002)	Belief in pseudosciences such as graphology, and astrology is fostered by the phenomenon of illusory correlation.
Difference between correlation and causation; recognizing spurious correlation	Baumeister, Campbell, Krueger, & Vohs (2003)	Educators have based many programs on the assumption that high self esteem leads to better achievement when the direction of cause, if it exists at all, is the opposite.
Understanding falsifiability as a context for confirmation; thinking of the alternative hypothesis	Wood, Nezworski, Lilienfeld, & Garb (2003); McHugh (2008)	Spurious associations are common in Rorschach interpretation, and pseudosciences such as recovered memory are maintained through unfalsifiable arguments.
Differentiating theory from evidence	Offit (2008); Spitz (1997)	The pseudoscience of facilitated communication as a treatment for autism was not critically assessed because of a failure to differentiate theory and evidence. The same is true in the famous Clever Hans case, a classic in behavioral science.
Appreciation of converging evidence	Begley, S. (2007); Jordan (2007); Nijhuis (2008)	The failure to appreciate the principle of converging evidence contributes to the denial of the evidence suggesting human-caused global warming.
Appreciating the limits of personal observation, testimonials, and single-case evidence	Lilienfeld (2007); Dawes (1994); Baker, McFall, & Shoham (2009)	Clinical psychologists continue to ignore more valid actuarial evidence in favor of personal experience and so-called "clinical intuition."

(Continued)

TABLE 10.2 Association Between Aspects of Rational Thought and Real-World Outcomes (*Continued*)

Components of Rational Thought

Crystallized Rationality: Crystallized Facilitators

Major Dimensions	Measurement Paradigms	Source for Association with Real-World Outcome	Association with Real-World Outcome
Rules of logical consistency and validity	Logical validity judgment tasks	Johnson-Laird (1982)	Government documents describing citizen benefits often require interpretation in terms of logical relationships.
Economic thinking	Cost/Benefit reasoning; limited resource reasoning	Sunstein (2002)	Environmental and other government regulations are written inefficiently because of a lack of attention to cost–benefit reasoning.
	Recognizing opportunity costs	Larrick, Nisbett, & Morgan (1993)	Salary levels were related to the ability to recognize opportunity costs.
	Avoiding sunk costs	Bruine de Bruin et al. (2007)	Committing the sunk cost fallacy was related to a Decision Outcomes Inventory of 41 negative outcomes such as loan default and drunk driving
	Understanding externalities	Heath (2001)	Most people in the United States do not realize that, because of externalities, gasoline prices are too low rather than too high.
	Awareness of the logic of exponential growth and compounding	Paulos (2003)	People save too little, fail to recognize the pitfalls of pyramid schemes, and invest foolishly because of ignorance of the mathematics of compounding.
	Understanding commons dilemmas, zero-sum, and nonzero-sum games	Bazerman, Baron, & Shonk (2001)	Oceans are overfished and traffic jams exacerbated because of the failure to recognize commons dilemmas.
	Recognizing regression effects	Malkiel (2008)	Failure to recognize regression effects in a random walk leads stock market investors to buy high and sell low.

Major Dimensions	Measurement Paradigms	Source for Association with Real-World Outcome	Association with Real-World Outcome
Appropriate mental accounting and understanding of fungibility		Thaler (1985, 1992)	Many people have money in savings accounts while simultaneously carrying credit card debt at much higher interest rates.
Crystallized Rationality: Crystallized Inhibitors			
Superstitious thinking and belief in the paranormal	Paranormal, Superstitious Thinking, and Luck Scales; Illusion of Control	Fenton-O'Creevy et al. (2003); Barber & Odean (2000)	A measure of illusion of control was (negatively) related to several measures of stock traders' performance, including their remuneration; personal investors trade too much and thus lower their investment returns.
Belief in the superiority of intuition	Faith in Intuition Scale	Epstein, Pacini, Denes-Raj, & Heier (1996)	Small observed correlations with depression, anxiety, and stress in nonselected samples.
Overreliance on folk wisdom	Folk psychology	Lilienfeld, Lynn, Ruscio, & Beyerstein (2010)	The many errors in folk psychology have been documented in publications like Lilienfeld et al. (2010): "we use only 10% of our brainpower"; left-brain right brain clichés; "opposites attract."
Belief in "special" expertise	High value placed on nongrounded knowledge sources	Toplak, Liu, Macpherson, Toneatto, & Stanovich (2007)	Problem gamblers are higher in measures of belief in phenomena not grounded in evidence.
Financial misconceptions	Financial literacy	Jarvis (2000); Valentine (1998)	The belief that reward can become decoupled from risk contributes to the proliferation of Ponzi and pyramid schemes.
Incorrigibility of introspection (overoptimistic Theories of one's own introspective powers)	Accuracy of affective forecasting	Schooler, Ariely, & Loewenstein (2003)	People who spent the most on their New Year's Eve celebrations were the most disappointed.
	Bias Blind Spot Test	Hilton (2003)	Professionals such as doctors and investment bankers have been shown to have little insight into which cues influence their decisions.

(Continued)

TABLE 10.2 Association Between Aspects of Rational Thought and Real-World Outcomes (*Continued*)

Components of Rational Thought

Crystallized Rationality: Crystallized Facilitators

Major Dimensions	Measurement Paradigms	Source for Association with Real-World Outcome	Association with Real-World Outcome
Dysfunctional personal beliefs	Measures of irrational personal beliefs	Epstein & Meier (1989)	Small-to-moderate correlations with alcohol and drug problems.
A notion of self that encourages egocentric processing	Unbiased processing of evidence	Forsythe, Nelson, Neumann, & Wright (1992)	Successful investors in a political prediction stock market exchange showed less of a tendency to overestimate the number of other people who shared their preferences.
	Self-perception biases, and unrealistic optimism	Dillard, Midboe, & Klein (2009)	Unrealistic optimism predicts negative events with alcohol longitudinally over a 2-year period after the incidence of earlier negative events is partialled out.

Their importance, and hence the necessity for assessment, stands or falls on the conceptual model, not on any future psychometric finding. An oversimplified example will illustrate the point. Imagine that highway safety researchers found that braking skill was causally associated with lifetime automobile accident frequency, that knowledge of the road rules was causally associated with lifetime automobile accident frequency, that city driving skill was causally associated with lifetime automobile accident frequency, that cornering skill was causally associated with lifetime automobile accident frequency, that defensive driving was causally associated with lifetime automobile accident frequency, and a host of other relationships. In short, collectively, these skills define a construct called "overall driver skill." Of course we could ask these researchers whether driving skill is a g-factor or whether it is really 50 little separate skills. But the point is that the outcome of the investigation of the structure of individual differences in driving skill would have no effect on the conceptual definition of what driving skill is. It may have logistical implications for measurement, however. Skills that are highly correlated might not all have to be assessed to get a good individual difference metric. But if they were all causally related to accident frequency, they would remain part of the conceptual definition of overall driver skill.

It is likewise with rational thinking. There is independent evidence in the literature of cognitive science that the cognitive components in Table 10–1 form part of the conceptual definition of rational thought. If several components or measurement paradigms turn out to be highly correlated, assessment will be more efficient and logistically easier. However, the outcome of such a correlational investigation will neither enhance nor diminish the status of these components as aspects of rational thought. Conversely, finding that many of the components or measurement paradigms are separable in individual difference analyses in no way detracts from the importance of the assessment of any component. It would, however, have logistical implications by making the comprehensive assessment of rational thought time-consuming and unwieldy. In short, the point is that psychometric findings do not trump what cognitive scientists have found are the conceptually essential features of rational thought and action.

The point that psychometric findings do not trump a concept that has theoretical or practical importance can be appreciated by simply looking at other areas of cognitive science that are as incompletely developed as rational thought. Take, for example, the important area of children's developing theory of mind (ToM; Goldman, 2006; Leslie, Friedman, & German, 2004; Nichols & Stich, 2003; Wellman & Liu, 2004). Like rationality, ToM has been found to have a variety of subcomponents (Baron-Cohen, 1995), and there is, as yet, less-than-complete agreement in characterizing them (Goldman, 2006; Nichols & Stich, 2003). No g-factor of ToM skills has yet been identified. The many laboratory tests of the construct remain important for theoretical purposes, although they have yet to yield a psychometric gold-standard standardized test. ToM has been linked to real-world outcomes such as school learning, but the causal nature of these links have not been established nor have the links been unambiguously shown to be independent of intelligence. Despite the nascent status of the concept, it remains an essential one in cognitive science with great promise for practical impact in educational psychology. We would not want to lesson the research effort on the concept just because its proponents cannot answer questions about its psychometric structure.

All of this is not to deny that it would obviously be useful to really know the structure of rational thinking skills from a psychometric point of view. Our research group has contributed to clarifying that structure. We have found that certain rational thinking tasks consistently correlate with each other even after cognitive ability has been partialled out. For example, we have found that the ability to avoid belief bias in syllogistic reasoning is related to the ability to reason statistically in the face of conflicting case evidence and that this relationship is maintained after intelligence is partialled out (Stanovich & West, 1998c; West et al., 2008). Additionally, our group has consistently found rational tasks that are predicted by thinking dispositions after cognitive ability has been partialled—particularly tasks involving statistical reasoning and informal argumentation (Kokis et al., 2002; Stanovich & West, 1997, 1998c; West et al., 2008).

Our point here is to emphasize that the importance of assessing rational thought is not contingent on any empirical outcome, and it especially is not contingent on any type of psychometric outcome. We want to spur efforts at assessing components of rational thought, and thus in this early stage of the endeavor we do not want the effort to be impeded by protests that it cannot be measured because its psychometric structure is uncertain. That structure will become clarified once our call for greater attention to the measurement of this domain is heeded. We do not fail to measure something because of lack of knowledge of the full structure of its domain. We would not fail to measure braking skill if we were ignorant of its precise relationship to cornering ability or knowledge of road rules.

If neither the fluid nor crystallized components of rational thought cluster in the manner of a g-factor (which we suspect), then rational thought will be a difficult concept to practically assess in its entirety. But again, we should not shirk from measuring something just because it is logistically difficult—particularly if the domain is important. Economists and public policy experts measured the size of their country's gross domestic product (GDP) in 1950 despite (by present standards) primitive statistical tools and data-gathering technology. The myriad components of the GDP (wheat, corn, ingots produced, heavy machinery produced, clothing, financial services, etc.) were each an important component of GDP in and of themselves. It was not an argument against measuring them that they were hard to measure, that there were myriad components, and that we did not know how all of the components hung together statistically. In 1950, economists measured what they could with the tools they had, and they simply hoped that better knowledge via better tools lay in the future. We are at a similar juncture in the measurement of the multifarious concept of rational thought.

We are at a similar nascent stage when it comes to determining the malleability of rational thinking—that is, when it comes to addressing the teachability and trainability of rational thinking skills. Nonetheless, there has been some progress on this question. Table 10–3 addresses the issue of the potential malleability of these skills. For each paradigm that partially defines a major dimension, we have listed at least one study that shows that the skill is possibly malleable via training, education, or experience. Each of the rational thinking skills in question has at least some direct or indirect evidence indicating that it is to some extent malleable.

The types of evidence listed in the Table 10–3 differ in terms of the strength of the inference that can be drawn. Some are true training studies using random assignment to experimental groups. Of course, such studies provide the strongest evidence that training does result in measurable increases in a rational thinking skill. Nevertheless, we have also

TABLE 10.3   Training, Education, Experience, and Knowledge Effects on the Components of Rational Thought

Components of Rational Thought

Fluid Rationality

Major Dimensions	Measurement Paradigms	Source for Training or Experiential Effect	Evidence for Training, Education, or Experiential Effect
Resistance to miserly information processing	Belief bias paradigms	Macpherson & Stanovich (2007); Evans, Newstead, Allen, & Pollard (1994)	Decontextualizing instructional set resulted in significantly less myside bias than nondirective instructions Debiasing instructions reduced belief bias on syllogistic reasoning tasks
	Attribute substitution (i.e., vividness substitution; affect substitution; denominator neglect)	Fong, Krantz, & Nisbett (1986); Fong & Nisbett (1991)	Rule training, training using examples, and a combination of rule training and training using examples resulted in significantly better performance on statistical reasoning problems involving vividness substitution (Saab/Volvo problem). These training effects were maintained after 2 weeks.
	Cognitive Reflection Test	Duckworth, Ragland, Sommerfeld, & Wyne (1974); Egeland (1974); Zelniker, Cochavi, & Yered (1974); Zelniker, Jeffrey, Ault, & Parsons (1972)	Training effects have been shown on tasks related to the Matching Familiar Figures Test (MFFT), a measure capturing the dimension of reflectivity and impulsivity.
	Disjunctive reasoning tasks	Evans, Newstead, & Byrne (1993)	Facilitation found on disjunctive reasoning tasks when it was made clear in the problem that alternatives needed to be generated and tested.
	Accurate perception of risks and benefits	Dieckmann, Slovic, & Peters (2009)	Participants with higher numeracy skills were more likely to rely on stated likelihoods and less likely to focus on narrative evidence in risk assessment than those with lower numeracy skills.

	Resistance to base-rate neglect	Case, Fantino, & Goodie (1999)	Base-rate training with case cues reduced base-rate neglect in a sample of college students.
	Outcome bias paradigms; status quo bias; endowment effects	Thaler & Sunstein (2008)	Status quo and endowment effects are easily remedied by changing default values—that is, by changing the environment rather than the cognition of individuals.
	Hindsight bias paradigms	Fischhoff (1982; 2002); Arkes, Faust, Guilmette, & Hart (1988)	Asking participants to consider alternative explanations and contrary evidence reduced hindsight bias.
	Diagnostic hypothesis testing	Moutier, Angeard, & Houdé (2002)	Participants trained to inhibit the matching bias on the selection task displayed better performance than participants who did not receive training.
	Accuracy of affective forecasting	Richard, van der Plight, & de Vries (1996)	Participants who were asked to focus on their anticipated, post-behavioral feelings in relation to unsafe sex and risk-taking behavior were more likely to generate negative feelings such as regret and reported adoption of safer sex practices than respondents who were asked to report on the behaviors themselves. Those respondents who had to focus on anticipated feelings showed less risky behavior 5 months after the initial experiment.
Resistance to myside thinking; accurate self-evaluation	Overconfidence paradigms; fairness paradigms; Argument Evaluation Test	Fischhoff (1982; 2002); Arkes, Christensen, Lai, & Blumer (1987)	Asking participants to consider alternative explanations and contrary evidence reduced overconfidence.
		Lichtenstein, & Fischhoff (1980)	Participants who received intensive training on probability assessment with feedback on performance significantly reduced overconfidence ratings.
	Unbiased processing of evidence	Macpherson & Stanovich (2007)	Decontextualizing instructional set resulted in significantly less myside bias than nondirective instructions
		Toplak & Stanovich (2003)	Increasing years of university education was correlated with less myside bias—that is, less of a tendency to generate more arguments and evidence in favor of a previously held position.

(Continued)

TABLE 10.3 Training, Education, Experience, and Knowledge Effects on the Components of Rational Thought (*Continued*)

Components of Rational Thought

Fluid Rationality

Major Dimensions	Measurement Paradigms	Source for Training or Experiential Effect	Evidence for Training, Education, or Experiential Effect
Absence of irrelevant context effects in decision making	Framing effects; preference reversals	Peters, Västfjäll, Slovic, Mertz, Mazzocco, & Dickert (2006) Almashat, Ayotte, Edelstein, & Margrett (2008)	Participants higher in numeracy skills were less susceptible to framing effects than participants lower in numeracy skills. Notably, numeracy skill effects were not eliminated when IQ was entered. Participants who were asked to list the advantages and disadvantages of hypothetical medical decision-making treatments did not show a framing effect, relative a control group who was not instructed to consider advantages and disadvantages.
	Avoidance of irrelevant anchoring	Galinsky & Mussweiler (2001) Mussweiler, Strack, & Pfeiffer (2000) Mumma & Wilson (1995)	Regarding the anchoring effect on first offers in buyer–seller negotiations, this study demonstrated that the anchoring effect can be eliminated if the negotiators considered the alternatives of one's opponent, and if the negotiators considered their own target prices and ideal outcomes. Anchoring effects were reduced when participants were prompted to use a "consider the opposite" strategy. Debiasing strategies of "consider the opposite" and cues to take notes on the cues prior to making judgments reduced anchoring effects.

Belief flexibility: actively open-minded thinking	Actively open-minded thinking scale; need for closure; dogmatism; belief identification; epistemological understanding	Schommer (1998)	Education was associated with epistemological beliefs related to the complexity and certainty of knowledge.
Value placed on reason and truth	The Master Rationality Motive Scale	Miller & Rollnick (2002); Miller & Rose (2009); Hodgins, Currie, Currie, & Fick, 2009)	One main component of motivational interviewing therapy involves the therapist assisting with creating and amplifying a discrepancy between clients' present behavior and their broader goals. This therapy has been shown to positively change a number of health and mental health outcomes, such as cardiovascular rehabilitation, diabetes management, hypertension, illicit drug use, problem drinking, gambling, and smoking.
Tendency to seek information, enjoy thought, and fully process information	Measures of need for cognition and typical intellectual engagement	Cacioppo, Petty, Feinstein, & Jarvis (1996)	Educational level is associated with need for cognition.
	Disjunctive reasoning tasks	Evans, Newstead, & Byrne (1993) Shanteau, Grier, Johnson, & Berner (1991)	Facilitation found on disjunctive reasoning task when it was made clear in the problem that alternatives needed to be generated and tested. Trainee nursing students were given scenarios to evaluate alternative choices of action with patients. With training using an alternative-by-outcome trade-off table that incorporated explicit consideration of all options and comparison of options the trainee nursing students made better choices.
Objective reasoning styles	Separating fact from opinion and theory from evidence; recognizing the validity and invalidity of informal arguments; argument evaluation test	Kuhn (1989, 1991)	College students generated more genuine evidence and alternative theories than noncollege students.

(Continued)

TABLE 10.3 Training, Education, Experience, and Knowledge Effects on the Components of Rational Thought (*Continued*)

Components of Rational Thought

Fluid Rationality

Major Dimensions	Measurement Paradigms	Source for Training or Experiential Effect	Evidence for Training, Education, or Experiential Effect
Sensitivity to contradiction; tendency to seek consistency in belief and argument	Informal reasoning and argument evaluation paradigms	Toplak & Stanovich (2003)	Increasing years of university education were correlated with less myside bias—that is, less of a tendency to generate more arguments and evidence in favor of a previously held position.
Sense of self-efficacy	Locus of Control Scales	Aronson, Fried, & Good (2002); Blackwell, Trzesniewski, & Dweck (2007)	Interventions that emphasized malleable, changeable aspects of learning, as compared to fixed abilities, resulted in significant improvements in grades and changes in motivation.
Prudently discounting the future	Temporal discounting of reward	Fishbach & Trope (2005)	Experimental manipulations of externally imposed self-control strategies helped participants overcome the unexpected short-term costs of decisions to pursue long-term benefits.
Self-control skills	Delay of gratification paradigms; time preference; future orientation	Diamond, Barnett, Thomas, & Munro (2007)	Executive function (EF) training curriculum resulted in significance increase in cognitive control skills, including inhibitory control, working memory and cognitive flexibility, as compared to a balanced literacy program in preschool children.
Fine-grained and controlled emotional regulation	Measures of Alexithymia	Elliott & Greenberg (2007); Pos, Greenberg, & Warwar (2009)	The focus of therapy based on process-experiential emotion theory is to help clients understand their emotions, to help them reflect and re-evaluate their emotions, and to expose them to more adaptive emotional responses. This therapy has been shown to improve symptoms in disorders of affective dysfunction, such as depression.

Major Dimensions	Measurement Paradigms	Source for Training or Experiential Effect	Evidence for Training, Education, or Experiential Effect
Emotional regulation related to reward	Iowa Gambling Task	Brand, Laier, Pawlikowski, & Markowitsch (2009)	In a task measuring decision making under risk (Game of Dice Task), participants who completed the task with feedback outperformed participants who received no feedback. Participants who used calculative decision strategies, such as using mathematical operations, also performed better than those who did not use such strategies.

Crystallized Rationality: Crystallized Facilitators

Major Dimensions	Measurement Paradigms	Source for Training or Experiential Effect	Evidence for Training, Education, or Experiential Effect
Probabilistic reasoning	Importance of sample size	Lehman & Nisbett (1990); Fong, Krantz, & Nisbett (1986); Fong & Nisbett (1991); Kosonen & Winne (1995)	Undergraduate training in social science and psychology significantly improved performance on statistical and methodological reasoning related to the law of large numbers. Training formal rule properties and presenting sample problems on the law of large numbers resulted in improved statistical reasoning performance.
	Consistent probability judgments	Agnoli & Krantz (1989); Moutier & Houdé (2003)	Participants who received training on concepts of algebra, such as using Venn diagrams to explain logical relations of inclusion, disjunction, and overlap, did significantly better on conjunction problems. Participants trained to inhibit the conjunction fallacy on a frequency judgment task displayed better performance on probability judgment.

(Continued)

TABLE 10.3 Training, Education, Experience, and Knowledge Effects on the Components of Rational Thought (*Continued*)

Components of Rational Thought

Crystallized Rationality: Crystallized Facilitators

Major Dimensions	Measurement Paradigms	Source for Training or Experiential Effect	Evidence for Training, Education, or Experiential Effect
	Resistance to base-rate neglect	Case, Fantino, & Goodie (1999)	Base-rate training with case cues reduced base-rate neglect in a sample of college students.
	Resistance to gambler's fallacy	Ladouceur, Sylvain, Boutin, Lachance, Doucet, Leblond, & Jacques (2001)	Pathological gamblers who received training in statistical concepts related to gambling, such as randomness and independence, met fewer diagnostic criteria for gambling, showed less desire to gamble, and gambled less frequently than a waitlist control group.
	Use of chance in explanatory frameworks; understanding random processes	Fong, Krantz, & Nisbett (1986)	Rule training, training using examples, and a combination of rule training and training using examples resulted in significantly better performance on statistical reasoning problems involving inferences about random variation.
	Understanding regression effects	Lehman & Nisbett (1990) Lehman, Lempert, & Nisbett (1988)	Undergraduate training in social science and psychology significantly improved performance on statistical and methodological reasoning. Graduate training in medicine and psychology was associated with better performance on statistical and methodological reasoning.
	Recognizing biased and unbiased samples	Lehman & Nisbett (1990) Lehman, Lempert, & Nisbett (1988)	Undergraduate training in social science and psychology significantly improved performance on statistical and methodological reasoning. Graduate training in medicine and psychology was associated with better performance on statistical and methodological reasoning.

	Diagnostic hypothesis testing	Platt & Griggs (1993)	Participants who were instructed to provide reasons for their selections and were provided with explicated rules displayed significant facilitation on selection task performance.
	Accurate perception of risks	Davids, Schapira, McAuliffe, & Nattinger (2004); Schwartz, Woloshin, Black, & Welch (1997)	Participants who had higher numeracy knowledge were better able to use risk reduction data to adjust risk estimates for understanding the risk of breast cancer.
Qualitative decision theory insights	Stable preferences; adherence to basic probability/utility trade-offs in SEU theory; preferences in line with SEU axioms	Donkers, Melenberg, & van Soest, (2001)	Study found that more educated subjects were more likely to choose options that maximized expected utility
Knowledge of scientific reasoning	Scientific control concepts; causal variable isolation; control group necessity; understanding placebo and selection effects	Schaller, Asp, Ceynar Roseil, & Heim (1996) Kuhn & Dean (2005)	Students received training in statistical concepts, including the logic of analysis of covariance, relative to a control group. One week later, participants who received the statistical training were better able to identify a confound in a presented task than the control group. Students who participated in a computer-based program on scientific enquiry skills were compared to students in a control group who participated in a typical science class. Students in the experimental group made significantly more valid inferences about manipulations than students in the control group.
	Avoidance of confirmation bias	Wiley (2005)	Participants who had high prior knowledge on a controversial issue were better able to recall arguments on both sides of the issue in comparison to participants who had low prior knowledge.
	Diagnostic covariation judgment	Klahr & Nigam (2004)	Direct explicit instruction about a strategy for the control of variables was helpful to children in Grades 3 and 4 who were learning experimental design.

(Continued)

TABLE 10.3 Training, Education, Experience, and Knowledge Effects on the Components of Rational Thought (*Continued*)

Components of Rational Thought

Crystallized Rationality: Crystallized Facilitators

Major Dimensions	Measurement Paradigms	Source for Training or Experiential Effect	Evidence for Training, Education, or Experiential Effect
	Covariation detection free of belief bias; avoidance of illusory correlations	Leshowitz, Jenkens, Heaton, & Bough (1993)	Students who received teacher directed lessons in evaluating the scientific basis of advertisements in magazines and newspapers outperformed the control group in evaluating the claims made in the new advertisements.
	Difference between Correlation and causation; recognizing spurious correlation	Leshowitz, DiCerbo, & Okun (2002)	Undergraduate students involved in an instructional program in methodological reasoning with an emphasis on understanding correlation and causation outperformed a control group.
	Understanding falsifiability as a context for confirmation; thinking of the alternative hypothesis	O'Brien & Overton (1980); Overton, Byrnes, & O'Brien, (1985)	Young adults benefited from contradiction training on conditional reasoning tasks.
	Differentiating theory from evidence	Kuhn & Pease (2008)	Students participated in a computer-based program on scientific enquiry skills that examined the forecasting of earthquakes. From pre- to post-test, students showed an increase in their reliance on using and integrating evidence to explain results and a decrease in exclusive reliance on a theory-based explanation.
	Appreciation of converging evidence	Halpern (2003); Stanovich (2010); Wade & Tavris (2008)	This concept is widely taught in critical thinking courses and scientific methodology courses under the assumption that it is teachable.

	Appreciating the limits of personal observation, testimonials, and single-case evidence	Kuhn & Pease (2008)	Students participated in a computer-based program on scientific enquiry skills that examined the forecasting of earthquakes. From pre– to post-test, students showed a decrease in their reliance on single case instances.
Rules of logical consistency and validity	Logical validity judgment tasks	Lehman & Nisbett (1990) Cheng, Holyoak, Nisbett, & Oliver (1986); Klaczynski & Laipple (1993) Klauer, Stegmaier, & Meiser (1997).	Undergraduate training in natural science and humanities training displayed significantly improved performance on problems in conditional logic. Training in applying logical rules plus application to concrete problems resulted in better performance on selection task problems. Training in a truth table evaluation task resulted in substantial performance improvements on propositional syllogistic reasoning.
Economic thinking	Cost/Benefit reasoning; limited resource reasoning	Larrick, Morgan, & Nisbett (1990)	Participants who were trained on cost–benefit rules (including the sunk cost principle and the derivative extra–cost principle) performed better on reasoning on these types of problems, in comparison to a group that received no training.
	Recognizing opportunity costs	Larrick, Nisbett, & Morgan (1993) Frederick, Novemsky, Wang, Dhar, & Nowlis (2009)	Students who had taken more economics courses were more likely to recognize opportunity costs. Explicit mention of lost opportunity cost on purchases resulted in more selections that acknowledged the lost opportunity, as compared to a condition that made no mention of lost opportunities.
	Avoiding sunk costs	Fennema & Perkins (2008	Participants trained in sunk costs in managerial accounting courses performed better on tasks requiring them to assess whether to proceed on projects or to discontinue because of sunk costs relative to untrained students.

(Continued)

TABLE 10.3 Training, Education, Experience, and Knowledge Effects on the Components of Rational Thought (*Continued*)

Components of Rational Thought

Crystallized Rationality: Crystallized Facilitators

Major Dimensions	Measurement Paradigms	Source for Training or Experiential Effect	Evidence for Training, Education, or Experiential Effect
	Understanding externalities	Burkett (2006)	This concept is widely taught in economics courses under the assumption that it is teachable.
	Awareness of the logic of exponential growth and compounding	Banks & Oldfield (2007)	Numeracy levels are associated with higher wealth.
	Understanding commons dilemmas, zero-sum, and nonzero-sum games	Axelrod & Hamilton (1981)	Players in iterative prisoner's dilemma games where the number of interactions is not known in advanced can learn a cooperative strategies such as TIT-FOR-TAT.
		McNeel (1973)	Participants playing prisoner's dilemma games were trained to cooperate when the outcomes are presented in terms of their own gains, as opposed to their gains relative to the other player.
		Dawes, Van de kragt, & Orbell (1988)	Participants were asked to make a single anonymous binary choice between cooperation and defection involving substantial amounts of money. They displayed high rates of cooperation when the benefits of cooperating accrued to members of a group that discussed the problem.
	Recognizing regression effects that encourage buying high and selling low	Lehman, Lempert, & Nisbett (1988)	Graduate training in medicine and psychology was associated with better performance on statistical and methodological reasoning.
	Appropriate mental accounting and understanding of fungibility	Larrick, Nisbett, & Morgan (1993)	Students who had taken more economics courses were more likely to recognize the net benefit rule.

Crystallized Rationality: Crystallized Inhibitors

Major Dimensions	Measurement Paradigms	Source for Training or Experiential Effect	Evidence for Training, Education, or Experiential Effect
Superstitious thinking and belief in the paranormal	Paranormal, Superstitious Thinking, and Luck Scales; illusion of control	Echeburua, Baez, & Fernandez-Montalvo (1996) Banziger (1983) Miller, Wozniak, Rust, Miller, & Slezak (1996)	Pathological gamblers in a treatment group receiving cognitive restructuring, such as challenging beliefs about illusion of control, had higher rates of abstinence from gambling 6 months after treatment compared to a waitlist control group. Older adults (median = 67 years) participated in a two-session course on parapsychology. Pre-/post-test comparisons on the Belief in the Paranormal Scale indicated an enduring shift toward skepticism. Counter-attitudinal advocacy was effective in increasing students' skepticism about paranormal beliefs.
Belief in the superiority of intuition	Faith in Intuition Scale	Kowalski & Taylor (2009)	A refutational approached that involved activating, then immediately countering, a misconception was found to decrease college students' agreement with common misconceptions such as "Human intuition is remarkably accurate and free from error."
Overreliance on folk wisdom and folk psychology	Folk Wisdom Tests	Kowalski & Taylor (2009)	A refutational approached that involved activating, then immediately countering, a misconception was found to decrease college students' agreement with common misconceptions such as "A schizophrenic is someone with a split personality."

(Continued)

TABLE 10.3 Training, Education, Experience, and Knowledge Effects on the Components of Rational Thought (*Continued*)

Crystallized Rationality: Crystallized Inhibitors

Major Dimensions	Measurement Paradigms	Source for Training or Experiential Effect	Evidence for Training, Education, or Experiential Effect
Belief in "special" expertise	High value placed on nongrounded knowledge sources	Furnham & McGill (2003)	Time spent in medical school was positively associated with increased skepticism about alternative medicine.
Financial misconceptions	Financial Literacy/Illiteracy Scales	Bhandari, Hassanein, & Deaves (2008)	Participants provided with textual feedback and graphical representations that provided information about investment options showed a lowered impact of investment-related cognitive biases, such as insufficient diversification in financial portfolios.
Incorrigibility of introspection (overoptimistic theories of one's own introspective powers)	Accuracy of affective forecasting	Richard, van der Plight, & de Vries (1996)	Participants who were asked to focus on their anticipated, postbehavioral feelings in relation to unsafe sex and risk-taking behavior were more likely to generate negative feelings such as regret and reported adoption of safer sex practices than respondents who were asked to report on the behaviors itself. Those respondents who had to focus on anticipated feelings showed less risky behavior five months after the initial experiment.
	Bias Blind Spot Test	Pronin, & Kugler (2007)	Participants who were educated about the role of nonconscious processes were more likely to avoid the bias blind spot error.

Dysfunctional personal beliefs	Measures of irrational personal beliefs	Kendall, Hudson, Gosch, Flannery-Schroeder & Suveg (2008) Bentz, Williamson, & Franks (2004)	Individual and family cognitive-behavioral therapy interventions addressing irrational anxieties were superior to a treatment using family-based education, attention, and support in children and adolescents with anxiety Participants who were in a group receiving instructions to consider alternative positive information displayed significantly reduced pessimistic predictions of future events relative to the control group.
A notion of self that encourages egocentric processing	Unbiased processing of evidence	Toplak & Stanovich (2003)	Increasing years of university education was correlated with less myside bias—that is, less of a tendency to generate more arguments and evidence in favor of a previously held position.
	Self-perception biases, and unrealistic optimism	Rose & Windschitl (2008)	Egocentric weighting and optimism decreased across rounds in a full feedback condition.

included other, weaker types of evidence in Table 10–3. For example, we have included some studies showing that levels of a rational thinking skill are correlated with educational level and/or experience. Such correlational evidence is of course suggestive, but it is not definitive evidence that the skill is teachable or trainable. Nonetheless, it is impressive that, given so many different areas of rational thought displayed in Table 10–3, there is at least some type of evidence suggesting the trainability of each one of them.

Of course, because the relationships among the components have yet to be worked out, it is presently unclear whether training on any one component of rational thought might improve others. In the domain of crystallized facilitators, there is certainly reason to believe that this might be the case. For example, the many components of the major dimension of "Knowledge of Scientific Reasoning" are often taught in courses as an interrelated set of thinking skills. Whether or not research has shown the training of any particular component to generalize to the learning of another, methodology instructors all over the world are certainly proceeding under the assumption that this is the case. They are also proceeding under the assumption that any given component in the list under this domain of knowledge is teachable. And this is true with respect to virtually all the areas of crystallized facilitator and inhibitors: probabilistic reasoning, decision theory insights, scientific reasoning, logic, economic thinking, and avoidance of various aspects of superstitious thinking. That is, whatever evidence exists in the actual scientific literature for the trainability of such skills, major societal institutions (schools) are proceeding under the pragmatic assumption that such skills are teachable. The same is not true in the domains of fluid rationality.

Our *a priori* expectation about the teachability of the various thinking styles comprising the category of fluid rationality is more complex. Some dimensions, such as actively open-minded thinking and objective reasoning styles, might be more like heritable personality traits (noting this is not, of course, to imply that heritability is necessarily correlated with lack of malleability). Other aspects of fluid rationality are harder to characterize. For example, the three major dimensions of rational thought that lead off the Table 10–3 (and Fig. 10–1) are: resistance to miserly information processing; resistance to myside thinking; and absence of irrelevant context effects. Components of all three of these major dimensions have been successfully trained by teaching variants of a "consider the opposite" or "consider the alternative" strategy (Almashat et al., 2008; Arkes et al., 1987; Arkes et al., 1988; Fischhoff, 1982, 2002; Galinsky & Mussweiler, 2001). Thus, perhaps the findings on training are indicating that these major dimensions are interrelated, something that will be determined by future research.

The nature of the significant training effect on these three dimensions does, however, highlight the complexity of classifying rational thinking skills. It might seem that, because the training strategy is essentially one of learning some declarative knowledge ("think of the opposite") and applying it, these dimensions of rational thought must be classified as crystallized and not fluid. We think not, because of a critical facet of the training. The use of the instruction must be triggered quickly and automatically in contexts where processing would be biased by one-sided thinking. The strategy must be so "highly compiled," so to speak, that it ends up operating in the manner of a thinking disposition. Consequently, the skills that ensure these three positive outcomes—resistance to miserly information processing; resistance to myside thinking; and absence of irrelevant context effects—actually do end up looking, from a processing point of view, like other of the dispositions of fluid rationality (need for cognition, actively open-minded thinking). Regardless of how these issues of classification are finally resolved, we acknowledge the taxonomic complexities here.

The Future of Research on Individual Differences in Rational Thought

The issues about assessment raised in this chapter represent the current point of our research program on individual differences in rational thought. We began by examining whether individual differences might have implications for the Great Rationality Debate in cognitive science (*see* Chapter 1). In the course of those investigations, we were led to the insight that individual differences in rational thought might be used to fractionate the notion of Type 2 processing (Chapters 2–4). In building an alternative, tripartite view of cognition, we elaborated the idea of the reflective mind. In addition to situating the concept of rationality within the tripartite model, our view also contextualizes the concept of intelligence and emphasizes that the concept should be defined as it is operationalized in cognitive science—not according to the broader but unoperationalized notions in folk psychology.

From the tri-process model of cognition, we were led to develop a taxonomy of rational thinking errors that have been revealed in the heuristics and biases literature (Chapter 6). Individual differences have been found in virtually every task in this taxonomy, and we have conducted numerous investigations of the structure of this variability. For example, over the years we have collected considerable data on the relationships between aspects of rational thought and intelligence. Given the high status of the latter concept in both the science of psychology and in the public mind, the associations tend to be surprisingly modest (Chapters 7 and 8). We have shown that this is to be expected when intelligence and rationality are properly situated within the tripartite model. Simply put, the data indicate that knowledge of a person's intelligence does very little to predict how they will do on measures of rational thinking. In Chapter 9, the social implications of this modest association were explored.

One such implication was that if we value the parts of cognition that are missed by IQ tests, we need to create assessment devices for the parts of cognition that are missing. In this chapter, we have tried to lay the foundations for such an effort. In this and previous chapters, we have shown that there is no conceptual obstacle to the development of such an assessment device. At present, of course, there is no IQ-type test for rationality—that is, a test of one's rationality quotient (RQ). However, we have shown that the field has in hand prototypes of the kinds of tasks that would be used in the domains of both instrumental rationality and epistemic rationality (*see* Table 10–1). In this chapter, we hope to have motivated other researchers to participate in developing versions of these prototypes that might be used as assessment devices. There is value in assessing rational thought because, as shown in this chapter, rational thought is related to real-world consequences and it can be taught.

References

Abelson, R. P. (1963). Computer simulation of "hot cognition". In S. Tomkins & S. Messick (Eds.), *Computer simulation of personality: Frontier of psychological theory* (pp. 277–298). New York: John Wiley.

Ackerman, P. L. (1994). Intelligence, attention, and learning: Maximal and typical performance. In D. K. Detterman (Ed.), *Current topics in human intelligence (Vol. 4)* (pp. 1–27). Norwood, NJ: Ablex.

Ackerman, P. L. (1996). A theory of adult development: Process, personality, interests, and knowledge. *Intelligence, 22,* 227–257.

Ackerman, P. L., & Heggestad, E. D. (1997). Intelligence, personality, and interests: Evidence for overlapping traits. *Psychological Bulletin, 121,* 219–245.

Ackerman, P. L., & Kanfer, R. (2004). Cognitive, affective, and conative aspects of adult intellect within a typical and maximal performance framework. In D. Y. Dai & R. J. Sternberg (Eds.), *Motivation, emotion, and cognition: Integrative perspectives on intellectual functioning and development* (pp. 119–141). Mahwah, NJ: Lawrence Erlbaum Associates.

Ackerman, P., Kyllonen, P., & Richards, R. (Eds.). (1999). *Learning and individual differences: Process, trait, and content determinants.* Washington, DC: American Psychological Association.

Adler, J. E. (1984). Abstraction is uncooperative. *Journal for the Theory of Social Behaviour, 14,* 165–181.

Adler, J. E. (1991). An optimist's pessimism: Conversation and conjunctions. In E. Eells & T. Maruszewski (Eds.), *Probability and rationality: Studies on L. Jonathan Cohen's philosophy of science* (pp. 251–282). Amsterdam: Editions Rodopi.

Agnoli, F., & Krantz, D. H. (1989). Suppressing natural heuristics by formal instruction: The case of the conjunction fallacy. *Cognitive Psychology, 21,* 515–550.

Ahluwalia, R., & Gurhan-Canli, Z. (2000). The effects of extensions on the family
brand name: An accessibility-diagnosticity perspective. *Journal of Consumer
Research, 27,* 371–381.

Ainslie, G. (1982). A behavioral economic approach to the defence mechanisms:
Freud's energy theory revisited. *Social Science Information, 21,* 735–780.

Ainslie, G. (1992). *Picoeconomics.* Cambridge: Cambridge University Press.

Ainslie, G. (2001). *Breakdown of will.* Cambridge: Cambridge University Press.

Ainslie, G. (2005). Precis of Breakdown of will. *Behavioral and Brain Sciences, 28,*
635–673.

Ajzen, I. (1977). Intuitive theories of events and the effects of base-rate information
on prediction. *Journal of Personality and Social Psychology, 35,* 303–314.

Almashat, S., Ayotte, B., Edelstein, B., & Margrett, J. (2008). Framing effect debiasing
in medical decision making. *Patient Education and Counseling, 71,* 102–107.

Alter, A. L., & Oppenheimer, D. M. (2009). Uniting the tribes of fluency to form a
metacognitive nation. *Personality and Social Psychology Review, 13,* 219–235.

Alter, A. L., Oppenheimer, D. M., Epley, N., & Eyre, R. N. (2007). Overcoming intuition: Metacognitive difficulty activates analytic reasoning. *Journal of Experimental
Psychology: General, 136,* 569–576.

Ameriks, J., Caplin, A., & Leahy, J. (2003). Wealth accumulation and the propensity to
plan. *Quarterly Journal of Economics, 118,* 1007–1047.

Anderson, J. R. (1990). *The adaptive character of thought.* Hillsdale, NJ: Erlbaum.

Anderson, M. (1998). Mental retardation, general intelligence, and modularity.
Learning and Individual Differences, 10, 159–178.

Anderson, M. (2005). Marrying intelligence and cognition: A developmental view.
In R. J. Sternberg & J. E. Pretz (Eds.), *Cognition and intelligence* (pp. 268–287).
New York: Cambridge University Press.

Ariely, D., & Wertenbroch, K. (2002). Procrastination, deadlines, and performance:
Self-control by precommitment. *Psychological Science, 13,* 219–224.

Arkes, H. R. (1991). Costs and benefits of judgment errors: Implications for debiasing. *Psychological Bulletin, 110,* 486–498.

Arkes, H. R., & Ayton, P. (1999). The sunk cost and Concorde effects: Are humans less
rational than lower animals? *Psychological Bulletin, 125,* 591–600.

Arkes, H. R., & Blumer, C. (1985). The psychology of sunk cost. *Organizational
Behavior and Human Decision Processes, 35,* 124–140.

Arkes, H. R., Christensen, C., Lai, C., & Blumer, C. (1987). Two methods of reducing
overconfidence. *Organizational Behavior and Human Decision Processes, 39,*
133–144.

Arkes, H., Faust, D., Guilmette, T., & Hart, K. (1988). Eliminating the hindsight bias.
Journal of Applied Psychology, 73, 305–307.

Aron, A. R. (2008). Progress in executive-function research: From tasks to functions
to regions to networks. *Current Directions in Psychological Science, 17,* 124–129.

Aronson, J., Fried, C., & Good, C. (2002). Reducing the effects of stereotype threat on African American college students by shaping theories of intelligence. *Journal of Experimental Social Psychology, 38*, 113–125.

Atance, C. M., & Jackson, L. K. (2009). The development and coherence of the future-oriented behaviors during the preschool years. *Journal of Experimental Child Psychology, 102*, 379–391.

Atance, C. M., & O'Neill, D. K. (2001). Episodic future thinking. *Trends in Cognitive Sciences, 5*, 533–539.

Atran, S. (1998). Folk biology and the anthropology of science: Cognitive universals and cultural particulars. *Behavioral and Brain Sciences, 21*, 547–609.

Atran, S. (2002). *In Gods we trust: The evolutionary landscape of religion*. Oxford: Oxford University Press.

Audi, R. (1993). *The structure of justification*. Cambridge: Cambridge University Press.

Audi, R. (2001). *The architecture of reason: The structure and substance of rationality*. Oxford: Oxford University Press.

Aunger, R. (Ed.). (2000). *Darwinizing culture: The status of memetics as a science*. Oxford: Oxford University Press.

Aunger, R. (2002). *The electric meme: A new theory of how we think*. New York: Free Press.

Aunger, R., & Curtis, V. (2008). Kinds of behaviour. *Biology & Philosophy, 23*, 317–345.

Austin, E. J., & Deary, I. J. (2002). Personality dispositions. In R. J. Sternberg (Ed.), *Why smart people can be so stupid* (pp. 187–211). New Haven, CT: Yale University Press.

Axelrod, R., & Hamilton, W. D. (1981). The evolution of cooperation. *Science, 211*, 1390–1396.

Ayduk, O., & Mischel, W. (2002). When smart people behave stupidly: Reconciling inconsistencies in social-emotional intelligence. In R. J. Sternberg (Ed.), *Why smart people can be so stupid* (pp. 86–105). New Haven, CT: Yale University Press.

Ayton, P., & Fischer, I. (2004). The hot hand fallacy and the gambler's fallacy: Two faces of subjective randomness? *Memory & Cognition, 32*, 1369–1378.

Baddeley, A. D. (1992). Working memory. *Science, 255*, 556–559.

Baddeley, A., Chincotta, D., & Adlam, A. (2001). Working memory and the control of action: Evidence from task switching. *Journal of Experimental Psychology: General, 130*, 641–657.

Bagassi, M., & Macchi, L. (2006). Pragmatic approach to decision making under uncertainty: The case of the disjunction effect. *Thinking and Reasoning, 12*, 329–350.

Bagby, R. M., Parker, J. D. A., & Taylor, G. J. (1994). The twenty-item Toronto Alexithymia Scale-I. Item selection and cross-validation of the factor structure. *Journal of Psychosomatic Research, 38*, 23–32.

Baker, T. B., McFall, R. M., & Shoham, V. (2009). Current status and future prospects of clinical psychology: Toward a scientifically principled approach to mental and behavioral health care. *Psychological Science In The Public Interest, 9*, 67–103.

Baldwin, D. A. (2000). Interpersonal understanding fuels knowledge acquisition. *Current Directions in Psychological Science, 9*, 40–45.

Baltes, P. B., & Staudinger, U. M. (2000). Wisdom: A metaheuristic (pragmatic) to orchestrate mind and virtue toward excellence. *American Psychologist, 55*, 122–136.

Banks, J., & Oldfield, Z. (2007). Understanding pensions: Cognitive function, numerical ability and retirement saving. *Fiscal Studies, 28*, 143–170.

Banziger, G. (1983). Normalizing the paranormal: Short-term and long-term change in belief in the paranormal among older learners during a short course. *Teaching of Psychology, 10*, 212–214.

Barber, B., & Odean, T. (2000). Trading is hazardous to your wealth: The common stock investment performance of individual investors. *Journal of Finance, 60*, 773–806.

Barbaresi, W., Katusic, S., Colligan, R., Weaver, A., & Jacobsen, S. (2005). The incidence of autism in Olmsted County, Minnesota, 1976-1997. *Archives of Pediatric and Adolescent Medicine, 159*, 37–44.

Bargh, J. A., & Chartrand, T. L. (1999). The unbearable automaticity of being. *American Psychologist, 54*, 462–479.

Bar-Hillel, M. (1980). The base-rate fallacy in probability judgments. *Acta Psychologica, 44*, 211–233.

Bar-Hillel, M. (1990). Back to base rates. In R. M. Hogarth (Ed.), *Insights into decision making: A tribute to Hillel J. Einhorn* (pp. 200–216). Chicago: University of Chicago Press.

Barkley, R. A. (1998). *Attention-deficit hyperactivity disorder: A handbook for diagnosis and treatment (Second Edition).* New York: Guilford Press.

Baron, J. (1985). *Rationality and intelligence.* Cambridge: Cambridge University Press.

Baron, J. (1991). Beliefs about thinking. In J. Voss, D. Perkins & J. Segal (Eds.), *Informal reasoning and education* (pp. 169–186). Hillsdale, NJ: Erlbaum.

Baron, J. (1993). *Morality and rational choice.* Dordrecht: Kluwer.

Baron, J. (1995). Myside bias in thinking about abortion. *Thinking and Reasoning, 1*, 221–235.

Baron, J. (1998). *Judgment misguided: Intuition and error in public decision making.* New York: Oxford University Press.

Baron, J. (1999). Utility maximization as a solution: Promise, difficulties, and impediments. *American Behavioral Scientist, 42*, 1301–1321.

Baron, J. (2008). *Thinking and deciding (Fourth Edition).* Cambridge, MA: Cambridge University Press.

Baron, J., Bazerman, M. H., & Shonk, K. (2006). Enlarging the societal pie through wise legislation. A psychological perspective. *Perspectives on Psychological Science, 1*, 123–132.

Baron, J., & Hershey, J. C. (1988). Outcome bias in decision evaluation. *Journal of Personality and Social Psychology, 54*, 569–579.

Baron, J., & Ritov, I. (2004). Omission bias, individual differences, and normality. *Organizational Behavior and Human Decision Processes, 94*, 74–85.

Baron-Cohen, S. (1995). *Mindblindness: An essay on autism and theory of mind.* Cambridge, MA: The MIT Press.

Barrett, H. C., & Kurzban, R. (2006). Modularity in cognition: Framing the debate. *Psychological Review, 113,* 628–647.

Barrett, J. L. (2004). *Why would anyone believe in God?.* Lanham, MD: AltaMira Press.

Barrett, L., Henzi, P., & Dunbar, R. (2003). Primate cognition: From "what now?" to "what if." *Trends in Cognitive Sciences, 7,* 494–497.

Bartels, D. M. (2006). Proportion dominance: The generality and variability of favouring relative savings over absolute savings. *Organizational Behavior and Human Decision Processes, 100,* 76–95.

Bateman, I., Dent, S., Peters, E., Slovic, P., & Starmer, C. (2007). The affect heuristic and the attractiveness of simple gambles. *Journal of Behavioral Decision Making, 20,* 365–380.

Bateman, I., Munro, A., Rhodes, B., Starmer, C., & Sugden, R. (1997). A test of the theory of reference-dependent preferences. *The Quarterly Journal of Economics, 116,* 479–506.

Bates, T. C., & Shieles, A. (2003). Crystallized intelligence as a product of speed and drive for experience: the relationship of inspection time and openness to g and Gc. *Intelligence, 31,* 275–287.

Baumeister, R. F., Campbell, J. D., Krueger, J. I., & Vohs, K. D. (2003). Does high self-esteem cause better performance, interpersonal success, happiness, or healthier lifestyles? *Psychological Science in the Public Interest, 4,* 1–44.

Baumeister, R. F., & Vohs, K. D. (2003). Willpower, choice and self-control. In G. Loewenstein, D. Read, & R. Baumeister (Eds.), *Time and decision: Economic and psychological perspectives on intertemporal choice* (pp. 201–216). New York, N.Y.: Russell Sage Foundation.

Baumeister, R. F., & Vohs, K. D. (Eds.). (2007). *Handbook of self-regulation: Research, theory, and applications.* New York: Guilford Press.

Bazerman, M. (2001). Consumer research for consumers. *Journal of Consumer Research, 27,* 499–504.

Bazerman, M., Baron, J., & Shonk, K. (2001). *"You can't enlarge the pie": Six barriers to effective government.* New York: Basic Books.

Bazerman, M., Tenbrunsel, A., & Wade-Benzoni, K. (1998). Negotiating with yourself and losing: Understanding and managing conflicting internal preferences. *Academy of Management Review, 23,* 225–241.

Bechara, A. (2005). Decision making, impulse control and loss of willpower to resist drugs: A neurocognitive perspective. *Nature Neuroscience, 8,* 1458–1463.

Bechara, A., Damasio, A. R., Damasio, H., & Anderson, S. (1994). Insensitivity to future consequences following damage to human prefrontal cortex. *Cognition, 50,* 7–15.

Bechara, A., Damasio, H., Tranel, D., & Anderson, S. (1998). Dissociation of working memory from decision making within the human prefrontal cortex. *Journal of Neuroscience, 18,* 428–437.

Beck, S. R., Riggs, K. J., & Gorniak, S. L. (2009). Relating developments in children's counterfactual thinking and executive functions. *Thinking and Reasoning, 15,* 337–354.

Begley, S. (2007 August, 13). The truth about denial. *Newsweek,* 20–29.

Belsky, G., & Gilovich, T. (1999). *Why smart people make big money mistakes—And how to correct them: Lessons from the new science of behavioral economics.* New York: Simon & Schuster.

Benjamin, D., & Shapiro, J. (2005 February, 25). *Does cognitive ability reduce psychological bias?* JEL manuscript: J24, D14, C91.

Bentz, B. G., Williamson, D. A., & Franks, S. F. (2004). Debiasing of pessimistic judgments associated with anxiety. *Journal of Psychopathology and Behavioral Assessment, 26,* 173–180.

Bering, J. M. (2006). The folk psychology of souls. *Behavioral and Brain Sciences, 29,* 453–498.

Bermudez, J. L. (2001). Normativity and rationality in delusional psychiatric disorders. *Mind & Language, 16,* 457–493.

Berner, E. S., & Graber, M. L. (2008). Overconfidence as a cause of diagnostic error in medicine. *American Journal of Medicine, 121,* S2–S23.

Berridge, K. C. (2003). Irrational pursuits: Hyper-incentives from a visceral brain. In I. Brocas & J. D. Carrillo (Eds.), *The psychology of economic decisions (Vol. 1): Rationality and well-being* (17–40). Oxford: Oxford University Press.

Best, J. R., Miller, P. H., & Jones, L. L. (2009). Executive functions after age 5: Changes and correlates. *Developmental Review, 29,* 180–200.

Bhandari, G., Hassanein, K., & Deaves, R. (2008). Debiasing investors with decision support systems: An experimental investigation. *Decision Support Systems, 46,* 399–410.

Bickerton, D. (1995). *Language and human behavior.* Seattle: University of Washington Press.

Birch, S. A. J. (2005). When knowledge is a curse: Children's and adult's reasoning about mental states. *Current Directions in Psychological Science, 14,* 25–29.

Birnbaum, M. H. (1999). Testing critical properties of decision making on the internet. *Psychological Science, 10,* 399–407.

Blackmore, S. (1999). *The meme machine.* New York: Oxford University Press.

Blackmore, S. (2000). The memes' eye view. In R. Aunger (Ed.), *Darwinizing culture: The status of memetics as a science,* (pp. 25–42). Oxford: Oxford University Press.

Blackmore, S. (2005). Can memes meet the challenge? In S. Hurley & N. Chater (Eds.), *Perspectives on imitation (Vol. 2)* (pp. 409–411). Cambridge, MA: MIT Press.

Blackwell, L., Trzesniewski, K., & Dweck, C. S. (2007). Implicit theories of intelligence predict achievement across an adolescent transition: A longitudinal study and an intervention. *Child Development, 78,* 246–263.

Bloom, P. (2004). *Descartes' baby.* New York: Basic Books.

Boring, E. G. (1923). Intelligence as the tests test it. *New Republic, 35,* 35–37.

Botvinick, M., Cohen, J. D., & Carter, C. S. (2004). Conflict monitoring and anterior cingulate cortex: An update. *Trends in Cognitive Sciences, 8*, 539–546.

Boyer, P. (2001). *Religion explained: The evolutionary origins of religious thought.* New York: Basic Books.

Boyer, P. (2003). Religious thought and behaviour as by-products of brain function. *Trends in Cognitive Sciences, 7*, 119–124.

Brainerd, C. J., & Reyna, V. F. (2001). Fuzzy-trace theory: Dual processes in memory, reasoning, and cognitive neuroscience. In H. W. Reese & R. Kail (Eds.), *Advances in child development and behavior (Vol. 28)* (pp. 41–100). San Diego: Academic Press.

Brand, M., Laier, C., Pawlikowski, M., & Markowitsch, H. J. (2009). Decision making with and without feedback: The role of intelligence, strategies, executive functions, and cognitive styles. *Journal of Clinical and Experimental Neuropsychology, 31*, 984–998.

Brandstatter, E., Gigerenzer, G., & Hertwig, R. (2006). The priority heuristic: Making choices without trade-offs. *Psychological Review, 113*, 409–432.

Brase, G. L. (2004). What we reason about and why: How evolution explains reasoning. In K. I. Manktelow & M. C. Chung (Eds.), *Psychology of reasoning: Theoretical and historical perspectives* (pp. 309–331). Hove, England: Psychology Press.

Bratman, M. E. (2003). Autonomy and heirarchy. *Social Philosophy & Policy, 20*, 156–176.

Broder, A., & Newell, B. R. (2008). Challenging some common beliefs: Empirical work within the adaptive toolbox metaphor. *Judgment and Decision Making, 3*, 205–214.

Bruine de Bruin, W., Parker, A. M., & Fischhoff, B. (2007). Individual differences in adult decision-making competence. *Journal of Personality and Social Psychology, 92*, 938–956.

Buckner, R. L., & Carroll, D. C. (2007). Self-projection and the brain. *Trends in Cognitive Sciences, 11*, 49–57.

Buehner, M., Krumm, S., & Pick, M. (2005). Reasoning [=] working memory [≠] attention. *Intelligence, 33*, 251–272.

Burkett, J. P. (2006). *Microeconomics: Optimization, experiments, and behavior.* New York: Oxford University Press.

Burns, B. D., & Corpus, B. (2004). Randomness and inductions from streaks: "Gambler's fallacy" versus "hot hand." *Psychonomic Bulletin & Review, 11*, 179–184.

Burns, W. C. (1997). *Spurious correlations.* Accessed July 29, 2009 at http://www.burns.com/wcbspurcorl.htm

Buss, D. M. (Ed.). (2005). *The handbook of evolutionary psychology.* Hoboken, NJ: John Wiley.

Buss, D. M. (2009). How can evolutionary psychology successfully explain personality and individual differences? *Perspectives on Psychological Science, 4*, 359–366.

Byrne, R. M. J. (2005). *The rational imagination: How people create alternatives to reality.* Cambridge, MA: MIT Press.

Cacioppo, J. T., Petty, R. E., Feinstein, J., & Jarvis, W. (1996). Dispositional differences in cognitive motivation: The life and times of individuals varying in need for cognition. *Psychological Bulletin, 119*, 197–253.

Camerer, C. F. (2000). Prospect theory in the wild: Evidence from the field. In D. Kahneman & A. Tversky (Eds.), *Choices, values, and frames* (pp. 288–300). Cambridge: Cambridge University Press.

Camerer, C., Issacharoff, S., Loewenstein, G., O'Donoghue, T., & Rabin, M. (2003). Regulation for conservatives: Behavioral economics and the case for "asymmetric paternalism." *University of Pennsylvania Law Review, 151*, 1211–1254.

Camerer, C., Loewenstein, G., & Prelec, D. (2005). Neuroeconomics: How neuroscience can inform economics. *Journal of Economic Literature, 34*, 9–64.

Camerer, C., Loewenstein, G., & Weber, M. (1989). The curse of knowledge in economic settings: An experimental analysis. *Journal of Political Economy, 97*, 1232–1254.

Capon, N., & Kuhn, D. (1979). Logical reasoning in the supermarket: Adult females' use of a proportional reasoning strategy in an everyday context. *Developmental Psychology, 15*, 450–452.

Carroll, J. B. (1993). *Human cognitive abilities: A survey of factor-analytic studies.* Cambridge: Cambridge University Press.

Carruthers, P. (2000). The evolution of consciousness. In P. Carruthers & A. Chamberlain (Eds.), *Evolution and the human mind: Modularity, language and meta-cognition* (pp. 254–275). Cambridge: Cambridge University Press.

Carruthers, P. (2002). The cognitive functions of language. *Behavioral and Brain Sciences, 25*, 657–726.

Carruthers, P. (2006). *The architecture of the mind.* New York: Oxford University Press.

Carruthers, P. (2009). How we know our own minds: The relationship between mindreading and metacognition. *Behavioral and Brain Sciences, 32*, 121–182.

Case, D. A., Fantino, E., & Goodie, A. S. (1999). Base-rate training without case cues reduces base-rate neglect. *Psychonomic Bulletin & Review, 6*, 319–327.

Cattell, R. B. (1963). Theory for fluid and crystallized intelligence: A critical experiment. *Journal of Educational Psychology, 54*, 1–22.

Cattell, R. B. (1998). Where is intelligence? Some answers from the triadic theory. In J. J. McArdle & R. W. Woodcock (Eds.), *Human cognitive abilities in theory and practice* (pp. 29–38). Mahwah, NJ: Erlbaum.

Cavedini, P., Riboldi, G., Keller, R., D'Annucci, A., & Bellodi, L. (2002). Frontal lobe dysfunction in pathological gambling patients. *Biological Psychiatry, 51*, 334–341.

Chaiken, S., Liberman, A., & Eagly, A. H. (1989). Heuristic and systematic information within and beyond the persuasion context. In J. S. Uleman & J. A. Bargh (Eds.), *Unintended thought* (pp. 212–252). New York: Guilford Press.

Chapman, G. B., & Elstein, A. S. (2000). Cognitive processes and biases in medical decision making. In G. B. Chapman & F. A. Sonnenberg (Eds.), *Decision making in health care: Theory, psychology, and applications* (pp. 183–210). New York: Cambridge University Press.

Chapman, L., & Chapman, J. (1969). Illusory correlation as an obstacle to the use of valid psychodiagnostic signs. *Journal of Abnormal Psychology, 74*, 271–280.

Chater, N., & Oaksford, M. (2001). Human rationality and the psychology of reasoning: Where do we go from here? *British Journal of Psychology, 92*, 193–216.

Chatillon, G. (1989). Acceptance of paranormal among two special groups. *Skeptical Inquirer, 13*(2), 216–217.

Chatterjee, S., Heath, T. B., Milberg, S. J., & France, K. R. (2000). The differential processing price in gains and losses: The effects of frame and need for cognition. *Journal of Behavioral Decision Making, 13*, 61–75.

Chen, H., & Volpe, R. P. (1998). An analysis of personal financial literacy among college students. *Financial Services Review, 7*, 107–128.

Cheng, P. W., Holyoak, K. J., Nisbett, R. E., & Oliver, L. M. (1986). Pragmatic versus syntactic approaches to training deductive reasoning. *Cognitive Psychology, 18*, 293–328.

Christiansen-Szalanski, J. J., & Williams, C. F. (1991). The hindsight bias: A meta-analysis. *Organizational Behavior and Human Decision Processes, 48*, 147–168.

Christie, R. (1991). Authoritarianism and related constructs. In J. P. Robinson, P. Shaver & L. S. Wrightsman (Eds.), *Measures of personality and social psychological attitudes* (pp. 501–571). San Diego, CA: Academic Press.

Churchland, P. M. (1988). *Matter and consciousness—Revised edition.* Cambridge, MA: MIT Press.

Clark, A. (1997). *Being there: Putting brain, body, and world together again.* Cambridge, MA: MIT Press.

Clark, A., & Karmiloff-Smith, A. (1993). The cognizer's innards: A psychological and philosophical perspective on the development of thought. *Mind and Language, 8*, 487–519.

Cohen, L. J. (1979). On the psychology of prediction: Whose is the fallacy? *Cognition, 7*, 385–407.

Cohen, L. J. (1981). Can human irrationality be experimentally demonstrated? *Behavioral and Brain Sciences, 4*, 317–370.

Cohen, L. J. (1982). Are people programmed to commit fallacies? Further thoughts about the interpretation of experimental data on probability judgment. *Journal for the Theory of Social Behavior, 12*, 251–274.

Cohen, L. J. (1986). *The dialogue of reason.* Oxford: Oxford University Press.

Colom, R., Rebollo, I., Palacios, A., Juan-Espinosa, M., & Kyllonen, P. C. (2004). Working memory is (almost) perfectly predicted by g. *Intelligence, 32*, 277–296.

Coltheart, M. (1999). Modularity and cognition. *Trends in Cognitive Sciences, 3*, 115–120.

Coltheart, M., & Davies, M. (Eds.). (2000). *Pathologies of belief.* Oxford: Blackwell Publishers.

Consumer Fraud Research Group. (2006 May, 12). *Investor fraud study final report*. Washington, DC: National Association of Securities Dealers.

Conway, A. R. A., Cowan, N., & Bunting, M. F. (2001). The cocktail party phenomenon revisited: The importance of working memory capacity. *Psychonomic Bulletin & Review, 8*, 331–335.

Conway, A. R. A., Cowan, N., Bunting, M. F., Therriault, D. J., & Minkoff, S. R. B. (2002). A latent variable analysis of working memory capacity, short-term memory capacity, processing speed, and general fluid intelligence. *Intelligence, 30*, 163–183.

Conway, A. R. A., Kane, M. J., & Engle, R. W. (2003). Working memory capacity and its relation to general intelligence. *Trends in Cognitive Science, 7*, 547–552.

Corballis, M. C. (2003). Recursion as the key to the human mind. In K. Sterelny & J. Fitness (Eds.), *From mating to mentality: Evaluating evolutionary psychology* (pp. 155–171). Hove, England: Psychology Press.

Cosmides, L., & Tooby, J. (1992). Cognitive adaptations for social exchange. In J. Barkow, L. Cosmides, & J. Tooby (Eds.), *The adapted mind*, (pp. 163–205). New York: Oxford University Press.

Cosmides, L., & Tooby, J. (1994). Better than rational: Evolutionary psychology and the invisible hand. *American Economic Review, 84*, 327–332.

Cosmides, L., & Tooby, J. (1996). Are humans good intuitive statisticians after all? Rethinking some conclusions from the literature on judgment under uncertainty. *Cognition, 58*, 1–73.

Cosmides, L., & Tooby, J. (2000). Consider the source: The evolution of adaptations for decoupling and metarepresentation. In D. Sperber (Eds.), *Metarepresentations: A multidisciplinary perspective* (pp. 53–115). Oxford: Oxford University Press.

Cosmides, L., & Tooby, J. (2005). Neurocognitive adaptations designed for social exchange. In D. M. Buss (Ed.), *The handbook of evolutionary psychology* (pp. 584–627). Hoboken, NJ: John Wiley.

Costa, P. T., & McCrae, R. R. (1992). *Revised NEO personality inventory*. Odessa, FL: Psychological Assessment Resources.

Coyle, T. R. (2003). A review of the worst performance rule: Evidence, theory, and alternative hypotheses. *Intelligence, 31*, 567–587.

Cronbach, L. J. (1949). *Essentials of psychological testing*. New York: Harper.

Croskerry, P. (2009a). A universal model of diagnostic reasoning. *Academic Medicine, 84*, 22–1028.

Croskerry, P. (2009b). Context is everything or how could I have been that stupid? *Healthcare Quarterly, 12*, 167–173.

Croson, R., & Sundali, J. (2005). The gambler's fallacy and the hot hand: Empirical data from casinos. *Journal of Risk and Uncertainty, 30*, 195–209.

Cummins, D. D. (1996). Evidence for the innateness of deontic reasoning. *Mind & Language, 11*, 160–190.

Cummins, D. D. (2002). The evolutionary roots of intelligence and rationality. In R. Elio (Ed.), *Common sense, reasoning, and rationality* (pp. 132–147). Oxford: Oxford University Press.

Currie, G., & Ravenscroft, I. (2002). *Recreative minds*. Oxford: Oxford University Press.

Damasio, A. R. (1994). *Descartes' error*. New York: Putnam.

Damasio, A. R. (1996). The somatic marker hypothesis and the possible functions of the prefrontal cortex. *Philosophical Transactions of the Royal Society (London), 351*, 1413–1420.

Daniel, M. H. (2000). Interpretation of intelligence test scores. In R. J. Sternberg (Ed.), *Handbook of intelligence* (pp. 477–491). Cambridge, MA: Cambridge University Press.

Daston, L. (1980). Probabilistic expectation and rationality in classical probability theory. *Historia Mathematica, 7*, 234–260.

Davids, S. L., Schapira, M. M., McAuliffe, T. L., & Nattinger, A. B. (2004). Predictors of pessimistic breast cancer risk perceptions in a primary care population. *Journal of General Internal Medicine, 19*, 310–315.

Davidson, D. (1980). *Essays on actions & events*. Oxford: Oxford University Press.

Davies, M. (2000). Interaction without reduction: The relationship between personal and sub-personal levels of description. *Mind & Society, 1*, 87–105.

Dawes, R. M. (1976). Shallow psychology. In J. S. Carroll & J. W. Payne (Eds.), *Cognition and social behavior* (pp. 3–11). Hillsdale, NJ: Erlbaum.

Dawes, R. M. (1994). *House of cards: Psychology and psychotherapy based on myth*. New York: Free Press.

Dawes, R. M. (1998). Behavioral decision making and judgment. In D. T. Gilbert, S. T. Fiske, & G. Lindzey (Eds.), *The handbook of social psychology (Vol. 1)* (pp. 497–548). Boston: McGraw-Hill.

Dawes, R. M., Van de Kragt, A. J. C., & Orbell, J. M. (1988). Not me or thee but we: The importance of group identity in eliciting cooperation in dilemma situations: Experimental manipulations. *Acta Psychologica, 68*, 83–97.

Dawkins, R. (1976/1989). *The selfish gene*. New York: Oxford University Press.

Dawkins, R. (1982). *The extended phenotype*. New York: Oxford University Press.

Dawkins, R. (1993). Viruses of the mind. In B. Dahlbom (Ed.), *Dennett and his critics*, (pp. 13–27). Cambridge, MA: Blackwell.

Deary, I. J. (2000). *Looking down on human intelligence: From psychometrics to the brain*. Oxford: Oxford University Press.

Deary, I. J. (2001). *Intelligence: A very short introduction*. Oxford: Oxford University Press.

Deary, I. J., Whiteman, M. C., Starr, J. M., Whalley, L. J., & Fox, H. C. (2004). The impact of childhood intelligence on later life: Following up the Scottish Mental Surveys of 1932 and 1947. *Journal of Personality and Social Psychology, 86*, 130–147.

Decety, J., & Grezes, J. (2006). The power of simulation: Imagining one's own and other's behavior. *Brain Research, 1079*, 4–14.

de Finetti, B. (1989). Probabilism. *Erkenntnis, 31*, 169–223.

DeMartino, B., Kumaran, D., Seymour, B., & Dolan, R. J. (2006). Frames, biases, and rational decision-making in the human brain. *Science, 313*, 684–687.

Denes-Raj, V., & Epstein, S. (1994). Conflict between intuitive and rational process-ing: When people behave against their better judgment. *Journal of Personality and Social Psychology, 66*, 819–829.

De Neys, W. (2006a). Automatic-heuristic and executive-analytic processing during reasoning: Chronometric and dual-task considerations. *Quarterly Journal of Experimental Psychology, 59*, 1070–1100.

De Neys, W. (2006b). Dual processing in reasoning—Two systems but one reasoner. *Psychological Science, 17*, 428–433.

De Neys, W., & Franssens, S. (2009). Belief inhibition during thinking: Not always winning but at least taking part. *Cognition, 113*, 45–61.

De Neys, W., & Glumicic, T. (2008). Conflict monitoring in dual process theories of thinking. *Cognition, 106*, 1248–1299.

De Neys, W., Moyens, E., & Vansteenwegen, D. (2010). Feeling we're biased: Autonomic arousal and reasoning conflict. *Cognitive, Affective, & Behavioral Neuroscience, 10*, 208-216.

De Neys, W., Vartanian, O., & Goel, V. (2008). Smarter than we think: When our brains detect that we are biased. *Psychological Science, 19*, 483–489.

Dennett, D. C. (1984). *Elbow room: The varieties of free will worth wanting.* Cambridge, MA: MIT Press.

Dennett, D. C. (1987). *The intentional stance.* Cambridge, MA: The MIT Press.

Dennett, D. C. (1988). Precis of "The Intentional Stance." *Behavioral and Brain Sciences, 11*, 493–544.

Dennett, D. C. (1991). *Consciousness explained.* Boston: Little Brown.

Dennett, D. C. (1995). *Darwin's dangerous idea: Evolution and the meanings of life.* New York: Simon & Schuster.

Dennett, D. C. (1996). *Kinds of minds: Toward an understanding of consciousness.* New York: Basic Books.

Dennett, D. C. (2006). From typo to thinko: When evolution graduated to semantic norms. In S. C. Levinson & P. Jaisson (Eds.), *Evolution and culture* (pp. 133–145). Cambridge, MA: MIT Press.

DeShon, R. P., Smith, M. R., Chan, D., & Schmitt, N. (1998). Can racial differences in cognitive test performance be reduced by presenting problems in a social context? *Journal of Applied Psychology, 83*, 438–451.

de Sousa, R. (2007). *Why think? Evolution and the rational mind.* Oxford: Oxford University Press.

Diamond, A., Barnett, W. S., Thomas, J., & Munro, S. (2007). Preschool program improves cognitive control. *Science, 318*, 1387–1388.

Dieckmann, N. F., Slovic, P., & Peters, E. M. (2009). The use of narrative evidence and explicit likelihood by decisionmakers varying in numeracy. *Risk Analysis, 29*, 1473–1488.

Dienes, Z., & Perner, J. (1999). A theory of implicit and explicit knowledge. *Behavioral and Brain Sciences, 22*, 735–808.

Dillard, A. J., Midboe, A. M., & Klein, W. (2009). The dark side of optimism: Unrealistic optimism about problems with alcohol predicts subsequent negative event experiences. *Personality and Social Psychology Bulletin, 35*, 1540–1550.

Distin, K. (2005). *The selfish meme.* Cambridge: Cambridge University Press.

Doherty, M. (2003). Optimists, pessimists, and realists. In S. L. Schneider & J. Shanteau (Eds.), *Emerging perspectives on judgment and decision research* (pp. 643–679). New York: Cambridge University Press.

Doherty, M. E., & Mynatt, C. (1990). Inattention to P(H) and to P(D/~H): A converging operation. *Acta Psychologica, 75*, 1–11.

Doherty, M. E., Mynatt, C., Tweney, R., & Schiavo, M. (1979). Pseudodiagnosticity. *Acta Psychologica, 43*, 111–121.

Doherty-Sneddon, G., Phelps, F., & Clark, J. K. (2007). Gaze aversion: A response to cognitive or social difficulty? *British Journal of Developmental Psychology, 25*, 513–526.

Dole, J. A., & Sinatra, G. M. (1998). Reconceptualizing change in the cognitive construction of knowledge. *Educational Psychologist, 33*, 109–128.

Donkers, B., Melenberg, B., & van Soest, A. (2001). Estimating risk attitudes using lotteries: A large sample approach. *The Journal of Risk and Uncertainty, 22*, 165–195.

Dörner, D. (1996). *The logic of failure: Why things go wrong and what we can do to make them right.* New York: Metropolitan Books.

Dougherty, M. R., Franco-Watkins, A. M., & Thomas, R. (2008). Psychological plausibility of the theory of probabilistic mental models and the fast and frugal heuristics. *Psychological Review, 115*, 199–213.

Dougherty, M. R. P., Gettys, C. F., & Thomas, R. P. (1997). The role of mental simulation in judgements of likelihood. *Organizational Behavior and Human Decision Processes, 70*(2), 135–148.

Duckworth, A. L. (2009). Over and beyond high-stakes testing. *American Psychologist, 64*, 279–280.

Duckworth, A. L., & Seligman, M. E. P. (2005). Self-discipline outdoes IQ in predicting academic performance of adolescents. *Psychological Science, 16*, 939–944.

Duckworth, S., Ragland, G. G., Sommerfeld, R. E., & Wyne, M. D. (1974). Modification of conceptual impulsivity in retarded children. *American Journal of Mental Deficiency, 79*, 59–63.

Dulany, D. E., & Hilton, D. J. (1991). Conversational implicature, conscious representation, and the conjunction fallacy. *Social Cognition, 9*, 85–110.

Dunbar, R. (1998). Theory of mind and the evolution of language. In J. R. Hurford, M. Studdert-Kennedy, & C. Knight (Eds.), *Approaches to the evolution of language* (pp. 92–110). Cambridge: Cambridge University Press.

Duncan, J., Emslie, H., Williams, P., Johnson, R., & Freer, C. (1996). Intelligence and the frontal lobe: The organization of goal-directed behavior. *Cognitive Psychology, 30*, 257–303.

Duncan, J., Parr, A., Woolgar, A., Thompson, R., Bright, P., Cox, S., Bishop, S., & Nimmo-Smith, I. (2008). Goal neglect and Spearman's g: Competing parts of a complex task. *Journal of Experimental Psychology: General, 137*, 131–148.

Duncan, J., Seitz, R. J., Kolodny, J., Bor, D., Herzog, H., Ahmed, A., Newell, F. N., & Emslie, H. (2000). A neural basis for general intelligence. *Science, 289*, 457–460.

Dworkin, G. (1988). *The theory and practice of autonomy.* Cambridge: Cambridge University Press.

Earman, J. (1992). *Bayes or bust.* Cambridge, MA: MIT Press.

Echeburua, E., Baez, C., & Fernandez-Montalvo, J. (1996). Comparative effectiveness of three therapeutic modalities in the psychological treatment of pathological gambling. *Behavioral and Cognitive Psychotherapy, 24*, 51–72.

Eckblad, M., & Chapman, L. J. (1983). Magical ideation as an indicator of schizotypy. *Journal of Consulting and Clinical Psychology, 51*, 215–225.

Edwards, W. (1954). The theory of decision making. *Psychological Bulletin, 51*, 380–417.

Edwards, W., & von Winterfeldt, D. (1986). On cognitive illusions and their implications. In H. R. Arkes & K. R. Hammond (Eds.), *Judgment and decision making* (pp. 642–679). Cambridge: Cambridge University Press.

Egeland, B. (1974). Training impulsive children in the use of more efficient scanning techniques. *Child Development, 45*, 165–171.

Ehrlinger, J., Gilovich, T., & Ross, L. (2005). Peering into the bias blind spot: People's assessments of bias in themselves and others. *Personality and Social Psychology Bulletin, 31*, 680–692.

Elliott, R., & Greenberg, L. S. (2007). The essence of process-experiential/emotion-focused therapy. *American Journal of Psychotherapy, 61*, 241–254.

Elster, J. (1983). *Sour grapes: Studies in the subversion of rationality.* Cambridge, England: Cambridge University Press.

Engle, R. W. (2002). Working memory capacity as executive attention. *Current Directions in Psychological Science, 11*, 19–23.

Engle, R. W., Tuholski, S. W., Laughlin, J. E., & Conway, A. R. A. (1999). Working memory, short-term memory, and general fluid intelligence: A latent-variable approach. *Journal of Experimental Psychology: General, 128*, 309–331.

Epley, N., & Gilovich, T. (2004). Are adjustments insufficient? *Personality and Social Psychology Bulletin, 30*, 447–460.

Epley, N., & Gilovich, T. (2006). The anchoring-and-adjustment heuristic: Why the adjustments are insufficient. *Psychological Science, 17*, 311–318.

Epley, N., Mak, D., & Chen Idson, L. (2006). Bonus or rebate? The impact of income framing on spending and saving. *Journal of Behavioral Decision Making, 19*, 213–227.

Epstein, S. (1994). Integration of the cognitive and the psychodynamic unconscious. *American Psychologist, 49*, 709–724.

Epstein, S., & Meier, P. (1989). Constructive thinking: A broad coping variable with specific components. *Journal of Personality and Social Psychology, 57*, 332–350.

Epstein, S., Pacini, R., Denes-Raj, V., & Heier, H. (1996). Individual differences in intuitive-experiential and analytical-rational thinking styles. *Journal of Personality and Social Psychology, 71*, 390–405.

Epstein, S., Pacini, R., Heier, H., & Denes-Raj, V. (1995). *Individual differences in intuitive and analytical information processing.* Manuscript.

Ericsson, K. A., & Charness, N. (1994). Expert performance: Its structure and acquisition. *American Psychologist, 49*, 725–747.

Eslinger, P. J., & Damasio, A. R. (1985). Severe disturbance of higher cognition after bilateral frontal lobe ablation: Patient EVR. *Neurology, 35*, 1731–1741.

Evans, J. St. B. T. (1972). Interpretation and matching bias in a reasoning task. *Quarterly Journal of Experimental Psychology, 24*, 193–199.

Evans, J. St. B. T. (1984). Heuristic and analytic processes in reasoning. *British Journal of Psychology, 75*, 451–468.

Evans, J. St. B. T. (1989). *Bias in human reasoning: Causes and consequences.* Hove, UK: Lawrence Erlbaum Associates.

Evans, J. St. B. T. (1996). Deciding before you think: Relevance and reasoning in the selection task. *British Journal of Psychology, 87*, 223–240.

Evans, J. St. B. T. (1998). Matching bias in conditional reasoning: Do we understand it after 25 years? *Thinking and Reasoning, 4*, 45–82.

Evans, J. St. B. T. (2002). The influence of prior belief on scientific thinking. In P. Carruthers, S. Stich, & M. Siegal (Eds.), *The cognitive basis of science* (pp. 193–210). Cambridge: Cambridge University Press.

Evans, J. St. B. T. (2003). In two minds: Dual-process accounts of reasoning. *Trends in Cognitive Sciences, 7*, 454–459.

Evans, J. St. B. T. (2004). History of the dual process theory of reasoning. In K. I. Manktelow & M. C. Chung (Eds.), *Psychology of reasoning: Theoretical and historical perspectives* (pp. 241–266). Hove, England: Psychology Press.

Evans, J. St. B. T. (2006a). Dual system theories of cognition: Some issues. *Proceedings of the 28th Annual Meeting of the Cognitive Science Society, Vancouver*, 202–207.

Evans, J. St. B. T. (2006b). The heuristic-analytic theory of reasoning: Extension and evaluation. *Psychonomic Bulletin and Review, 13*, 378–395.

Evans, J. St. B. T. (2007a). *Hypothetical thinking: Dual processes in reasoning and judgment.* New York: Psychology Press.

Evans, J. St. B. T. (2007b). On the resolution of conflict in dual process theories of reasoning. *Thinking and Reasoning, 13*, 321–339.

Evans, J. St. B. T. (2008). Dual-processing accounts of reasoning, judgment and social cognition. *Annual Review of Psychology, 59*, 255–278.

Evans, J. St. B. T. (2009). How many dual-process theories do we need? One, two, or many? In J. Evans & K. Frankish (Eds.), *In two minds: Dual processes and beyond* (pp. 33–54). Oxford: Oxford University Press.

Evans, J. St. B. T., Barston, J., & Pollard, P. (1983). On the conflict between logic and belief in syllogistic reasoning. *Memory & Cognition, 11*, 295–306.

Evans, J. St. B. T., & Curtis-Holmes, J. (2005). Rapid responding increases belief bias: Evidence for the dual-process theory of reasoning. *Thinking and Reasoning, 11*, 382–389.

Evans, J. St. B. T., & Feeney, A. (2004). The role of prior belief in reasoning. In J. P. Leighton & R. J. Sternberg (Eds.), *The nature of reasoning* (pp. 78–102). Cambridge: Cambridge University Press.

Evans, J. St. B. T., & Frankish, K. (Eds.). (2009). *In two minds: Dual processes and beyond.* Oxford: Oxford University Press.

Evans, J. St. B. T., Handley, S. J., Harper, C., & Johnson-Laird, P. N. (1999). Reasoning about necessity and possibility: A test of the mental model theory of deduction. *Journal of Experimental Psychology: Learning, Memory, and Cognition, 25*, 1495–1513.

Evans, J. St. B. T., & Lynch, J. S. (1973). Matching bias in the selection task. *British Journal of Psychology, 64*, 391–397.

Evans, J. St. B. T., Newstead, S. E., & Byrne, R. M. J. (1993). *Human reasoning: The psychology of deduction.* Hove, England: Erlbaum.

Evans, J. St. B. T., Newstead, S., Allen, J., & Pollard, P. (1994). Debiasing by instruction: The case of belief bias. *European Journal of Cognitive Psychology, 6*, 263–285.

Evans, J. St. B. T., & Over, D. E. (1996). *Rationality and reasoning.* Hove, England: Psychology Press.

Evans, J. St. B. T., & Over, D. E. (1999). Explicit representations in hypothetical thinking. *Behavioral and Brain Sciences, 22*, 763–764.

Evans, J. St. B. T., & Over, D. E. (2004). *If.* Oxford: Oxford University Press.

Evans, J. St. B. T., & Over, D. E. (2010). Heuristic thinking and human intelligence: A commentary on Marewski, Gaissmaier and Gigerenzer. *Cognitive Processing, 11*, 171–175.

Evans, J. St. B. T., Over, D. E., & Handley, S. J. (2003). A theory of hypothetical thinking. In D. Hardman & L. Maachi (Eds.), *Thinking: Psychological perspectives on reasoning* (pp. 3–22). Chicester: Wiley.

Evans, J. St. B. T., & Wason, P. C. (1976). Rationalization in a reasoning task. *British Journal of Psychology, 67*, 479–486.

Facione, P. (1990). *Critical thinking: A statement of expert consensus for purposes of educational assessment and instruction (Executive Summary of the Delphi Report).* La Cruz, CA: California Academic Press.

Feldman Barrett, L. F., Tugade, M. M., & Engle, R. W. (2004). Individual differences in working memory capacity and dual-process theories of the mind. *Psychological Bulletin, 130*, 553–573.

Fennema, M. G., & Perkins, J. D. (2008). Mental budgeting versus marginal decision making: Training, experience and justification effects on decisions involving sunk costs. *Journal of Behavioral Decision Making, 21*, 225–239.

Fenton-O'Creevy, M., Nicholson, N., Soane, E., & Willman, P. (2003). Trading on illusions: Unrealistic perceptions of control and trading performance. *Journal of Occupational and Organizational Psychology, 76*, 53–68.

Ferguson, M. J., & Zayas, V. (2009). Automatic evaluation. *Current Directions in Psychological Science, 18*, 362–366.

Ferreira, M. B., Garcia-Marques, L., Sherman, S. J., & Sherman, J. W. (2006). Automatic and controlled components of judgment and decision making. *Journal of Personality and Social Psychology, 91*, 797–813.

Fiedler, K. (2004). Illusory correlation. In R. Pohl (Ed.), *Cognitive illusions: A handbook on fallacies and biases in thinking, judgment and memory* (pp. 97–114). Hove, England: Psychology Press.

Finucane, M. L., Alhakami, A., Slovic, P., & Johnson, S. M. (2000). The affect heuristic in judgments of risks and benefits. *Journal of Behavioral Decision Making, 13*, 1–17.

Fischhoff, B. (1975). Hindsight ≠ foresight: The effect of outcome knowledge on judgment under uncertainty. *Journal of Experimental Psychology: Human Perception and Performance, 1*, 288–299.

Fischhoff, B. (1982). Debiasing. In D. Kahneman, P. Slovic & A. Tversky (Eds.), *Judgment under uncertainty: Heuristics and biases* (pp. 422–444). New York: Cambridge University Press.

Fischhoff, B. (2002). Heuristics and biases in application. In T. Gilovich, D. Griffin & D. Kahneman (Eds.), *Heuristics and biases: The psychology of intuitive judgment* (pp. 730–748). New York: Cambridge University Press.

Fischhoff, B., & Beyth-Marom, R. (1983). Hypothesis evaluation from a Bayesian perspective. *Psychological Review, 90*, 239–260.

Fischhoff, B., Slovic, P., & Lichtenstein, S. (1977). Knowing with certainty: The appropriateness of extreme confidence. *Journal of Experimental Psychology: Human Perception and Performance, 3*, 552–564.

Fischhoff, B., Slovic, P., & Lichtenstein, S. (1979). Subjective sensitivity analysis. *Organizational Behavior and Human Performance, 23*, 339–359.

Fishbach, A., & Trope, Y. (2005). The substitutability of external control and self-control. *Journal of Experimental Social Psychology, 41*, 256–270.

Fishburn, P. C. (1981). Subjective expected utility: A review of normative theories. *Theory and Decision, 13*, 139–199.

Fishburn, P. C. (1999). The making of decision theory. In J. Shanteau, B. A. Mellers, & D. A. Schum (Eds.), *Decision science and technology: Reflections on the contributions of Ward Edwards,*. Boston: Kluwer Academic Publishers.

Flanagan, O. (1996). *Self expressions: Mind, morals, and the meaning of life.* New York: Oxford University Press.

Fleischhauer, M., Enge, S., Brocke, B., Ullrich, J., Strobel, A., & Strobel, A. (2010). Same or different? Clarifying the relationship of need for cognition to personality and intelligence. *Personality and Social Psychology Bulletin, 36*, 82–96.

Flynn, J. R. (1984). The mean IQ of Americans: Massive gains 1932 to 1978. *Psychological Bulletin, 95*, 29–51.

Flynn, J. R. (1987). Massive IQ gains in 14 nations: What IQ tests really measure. *Psychological Bulletin, 101*, 171–191.

Flynn, J. R. (1998). IQ gains over time: Toward finding the causes. In U. Neisser (Ed.), *The rising curve: Long-term changes in IQ and related measures* (pp. 25–66). Washington, DC: American Psychological Association.

Flynn, J. R. (2007). *What is intelligence?* Cambridge: Cambridge University Press.

Fodor, J. A. (1983). *The modularity of mind.* Cambridge, MA: MIT University Press.

Foley, R. (1987). *The theory of epistemic rationality.* Cambridge, MA: Harvard University Press.

Fong, G. T., Krantz, D. H., & Nisbett, R. E. (1986). The effects of statistical training on thinking about everyday problems. *Cognitive Psychology, 18,* 253–292.

Fong, G. T., & Nisbett, R. E. (1991). Immediate and delayed transfer of training effects in statistical reasoning. *Journal of Experimental Psychology: General, 120,* 34–45.

Forsythe, R., Nelson, F., Neumann, G., & Wright, J. (1992). Anatomy of an experimental political stock market. *American Economic Review, 82,* 1142–1161.

Frank, M. J., Cohen, M., & Sanfey, A. G. (2009). Multiple systems in decision making. *Current Directions in Psychological Science, 18,* 73–77.

Frankfurt, H. (1971). Freedom of the will and the concept of a person. *Journal of Philosophy, 68,* 5–20.

Frankish, K. (2004). *Mind and supermind.* Cambridge: Cambridge University Press.

Frankish, K. (2009). Systems and levels: Dual-system theories and the personal-subpersonal distinction. In J. S. B. T. Evans & K. Frankish (Eds.), *In two minds: Dual processes and beyond* (pp. 89–107). Oxford: Oxford University Press.

Franklin, S. (1995). *Artificial Minds.* Cambridge, MA: MIT Press.

Franssens, S., & De Neys, W. (2009). The effortless nature of conflict detection during thinking. *Thinking & Reasoning, 15,* 105–128.

Frederick, S. (2005). Cognitive reflection and decision making. *Journal of Economic Perspectives, 19,* 25–42.

Frederick, S., Novemsky, N., Wang, J., Dhar, R., & Nowlis, S. (2009). Opportunity cost neglect. *Journal of Consumer Research, 36,* 553–561.

Friedman, N. P., Haberstick, B. C., Willcutt, E. G., Miyake, A., Young, S. E., Corley, R. P., & Hewitt, J. K. (2007). Greater attention problems during childhood predict poorer executive functioning in late adolescence. *Psychological Science, 18,* 893–900.

Friedman, N. P., Miyake, A., Corley, R. P., Young, S. E., DeFries, J. C., & Hewitt, J. K. (2006). Not all executive functions are related to intelligence. *Psychological Science, 17,* 172–179.

Friedman, N. P., Miyake, A., Young, S. E., DeFries, J. C., Corley, R. P., & Hewitt, J. K. (2008). Individual differences in executive functions are almost entirely genetic in origin. *Journal of Experiment Psychology: General, 137,* 201–225.

Friend, M. (2005). *Special education: Contemporary perspectives for school professionals.* Boston: Pearson Education.

Frisch, D. (1993). Reasons for framing effects. *Organizational Behavior and Human Decision Processes, 54,* 399–429.

Funder, D. C., & Block, J. (1989). The role of ego-control, ego-resiliency, and IQ in delay of gratification in adolescence. *Journal of Personality and Social Psychology, 57,* 1041–1050.

Furnham, A., & McGill, C. (2003). Medical students' attitudes about complementary and alternative medicine. *The Journal of Alternative and Complementary Medicine, 9,* 275–284.

Fuster, J. M. (1990). Prefrontal cortex and the bridging of temporal gaps in the perception-action cycle. In A. Diamond (Ed.), *The development and neural bases of higher cognitive functions* (pp. 318–336). New York: New York Academy of Sciences.

Gailliot, M. T., & Baumeister, R. F. (2007). The physiology of willpower: Linking blood glucose to self-control. *Personality and Social Psychology Review, 11,* 303–327.

Gale, M., & Ball, L. J. (2006). Dual-goal facilitation in Wason's 2-4-6 task: What mediates successful rule discovery? *The Quarterly Journal of Experimental Psychology, 59,* 873–885.

Gale, M., & Ball, L. J. (2009). Exploring the determinants of dual goal facilitation in a rule discovery task. *Thinking & Reasoning, 15,* 294–315.

Galinsky, A. D., & Mussweiler, T. (2001). First offers as anchors: The role of perspective-taking and negotiator focus. *Journal of Personality and Social Psychology, 81,* 657–669.

Galton, F. (1883). *Inquiry into human faculty and its development.* London: Macmillan.

Gardner, H. (1983). *Frames of mind.* New York: Basic Books.

Gardner, H. (1999). *Intelligence reframed.* New York: Basic Books.

Gauthier, D. (1975). Reason and maximization. *Canadian Journal of Philosophy, 4,* 411–433.

Gauthier, D. (1986). *Morals by agreement.* Oxford: Oxford University Press.

Gawronski, B., & Bodenhausen, G. V. (2006). Associative and propositional processes in evaluation: An integrative review of implicit and explicit attitude change. *Psychological Bulletin, 132,* 692–731.

Geary, D. C. (2005). *The origin of the mind: Evolution of brain, cognition, and general intelligence.* Washington, DC: American Psychological Association.

Gebauer, G., & Laming, D. (1997). Rational choices in Wason's selection task. *Psychological Research, 60,* 284–293.

Gernsbacher, M. A., Dawson, M., & Goldsmith, H. H. (2005). Three reasons not to believe in an autism epidemic. *Psychological Science, 14,* 55–58.

Gernsbacher, M. A., & Faust, M. E. (1991). The mechanism of suppression: A component of general comprehension skill. *Journal of Experimental Psychology: Learning, Memory, and Cognition., 17,* 245–262.

Gibbard, A. (1990). *Wise choices, apt feelings: A theory of normative judgment.* Cambridge, MA: Harvard University Press.

Gibson, B., Sanbonmatsu, D. M., & Posavac, S. S. (1997). The effects of selective hypothesis testing on gambling. *Journal of Experimental Psychology: Applied, 3,* 126–142.

Gigerenzer, G. (1991). How to make cognitive illusions disappear: Beyond "heuristics and biases." *European Review of Social Psychology, 2,* 83–115.

Gigerenzer, G. (1996). On narrow norms and vague heuristics: A reply to Kahneman and Tversky (1996). *Psychological Review, 103*, 592–596.

Gigerenzer, G. (2002). *Calculated risks: How to know when numbers deceive you.* New York: Simon & Schuster.

Gigerenzer, G. (2006). Out of the frying pan into the fire: Behavioral reactions to terrorist attacks. *Risk Analysis, 26*, 347–351.

Gigerenzer, G. (2007). *Gut feelings: The intelligence of the unconscious.* New York: Viking Penguin.

Gigerenzer, G. (2008). Why heuristics work. *Perspectives on Psychological Science, 3*, 20–29.

Gigerenzer, G., & Brighton, H. (2009). Homo heuristicus: Why biased minds make better inferences. *Topics in Cognitive Science, 1*, 107–143.

Gigerenzer, G., Hoffrage, U., & Ebert, A. (1998). AIDS counselling for low-risk clients. *AIDS Care, 10*, 197–211.

Gignac, G. E. (2005). Openness to experience, general intelligence and crystallized intelligence: A methodological extension. *Intelligence, 33*, 161–167.

Gilbert, D. T. (1991). How mental systems believe. *American Psychologist, 46*, 107–119.

Gilbert, D. T. (1999). What the mind's not. In S. Chaiken & Y. Trope (Eds.), *Dual-process theories in social psychology* (pp. 3–11). New York: Guilford Press.

Gilbert, D. T. (2006). *Stumbling on happiness.* New York: Alfred A. Knopf.

Gilhooly, K. J., & Fioratou, E. (2009). Executive functions in insight versus non-insight problem solving: An individual differences approach. *Thinking and Reasoning, 15*, 355–376.

Gilhooly, K. J., & Murphy, P. (2005). Differentiating insight from non-insight problems. *Thinking and Reasoning, 11*, 279–302.

Gilinsky, A., & Judd, B. B. (1994). Working memory and bias in reasoning across the life span. *Psychology and Aging, 9*, 356–371.

Gilovich, T. (1991). *How we know what isn't so.* New York: Free Press.

Gilovich, T., Griffin, D., & Kahneman, D. (Eds.). (2002). *Heuristics and biases: The psychology of intuitive judgment.* New York: Cambridge University Press.

Gilovich, T., Medvec, V. H., & Sativsky, K. (1998). The illusion of transparency: Biased assessment of others' ability to read one's emotional states. *Journal of Personality and Social Psychology, 75*, 332–346.

Gilovich, T., & Savitsky, K. (2002). Like goes with like: The role of representativeness in erroneous and pseudo-scientific beliefs. In T. Gilovich, D. Griffin & D. Kahneman (Eds.), *Heuristics and biases: The psychology of intuitive judgment* (pp. 617–624). New York: Cambridge University Press.

Girotto, V. (2004). Task understanding. In J. P. Leighton & R. J. Sternberg (Eds.), *The nature of reasoning* (pp. 103–125). Cambridge: Cambridge University Press.

Girotto, V., & Tentori, K. (2008). Is domain-general thinking a domain-specific adaptation. *Mind & Society, 7*, 167–175.

Glenberg, A. M. (1997). What memory is for. *Behavioral and Brain Sciences, 20*, 1–55.

Goel, V., & Dolan, R. J. (2003). Explaining modulation of reasoning by belief. *Cognition, 87,* B11–B22.

Goff, M., & Ackerman, P. L. (1992). Personality-intelligence relations: Assessment of typical intellectual engagement. *Journal of Educational Psychology, 84,* 537–552.

Goldman, A. I. (1995). In defense of the simulation theory. In M. Davies & T. Stone (Eds.), *Folk psychology* (pp. 191–206). Oxford: Blackwell.

Goldman, A. I. (2006). *Simulating minds: The philosophy, psychology, and neuroscience of mindreading.* Oxford: Oxford University Press.

Goldman-Rakic, P. S. (1992). Working memory and the mind. *Scientific American, 267,* 111–117.

Goody, E. N. (Ed.). (1995). *Social intelligence and interaction: Expressions and implications of the social bias in human intelligence.* Cambridge: Cambridge University Press.

Gordon, M., Lewandowski, L., & Keiser, S. (1999). The LD label for relatively well-functioning students: A critical analysis. *Journal of Learning Disabilities, 32,* 485–490.

Gould, S. J. (1991). *Bully for the Brontosaurus.* New York: Norton.

Gray, J. R., Chabris, C. F., & Braver, T. S. (2003). Neural mechanisms of general fluid intelligence. *Nature Neuroscience, 6,* 316–322.

Green, L., & Myerson, J. (2004). A discounting framework for choice with delayed and probabilistic rewards. *Psychological Bulletin, 130,* 769–792.

Greene, J. (2005). Cognitive neuroscience and the structure of the moral mind. In P. Carruthers, S. Laurence, & S. Stich (Eds.), *The innate mind* (pp. 338–352). Oxford: Oxford University Press.

Greene, J., Nystrom, L. E., Engell, A. D., Darley, J. M., & Cohen, J. D. (2004). The neural bases of cognitive conflict and control in moral judgment. *Neuron, 44,* 389–400.

Greenfield, P. M. (1998). The cultural evolution of IQ. In U. Neisser (Ed.), *The rising curve: Long-term changes in IQ and related measures* (pp. 81–123). Washington, DC: American Psychological Association.

Greenhoot, A. F., Semb, G., Colombo, J., & Schreiber, T. (2004). Prior beliefs and methodological concepts in scientific reasoning. *Applied Cognitive Psychology, 18,* 203–221.

Griffin, D., & Tversky, A. (1992). The weighing of evidence and the determinants of confidence. *Cognitive Psychology, 24,* 411–435.

Groopman, J. (2007). *How doctors think.* Boston: Houghton Mifflin.

Haidt, J. (2001). The emotional dog and its rational tail: A social intuitionist approach to moral judgment. *Psychological Review, 108,* 814–834.

Halpern, D. (2008). *Halpern Critical thinking assessment: Background and scoring standards.* Unpublished manuscript. Claremont, CA: Claremont McKenna College.

Handley, S. J., Capon, A., Beveridge, M., Dennis, I., & Evans, J. St. B. T. (2004). Working memory, inhibitory control and the development of children's reasoning. *Thinking and Reasoning, 10,* 175–195.

Hardman, D. (1998). Does reasoning occur on the selection task? A comparison of relevance-based theories. *Thinking and Reasoning, 4,* 353–376.

Harman, G. (1995). Rationality. In E. E. Smith & D. N. Osherson (Eds.), *Thinking (Vol. 3)* (pp. 175–211). Cambridge, MA: The MIT Press.

Harnishfeger, K. K., & Bjorklund, D. F. (1994). A developmental perspective on individual differences in inhibition. *Learning and Individual Differences, 6,* 331–356.

Hasher, L., Lustig, C., & Zacks, R. (2007). Inhibitory mechanisms and the control of attention. In A. Conway, C. Jarrold, M. Kane, A. Miyake, & J. Towse (Eds.), *Variation in working memory* (pp. 227–249). New York: Oxford University Press.

Hasher, L., Zacks, R. T., & May, C. P. (1999). Inhibitory control, circadian arousal, and age. In D. Gopher & A. Koriat (Eds.), *Attention & Performance XVII, Cognitive Regulation of Performance: Interaction of Theory and Application* (pp. 653–675). Cambridge, MA: MIT Press.

Hastie, R., & Dawes, R. M. (2001). *Rational choice in an uncertain world.* Thousand Oaks, CA: Sage.

Hastie, R., & Pennington, N. (2000). Explanation-based decision making. In T. Connolly, H. R. Arkes & K. R. Hammond (Eds.), *Judgment and decision making: An interdisciplinary reader (Second Edition)* (pp. 212–228). Cambridge, MA: Cambridge University Press.

Hawking, S. (1988). *A brief history of time.* New York: Bantam Books.

Heath, J. (2001). *The efficient society.* Toronto: Penguin Books.

Heaton, R., Chelune, G., Talley, J., Kay, G., & Curtiss, G. (1993). *Wisconsin Card Sorting Test - Revised and expanded.* Lutz, FL: Psychological Assessment Resource.

Henig, R. M. (2007, March 4). Darwin's God. *The New York Times.* Retrieved from http://www.nytimes.com/2007/03/04/magazine/04evolution.t.html?_r=1& oref=slogin&pagewanted=print (March 9, 2007).

Herrmann, E., Call, J., Hernandez-Lloreda, M. V., Hare, B., & Tomasello, M. (2007, September 7). Humans have evolved specialized skills of social cognition: The cultural intelligence hypothesis. *Science, 317,* 1360–1366.

Herrnstein, R. J. (1990). Rational choice theory: Necessary but not sufficient. *American Psychologist, 45,* 356–367.

Hertwig, R., Benz, B., & Krauss, S. (2008). The conjunction fallacy and the many meanings of *and. Cognition, 108,* 740–753.

Higgins, D. M., Peterson, J. B., Pihl, R. O., & Lee, A. G. M. (2007). Prefrontal cognitive ability, intelligence, big five personality, and the prediction of advanced academic and workplace performance. *Journal of Personality and Social Psychology, 93,* 298–319.

Hilbig, B. E., & Pohl, R. F. (2008). Recognizing users of the recognition heuristic. *Experimental Psychology, 55,* 394–401.

Hilton, D. J. (1995). The social context of reasoning: Conversational inference and rational judgment. *Psychological Bulletin, 118,* 248–271.

Hilton, D. J. (2003). Psychology and the financial markets: Applications to understanding and remedying irrational decision-making. In I. Brocas & J. D. Carrillo (Eds.), *The psychology of economic decisions (Vol. 1): Rationality and well-being* (pp. 273–297). Oxford: Oxford University Press.

Hodgins, D. C., Currie, S. R., Currie, G., & Fick, G. H. (2009). Randomized trial of brief motivational treatments for pathological gamblers: More is not necessarily better. *Journal of Consulting and Clinical Psychology, 77,* 950–960.

Hofmann, W., Friese, M., & Strack, F. (2009). Impulse and self-control from a dual-systems perspective. *Perspectives in Psychological Science, 4,* 162–176.

Hood, B. M. (2009). *Supersense: Why we believe in the unbelievable.* New York: HarperOne.

Horn, J. L., & Cattell, R. B. (1967). Age differences in fluid and crystallized intelligence. *Acta Psychologica, 26,* 1–23.

Horn, J. L., & Noll, J. (1997). Human cognitive capabilities: Gf-Gc theory. In D. Flanagan, J. Genshaft, & P. Harrison (Eds.), *Contemporary intellectual assessment: Theories, tests, and issues* (pp. 53–91). New York: Guilford Press.

Howson, C., & Urbach, P. (1993). *Scientific reasoning: The Bayesian approach (Second Edition).* Chicago: Open Court.

Hsee, C. K. (1996). The evaluability hypothesis: An explanation of preference reversals between joint and separate evaluations of alternatives. *Organizational Behavior and Human Decision Processes, 46,* 247–257.

Hsee, C. K., & Hastie, R. (2006). Decision and experience: Why don't we choose what makes us happy? *Trends in Cognitive Sciences, 10,* 31–37.

Hsee, C. K., Loewenstein, G. F., Blount, S., & Bazerman, M. H. (1999). Preference reversals between joint and separate evaluations of options: A review and theoretical analysis. *Psychological Bulletin, 125,* 576–590.

Hsee, C. K., & Zhang, J. (2004). Distinction bias: Misprediction and mischoice due to joint evaluation. *Journal of Personality and Social Psychology, 86,* 680–695.

Hull, D. L. (2000). Taking memetics seriously: Memetics will be what we make it. In R. Aunger (Eds.), *Darwinizing culture: The status of memetics as a science* (pp. 43–67). Oxford: Oxford University Press.

Hull, D. L. (2001). *Science and selection: Essays on biological evolution and the philosophy of science.* Cambridge: Cambridge University Press.

Humphrey, N. (1976). The social function of intellect. In P. P. G. Bateson & R. A. Hinde (Eds.), *Growing points in ethology* (pp. 303–317). London: Faber & Faber.

Humphrey, N. (1986). *The inner eye.* London: Faber & Faber.

Hurley, S. L. (1989). *Natural reasons: Personality and polity.* New York: Oxford University Press.

Hurley, S., & Nudds, M. (2006). The questions of animal rationality: Theory and evidence. In S. Hurley & M. Nudds (Eds.), *Rational animals?* (pp. 1–83). Oxford: Oxford University Press.

Jackendoff, R. (1996). How language helps us think. *Pragmatics and Cognition, 4*, 1–34.

Jacobs, J. E., & Potenza, M. (1991). The use of judgment heuristics to make social and object decisions: A developmental perspective. *Child Development, 62*, 166–178.

Jacowitz, K. E., & Kahneman, D. (1995). Measures of anchoring in estimation tasks. *Personality and Social Psychology Bulletin, 21*, 1161–1167.

Jaeggi, S. M., Buschkuehl, M., Jonides, J., & Perrig, W. J. (2008). Improved fluid intelligence with training in working memory. *Proceedings of the National Academy of Sciences, 105*, 6829–6833.

Jarvis, C. (2000). The rise and fall of Albania's pyramid schemes. *Finance & Development, 37*(1), 46–49.

Jeffrey, R. C. (1983). *The logic of decision (Second Ed.)*. Chicago: University of Chicago Press.

Jepson, C., Krantz, D., & Nisbett, R. (1983). Inductive reasoning: Competence or skill? *Behavioral and Brain Sciences, 6*, 494–501.

Johnson, E. J., & Goldstein, D. G. (2006). Do defaults save lives? In S. Lichtenstein & P. Slovic (Eds.), *The construction of preference* (pp. 682–688). Cambridge: Cambridge University Press.

Johnson, E. J., Hershey, J., Meszaros, J., & Kunreuther, H. (2000). Framing, probability distortions, and insurance decisions. In D. Kahneman & A. Tversky (Eds.), *Choices, values, and frames* (pp. 224–240). Cambridge: Cambridge University Press.

Johnson-Laird, P. N. (1982). Thinking as a skill. *Quarterly Journal of Experimental Psychology, 34A*, 1–29.

Johnson-Laird, P. N. (1983). *Mental models*. Cambridge, MA: Harvard University Press.

Johnson-Laird, P. N. (1999). Deductive reasoning. *Annual Review of Psychology, 50*, 109–135.

Johnson-Laird, P. N. (2005). Mental models and thought. In K. J. Holyoak & R. G. Morrison (Eds.), *The Cambridge handbook of thinking and reasoning* (pp. 185–208). New York: Cambridge University Press.

Johnson-Laird, P. N. (2006). *How we reason*. Oxford: Oxford University Press.

Johnson-Laird, P. N., & Byrne, R. M. J. (1993). Models and deductive rationality. In K. Manktelow & D. Over (Eds.), *Rationality: Psychological and philosophical perspectives* (pp. 177–210). London: Routledge.

Jordan, S. D. (2007, May). Global climate change triggered by global warming. *Skeptical Inquirer, 31*, 32–45.

Jungermann, H. (1986). The two camps on rationality. In H. R. Arkes & K. R. Hammond (Eds.), *Judgment and decision making* (pp. 627–641). Cambridge: Cambridge University Press.

Jurado, M. B., & Rosselli, M. (2007). The elusive nature of executive Functions: A review of our current understanding. *Neuropsychology Review, 17*, 213–233.

Juslin, P., Nilsson, H., & Winman, A. (2009). Probability theory, not the very guide of life. *Psychological Review, 116*, 856–874.

Kagan, J., Rosman, B. L., Day, D., Albert, J., & Philips, W. (1964). Information processing in the child: Significance of analytic and reflective attitudes. *Psychological Monographs*, 78(578).

Kahneman, D. (1973). *Attention and effort*. Englewood Cliffs, NJ: Prentice Hall.

Kahneman, D. (1994). New challenges to the rationality assumption. *Journal of Institutional and Theoretical Economics*, *150*, 18–36.

Kahneman, D. (1999). Objective happiness. In D. Kahneman, E. Diener, & N. Schwarz (Eds.), *Well-being: The foundations of hedonic psychology* (pp. 3–25). Thousand Oaks, CA: Sage.

Kahneman, D. (2000). A psychological point of view: Violations of rational rules as a diagnostic of mental processes. *Behavioral and Brain Sciences*, *23*, 681–683.

Kahneman, D. (2003). A perspective on judgment and choice: Mapping bounded rationality. *American Psychologist*, *58*, 697–720.

Kahneman, D., Diener, E., & Schwarz, N. (Eds.). (1999). *Well-being: The foundations of hedonic psychology*. Thousand Oaks, CA: Sage.

Kahneman, D., & Frederick, S. (2002). Representativeness revisited: Attribute substitution in intuitive judgment. In T. Gilovich, D. Griffin, & D. Kahneman (Eds.), *Heuristics and biases: The psychology of intuitive judgment* (pp. 49–81). New York: Cambridge University Press.

Kahneman, D., & Frederick, S. (2005). A model of heuristic judgment. In K. J. Holyoak & R. G. Morrison (Eds.), *The Cambridge handbook of thinking and reasoning* (pp. 267–293). New York: Cambridge University Press.

Kahneman, D., & Klein, G. (2009). Conditions for intuitive expertise: A failure to disagree. *American Psychologist*, *64*, 515–526.

Kahneman, D., Knetsch, J. L., & Thaler, R. H. (1990). Experimental tests of the endowment effect and the Coase theorem. *Journal of Political Economy*, *98*, 1325–1348.

Kahneman, D., Knetsch, J. L., & Thaler, R. H. (1991). The endowment effect, loss aversion, and status quo bias. *Journal of Economic Perspectives*, *5*, 193–206.

Kahneman, D., Krueger, A. B., Schkade, D., Schwarz, N., & Stone, A. (2006). Would you be happier if you were richer? A focusing illusion. *Science*, *312*, 1908–1910.

Kahneman, D., & Tversky, A. (1972). Subjective probability: A judgment of representativeness. *Cognitive Psychology*, *3*, 430–454.

Kahneman, D., & Tversky, A. (1973). On the psychology of prediction. *Psychological Review*, *80*, 237–251.

Kahneman, D., & Tversky, A. (1979). Prospect theory: An analysis of decision under risk. *Econometrica*, *47*, 263–291.

Kahneman, D., & Tversky, A. (1982a). On the study of statistical intuitions. *Cognition*, *11*, 123–141.

Kahneman, D., & Tversky, A. (1982b). The simulation heuristic. In D. Kahneman, P. Slovic, & A. Tversky (Eds.), *Judgment under uncertainty: Heuristics and biases* (pp. 201–208). Cambridge: Cambridge University Press.

Kahneman, D., & Tversky, A. (1983). Can irrationality be intelligently discussed? *Behavioral and Brain Sciences*, *6*, 509–510.

Kahneman, D., & Tversky, A. (1984). Choices, values, and frames. *American Psychologist, 39*, 341–350.

Kahneman, D., & Tversky, A. (1996). On the reality of cognitive illusions. *Psychological Review, 103*, 582–591.

Kahneman, D., & Tversky, A. (Eds.). (2000). *Choices, values, and frames.* Cambridge: Cambridge University Press.

Kahneman, D., Wakker, P. P., & Sarin, R. (1997). Back to Bentham? Explorations of experienced utility. *The Quarterly Journal of Economics, 112*(2), 375–405.

Kaminski, J., Call, J., & Tomasello, M. (2008). Chimpanzees know what others know, but not what they believe. *Cognition, 109*, 224–234.

Kanazawa, S. (2004). General intelligence as a domain-specific adaptation. *Psychological Review, 111*, 512–523.

Kane, M. J. (2003). The intelligent brain in conflict. *Trends in Cognitive Sciences, 7*, 375–377.

Kane, M. J., Bleckley, M., Conway, A., & Engle, R. W. (2001). A controlled-attention view of WM capacity. *Journal of Experimental Psychology: General, 130*, 169–183.

Kane, M. J., Brown, L. H., McVay, J. C., Silvia, P. J., Myin-Germeys, I., & Kwapil, T. R. (2007). For whom the mind wanders, and when: An experience-sampling study of working memory and executive control in daily life. *Psychological Science, 18*, 614–621.

Kane, M. J., & Engle, R. W. (2002). The role of prefrontal cortex working-memory capacity, executive attention, and general fluid intelligence: An individual-differences perspective. *Psychonomic Bulletin and Review, 9*, 637–671.

Kane, M. J., & Engle, R. W. (2003). Working-memory capacity and the control of attention: The contributions of goal neglect, response competition, and task set to Stroop interference. *Journal of Experimental Psychology: General, 132*, 47–70.

Kane, M. J., Hambrick, D. Z., & Conway, A. R. A. (2005). Working memory capacity and fluid intelligence are strongly related constructs: Comment on Ackerman, Beier, and Boyle (2005). *Psychological Bulletin, 131*, 66–71.

Kane, M. J., Hambrick, D. Z., Tuholski, S. W., Wilhelm, O., Payne, T., & Engle, R. W. (2004). The generality of working memory capacity: A latent-variable approach to verbal and visuospatial memory span and reasoning. *Journal of Experimental Psychology: General, 133*, 189–217.

Kardash, C. M., & Scholes, R. J. (1996). Effects of pre-existing beliefs, epistemological beliefs, and need for cognition on interpretation of controversial issues. *Journal of Educational Psychology, 88*, 260–271.

Kelman, M., & Lester, G. (1997). *Jumping the queue: An inquiry into the legal treatment of students with learning disabilities.* Cambridge, MA: Harvard University Press.

Kendall, P. C., Hudson, J. L., Gosch, E., Flannery-Schroeder, E., & Suveg, C. (2008). Cognitive-behavioral therapy for anxiety disordered youth: A randomized clinical trial evaluating child and family modalities. *Journal of Consulting and Clinical Psychology, 76*, 282–297.

Keren, G. (1994). The rationality of gambling: Gamblers' conceptions of probability, chance and luck. In G. W. P. Ayton (Ed.), *Subjective probability* (Vol. 60, pp. 485–499). Chichester, UK: Wiley.

Kermer, D. A., Driver-Linn, E., Wilson, T. D., & Gilbert, D. T. (2006). Loss aversion is an affective forecasting error. *Psychological Science, 17*, 649–653.

Kern, L., & Doherty, M. E. (1982). "Pseudodiagnosticity" in an idealized medical problem-solving environment. *Journal of Medical Education, 57*, 100–104.

Keys, D. J., & Schwartz, B. (2007). "Leaky" rationality: How research on behavioral decision making challenges normative standards of rationality. *Perspectives on Psychological Science, 2*, 162–180.

Keysar, B., & Barr, D. J. (2002). Self-anchoring in conversation: Why language users do not do what they "should." In T. Gilovich, D. Griffin & D. Kahneman (Eds.), *Heuristics and biases: The psychology of intuitive judgment* (pp. 150–166). New York: Cambridge University Press.

Kimberg, D. Y., D'Esposito, M., & Farah, M. J. (1998). Cognitive functions in the prefrontal cortex—working memory and executive control. *Current Directions in Psychological Science, 6*, 185–192.

King, R. N., & Koehler, D. J. (2000). Illusory correlations in graphological inference. *Journal of Experimental Psychology: Applied, 6*, 336–348.

Kirby, K. N. (2009). One-year temporal stability of delay-discount rates. *Psychonomic Bulletin & Review, 16*, 457–462.

Kirby, K. N., & Herrnstein, R. J. (1995). Preference reversals due to myopic discounting of delayed reward. *Psychological Science, 6*, 83–89.

Kirby, K. N., Petry, N. N., & Bickel, W. K. (1999). Heroin addicts have higher discount rates for delayed rewards than non-drug-using controls. *Journal of Experimental Psychology: General, 128*, 78–87.

Kirby, K. N., Winston, G. C., & Santiesteban, M. (2005). Impatience and grades: Delay-discount rates correlate negatively with college GPA. *Learning and Individual Differences, 15*, 213–222.

Kirkpatrick, L., & Epstein, S. (1992). Cognitive-experiential self-theory and subjective probability: Evidence for two conceptual systems. *Journal of Personality and Social Psychology, 63*, 534–544.

Klaczynski, P. A. (1997). Bias in adolescents' everyday reasoning and its relationship with intellectual ability, personal theories, and self-serving motivation. *Developmental Psychology, 33*, 273–283.

Klaczynski, P. A. (2000). Motivated scientific reasoning biases, epistemological beliefs, and theory polarization: A two-process approach to adolescent cognition. *Child Development, 71*, 1347–1366.

Klaczynski, P. A. (2001). Analytic and heuristic processing influences on adolescent reasoning and decision making. *Child Development, 72*, 844–861.

Klaczynski, P. A., & Gordon, D. H. (1996). Self-serving influences on adolescents' evaluations of belief-relevant evidence. *Journal of Experimental Child Psychology, 62*, 317–339.

Klaczynski, P. A., Gordon, D. H., & Fauth, J. (1997). Goal-oriented critical reasoning and individual differences in critical reasoning biases. *Journal of Educational Psychology, 89,* 470–485.

Klaczynski, P. A., & Laipple, J. (1993). Role of content domain, logic training, and IQ in rule acquisition and transfer. *Journal of Experimental Psychology: Learning, Memory, and Cognition, 19,* 653–672.

Klaczynski, P. A., & Lavallee, K. L. (2005). Domain-specific identity, epistemic regulation, and intellectual ability as predictors of belief-based reasoning: A dual-process perspective. *Journal of Experimental Child Psychology, 92,* 1–24.

Klaczynski, P. A., & Narasimham, G. (1998). Development of scientific reasoning biases: Cognitive versus ego-protective explanations. *Developmental Psychology, 34,* 175–187.

Klaczynski, P. A., & Robinson, B. (2000). Personal theories, intellectual ability, and epistemological beliefs: Adult age differences in everyday reasoning tasks. *Psychology and Aging, 15,* 400–416.

Klahr, D., & Nigam, M. (2004). The equivalence of learning paths in early science instruction: Effects of direct instruction and discovery learning. *Psychological Science, 15,* 661–667.

Klauer, K. C., Musch, J., & Naumer, B. (2000). On belief bias in syllogistic reasoning. *Psychological Review, 107,* 852–884.

Klauer, K. C., Stahl, C., & Erdfelder, E. (2007). The abstract selection task: New data and an almost comprehensive model. *Journal of Experimental Psychology: Learning, Memory, and Cognition, 33,* 688–703.

Klauer, K. C., Stegmaier, R., & Meiser, T. (1997). Working memory involvement in propositional and spatial reasoning. *Thinking and Reasoning, 3,* 9–47.

Klayman, J., & Ha, Y. (1987). Confirmation, disconfirmation, and information in hypothesis testing. *Psychological Review, 94,* 211–228.

Klein, G. (1998). *Sources of power: How people make decisions.* Cambridge, MA: MIT Press.

Klein, P. (1997). Multipying the problems of intelligence by eight: A critique of Gardner's theory. *Canadian Journal of Education, 22,* 377–394.

Kleindorfer, P. R., Kunreuther, H. C., & Schoemaker, P. J. H. (1993). *Decision sciences: An integrative perspective.* Cambridge: Cambridge University Press.

Koehler, D. J., Brenner, L., & Griffin, D. (2002). The calibration of expert judgment: Heuristics and biases beyond the laboratory. In T. Gilovich, D. Griffin & D. Kahneman (Eds.), *Heuristics and biases: The psychology of intuitive judgment* (pp. 686–715). New York: Cambridge University Press.

Koehler, D. J., & Harvey, N. (Eds.). (2004). *Blackwell handbook of judgment and decision making.* Oxford, England: Blackwell.

Koehler, D. J., & James, G. (2009). Probability matching in choice under uncertainty: Intuition versus deliberation. *Cognition, 113,* 123–127.

Koehler, J. J. (1996). The base rate fallacy reconsidered: Descriptive, normative and methodological challenges. *Behavioral and Brain Sciences, 19,* 1–53.

Kokis, J., Macpherson, R., Toplak, M., West, R. F., & Stanovich, K. E. (2002). Heuristic and analytic processing: Age trends and associations with cognitive ability and cognitive styles. *Journal of Experimental Child Psychology*, *83*, 26–52.

Komorita, S. S., & Parks, C. D. (1994). *Social dilemmas*. Boulder, CO: Westview Press.

Kosonen, P., & Winne, P. H. (1995). Effects of teaching statistical laws on reasoning about everyday problems. *Journal of Educational Psychology*, *87*, 33–46.

Kowalski, P., & Taylor, A. K. (2009). The effect of refuting misconceptions in the introductory psychology class. *Teaching of Psychology*, *36*, 153–159.

Kramer, W., & Gigerenzer, G. (2005). How to confuse with statistics or: The use and misuse of conditional probabilities. *Statistical Science*, *20*, 223–230.

Krueger, J., & Funder, D. C. (2004). Towards a balanced social psychology: Causes, consequences and cures for the problem-seeking approach to social cognition and behavior. *Behavioral and Brain Sciences*, *27*, 313–376.

Kruglanski, A. W., & Webster, D. M. (1996). Motivated closing of the mind: "Seizing" and "freezing." *Psychological Review*, *103*, 263–283.

Ku, K., & Ho, I. T. (2010). Dispositional factors predicting Chinese students' critical thinking performance. *Personality and Individual Differences*, *48*, 54–58.

Kuhberger, A. (1998). The influence of framing on risky decisions: A meta-analysis. *Organizational Behavior and Human Decision Processes*, *75*, 23–55.

Kuhberger, A. (2002). The rationality of risky decisions: A changing message. *Theory & Psychology*, *12*, 427–452.

Kuhn, D. (1989). Children and adults as intuitive scientists. *Psychological Review*, *96*, 674–689.

Kuhn, D. (1991). *The skills of argument*. Cambridge: Cambridge University Press.

Kuhn, D. (1992). Thinking as argument. *Harvard Educational Review*, *62*, 155–178.

Kuhn, D. (2001). How do people know? *Psychological Science*, *12*, 1–8.

Kuhn, D., Cheney, R., & Weinstock, M. (2000). The development of epistemological understanding. *Cognitive Development*, *15*, 309–328.

Kuhn, D., & Dean, D. J. (2005). Is developing scientific thinking all about learning to control variables? *Psychological Science*, *16*, 866–870.

Kuhn, D., & Pease, M. (2008). What needs to develop in the development of inquiry skills? *Cognition and Instruction*, *26*, 512–559.

Kummer, H., Daston, L., Gigerenzer, G., & Silk, J. B. (1997). The social intelligence hypothesis. In P. Weingart, S. D. Mitchell, P. J. Richerson & S. Maasen (Eds.), *Human by nature: Between biology and the social sciences* (pp. 157–179). Mahwah, NJ: Lawrence Erlbaum Associates.

Kyllonen, P. C., & Christal, R. E. (1990). Reasoning ability is (little more than) working memory capacity! *Intelligence*, *14*, 389–433.

Labudda, K., Frigge, K., Horstmann, S., Aengenendt, J., Woermann, F. G., Ebner, A., Markowitsch, H. J., & Brand, M. (2009). Decision making in patients with temporal lobe epilepsy. *Neuropsychologia*, 47, 50–58.

Ladouceur, R., Sylvain, C., Boutin, C., Lachance, S., Doucet, C., Leblond, J., et al. (2001). Cognitive treatment of pathological gambling. *The Journal of Nervous and Mental Disease, 189,* 774–780.

Laland, K. N., & Brown, G. R. (2002). *Sense and nonsense: Evolutionary perspectives on human behaviour.* Oxford: Oxford University Press.

Lambdin, C., & Shaffer, V. A. (2009). Are within-subjects designs transparent? *Judgment and Decision Making, 4,* 554–566.

Larrick, R. P., Morgan, J. N., & Nisbett, R. E. (1990). Teaching the use of cost-benefit reasoning in everyday life. *Psychological Science, 1,* 362–370.

Larrick, R. P., Nisbett, R. E., & Morgan, J. N. (1993). Who uses the cost-benefit rules of choice? Implications for the normative status of microeconomic theory. *Organizational Behavior and Human Decision Processes, 56,* 331–347.

Leary, M. R., Shepperd, J. A., McNeil, M. S., Jenkins, B., & Barnes, B. D. (1986). Objectivism in information utilization: Theory and measurement. *Journal of Personality Assessment, 50,* 32–43.

LeBoeuf, R. A., & Shafir, E. (2003). Deep thoughts and shallow frames: On the susceptibility to framing effects. *Journal of Behavioral Decision Making, 16,* 77–92.

Lee, C. J. (2006). Gricean charity: The Gricean turn in psychology. *Philosophy of the Social Sciences, 36,* 193–218.

Lee, L., Amir, O., & Ariely, D. (2009). In search of homo economicus: Cognitive noise and the role of emotion in preference consistency. *Journal of Consumer Research, 36,* 173–187.

Lefcourt, H. M. (1991). Locus of control. In J. P. Robinson, P. Shaver & L. S. Wrightsman (Eds.), *Measures of personality and social psychological attitudes* (pp. 413–499). San Diego, CA: Academic Press.

Legrenzi, P., Girotto, V., & Johnson-Laird, P. N. (1993). Focussing in reasoning and decision making. *Cognition, 49,* 37–66.

Lehman, D. R., Lempert, R. O., & Nisbett, R. E. (1988). The effect of graduate training on reasoning. *American Psychologist, 43,* 431–442.

Lehman, D. R., & Nisbett, R. E. (1990). A longitudinal study of the effects of undergraduate training on reasoning. *Developmental Psychology, 26,* 952–960.

Lehrer, K. (1990). *Theory of knowledge.* London: Routledge.

Lehrer, K. (1997). *Self-trust: A study of reason, knowledge, and autonomy.* Oxford: Oxford University Press.

Lepine, R., Barrouillet, P., & Camos, V. (2005). What makes working memory spans so predictive of high-level cognition? *Psychonomic Bulletin & Review, 12,* 165–170.

Leshowitz, B., DiCerbo, K. E., & Okun, M. A. (2002). Effects of instruction in methodological reasoning on information evaluation. *Teaching of Psychology, 29,* 5–10.

Leshowitz, B., Jenkens, K., Heaton, S., & Bough, T. L. (1993). Fostering critical thinking skills in students with learning disabilities: An instructional program. *Journal of Learning Disabilities, 26,* 483–490.

Leslie, A. M. (1987). Pretense and representation: The origins of "Theory of Mind." *Psychological Review, 94*, 412–426.

Leslie, A. M., Friedman, O., & German, T. P. (2004). Core mechanisms in theory of mind. *Trends in Cognitive Sciences, 8*, 528–533.

Levesque, H. J. (1986). Making believers out of computers. *Artificial Intelligence, 30*, 81–108.

Levesque, H. J. (1989). Logic and the complexity of reasoning. In R. H. Thomason (Ed.), *Philosophical logic and artificial intelligence* (pp. 73–107). Kluwer Academic Publishers.

Levi, I. (1983). Who commits the base rate fallacy? *Behavioral and Brain Sciences, 6*, 502–506.

Levin, I. P., Gaeth, G. J., Schreiber, J., & Lauriola, M. (2002). A new look at framing effects: Distribution of effect sizes, individual differences, and independence of types of effects. *Organizational Behavior and Human Decision Processes, 88*, 411–429.

Levin, I. P., & Hart, S. S. (2003). Risk preferences in young children: Early evidence of individual differences in reaction to potential gains and losses. *Journal of Behavioral Decision Making, 16*, 397–413.

Levin, I. P., Hart, S. S., Weller, J. A., & Harshman, L. A. (2007). Stability of choices in a risky decision-making task: A 3-year longitudinal study with children and adults. *Journal of Behavioral Decision Making, 20*, 241–252.

Levinson, S. C. (1995). Interactional biases in human thinking. In E. Goody (Eds.), *Social intelligence and interaction* (pp. 221–260). Cambridge: Cambridge University Press.

Lewis, D. (1989). Dispositional theories of value. *Proceedings of the Aristotelian Society, Supplementary Volume 63*, 113–137.

Lezak, M. D. (1983). *Neuropsychological assessment (Second Edition)*. New York: Oxford University Press.

Li, M., & Chapman, G. B. (2009). "100% of anything looks good": The appeal of one hundred percent. *Psychonomic Bulletin & Review, 16*, 156–162.

Liberman, N., & Klar, Y. (1996). Hypothesis testing in Wason's selection task: Social exchange cheating detection or task understanding. *Cognition, 58*, 127–156.

Lichtenstein, S., & Fischhoff, B. (1980). Training for calibration. *Organizational Behavior and Human Performance, 26*, 149–171.

Lichtenstein, S., & Slovic, P. (1971). Reversal of preferences between bids and choices in gambling decisions. *Journal of Experimental Psychology, 89*, 46–55.

Lichtenstein, S., & Slovic, P. (1973). Response-induced reversals of preference in gambling: An extended replication in Las Vegas. *Journal of Experimental Psychology, 101*, 16–20.

Lichtenstein, S., & Slovic, P. (Ed.). (2006). *The construction of preference*. Cambridge: Cambridge University Press.

Lichtenstein, S., Slovic, P., Fischhoff, B., Layman, M., & Combs, B. (1978). Judged frequency of lethal events. *Journal of Experimental Psychology: Human Learning and Memory, 4*, 551–578.

Lieberman, M. D. (2000). Intuiton: A social cognitive neuroscience approach. *Psychological Bulletin, 126*, 109–137.

Lieberman, M. D. (2003). Reflexive and reflective judgment processes: A social cognitive neuroscience approach. In J. P. Forgas, K. R. Williams, & W. von Hippel (Eds.), *Social judgments: Implicit and explicit processes* (pp. 44–67). New York: Cambridge University Press.

Lieberman, M. D. (2007). Social cognitive neuroscience: A review of core processes. *Annual Review of Psychology, 58*, 259–289.

Lieberman, M. D. (2009). What zombies can't do: A social cognitive neuroscience approach to the irreducibility of reflective consciousness. In J. St. B. T. Evans & K. Frankish (Eds.), *In two minds: Dual processes and beyond* (pp. 293–316). Oxford: Oxford University Press.

Lilienfeld, S. O. (2007). Psychological treatments that cause harm. *Perspectives on Psychological Science, 2*, 53–70.

Lilienfeld, S. O., Ammirati, R., & Landfield, K. (2009). Giving debiasing away: Can psychological research on correcting cognitive errors promote human welfare? *Perspectives on Psychological Science, 4*, 390–398.

Lilienfeld, S. O., & Arkowitz, H. (2007, April). Autism: An epidemic. *Scientific American Mind, 18*, 82–83.

Lilienfeld, S. O., Lynn, S. J., Ruscio, J., & Beyerstein, B. L. (2010). *50 Great myths of popular psychology*. Malden, MA: Wiley-Blackwell.

Lillard, A. (2001). Pretend play as twin Earth: A social-cognitive analysis. *Developmental Review, 21*, 495–531.

Lindner, H., Kirkby, R., Wertheim, E., & Birch, P. (1999). A brief assessment of irrational thinking: The Shortened General Attitude and Belief Scale. *Cognitive Therapy and Research, 23*, 651–663.

Lipstadt, D. (1994). *Denying the Holocaust*. New York: Plume.

Loewenstein, G. F. (1996). Out of control: Visceral influences on behavior. *Organizational Behavior and Human Decision Processes, 65*, 272–292.

Loewenstein, G. F., Read, D., & Baumeister, R. (Eds.). (2003). *Time and decision: Economic and psychological perspectives on intertemporal choice*. New York: Russell Sage.

Loewenstein, G. F., Weber, E. U., Hsee, C. K., & Welch, N. (2001). Risk as feelings. *Psychological Bulletin, 127*, 267–286.

Logan, G. D. (1994). On the ability to inhibit thought and action: A user's guide to the stop signal paradigm. In D. Dagenbach & T. H. Carr (Eds.), *Inhibitory processes in attention, memory, and language* (pp. 189–239). San Diego: Academic Press.

Lopes, L. (1991). The rhetoric of irrationality. *Theory & Psychology, 1*, 65–82.

Lubinski, D. (2000). Scientific and social significance of assessing individual differences: "Sinking shafts at a few critical points." *Annual Review of Psychology, 51*, 405–444.

Lubinski, D. (2004). Introduction to the special section on cognitive abilities: 100 years after Spearman's (1904) "General Intelligence, Objectively Determined and Measured." *Journal of Personality and Social Psychology, 86*, 96–111.

Lubinski, D., & Humphreys, L. G. (1997). Incorporating general intelligence into epidemiology and the social sciences. *Intelligence, 24*, 159–201.

Lucas, E. J., & Ball, L. J. (2005). Think-aloud protocols and the selection task: Evidence for relevance effects and rationalisation processes. *Thinking and Reasoning, 11*, 35–66.

Luce, R. D., & Raiffa, H. (1957). *Games and decisions.* New York: Wiley.

Lumley, M. A., & Roby, K. J. (1995). Alexithymia and pathological gambling. *Psychotherapy and Psychosomatics, 63*, 201–206.

Lynch, A. (1996). *Thought contagion.* New York: Basic Books.

Lyon, D., & Slovic, P. (1976). Dominance of accuracy information and neglect of base rates in probability estimation. *Acta Psychologica, 40*, 287–298.

MacDonald, A. W., Cohen, J. D., Stenger, V. A., & Carter, C. S. (2000). Dissociating the role of the dorsolateral prefrontal and anterior cingulate cortex in cognitive control. *Science, 288*, 1835–1838.

Mackintosh, N. J., & Bennett, E. S. (2003). The fractionation of working memory maps onto different components of intelligence. *Intelligence, 31*, 519–531.

Macpherson, R., & Stanovich, K. E. (2007). Cognitive ability, thinking dispositions, and instructional set as predictors of critical thinking. *Learning and Individual Differences, 17*, 115–127.

Maher, P. (1993). *Betting on theories.* Cambridge: Cambridge University Press.

Malkiel, B. G. (2008). *A random walk down Wall Street.* New York: Norton.

Mandell, L. (2009). *The financial literacy of young American adults.* Washington, DC: JumpStart Coalition for Personal Financial Literacy. Items at: http://www.jumpstart.org/upload/2009_FinLit-Mandell.pdf

Manktelow, K. I. (2004). Reasoning and rationality: The pure and the practical. In K. I. Manktelow & M. C. Chung (Eds.), *Psychology of reasoning: Theoretical and historical perspectives* (pp. 157–177). Hove, England: Psychology Press.

Margolis, H. (1987). *Patterns, thinking, and cognition.* Chicago: University of Chicago Press.

Margolis, H. (1996). *Dealing with risk.* Chicago: University of Chicago Press.

Markovits, H., & Nantel, G. (1989). The belief-bias effect in the production and evaluation of logical conclusions. *Memory & Cognition, 17*, 11–17.

Matthews, G., Zeidner, M., & Roberts, R. D. (2002). *Emotional intelligence: Science & myth.* Cambridge, MA: MIT Press.

Maule, J., & Villejoubert, G. (2007). What lies beneath: Reframing framing effects. *Thinking and Reasoning, 13*, 25–44.

McArdle, J. J., Ferrer-Caja, E., Hamagami, F., & Woodcock, R. W. (2002). Comparative longitudinal structural analyses of the growth and decline of multiple intellectual abilities over the life span. *Developmental Psychology, 38*, 115–142.

McCarthy, R. A., & Warrington, E. K. (1990). *Cognitive neuropsychology: A clinical introduction.* San Diego: Academic Press.

McClure, S. M., Laibson, D. I., Loewenstein, G., & Cohen, J. D. (2004). Separate neural systems value immediate and delayed monetary rewards. *Science, 306*, 503–507.

McElroy, T., & Seta, J. J. (2003). Framing effects: An analytic-holistic perspective. *Journal of Experimental Social Psychology, 39*, 610–617.

McFadden, D. (1999). Rationality for economists? *Journal of Risk and Uncertainty, 19*, 73–105.

McGrew, K. S. (1997). Analysis of major intelligence batteries according to a proposed comprehensive Gf-Gc framework. In D. Flanagan, J. Genshaft, & P. Harrison (Eds.), *Contemporary intellectual assessment: Theories, tests, and issues* (pp. 151–180). New York: Guilford Press.

McGrew, K. S., & Woodcock, R. W. (2001). *Technical Manual: Woodcock-Johnson III.* Itasca, IL: Riverside Publishing.

McHugh, P. (2008). *The memory wars: Psychiatry's clash over meaning, memory, and mind.* Washington, DC: The Dana Foundation.

McKay, R. T., & Dennett, D. C. (2010). The evolution of misbelief. *Behavioral and Brain Sciences 32*, 493–561.

McNeel, S. P. (1973). Training cooperation in the prisoner's dilemma. *Journal of Experimental Social Psychology, 9*, 335–348.

Mealey, L. (1995). The sociobiology of sociopathy: An integrated evolutionary model. *Behavioral and Brain Sciences, 18*, 523–599.

Mellers, B., Hertwig, R., & Kahneman, D. (2001). Do frequency representations eliminate conjunction effects? An exercise in adversarial collaboration. *Psychological Science, 12*, 269–275.

Meserve, R. J., West, R. F., & Stanovich, K. E. (2008, May). *You're biased but I'm not: Cognitive ability and the bias blind spot.* Paper presented at the annual meeting of the Association for Psychological Science, Chicago.

Mesoudi, A., Whiten, A., & Laland, K. N. (2006). Towards a unified science of cultural evolution. *Behavioral and Brain Sciences, 29*, 329–383.

Messick, D. M., & Sentis, K. P. (1979). Fairness and preference. *Journal of Experimental Social Psychology, 15*, 418–434.

Metcalfe, J., & Mischel, W. (1999). A hot/cool-system analysis of delay of gratification: Dynamics of will power. *Psychological Review, 106*, 3–19.

Milkman, K. L., Chugh, D., & Bazerman, M. H. (2009). How can decision making be improved? *Perspectives on Psychological Science, 4*, 379–383.

Milkman, K. L., Rogers, T., & Bazerman, M. H. (2008). Harnessing our inner angels and demons. *Perspectives on Psychological Science, 3*, 324–338.

Miller, R. L., Wozniak, W. J., Rust, M. R., Miller, B. R., & Slezak, J. (1996). Counterattitudinal advocacy as a means of enhancing instructional effectiveness: How to teach students what they do not want to know. *Teaching of Psychology, 23*, 215–219.

Miller, W. R., & Rollnick, S. (2002). *Motivational interviewing: Preparing people for change* (2nd ed.). New York: The Guilford Press.

Miller, W. R., & Rose, G. S. (2009). Toward a theory of motivational interviewing. *American Psychologist, 64*, 527–537.

Millgram, E. (Ed.). (2001). *Varieties of practical reasoning*. Cambridge, MA: The MIT Press.

Minsky, M. (1985). *The society of mind*. New York: Simon & Schuster.

Mischel, W., & Ebbesen, E. B. (1970). Attention in delay of gratification. *Journal of Personality and Social Psychology, 16*, 329–337.

Mischel, W., Shoda, Y., & Rodriguez, M. L. (1989 May, 26). Delay of gratification in children. *Science, 244*, 933–938.

Mitchell, G. (2005). Libertarian paternalism is an oxymoron. *Northwestern University Law Review, 99*, 1245–1278.

Mitchell, J. P., Heatherton, T. F., Kelley, W. M., Wyland, C. L., Wegner, D. M., & Macrae, C. N. (2007). Separating sustained from transient aspects of cognitive control during thought suppression. *Psychological Science, 18*, 292–297.

Mithen, S. (1996). *The prehistory of mind: The cognitive origins of art and science*. London: Thames and Hudson.

Mithen, S. (2000). Palaeoanthropological perspectives on the theory of mind. In S. Baron-Cohen, H. Tager-Flusber(Miyake et al., 2001)g, & D. J. Cohen (Eds.), *Understanding other minds: Perspectives from developmental cognitive neuroscience (2nd Ed.)* (pp. 488–502). Oxford: Oxford University Press.

Mithen, S. (2002). Human evolution and the cognitive basis of science. In P. Carruthers, S. Stich, & M. Siegel (Eds.), *The cognitive basis of science* (pp. 23–40). Cambridge: Cambridge University Press.

Miyake, A., Friedman, N., Emerson, M. J., & Witzki, A. H. (2000). The utility and diversity of executive functions and their contributions to complex "frontal lobe" tasks: A latent variable analysis. *Cognitive Psychology, 41*, 49–100.

Miyake, A., Friedman, N. P., Rettinger, D. A., Shah, P., & Hegarty, M. (2001). How are visuospatial working memory, executive functioning, and spatial abilities related? A latent-variable analysis. *Journal of Experimental Psychology: General, 130*, 621–640.

Moore, D. A. (1999). Order effects in preference judgments: Evidence for context dependence in the generation of preferences. *Organizational Behavior and Human Decision Processes, 78*, 146–165.

Moutier, S., Angeard, N., & Houdé, O. (2002). Deductive reasoning and matching-bias inhibition training: Evidence from a debiasing paradigm. *Thinking and Reasoning, 8*, 205–224.

Moutier, S., & Houdé, O. (2003). Judgement under uncertainty and conjunction fallacy inhibition training. *Thinking and Reasoning, 9*, 185–201.

Mumma, G. T., & Wilson, S. B. (1995). Procedural debiasing of primacy/anchoring effects in clinical-like judgments. *Journal of Clinical Psychology, 51*, 841–853.

Murphy, D., & Stich, S. (2000). Darwin in the madhouse: Evolutionary psychology and the classification of mental disorders. In P. Carruthers & A. Chamberlain (Eds.), *Evolution and the human mind: Modularity, language and meta-cognition* (pp. 62–92). Cambridge: Cambridge University Press.

Mussweiler, T., Strack, F., & Pfeiffer, T. (2000). Overcoming the inevitable anchoring effect: Considering the opposite compensates for selective accessibility. *Personality and Social Psychology Bulletin, 26*, 1142–1150.

Myers, D. G. (2002). *Intuition: Its powers and perils.* New Haven, CT: Yale University Press.

Mynatt, C. R., Doherty, M. E., & Dragan, W. (1993). Information relevance, working memory, and the consideration of alternatives. *Quarterly Journal of Experimental Psychology, 46A*, 759–778.

Myrseth, K. O. R., & Fishbach, A. (2009). Self-control: A function of knowing when and how to exercise restraint. *Current Directions In Psychological Science, 18*, 247–252.

Nakamura, M., Nestor, P. G., Levitt, J. J., Cohen, A. S., Kawashima, T., Shenton, M. E., & McCarley, R. W. (2008). Orbitofrontal volume deficit in schizophrenia and thought disorder. *Brain, 131*, 180–195.

Navon, D. (1989). The importance of being visible: On the role of attention in a mind viewed as an anarchic intelligence system. *European Journal of Cognitive Psychology, 1*, 191–238.

NCEE (National Council for Economic Education) (2005), *What American teens & adults know about economics.* Accessed July 28, 2009 at http://www.ncee.net/cel/ WhatAmericansKnowAboutEconomics_042605-3.pdf

Neisser, U. (Ed.). (1998). *The rising curve: Long-term changes in IQ and related measures.* Washington, DC: American Psychological Association.

Neisser, U., Boodoo, G., Bouchard, T., Boykin, A. W., Brody, N., Ceci, S. J., Halpern, D., Loehlin, J., Perloff, R., Sternberg, R., & Urbina, S. (1996). Intelligence: Knowns and unknowns. *American Psychologist, 51*, 77–101.

Neubauer, A., & Fink, A. (2005). Basic information processing and the psychophysiology of intelligence. In R. J. Sternberg & J. E. Pretz (Eds.), *Cognition and intelligence* (pp. 68–87). New York: Cambridge University Press.

Neurath, O. (1932/33). Protokollsatze. *Erkenntis, 3*, 204–214.

Newell, B. R. (2005). Re-visions of rationality? *Trends in Cognitive Sciences, 9*, 11–15.

Newstead, S. E., & Evans, J. St. B. T. (Eds.). (1995). *Perspectives on thinking and reasoning.* Hove, England: Erlbaum.

Newstead, S. E., Handley, S. J., Harley, C., Wright, H., & Farrelly, D. (2004). Individual differences in deductive reasoning. *Quarterly Journal of Experimental Psychology, 57A*, 33–60.

Nichols, S., & Stich, S. P. (2003). *Mindreading: An integrated account of pretence, self-awareness, and understanding other minds.* Oxford: Oxford University Press.

Nickerson, R. S. (1998). Confirmation bias: A ubiquitous phenomenon in many guises. *Review of General Psychology, 2*, 175–220.

Nickerson, R. S. (2004). *Cognition and chance: The psychology of probabilistic reasoning.* Mahwah, NJ: Erlbaum.

Nickerson, R. S. (2008). *Aspects of rationality.* New York: Psychology Press.

Nigg, J. T. (2000). On inhibition/disinhibition in developmental psychopathology: Views from cognitive and personality psychology and a working inhibition taxonomy. *Psychological Bulletin, 126*, 220–246.

Nigg, J. T. (2001). Is ADHD a disinhibitory disorder? *Psychological Bulletin, 127*, 571–598.

Nijhuis, M. (2008, June/July). The doubt makers. *Miller-McCune, 1*, 26–35.

Nisbett, R. E. (1993). *Rules for reasoning.* Hillsdale, NJ: Lawrence Erlbaum Associates.

Nisbett, R. E., Krantz, D. H., Jepson, C., & Kunda, Z. (1983). The use of statistical heuristics in everyday inductive reasoning. *Psychological Review, 90*, 339–363.

Nisbett, R. E., & Ross, L. (1980). *Human inference: Strategies and shortcomings of social judgment.* Englewood Cliffs, NJ: Prentice-Hall.

Nisbett, R. E., & Wilson, T. D. (1977). Telling more than we can know: Verbal reports on mental processes. *Psychological Review, 84*, 231–259.

Noftle, E. E., & Robins, R. W. (2007). Personality predictors of academic outcomes: Big five correlates of GPA and SAT scores. *Journal of Personality and Social Psychology, 93*, 116–130.

Norman, D. A., & Shallice, T. (1986). Attention to action: Willed and automatic control of behavior. In R. J. Davidson, G. E. Schwartz, & D. Shapiro (Eds.), *Consciousness and self-regulation* (pp. 1–18). New York: Plenum.

Norris, S. P., & Ennis, R. H. (1989). *Evaluating critical thinking.* Pacific Grove, CA: Midwest Publications.

Northcraft, G. B., & Neale, M. A. (1987). Experts, amateurs, and real estate: An anchoring-and-adjustment perspective on property pricing decisions. *Organizational Behavior And Human Decision Processes, 39*, 84–97.

Nozick, R. (1993). *The nature of rationality.* Princeton, NJ: Princeton University Press.

Nussbaum, E. M., & Kardash, C. A. M. (2005). The effects of goal instructions and text on the generation of counterarguments during writing. *Journal of Educational Psychology, 97*, 157–169.

Oaksford, M., & Chater, N. (1994). A rational analysis of the selection task as optimal data selection. *Psychological Review, 101*, 608–631.

Oaksford, M., & Chater, N. (1998). An introduction to rational models of cognition. In M. Oaksford & N. Chater (Eds.), *Rational models of cognition* (pp. 1–18). New York: Oxford University Press.

Oaksford, M., & Chater, N. (2007). *Bayesian rationality: The probabilistic approach to human reasoning.* Oxford: Oxford University Press.

Oatley, K. (1992). *Best laid schemes: The psychology of emotions.* Cambridge: Cambridge University Press.

Oatley, K. (1999). Why fiction may be twice as true as fact: Fiction as cognitive and emotional simulation. *Review of General Psychology, 3*, 101–117.

O'Brien, D., & Overton, W. F. (1980). Conditional reasoning following contradictory evidence: A developmental analysis. *Journal of Experimental Child Psychology, 30*, 44–61.

Odean, T. (1998). Volume, volatility, price, and profit when all traders are above average. *Journal of Finance, 53*, 1887–1934.

O'Donoghue, T., & Rabin, M. (2000). The economics of immediate gratification. *Journal of Behavioral Decision Making, 13*, 233–250.

Offit, P. A. (2008). *Autism's false prophets.* New York: Columbia University Press.

Ohman, A., & Mineka, S. (2001). Fears, phobias, and preparedness: Toward an evolved module of fear and fear learning. *Psychological Review, 108*, 483–522.

Oppenheimer, D. M. (2003). Not so fast! (and not so frugal!): Rethinking the recognition heuristic. *Cognition, 90*, B1–B9.

Oreg, S., & Bayazit, M. (2009). Prone to bias: Development of a bias taxonomy from an individual differences perspective. *Review of General Psychology, 13*, 175–193.

Orwell, G. (1968). *As I Please, 1943-1945: The Collected Essays, Journalism and Letters of George Orwell* (Vol. 3), S. Orwell & I. Angus (Eds.). New York: Harcourt Brace Jovanovich.

Osman, M. (2007). Can tutoring improve performance on a reasoning task under deadline conditions? *Memory & Cognition, 35*, 342–351.

Osman, M., & Laming, D. (2001). Misinterpretation of conditional statements in Wason's selection task. *Psychological Research, 65*, 128–144.

Oswald, M. E., & Grosjean, S. (2004). Confirmation bias. In R. Pohl (Eds.), *Cognitive illusions: A handbook on fallacies and biases in thinking, judgment and memory* (pp. 81–96). Hove, England: Psychology Press.

Over, D. E. (2000). Ecological rationality and its heuristics. *Thinking and Reasoning, 6*, 182–192.

Over, D. E. (2002). The rationality of evolutionary psychology. In J. L. Bermudez & A. Millar (Eds.), *Reason and nature: Essays in the theory of rationality* (pp. 187–207). Oxford: Oxford University Press.

Over, D. E. (2004). Rationality and the normative/descriptive distinction. In D. J. Koehler & N. Harvey (Eds.), *Blackwell handbook of judgment and decision making* (pp. 3–18). Malden, MA: Blackwell Publishing.

Overton, W. F., Byrnes, J. P., & O'Brien, D. P. (1985). Developmental and individual differences in conditional reasoning: The role of contradiction training and cognitive style. *Developmental Psychology, 21*, 692–701.

Pacini, R., & Epstein, S. (1999). The relation of rational and experiential information processing styles to personality, basic beliefs, and the ratio-bias phenomenon. *Journal of Personality and Social Psychology, 76*, 972–987.

Parker, A. M., & Fischhoff, B. (2005). Decision-making competence: External validation through an individual differences approach. *Journal of Behavioral Decision Making, 18*, 1–27.

Parsell, D. (2004 November, 13). Assault on autism. *Science News, 166*, 311–312.

Pashler, H., McDaniel, M., Rohrer, D., & Bjork, R. (2009). Learning styles: Concepts and evidence. *Psychological Science in the Public Interest, 9*, 105–119.

Paulos, J. A. (2003). *A mathematician plays the stock market.* New York: Basic Books.

Penke, L., Denissen, J., & Miller, G. F. (2007). The evolutionary genetics of personality. *European Journal of Personality, 21,* 549–587.

Penn, D. C., Holyoak, K. J., & Povinelli, D. J. (2008). Darwin's mistake: explaining the discontinuity between human and nonhuman minds. *Behavioral and Brain Sciences, 31,* 109–178.

Penn, D. C., Holyoak, K. J., & Povinelli, D. J. (2009). Universal grammar and mental continuity: Two modern myths. *Behavioral and Brain Sciences, 32,* 462–464.

Pennington, B. F., & Ozonoff, S. (1996). Executive functions and developmental psychopathology. *Journal of Child Psychology and Psychiatry, 37,* 51–87.

Perkins, D. N. (1985). Postprimary education has little impact on informal reasoning. *Journal of Educational Psychology, 77,* 562–571.

Perkins, D. N. (1995). *Outsmarting IQ: The emerging science of learnable intelligence.* New York: Free Press.

Perkins, D. N. (2002). The engine of folly. In R. J. Sternberg (Eds.), *Why smart people can be so stupid* (pp. 64–85). New Haven, CT: Yale University Press.

Perkins, D. N., Farady, M., & Bushey, B. (1991). Everyday reasoning and the roots of intelligence. In J. Voss, D. Perkins, & J. Segal (Eds.), *Informal reasoning and education* (pp. 83–105). Hillsdale, NJ: Erlbaum.

Perkins, D. N., & Ritchhart, R. (2004). When is good thinking? In D. Y. Dai & R. J. Sternberg (Eds.), *Motivation, emotion, and cognition: Integrative perspectives on intellectual functioning and development* (pp. 351–384). Mahwah, NJ: Lawrence Erlbaum Associates.

Perner, J. (1991). *Understanding the representational mind.* Cambridge, MA: MIT Press.

Perner, J. (1998). The meta-intentional nature of executive functions and theory of mind. In P. Carruthers & J. Boucher (Eds.), *Language and thought: Interdisciplinary themes* (pp. 270–283). Cambridge: Cambridge University Press.

Peters, E., Vastfjall, D., Slovic, P., Mertz, C. K., Mazzocco, K., & Dickert, S. (2006). Numeracy and decision making. *Psychological Science, 17,* 407–413.

Petry, N. M., Bickel, W. K., & Arnett, M. (1998). Shortened time horizons and insensitivity to future consequences in heroin addicts. *Addiction, 93,* 729–738.

Pinker, S. (1997). *How the mind works.* New York: Norton.

Pinker, S. (2009 January, 11). My genome, my self. *New York Times Magazine,* 24-31, 46–50.

Plato (1945). *The republic.* Translated by Francis MacDonald Cornford. New York: Oxford University Press.

Platt, R. D., & Griggs, R. A. (1993). Facilitation in the abstract selection task: The effects of attentional and instructional factors. *Quarterly Journal of Experimental Psychology Section A, 46,* 591–613.

Pohl, R. (2004). Hindsight bias. In R. Pohl (Ed.), *Cognitive illusions: A handbook on fallacies and biases in thinking, judgment and memory* (pp. 363–378). Hove, England: Psychology Press.

Politzer, G., & Macchi, L. (2000). Reasoning and pragmatics. *Mind & Society, 1,* 73–93.

Politzer, G., & Noveck, I. A. (1991). Are conjunction rule violations the result of conversational rule violations? *Journal of Psycholinguistic Research, 20*, 83–103.

Pollock, J. L. (1991). OSCAR: A general theory of rationality. In J. Cummins & J. L. Pollock (Eds.), *Philosophy and AI: Essays at the interface* (pp. 189–213). Cambridge, MA: MIT Press.

Pollock, J. L. (1995). *Cognitive carpentry.* Cambridge, MA: The MIT Press.

Pos, A. E., Greenberg, L. S., & Warwar, S. H. (2009). Testing a model of change in the experiential treatment of depression. *Journal of Consulting and Clinical Psychology, 77*, 1055–1066.

Posner, M. I., & Snyder, C. R. R. (1975). Attention and cognitive control. In R. L. Solso (Ed.), *Information processing and cognition: The Loyola Symposium* (pp. 55–85). New York: Wiley.

Postman, N. (1988). *Conscientious objections.* New York: Vintage Books.

Povinelli, D. J., & Bering, J. M. (2002). The mentality of apes revisited. *Current Directions in Psychological Science, 11*, 115–119.

Povinelli, D. J., & Giambrone, S. (2001). Reasoning about beliefs: A human specialization? *Child Development, 72*, 691–695.

Prado, J., & Noveck, I. A. (2007). Overcoming perceptual features in logical reasoning: A parametric functional magnetic resonance imaging study. *Journal of Cognitive Neuroscience, 19*, 642–657.

Pratt, J. W., Raiffa, H., & Schlaifer, R. (1995). *Introduction to statistical decision theory.* Cambridge, MA: MIT Press.

Prentice, R. A. (2003). Chicago man, K-T man, and the future of behavioral law and economics. *Vanderbilt Law Review, 56*, 1663–1777.

Pronin, E. (2006). Perception and misperception of bias in human judgment. *Trends in Cognitive Sciences, 11*, 37–43.

Pronin, E., Berger, J., & Molouki, S. (2007). Alone in a crowd of sheep: Asymmetric perceptions of conformity and their roots in an introspection illusion. *Journal of Personality and Social Psychology, 92*, 585–595.

Pronin, E., & Kugler, M. B. (2007). Valuing thoughts, ignoring behavior: The introspection illusion as a source of the bias blind spot. *Journal of Experimental Social Psychology, 43*, 565–578.

Pronin, E., Lin, D. Y., & Ross, L. (2002). The bias blind spot: Perceptions of bias in self versus others. *Journal of Personality and Social Psychology Bulletin, 28*, 369–381.

Pronk, T. M., Karremans, J. C., Overbeek, G., Vermulst, A. A., & Wigboldus, D. (2010). What it takes to forgive: When and why executive functioning facilitates forgiveness. *Journal of Personality and Social Psychology, 98*, 119–131.

Quine, W. (1960). *Word and object.* Cambridge, MA: MIT Press.

Rachlin, H. (1995). Self-control: Beyond commitment. *Behavioral and Brain Sciences, 18*, 109–159.

Rachlin, H. (2000). *The science of self-control.* Cambridge, MA: Harvard University Press.

Reber, A. S. (1992). An evolutionary context for the cognitive unconscious. *Philosophical Psychology, 5*, 33–51.

Reber, A. S. (1993). *Implicit learning and tacit knowledge*. New York: Oxford University Press.

Reber, A. S., Walkenfeld, F. F., & Hernstadt, R. (1991). Implicit and Explicit Learning: Individual Differences and IQ. *Journal of Experimental Psychology: Learning, Memory, and Cognition, 17*, 888–896.

Redelmeier, D. A., & Shafir, E. (1995). Medical decision making in situations that offer multiple alternatives. *JAMA, 273*, 302–305.

Reitan, R. M. (1955). The relation of the Trail Making Test to organic brain damage. *Journal of Consulting Psychology, 19*, 393–394.

Reitan, R. M. (1958). Validity of the Trail Making Test as an indicator of organic brain damage. *Perceptual and Motor Skills, 8*, 271–276.

Rescher, N. (1988). *Rationality: A philosophical inquiry into the nature and rationale of reason*. Oxford: Oxford University Press.

Reyna, V. F., Adam, M. B., Poirier, K., LeCroy, C., & Brainerd, C. J. (2005). Risky decision making in childhood and adoelescence: A fuzzy-trace theory approach. In J. E. Jacobs & P. A. Klaczynski (Eds.), *The development of judgment and decision making in children and adolescents* (pp. 77–106). Mahwah, NJ: Lawrence Erlbaum Associates.

Reyna, V. F., & Ellis, S. (1994). Fuzzy-trace theory and framing effects in children's risky decision making. *Psychological Science, 5*, 275–279.

Reyna, V. F., & Lloyd, F. J. (2006). Physician decision making and cardiac risk: Effects of knowledge, risk perception, risk tolerance, and fuzzy processing. *Journal of Experimental Psychology: Applied, 12*, 179–195.

Reyna, V. F., Lloyd, F. J., & Brainerd, C. J. (2003). Memory, development, and rationality: An integrative theory of judgment and decision making. In S. L. Schneider & J. Shanteau (Eds.), *Emerging perspectives on judgment and decision research* (pp. 201–245). New York: Cambridge University Press.

Reyna, V. F., Nelson, W. L., Han, P. K., & Dieckmann, N. F. (2009). How numeracy influences risk comprehension and medical decision making. *Psychological Bulletin, 135*, 943–973.

Rhodes, M. G. (2004). Age-related differences in performance on the Wisconsin Card Sorting Test: A meta-analytic review. *Psychology and Aging, 19*, 482–494.

Ricco, R. B. (2007). Individual differences in the analysis of informal reasoning fallacies. *Contemporary Educational Psychology, 32*, 459–484.

Richard, R., van der Plight, J., & de Vries, N. (1996). Anticipated regret and time perspective: Changing sexual risk-taking behavior. *Journal of Behavioral Decision Making, 9*, 185–199.

Richerson, P. J., & Boyd, R. (2005). *Not by genes alone: How culture transformed human evolution*. Chicago, IL: University of Chicago Press.

Rips, L. J. (1994). *The logic of proof*. Cambridge, MA: MIT Press.

Ritchhart, R., & Perkins, D. N. (2005). Learning to think: The challenges of teaching thinking. In K. J. Holyoak & R. G. Morrison (Eds.), *The Cambridge handbook of thinking and reasoning* (pp. 775–802). New York: Cambridge University Press.

Roberts, M. J., & Newton, E. J. (2001). Inspection times, the change task, and the rapid-response selection task. *Quarterly Journal of Experimental Psychology, 54A,* 1031–1048.

Rodriguez, M. L., Mischel, W., & Shoda, Y. (1989). Cognitive person variables in delay of gratification of older children at risk. *Journal of Personality and Social Psychology, 57,* 358–367.

Roese, N. (1997). Counterfactual thinking. *Psychological Bulletin, 121,* 131–148.

Rogers, P. (1998). The cognitive psychology of lottery gambling: A theoretical review. *Journal of Gambling Studies, 14,* 111–134.

Rokeach, M. (1960). *The open and closed mind.* New York: Basic Books.

Roney, C. J. R., & Trick, L. M. (2009). Sympathetic magic and perceptions of randomness: The hot hand versus the gambler's fallacy. *Thinking & Reasoning, 15,* 197–210.

Rose, J. P., & Windschitl, P. D. (2008). How egocentrism and optimism change in response to feedback in repeated competitions. *Organizational Behavior and Human Decision Processes, 105,* 201–220.

Royzman, E. B., Cassidy, K. W., & Baron, J. (2003). "I know, you know": Epistemic egocentrism in children and adults. *Review of General Psychology, 7,* 38–65.

Sá, W., Kelley, C., Ho, C., & Stanovich, K. E. (2005). Thinking about personal theories: Individual differences in the coordination of theory and evidence. *Personality and Individual Differences, 38,* 1149–1161.

Sá, W., West, R. F., & Stanovich, K. E. (1999). The domain specificity and generality of belief bias: Searching for a generalizable critical thinking skill. *Journal of Educational Psychology, 91,* 497–510.

Sackett, P. R., Zedeck, S., & Fogli, L. (1988). Relations between measures of typical and maximum job performance. *Journal of Applied Psychology, 73,* 482–486.

Saffran, J. R., Aslin, R. N., & Newport, E. L. (1996). Statistical learning by 8-month-old infants. *Science, 274,* 1926–1928.

Salthouse, T. A., Atkinson, T. M., & Berish, D. E. (2003). Executive functioning as a potential mediator of age-related cognitive decline in normal adults. *Journal of Experimental Psychology: General, 132,* 566–594.

Salthouse, T. A., & Davis, H. P. (2006). Organization of cognitive abilities and neuropsychological variables across the lifespan. *Developmental Review, 26,* 31–54.

Salthouse, T. A., & Pink, J. E. (2008). Why is working memory related to fluid intelligence? *Psychonomic Bulletin & Review, 15,* 364–371.

Samuels, R. (2005). The complexity of cognition: Tractability arguments for massive modularity. In P. Carruthers, S. Laurence, & S. Stich (Eds.), *The innate mind* (pp. 107–121). Oxford: Oxford University Press.

Samuels, R. (2009). The magical number two, plus or minus: Dual-process theory as a theory of cognitive kinds. In J. St. B. T. Evans & K. Frankish (Eds.), *In two minds: Dual processes and beyond* (pp. 129–146). Oxford: Oxford University Press.

Samuels, R., & Stich, S. P. (2004). Rationality and psychology. In A. R. Mele & P. Rawling (Eds.), *The Oxford handbook of rationality* (pp. 279–300). Oxford: Oxford University Press.

Samuels, R., Stich, S. P., & Bishop, M. (2002). Ending the rationality wars: How to make disputes about human rationality disappear. In R. Elio (Ed.), *Common sense, reasoning and rationality* (pp. 236–268). New York: Oxford University Press.

Samuels, R., Stich, S. P., & Tremoulet, P. D. (1999). Rethinking rationality: From bleak implications to Darwinian modules. In E. Lepore & Z. Pylyshyn (Eds.), *What is cognitive science?* (pp. 74–120). Oxford: Blackwell.

Samuelson, W., & Zeckhauser, R. J. (1988). Status quo bias in decision making. *Journal of Risk and Uncertainty, 1,* 7–59.

Sanfey, A. G. (2007). Decision neuroscience: New directions in studies of judgment and decision making. *Current Perceptions in Psychological Science, 16,* 151–155.

Sanfey, A. G., Loewenstein, G., McClure, S. M., & Cohen, J. D. (2006). Neuroeconomics: Cross-currents in research on decision-making. *Trends in Cognitive Sciences, 10,* 108–116.

Satpute, A. B., & Lieberman, M. D. (2006). Integrating automatic and controlled processes into neurocognitive models of social cognition. *Brain Research, 1079,* 86–97.

Savage, L. J. (1954). *The foundations of statistics.* New York: Wiley.

Schacter, D. L., & Addis, D. R. (2007). The cognitive neuroscience of constructive memory: Remembering the past and imagining the future. *Philosophical Transactions of the Royal Society (London) B, 362,* 773–786.

Schaller, M., Asp, C. H., Roseil, M. C., & Heim, S. J. (1996). Training in statistical reasoning inhibits the formation of erroneous group stereotypes. *Personality and Social Psychology Bulletin, 22,* 829–844.

Schelling, T. C. (1984). *Choice and consequence: Perspectives of an errant economist.* Cambridge, MA: Harvard University Press.

Schkade, D. A., & Kahneman, D. (1998). Does living in California make people happy? *Psychological Science, 9,* 340–346.

Schmiedek, F., Oberauer, K., Wilhelm, O., Sub, H. M., & Wittmann, W. W. (2007). Individual differences in components of reaction time distributions and their relations to working memory and intelligence. *Journal of Experimental Psychology: General, 136,* 414–429.

Schneider, S. L., Burke, M. D., Solomonson, A. L., & Laurion, S. K. (2005). Incidental framing effects and associative processes: A study of attribute frames in broadcast news stories. *Journal of Behavioral Decision Making, 18,* 261–280.

Schneider, W., & Chein, J. (2003). Controlled and automatic processing: Behavior, theory, and biological processing. *Cognitive Science, 27,* 525–559.

Schommer, M. (1990). Effects of beliefs about the nature of knowledge on comprehension. *Journal of Educational Psychology, 82,* 498–504.

Schommer, M. (1998). The influence of age and education on epistemological beliefs. *British Journal of Educational Psychology, 68,* 551–562.

Schooler, C. (1998). Environmental complexity and the Flynn effect. In U. Neisser (Ed.), *The rising curve: Long-term changes in IQ and related measures* (pp. 67–79). Washington, DC: American Psychological Association.

Schooler, J. W., Ariely, D., & Loewenstein, G. (2003). The pursuit and assessment of happiness can be self-defeating. In I. Brocas & J. D. Carrillo (Eds.), *The psychology of economic decisions (Vol. 1): Rationality and well-being* (pp. 41–70). Oxford: Oxford University Press.

Schwartz, L. M., Woloshin, S., Black, W. C., & Welch, H. G. (1997). The role of numeracy in understanding the benefit of screening mammography. *Annals of Internal Medicine, 127,* 966–972.

Shafir, E. (1994). Uncertainty and the difficulty of thinking through disjunctions. *Cognition, 50,* 403–430.

Shafir, E. (1998). Philosophical intuitions and cognitive mechanisms. In M. R. DePaul & W. Ramsey (Eds.), *Rethinking intuition: The psychology of intuition and its role in philosophical inquiry* (pp. 59–83). Lanham, MD: Rowman & Littlefield Publishers, Inc.

Shafir, E., & LeBoeuf, R. A. (2002). Rationality. *Annual Review of Psychology, 53,* 491–517.

Shafir, E., & Tversky, A. (1992). Thinking through uncertainty: Nonconsequential reasoning and choice. *Cognitive Psychology, 24,* 449–474.

Shah, A. K., & Oppenheimer, D. M. (2008). Heuristics made easy: An effort-reduction framework. *Psychological Bulletin, 134,* 207–222.

Shallice, T. (1988). *From neuropsychology to mental structure.* Cambridge: Cambridge University Press.

Shamosh, N. A., DeYoung, C. G., Green, A. E., Reis, D. L., Johnson, M. R., Conway, A., Engle, R., Braver, T., & Gray, J. (2008). Individual differences in delay discounting relation to intelligence, working memory, and anterior prefrontal cortex. *Psychological Science, 19,* 904–911.

Shamosh, N. A., & Gray, J. R. (2008). Delay discounting and intelligence: A meta-analysis. *Intelligence, 36,* 289–305.

Shanteau, J., Grier, M., Johnson, J., & Berner, E. (1991). Teaching decision-making skills to student nurses. In J. Baron & R. V. Brown (Eds.), *Teaching decision making to adolescents* (pp. 185–206). Hillsdale, NJ: Lawrence Erlbaum Associates, Inc.

Shermer, M. (1997). *Why people believe weird things.* New York: WH Freeman.

Shiffrin, R. M., & Schneider, W. (1977). Controlled and automatic human information processing: II. Perceptual learning, automatic attending, and a general theory. *Psychological Review, 84,* 127–190.

Shiloh, S., Salton, E., & Sharabi, D. (2002). Individual differences in rational and intuitive thinking styles as predictors of heuristic responses and framing effects. *Personality and Individual Differences, 32,* 415–429.

Shiv, B., Loewenstein, G., Bechara, A., Damasio, H., & Damasio, A. R. (2005). Investment behavior and the negative side of emotion. *Psychological Science, 16,* 435–439.

Simon, A. F., Fagley, N. S., & Halleran, J. G. (2004). Decision framing: Moderating effects of individual differences and cognitive processing. *Journal of Behavioral Decision Making, 17,* 77–93.

Simon, H. A. (1955). A behavioral model of rational choice. *The Quarterly Journal of Economics, 69,* 99–118.

Simon, H. A. (1956). Rational choice and the structure of the environment. *Psychological Review, 63,* 129–138.

Simoneau, M., & Markovits, H. (2003). Reasoning with premises that are not empirically true: Evidence for the role of inhibition and retrieval. *Developmental Psychology, 39,* 964–975.

Sinatra, G. M., & Pintrich, P. R. (Eds.). (2003). *Intentional conceptual change.* Mahwah, NJ: Erlbaum.

Sinz, H., Zamarian, L., Benke, T., Wenning, G. K., & Delazer, M. (2008). Impact of ambiguity and risk on decision making in mild Alzheimer's disease. *Neuropsychologia, 46,* 2043–2055.

Sivak, M., & Flannagan, M. J. (2003). Flying and driving after the September 11 attacks. *American Scientist, 91,* 6–7.

Sloman, A. (1993). The mind as a control system. In C. Hookway & D. Peterson (Eds.), *Philosophy and cognitive science* (pp. 69–110). Cambridge: Cambridge University Press.

Sloman, A., & Chrisley, R. (2003). Virtual machines and consciousness. *Journal of Consciousness Studies, 10,* 133–172.

Sloman, S. A. (1996). The empirical case for two systems of reasoning. *Psychological Bulletin, 119,* 3–22.

Sloman, S. A. (2002). Two systems of reasoning. In T. Gilovich, D. Griffin, & D. Kahneman (Eds.), *Heuristics and biases: The psychology of intuitive judgment* (pp. 379–396). New York: Cambridge University Press.

Sloman, S. A., Over, D., Slovak, L., & Stibel, J. M. (2003). Frequency illusions and other fallacies. *Organizational Behavior and Human Decision Processes, 91,* 296–309.

Slovic, P., Finucane, M. L., Peters, E., & MacGregor, D. G. (2002). The affect heuristic. In T. Gilovich, D. Griffin, & D. Kahneman (Eds.), *Heuristics and biases: The psychology of intuitive judgment* (pp. 397–420). New York: Cambridge University Press.

Slovic, P., & Peters, E. (2006). Risk perception and affect. *Current Directions in Psychological Science, 15,* 322–325.

Slovic, P., & Tversky, A. (1974). Who accepts Savage's axiom? *Behavioral Science, 19,* 368–373.

Slugoski, B. R., Shields, H. A., & Dawson, K. A. (1993). Relation of conditional reasoning to heuristic processing. *Personality and Social Psychology Bulletin, 19,* 158–166.

Smallwood, J., & Schooler, J. W. (2006). The restless mind. *Psychological Bulletin, 132,* 946–958.

Smith, E. E., Patalino, A. L., & Jonides, J. (1998). Alternative strategies of categorization. In S. A. Sloman & L. J. Rips (Eds.), *Similarity and symbols in human thinking* (pp. 81–110). Cambridge, MA: MIT Press.

Smith, E. R., & DeCoster, J. (2000). Dual-process models in social and cognitive psychology: Conceptual integration and links to underlying memory systems. *Personality and Social Psychology Review, 4,* 108–131.

Smith, S. M., & Levin, I. P. (1996). Need for cognition and choice framing effects. *Journal of Behavioral Decision Making, 9*, 283–290.

Song, H., & Schwarz, N. (2009). If it's difficult to pronounce, it must be risky. *Psychological Science, 20*, 135–138.

Sonuga-Barke, E. (2002). Psychological heterogeneity in AD/HD - a dual pathway model of behavior and cognition. *Behavioural Brain Research, 130*, 29–36.

Sonuga-Barke, E. (2003). The dual pathway model of AD/HD: An elaboration of neurodevelopmental characteristics. *Neuroscience and Biobehavioral Reviews, 27*, 593–604.

Spearman, C. (1904). General intelligence, objectively determined and measured. *American Journal of Psychology, 15*, 201–293.

Sperber, D. (1994). The modularity of thought and the epidemiology of representations. In L. A. Hirschfeld & S. A. Gelman (Eds.), *Mapping the mind: Domain specificity in cognition and culture* (pp. 39–67). Cambridge: Cambridge University Press.

Sperber, D. (2000). Metarepresentations in evolutionary perspective. In D. Sperber (Ed.), *Metarepresentations: A Multidisciplinary Perspective* (pp. 117–137). Oxford: Oxford University Press.

Sperber, D., Cara, F., & Girotto, V. (1995). Relevance theory explains the selection task. *Cognition, 57*, 31–95.

Spitz, H. H. (1997). *Nonconscious movements: From mystical messages to facilitated communication.* Mahwah, NJ: Lawrence Erlbaum Associates.

Stanovich, K. E. (1989). Implicit philosophies of mind - the dualism scale and its relation to religiosity and belief in extrasensory perception. *Journal of Psychology, 123*, 5–23.

Stanovich, K. E. (1999). *Who is rational? Studies of individual differences in reasoning.* Mahwah, NJ: Erlbaum.

Stanovich, K. E. (2000). *Progress in understanding reading: Scientific foundations and new frontiers.* New York: Guilford Press.

Stanovich, K. E. (2001). Reductionism in the study of intelligence: Review of "Looking Down on Human Intelligence" by Ian Deary. *Trends in Cognitive Sciences, 5*(2), 91–92.

Stanovich, K. E. (2002). Rationality, intelligence, and levels of analysis in cognitive science: Is dysrationalia possible? In R. J. Sternberg (Ed.), *Why smart people can be so stupid* (pp. 124–158). New Haven, CT: Yale University Press.

Stanovich, K. E. (2003). The fundamental computational biases of human cognition: Heuristics that (sometimes) impair decision making and problem solving. In J. E. Davidson & R. J. Sternberg (Eds.), *The psychology of problem solving* (pp. 291–342). New York: Cambridge University Press.

Stanovich, K. E. (2004). *The robot's rebellion: Finding meaning in the age of Darwin.* Chicago: University of Chicago Press.

Stanovich, K. E. (2005). The future of a mistake: Will discrepancy measurement continue to make the learning disabilities field a pseudoscience? *Learning Disability Quarterly, 28*, 103–106.

Stanovich, K. E. (2008). Higher-order preferences and the Master Rationality Motive. *Thinking & Reasoning, 14*, 111–127.

Stanovich, K. E. (2009a). Distinguishing the reflective, algorithmic, and autonomous minds: Is it time for a tri-process theory? In J. Evans & K. Frankish (Eds.), *In two minds: Dual processes and beyond*. Oxford: Oxford University Press.

Stanovich, K. E. (2009b). *What intelligence tests miss: The psychology of rational thought*. New Haven, CT: Yale University Press.

Stanovich, K. E. (2010a). *Decision making and rationality in the modern world*. New York: Oxford University Press.

Stanovich, K. E. (2010b). *How to think straight about psychology* (Ninth Edition). Boston: Allyn & Bacon.

Stanovich, K. E., Grunewald, M., & West, R. F. (2003). Cost-benefit reasoning in students with multiple secondary school suspensions. *Personality and Individual Differences, 35*, 1061–1072.

Stanovich, K. E., Toplak, M. E., & West, R. F. (2008). The development of rational thought: A taxonomy of heuristics and biases. *Advances in child development and behavior, 36*, 251–285.

Stanovich, K. E., & West, R. F. (1997). Reasoning independently of prior belief and individual differences in actively open-minded thinking. *Journal of Educational Psychology, 89*, 342–357.

Stanovich, K. E., & West, R. F. (1998a). Cognitive ability and variation in selection task performance. *Thinking and Reasoning, 4*, 193–230.

Stanovich, K. E., & West, R. F. (1998b). Individual differences in framing and conjunction effects. *Thinking and Reasoning, 4*, 289–317.

Stanovich, K. E., & West, R. F. (1998c). Individual differences in rational thought. *Journal of Experimental Psychology: General, 127*, 161–188.

Stanovich, K. E., & West, R. F. (1998d). Who uses base rates and P(D/~H)? An analysis of individual differences. *Memory & Cognition, 26*, 161–179.

Stanovich, K. E., & West, R. F. (1999). Discrepancies between normative and descriptive models of decision making and the understanding/acceptance principle. *Cognitive Psychology, 38*, 349–385.

Stanovich, K. E., & West, R. F. (2000). Individual differences in reasoning: Implications for the rationality debate? *Behavioral and Brain Sciences, 23*, 645–726.

Stanovich, K. E., & West, R. F. (2003). Evolutionary versus instrumental goals: How evolutionary psychology misconceives human rationality. In D. E. Over (Ed.), *Evolution and the psychology of thinking: The debate* (pp. 171–230). Hove; New York: Psychology Press.

Stanovich, K. E., & West, R. F. (2007). Natural myside bias is independent of cognitive ability. *Thinking & Reasoning, 13*, 225–247.

Stanovich, K. E., & West, R. F. (2008a). On the failure of intelligence to predict myside bias and one-sided bias. *Thinking & Reasoning, 14*, 129–167.

Stanovich, K. E., & West, R. F. (2008b). On the relative independence of thinking biases and cognitive ability. *Journal of Personality and Social Psychology, 94*, 672–695.

Steen, L. A. (1990). Numeracy. *Daedalus, 119*, 211–231.

Stein, E. (1996). *Without good reason: The rationality debate in philosophy and cognitive science.* Oxford: Oxford University Press.

Steinberg, L., Graham, S., O'Brien, L., Woolard, J., Cauffman, E., & Banich, M. (2009). Age differences in future orientation and delay discounting. *Child Development, 80*, 28–44.

Stenning, K., & van Lambalgen, M. (2004a). A little logic goes a long way: basing experiment on semantic theory in the cognitive science of conditional reasoning. *Cognitive Science, 28*, 481–429.

Stenning, K., & van Lambalgen, M. (2004b). The natural history of hypotheses about the selection task: Towards a philosophy of science for investigating human reasoning. In K. I. Manktelow & M. C. Chung (Eds.), *Psychology of reasoning: Theoretical and historical perspectives* (pp. 127–156). Hove, England: Psychology Press.

Sterelny, K. (2001). *The evolution of agency and other essays.* Cambridge: Cambridge University Press.

Sterelny, K. (2003). *Thought in a hostile world: The evolution of human cognition.* Malden, MA: Blackwell Publishing.

Sternberg, R. J. (1997a). *Successful intelligence: How practical and creative intelligence determine success in life.* New York: Plume.

Sternberg, R. J. (1997b). The concept of intelligence and its role in lifelong learning and success. *American Psychologist, 52*, 1030–1037.

Sternberg, R. J. (1997c). *Thinking styles.* Cambridge: Cambridge University Press.

Sternberg, R. J. (2000). The concept of intelligence. In R. J. Sternberg (Ed.), *Handbook of intelligence* (pp. 3–15). New York: Cambridge University Press.

Sternberg, R. J. (2001). Why schools should teach for wisdom: The balance theory of wisdom in educational settings. *Educational Psychologist, 36*, 227–245.

Sternberg, R. J. (2003). *Wisdom, intelligence, and creativity synthesized.* Cambridge: Cambridge University Press.

Sternberg, R. J. (2004). Theory-based university admissions testing for a new millennium. *Educational Psychologist, 39*, 185–198.

Sternberg, R. J. (Ed.). (2005). *The psychology of hate.* Washington, DC: American Psychological Association.

Sternberg, R. J., & Detterman, D. K. (Eds.). (1986). *What is intelligence?* Norwood, NJ: Ablex.

Sternberg, R. J., & Grigorenko, E. L. (1997). Are cognitive styles still in style? *American Psychologist, 52*, 700–712.

Sternberg, R. J., & Kaufman, J. C. (1998). Human abilities. *Annual Review of Psychology, 49*, 479–502.

Stewart, N. (2009). The cost of anchoring on credit-card minimum repayments. *Psychological Science, 20*, 39–41.

Stich, S. P. (1990). *The fragmentation of reason.* Cambridge: MIT Press.

Stich, S. P., & Nisbett, R. E. (1980). Justification and the psychology of human reasoning. *Philosophy of Science, 47*, 188–202.

Strack, F., & Deutsch, R. (2004). Reflective and impulsive determinants of social behavior. *Personality and Social Psychology Review, 8,* 220–247.

Strathman, A., Gleicher, F., Boninger, D. S., & Scott Edwards, C. (1994). The consideration of future consequences: Weighing immediate and distant outcomes of behavior. *Journal of Personality and Social Psychology, 66,* 742–752.

Stroud, S., & Tappolet, C. (Eds.). (2003). *Weakness of will and practical irrationality.* Oxford: Oxford University Press.

Stuebing, K., Barth, A., Molfese, P. J., Weiss, B., & Fletcher, J. M. (2009). IQ is not strongly related to response to reading instruction: A meta-analytic interpretation. *Exceptional Children, 76,* 31–51.

Stuebing, K., Fletcher, J. M., LeDoux, J. M., Lyon, G. R., Shaywitz, S. E., & Shaywitz, B. A. (2002). Validity of IQ-discrepancy classification of reading difficulties: A meta-analysis. *American Educational Research Journal, 39,* 469–518.

Sub, H.-M., Oberauer, K., Wittmann, W. W., Wilhelm, O., & Schulze, R. (2002). Working-memory capacity explains reasoning ability - and a little bit more. *Intelligence, 30,* 261–288.

Suddendorf, T. (1999). The rise of the metamind. In M. C. Corballis & S. Lea (Eds.), *The descent of mind: Psychological perspectives on hominid evolution* (pp. 218–260). Oxford: Oxford University Press.

Suddendorf, T., & Corballis, M. C. (2007). The evolution of foresight: What is mental time travel and is it unique to humans? *Behavioral and Brain Sciences, 30,* 299–351.

Suddendorf, T., & Whiten, A. (2001). Mental evolution and development: Evidence for secondary representation in children, great apes, and other animals. *Psychological Bulletin, 127,* 629–650.

Sun, R., Lane, S. M., & Mathews, R. C. (2009). The two systems of learning: An architectural perspective. In J. St. B. T. Evans & K. Frankish (Eds.), *In two minds: Dual processes and beyond* (pp. 239–262). Oxford: Oxford University Press.

Sundali, J., & Croson, R. (2006). Biases in casino betting: The hot hand and the gambler's fallacy. *Judgment and Decision Making, 1,* 1–12.

Sunstein, C. R. (2002). *Risk and reason: Safety, law, and the environment.* Cambridge: Cambridge University Press.

Sunstein, C. R. (2005). Moral heuristics. *Behavioral and Brain Sciences, 28,* 531–573.

Sunstein, C. R., & Thaler, R. H. (2003). Libertarian paternalism is not an oxymoron. *University of Chicago Law Review, 70,* 1159–1202.

Taber, C. S., & Lodge, M. (2006). Motivated skepticism in the evaluation of political beliefs. *American Journal of Political Science, 50,* 755–769.

Taleb, N. N. (2001). *Fooled by randomness.* New York: Texere.

Taleb, N. (2007). *The black swan: The impact of the highly improbable.* New York: Random House.

Taub, G. E., & McGrew, K. S. (2004). A confirmatory factor analysis of Cattell-Horn-Carroll theory and cross-age invariance of the Woodcock-Johnson Tests of Cognitive Abilities III. *School Psychology Quarterly, 19,* 72–87.

Tavris, C., & Aronson, E. (2007). *Mistakes were made (but not by me)*. Orlando, FL: Harcourt.

Taylor, C. (1989). *Sources of the self: The making of modern identity*. Cambridge, MA: Harvard University Press.

Taylor, S. E. (1981). The interface of cognitive and social psychology. In J. H. Harvey (Ed.), *Cognition, social behavior, and the environment* (pp. 189–211). Hillsdale, NJ: Erlbaum.

Terjesen, M. D., Salhany, J., & Sciutto, M. J. (2009). A psychometric review of measures of irrational beliefs: Implications for psychotherapy. *Journal of Rational-Emotive & Cognitive-Behavior Therapy, 27*, 83–96.

Tetlock, P. E. (2005). *Expert political judgment*. Princeton, NJ: Princeton University Press.

Tetlock, P. E., & Mellers, B. A. (2002). The great rationality debate. *Psychological Science, 13*, 94–99.

Thagard, P. (1982). From the descriptive to the normative in philosophy and logic. *Philosophy of Science, 49*, 24–42.

Thaler, R. H. (1980). Toward a positive theory of consumer choice. *Journal of Economic Behavior and Organization, 1*, 39–60.

Thaler, R. H. (1985). Mental accounting and consumer choice. *Marketing Science, 4*, 199–214.

Thaler, R. H. (1987). The psychology of choice and the assumptions of economics. In A. E. Roth (Ed.), *Laboratory experimentation in economics: Six points of view* (pp. 99–130). Cambridge: University of Cambridge Press.

Thaler, R. H. (1992). *The winner's curse: Paradoxes and anomalies of economic life*. New York: Free Press.

Thaler, R. H., & Benartzi, S. (2004). Save more tomorrow: Using behavioral economics to increase employee saving. *Journal of Political Economy, 112*, s164–s187.

Thaler, R. H., & Shefrin, H. M. (1981). An economic theory of self-control. *Journal of Political Economy, 89*, 392–406.

Thaler, R. H., & Sunstein, C. R. (2008). *Nudge: Improving decisions about health, wealth, and happiness*. New Haven, CT: Yale University Press.

Thompson, S. C. (2004). Illusions of control. In R. Pohl (Ed.), *Cognitive illusions: A handbook on fallacies and biases in thinking, judgment and memory* (pp. 115–126). Hove, England: Psychology Press.

Thompson, V. A. (2009). Dual-process theories: A metacognitive perspective. In J. Evans & K. Frankish (Eds.), *In two minds: Dual processes and beyond* (pp. 171–195). Oxford: Oxford University Press.

Thurstone, L. L. (1927). *The nature of intelligence*. New York: Harcourt, Brace and Company.

Toates, F. (2005). Evolutionary psychology: Towards a more integrative model. *Biology and Philosophy, 20*, 305–328.

Toates, F. (2006). A model of the hierarchy of behavior, cognition, and consciousness. *Consciousness & Cognition, 15*, 75–118.

Tobacyk, J., & Milford, G. (1983). Belief in paranormal phenomena. *Journal of Personality and Social Psychology, 44,* 1029–1037.

Todd, P. M., & Gigerenzer, G. (2000). Precis of Simple Heuristics that Make Us Smart. *Behavioral and Brain Sciences, 23,* 727–780.

Todd, P. M., & Gigerenzer, G. (2007). Environments that make us smart: Ecological rationality. *Current Directions in Psychological Science, 16,* 167–171.

Todd, P. M., Hertwig, R., & Hoffrage, U. (2005). Evolutionary cognitive psychology. In D. M. Buss (Eds.), *The handbook of evolutionary psychology* (pp. 776–802). Hoboken, NJ: John Wiley.

Tomasello, M. (1998). Social cognition and the evolution of culture. In J. Langer & M. Killen (Eds.), *Piaget, evolution, and development* (pp. 221–245). Mahwah, NJ: Lawrence Erlbaum Associates.

Tomasello, M. (1999). *The cultural origins of human cognition.* Cambridge, MA: Harvard University Press.

Toneatto, T. (1999). Cognitive psychopathology of problem gambling. *Substance Use and Misuse, 34,* 1593–1604.

Toplak, M., Liu, E., Macpherson, R., Toneatto, T., & Stanovich, K. E. (2007). The reasoning skills and thinking dispositions of problem gamblers: A dual-process taxonomy. *Journal of Behavioral Decision Making, 20,* 103–124.

Toplak, M., Sorge, G. B., Benoit, A., West, R. F., & Stanovich, K. E. (2010). Decision-making and cognitive abilities: A review of associations between Iowa Gambling Task performance, executive functions, and intelligence. *Clinical Psychology Review, 30,* 562–581.

Toplak, M. E., & Stanovich, K. E. (2002). The domain specificity and generality of disjunctive reasoning: Searching for a generalizable critical thinking skill. *Journal of Educational Psychology, 94,* 197–209.

Toplak, M. E. & Stanovich, K. E. (2003). Associations between myside bias on an informal reasoning task and amount of post-secondary education. *Applied Cognitive Psychology, 17,* 851–860.

Torrens, D., Thompson, V. A., & Cramer, K. M. (1999). Individual differences and the belief bias effect: Mental models, logical necessity, and abstract reasoning. *Thinking and Reasoning, 5,* 1–28.

Towse, J. N., & Neil, D. (1998). Analyzing human random generation behavior: A review of methods used and a computer program for describing performance. *Behavior Research Methods, Instruments & Computers, 30,* 583–591.

Tschirgi, J. E. (1980). Sensible reasoning: A hypothesis about hypotheses. *Child Development, 51,* 1–10.

Tversky, A., & Kahneman, D. (1971). Belief in the law of small numbers. *Psychological Bulletin, 76,* 105–110.

Tversky, A., & Kahneman, D. (1973). Availability: A heuristic for judging frequency and probability. *Cognitive Psychology, 5,* 207–232.

Tversky, A., & Kahneman, D. (1974). Judgment under uncertainty: Heuristics and biases. *Science, 185,* 1124–1131.

Tversky, A., & Kahneman, D. (1979). Causal schemas in judgmnents under uncertainty. In M. Fishbein (Ed.), *Progress in social psychology* (pp. 1–30). Hillsdale, NJ: Erlbaum.

Tversky, A., & Kahneman, D. (1981). The framing of decisions and the psychology of choice. *Science, 211*, 453–458.

Tversky, A., & Kahneman, D. (1982). Evidential impact of base rates. In D. Kahneman, P. Slovic, & A. Tversky (Eds.), *Judgment under uncertainty: Heuristics and biases* (pp. 153–160). Cambridge: Cambridge University Press.

Tversky, A., & Kahneman, D. (1983). Extensional versus intuitive reasoning: The conjunction fallacy in probability judgment. *Psychological Review, 90*, 293–315.

Tversky, A., & Kahneman, D. (1986). Rational choice and the framing of decisions. *Journal of Business, 59*, 251–278.

Tversky, A., & Kahneman, D. (1991). Loss aversion in riskless choice: A reference-dependent model. *The Quarterly Journal of Economics, 106*, 1039–1061.

Twachtman-Cullen, D. (1997). *A passion to believe.* Boulder, CO: Westview.

Tweney, R. D., Doherty, M. E., Warner, W. J., & Pliske, D. (1980). Strategies of rule discovery in an inference task. *Quarterly Journal of Experimental Psychology, 32*, 109–124.

Tweney, R. D., & Yachanin, S. (1985). Can scientists rationally assess conditional inferences? *Social Studies of Science, 15*, 155–173.

Ubel, P. A. (2000). *Pricing life: Why it's time for health care rationing.* Cambridge, MA: MIT Press.

Unsworth, N., & Engle, R. W. (2005). Working memory capacity and fluid abilities: Examining the correlation between Operation Span and Raven. *Intelligence, 33*, 67–81.

Unsworth, N., & Engle, R. W. (2007). The nature of individual differences in working memory capacity: Active maintenance in primary memory and controlled search from secondary memory. *Psychological Review, 114*, 104–132.

Valentine, D. A. (1998 May, 13). *Pyramid schemes.* Presented at the International Monetary Fund Seminar on Current Legal Issues Affecting Central Banks. Washington, DC: IMF. Retreived from http://www.ftc.gov/speeches/other/dvimf16.shtm on August 29, 2007.

Valentine, E. R. (1975). Performance on two reasoning tasks in relation to intelligence, divergence and interference proneness: Content and context effects in reasoning. *British Journal of Educational Psychology, 45*, 198–205.

van Veen, V., & Carter, C. S. (2006). Conflict and cognitive control in the brain. *Current Directions in Psychological Science, 15*, 237–240.

Velleman, J. D. (1992). What happens when somebody acts? *Mind, 101*, 461–481.

Vellutino, F., Fletcher, J. M., Snowling, M., & Scanlon, D. M. (2004). Specific reading disability (dyslexia): What have we learned in the past four decades? *Journal of Child Psychology and Psychiatry, 45*, 2–40.

Verplanken, B. (1993). Need for cognition and external information search: Responses to time pressure during decision-making. *Journal of Research in Personality, 27*, 238–252.

Vinter, A., & Detable, C. (2003). Implicit learning in children and adolescents with mental retardation. *American Journal of Mental Retardation, 108,* 94–107.

Vinter, A., & Perruchet, P. (2000). Implicit learning in children is not related to age: Evidence from drawing behavior. *Child Development, 71,* 1223–1240.

von Neumann, J., & Morgenstern, O. (1944). *The theory of games and economic behavior.* Princeton: Princeton University Press.

Vranas, P. B. M. (2000). Gigerenzer's normative critique of Kahneman and Tversky. *Cognition, 76,* 179–193.

Wade, C., & Tavris, C. (2008). *Psychology (Ninth Edition).* Upper Saddle River, NJ: Pearson Education.

Wagenaar, W. A. (1988). *Paradoxes of gambling behavior.* Hove, England: Erlbaum.

Wagenaar, W. A., & Sagaria, S. D. (1975). Misperception of exponential growth. *Perception and Psychophysics, 18,* 416–422.

Wainer, H. (1993). Does spending money on education help? A reaction to the Heritage Foundation and the *Wall Street Journal. Educational Researcher, 22*(9), 22–24.

Wang, L. (2009). Money and fame: Vividness effects in the National Basketball Association. *Journal of Behavioral Decision Making, 22,* 20–44.

Wason, P. C. (1966). Reasoning. In B. Foss (Ed.), *New horizons in psychology* (pp. 135–151). Harmonsworth, England: Penguin.

Wason, P. C., & Evans, J. St. B. T. (1975). Dual processes in reasoning? *Cognition, 3,* 141–154.

Wasserman, E. A., Dorner, W. W., & Kao, S. F. (1990). Contributions of specific cell information to judgments of interevent contingency. *Journal of Experimental Psychology: Learning, Memory, and Cognition, 16,* 509–521.

Watson, G. (1975). Free agency. *Journal of Philosophy, 72,* 205–220.

Watson, G., & Glaser, E. M. (1980). *Watson-Glaser Critical Thinking Appraisal.* New York: Psychological Corporation.

Watson, G., & Glaser, E. M. (2006). *Watson-Glaser Critical Thinking Appraisal: Short Form Manual.* Orlando, FL: Harcourt.

Wegner, D. M. (1994). Ironic processes of mental control. *Psychological Review, 101,* 34–52.

Wegner, D. M. (2002). *The illusion of conscious will.* Cambridge, MA: MIT Press.

Weinstein, N. (1980). Unrealistic optimism about future life events. *Journal of Personality and Social Psychology, 39,* 806–820.

Weller, J. A., Levin, I. P., Shiv, B., & Bechara, A. (2007). Neural correlates of adaptive decision making for risky gains and losses. *Psychological Science, 18,* 958–964.

Wellman, H. M., & Liu, D. (2004). Scaling of theory-of-mind tasks. *Child Development, 75,* 523–541.

West, R. F., & Stanovich, K. E. (2003). Is probability matching smart? Associations between probabilistic choices and cognitive ability. *Memory & Cognition, 31,* 243–251.

West, R. F., Toplak, M. E., & Stanovich, K. E. (2008). Heuristics and biases as measures of critical thinking: Associations with cognitive ability and thinking dispositions. *Journal of Educational Psychology, 100,* 930–941.

Westen, D., Blagov, P., Kilts, C., & Hamann, S. (2006). Neural bases of motivated reasoning: An fMRI study of emotional constraints on partisan political judgment in the 2004 U.S. Presidential Election. *Journal of Cognitive Neuroscience, 18,* 1947–1958.

Whiten, A. (2001). Meta-representation and secondary representation. *Trends in Cognitive Sciences, 5,* 378.

Whiten, A., & Byrne, R. W. (Eds.) (1997). *Machiavellian intelligence II: Extensions and evaluations.* Cambridge: Cambridge University Press.

Whitney, P., Rinehart, C. A., & Hinson, J. M. (2008). Framing effects under cognitive load: The role of working memory in risky decisions. *Psychonomic Bulletin & Review, 15,* 1179–1184.

Wiley, J. (2005). A fair and balanced look at the news: What affects memory for controversial arguments? *Journal of Memory and Language, 53,* 95–109.

Williams, W. M. (1998). Are we raising smarter children today? School and home-related influences on IQ. In U. Neisser (Ed.), *The rising curve: Long-term changes in IQ and related measures* (pp. 125–154). Washington, DC: American Psychological Association.

Willingham, D. T. (1998). A neuropsychological theory of motor-skill learning. *Psychological Review, 105,* 558–584.

Willingham, D. T. (1999). The neural basis of motor-skill learning. *Current Directions in Psychological Science, 8,* 178–182.

Willingham, D. T. (2004). Reframing the mind. *Education Next, 4*(3), 19–24.

Wilson, D. S. (2002). *Darwin's cathedral.* Chicago: University of Chicago Press.

Wilson, M. (2002). Six views of embodied cognition. *Psychonomic Bulletin and Review, 9,* 625–636.

Wilson, T. D. (2002). *Strangers to ourselves.* Cambridge, MA: Harvard University Press.

Wilson, T. D., & Gilbert, D. T. (2005). Affective forecasting: Knowing what to want. *Current Directions in Psychological Science, 14,* 131–134.

Wilson, T. D., Wheatley, T., Meyers, J. M., Gilbert, D. T., & Axsom, D. (2000). Focalism: A source of durability bias in affective forecasting. *Journal of Personality and Social Psychology, 78,* 821–836.

Wolfe, C. R., & Britt, M. A. (2008). The locus of the myside bias in written argumentation. *Thinking and Reasoning, 14,* 1–27.

Wood, J. M., Nezworski, M. T., Lilienfeld, S. O., & Garb, H. N. (2003). *What's wrong with the Rorschach?* San Francisco: Jossey-Bass.

Wu, G., Zhang, J., & Gonzalez, R. (2004). Decision under risk. In D. J. Koehler & N. Harvey (Eds.), *Blackwell handbook of judgment and decision making* (399–423). Malden, MA: Blackwell Publishing.

Yechiam, E., Kanz, J., Bechara, A., Stout, J. C., Busemeyer, J. R., Altmaier, E., & Paulsen, J. (2008). Neurocognitive deficits related to poor decision making in people behind bars. *Psychonomic Bulletin & Review, 15,* 44–51.

Zacks, R. T., Hasher, L., & Sanft, H. (1982). Automatic encoding of event frequency: Further findings. *Journal of Experimental Psychology: Learning, Memory, and Cognition, 8*, 106–116.

Zagorsky, J. L. (2007). Do you have to be smart to be rich? The impact of IQ on wealth, income and financial distress. *Intelligence, 35,* 489–501.

Zelazo, P. D. (2004). The development of conscious control in childhood. *Trends in Cognitive Sciences, 8,* 12–17.

Zelniker, T., Cochavi, D., & Yered, J. (1974). The relationship between speed of performance and conceptual style: The effect of imposed modification of response latency. *Child Development, 45,* 779–784.

Zelniker, T., Jeffrey, W. E., Ault, R., & Parsons, J. (1972). Analysis and modification of search strategies of impulsive and reflective children on the Matching Familiar Figures Test. *Child Development, 43,* 321–335.

Author Index

Colombo, J., 113n8, 136n7
Coltheart, M., 20n8, 119
Conway, A. R. A., 53n5, 54, 57n7, 142n12, 182
Corballis, M. C., 47n1, 48n2, 82n2
Corley, R. P., 57n7, 74n2
Corpus, B., 104, 201t
Cosmides, L., 8, 23n10, 48n2, 171, 172
Costa, P. T., 43, 88t
Cowan, N., 53n5
Coyle, T. R., 54
Cramer, K. M., 136n7
Cronbach, L. J., 39, 72
Croskerry, P., 31n2, 222t
Croson, R., 104, 221t
Cummins, D. D., 91n7
Currie, G., 47n1, 233
Currie, S. R., 233
Curtis, V., 16, 20n8
Curtis-Holmes, J., 40, 213
Curtiss, G., 58

Damasio, A. R., 116, 117, 119, 119n10
Damasio, H., 116, 117, 119n10
Daniel, M. H., 52n4
D'Annucci, A., 119
Darley, J. M., 17n6
Daston, L., 91n7, 112
Davids, S. L., 82n1, 237t
Davidson, D., 82n1
Davies, M., 5, 37, 119
Davis, H. P., 53n5, 58, 142n12
Dawes, R. M., 6, 29, 31n2, 132n5, 188n4, 213, 223t, 240t
Dawkins, R., 22n9, 23, 83, 89, 103n4, 170, 171
Dawson, K. A., 216
Dawson, M., 184n3
Day, D., 35
Dean, D. J., 237t
Deary, I. J., 54, 139n9, 160
Deaves, R., 242t
Decety, J., 47n1

DeCoster, J., 17n6, 18t
DeFries, J. C., 57n7, 74n2
DeMartino, B., 17n6, 75n3
Denes-Raj, V., 87, 88t, 110, 111, 161, 194t, 225t
DeNeys, W., 76, 124, 147, 148, 151
Denissen, J., 72
Dennett, D. C., 22n9, 23, 32, 48n2, 51n3, 82n2, 83, 90, 103, 103n4, 168, 170
Dennis, I., 124, 136n7
Dent, S., 132
DeShon, R. P., 124n3
DeSousa, R., 3, 4
D'Esposito, M., 116n9
Detable, C., 37n6, 155n1
Detterman, D. K., 175, 175n1
Deutsch, R., 18t
DeVries, N., 231t, 242t
Dhar, R., 239t
Diamond, A., 234t
DiCerbo, K. E., 238t
Dickert, S., 232t
Dieckmann, N. F., 230t
Diener, E., 114
Dienes, Z., 48n2, 50, 82n2
Dillard, A. J., 226t
Distin, K., 22n9, 103n4, 170
Doherty, M. E., 9, 196, 202, 219t
Doherty-Sneddon, G., 50
Dolan, R. J., 17n6, 75n3
Dole, J. A., 35n5
Donkers, B., 237t
Dörner, D., 207
Dorner, W. W., 204t
Doucet, C., 236t
Dougherty, M. R. P., 30n1, 47n1
Driver-Linn, E., 196t, 210t, 219t
Duckworth, A. L., 32n3, 39, 45, 215, 221t
Duckworth, S., 230t
Dulany, D. E., 101n3
Dunbar, R., 47n1, 91n7

Subject Index

Note: Page references followed by "*f*" and "*t*" denote figures and tables, respectively.

and real-life functioning, 51
sustained, 51–52, 55
Cognitive misers, 98–100. *See also*
    Miserly processing
    and focal bias, 65–71
    hostile and benign environments
        for, 20–21
    humans as, 21, 29
    and intelligence, 156
    and serial associative cognition,
        65, 100
Cognitive quarantine, 49
Cognitive reflection test, 158*n*2, 194*t*,
    218*t*, 230*t*
Cognitive science
    Great Rationality Debate in, 9
    rationality in, 3, 4
Cognitive simulation, 22, 26, 47, 48, 50
Cognitive sophistication, individual
    differences in, 14–15
Cognitive styles. *See* Thinking
    dispositions
Coherence rationality, 139, 141
"Cold override," 159, 161
Competence
    and performance, distinction, 165,
        166–67
Comprehension, errors of, 141
Confirmation bias, 115. *See also* Bias
    avoidance of, 203*t*, 223*t*, 237*t*
Conflict detection, 78
Conjunction errors, 112–13
    and intelligence, 127, 129*t*, 130
Consciousness, and rightness, 79
Consistency
    in belief and argument, 198*t*, 234*t*
    checking, 90
    probability judgments, 200*t*,
        221*t*, 235*t*
Conspecifics, 90
Contaminated mindware, 102–4, 193
    and intelligence, 162
    skepticism about, 170

Converging evidence, 206*t*
    appreciation of, 205*t*, 223*t*, 238*t*
    in dual-process theory, 72–80
Cost/benefit reasoning, 207*t*,
    224*t*, 239*t*
Critical thinking, 135
    in algorithmic and reflective mind
        partition, 39–43
    definition of, 39
    and intelligence, 180
    tests, 39–43
    and thinking dispositions, 42
Crystallized intelligence, 53, 96, 97
Crystallized rationality, 192, 193
Culture, 171, 173
"Curse of knowledge" effects, 149, 161

Decision-making, 8*n*2, 101, 213, 197*t*,
    219*t*, 232*t*
    evaluation, 44, 45
Decoupling, 47–51, 73–80, 91–94
Delay of gratification
    and intelligence, 159–60
    paradigms, 199*t*, 221*t*, 234*t*
Delayed-discounting, and
    intelligence, 160–61
Denominator neglect, 110–11
Descriptive invariance, 109
Descriptive models, 10–16
Desires
    first-order, 84
    higher-order, 83
    second-order, 83–84
Diagnostic covariation judgment,
    204*t*, 223*t*, 237*t*
Diagnostic hypothesis testing, 196*t*,
    202*t*, 219*t*, 222*t*, 231*t*, 237*t*
Disjunctive reasoning, 68, 157, 194*t*,
    218*t*, 230*t*
Dorsal anterior cingulate cortex
    (dACC), 77, 78
Dorsolateral prefrontal cortex
    (DLPFC), 75–77

Printed in the USA/Agawam, MA
August 15, 2014

595246.023